State	Population (1000's in 2006)[c]	Per Capita Personal Income (2005)[d]	Obama/McCain Vote 2008 (%)[e]	Conservatism (rank)[f]
Alabama	4,599	$29,623	39/61	8
Alaska	670	$35,433	36/62	22
Arizona	6,166	$30,157	45/54	28
Arkansas	2,811	$26,641	39/59	6
California	36,458	$36,890	61/37	43
Colorado	4,753	$37,459	53/46	36
Connecticut	3,505	$47,519	62/36	47
Delaware	853	$37,084	61/38	42
Florida	18,090	$34,099	51/49	31
Georgia	9,364	$31,191	47/52	18
Hawaii	1,285	$34,468	72/27	48
Idaho	1,466	$28,398	36/62	12
Illinois	12,832	$36,264	62/37	40
Indiana	6,314	$31,150	50/49	16
Iowa	2,982	$31,795	54/45	23
Kansas	2,764	$32,948	41/57	10
Kentucky	4,206	$28,317	41/58	19
Louisiana	4,288	$24,582	40/59	7
Maine	1,322	$30,808	58/40	37
Maryland	5,616	$41,996	61/38	41
Massachusetts	6,437	$43,702	62/36	49
Michigan	10,096	$32,735	57/41	32
Minnesota	5,167	$37,322	54/44	38
Mississippi	2,911	$24,925	43/57	1
Missouri	5,843	$31,299	49/50	20
Montana	945	$28,906	47/50	17
Nebraska	1,768	$32,988	41/57	14
Nevada	2,496	$35,780	55/43	21
New Hampshire	1,315	$37,835	55/44	39
New Jersey	8,725	$43,822	57/42	45
New Mexico	1,955	$27,912	57/42	35
New York	19,306	$40,072	62/37	46
North Carolina	8,857	$31,029	50/49	15
North Dakota	636	$31,230	45/53	2
Ohio	11,478	$31,867	52/47	26
Oklahoma	3,579	$29,908	34/66	3
Oregon	3,701	$32,174	55/43	33
Pennsylvania	12,441	$34,848	55/44	30
Rhode Island	10,068	$35,219	64/35	43
South Carolina	4,321	$28,212	45/54	9
South Dakota	782	$32,642	45/53	4
Tennessee	6,039	$30,952	42/57	13
Texas	23,508	$32,604	44/55	10
Utah	2,550	$27,497	34/63	5
Vermont	624	$32,731	67/31	50
Virginia	7,643	$37,552	52/47	24
Washington	6,396	$35,234	58/41	34
West Virginia	1,818	$26,029	43	27
Wisconsin	5,557	$33,251	56	
Wyoming	515	$37,270	33	

Sources:
[c] Hovey, Kendra A., and Harold A. Hovey. 2007. *CQ's State Fact Finder 2007*. Washington, DC: CQ Press,
[d] Hovey and Hovey 2007, 44.
[e] CNN Election Center 2008 website (http://www.cnn.com/election/2008/results)—as of November
[f] Adapted from: Erikson, Robert S., Gerald C. Wright, and John P. McIver. 2006. "Public Opinion in the States: A Quarter Century of Change and Stability." In *Public Opinion in State Politics*, ed. Jeffrey E. Cohen. Stanford, CA: Stanford University Press.

STATE & LOCAL POLITICS

STATE & LOCAL

★★★★★★
POLITICS
Institutions & Reform
★ *The Essentials* ★

VOTE

Todd
Donovan

★★★★★★★
Christopher Z.
Mooney
★★★★★★★

Daniel A.
Smith
★ ★ ★

WADSWORTH
CENGAGE Learning™

Australia • Brazil • Canada • Mexico • Singapore • Spain • United Kingdom • United States

WADSWORTH
CENGAGE Learning

State and Local Politics:
Institutions and Reform
The Essentials
Todd Donovan, Christopher Z.
Mooney, Daniel A. Smith

Executive Editor: Carolyn Merrill

Development Editor: Rebecca Green

Assistant Editor: Katherine Hayes

Editorial Assistant: Nathan Gamache

Associate Development Manager:
  Caitlin Holroyd

Marketing Manager: Amy Whitaker

Marketing Communications
  Manager: Heather Baxley

Senior Content Project Manager:
  Josh Allen

Art Director: Linda Helcher

Print Buyer: Linda Hsu

Permissions Editor: Roberta Broyer

Production Service: Rathi Thirumalai,
  Pre-PressPMG

Image Acquisitions Manager:
  Mandy Groszko

Cover Designer: Beckmeyer Design

Cover Image: ©Shutterstock

Compositor: Pre-PressPMG

For product information and technology assistance, contact us at
Cengage Learning Customer & Sales Support, 1-800-354-9706
For permission to use material from this text or product, submit all requests online at **www.cengage.com/permissions.**
Further permissions questions can be emailed to
permissionrequest@cengage.com.

Library of Congress Control Number: 2008939030

Student Edition:

ISBN-13: 978-0-495-56789-9

ISBN-10: 0-495-56789-2

Wadsworth
20 Channel Center Street
Boston, MA 02210
USA

Cengage Learning products are represented in Canada by Nelson Education, Ltd.

For your course and learning solutions, visit **www.cengage.com.**

Purchase any of our products at your local college store or at our preferred online store **www.ichapters.com.**

Printed in the United States of America
1 2 3 4 5 6 7 12 11 10 09

To our families, with love: Deborah, Fiona, and Ian; Laura, Allison, and Charlie; and Brenda, Eliot, and Safi.

Contents

TODD DONOVAN (Ph. D., University of California, Riverside) is a professor of political science at Western Washington University, where he teaches state and local politics, American politics, parties, campaigns and elections, comparative electoral systems, and introductory research  methods and statistics. His research interests include direct democracy, election systems and representation, political behavior, subnational politics, and the political economy of local development. He has published extensively in academic journals; written a number of books on direct democracy, elections, institutions, and reform; and has received numerous grants and awards for his work. With Ken Hoover, he is the coauthor of *The Elements of Social Scientific Thinking,* also with Cengage.

CHRISTOPHER Z. MOONEY (Ph.D., University of Wisconsin–Madison) is professor of political studies at the University of Illinois at Springfield and research fellow at the Institute of Government and Public Affairs at the University  of Illinois. He is the founding editor of *State Politics and Policy Quarterly*, the official journal of the State Politics and Policy section of the American Political Science Association. He has published many books and articles on legislative politics, morality policy, and research methods. He can be heard each week as a regular panelist on *State Week in Review*, an NPR radio program broadcast statewide in Illinois.

DANIEL A. SMITH (Ph.D., University of Wisconsin–Madison) is associate professor of political science at the University of Florida and the interim director of the M.A. Political Campaigning Program. He teaches courses  on state and local politics, political parties, interest groups, campaign finance, and direct democracy. He has published numerous articles on direct democracy, political parties, interests groups, and campaign finance as well as two books on the politics and processes of ballot initiatives. Smith, a former Fulbright Scholar, serves on the Board of Directors of the Ballot Initiative Strategy Center Foundation (BISCF) and is a senior research fellow at the Initiative and Referendum Institute.

Studying State and Local Government

American state and local governments provide perhaps the best opportunity to study political phenomena in the world. They give political scientists a manageable number of cases similar enough in social structure, economics, politics, and government to make meaningful comparisons of them without becoming overwhelmed by extraneous variation. But they are also different enough from one another in theoretically and substantively important ways to allow us to test a wide range of questions concerning political behavior and policy making central to our understanding of politics. For example, what is the best way to choose our leaders? How should we make public policy? What are the impacts of public policy on policy problems, people, businesses, the economy, or anything else? These and other fundamental questions not only can be explored more productively by studying the American states and communities but can also be explored best there.

The study of state and local government can be just as productive and interesting for students as it is for political scientists. But as we all know, an undergraduate state and local government class is usually not the highlight of a student's college career. It is often taught as a large service course required by a variety of majors—everything from education to journalism to social work—or as a social science general education course. Ironically, state and local governments will have a greater impact on most students for the duration of their lives than almost any other topic they study in a political science class. For example, teachers and social workers will be working for these governments, and many journalists will at least begin their careers by covering them. Even American college students not pursuing these majors will be deeply affected by the politics and government of the states and local communities. Laws, ordinances, and regulations about their driver's licenses, the clubs and restaurants where they work and play, landlord-renter relationships, and even the large state universities many of them attend are all in the bailiwick of these governments. Furthermore, college students tend to move more often than the average American, and in going from place to place for college, a new job, or just spring break, they are frequently exposed to the diversity of state and local government laws around the country—the differing speed limits, gambling laws, alcohol sales regulations, tax structures, and so forth. For the untrained person, these variations can be just confusing annoyances, but for those students who have taken a good state and local government class—and for those students who have read this book—the exposure to these variations comprises teachable moments. Such students are more likely both to notice and to understand these differences, making them better citizens in the process and for the long run.

Approach of the Book

We wrote this essentials edition with these teachable moments in mind, packing each chapter with lively and wide-ranging examples pulled from headlines across the nation to illuminate our points. From the outset, we have made every effort to engage, excite, and inform students about American state and local government and politics and to help them develop the critical thinking skills needed to make them better political scientists and better citizens. Our aim with this essentials edition is to provide an affordable and flexible alternative without compromising on substance, scholarship, or style.

Theme

To accomplish this task, the book's central theoretical theme is that institutions matter. The states and communities are especially well-suited for testing and demonstrating this proposition, and we want students to understand why and how this is so. Throughout the book, we show countless ways in which state and local governmental institutions affect students' lives every day.

Approaches

Up-to-Date Scholarship Since 1990, there has been a renaissance in political science scholarship using the states and communities to understand political processes and behavior. We have integrated the insights of this literature throughout the book so that students and instructors have access to the most current research available on the subject. We have meticulously documented our sources to assist students working on class assignments as well as to help instructors wanting to keep abreast of this important and extensive literature.

Political Science Methods This is a political science textbook, not a government textbook. We very self-consciously show students how to use the variation among the states and communities to develop and test hypotheses about political behavior and policy making. Rather than simply describing how things are, we expose students to a multitude of differences among the states and communities and ask them to think about their causes and effects. In doing so, students will not only learn much about American states and communities but also learn how to think like political scientists. That is a skill that will help them in any college course they take thereafter as well as throughout the rest of their lives.

Unique Chapter on Direct Democracy Not only have ballot measures been at the center of some of the most significant political battles in the country in recent years, but they have also recently generated a great deal of high-quality scholarship and are sure to engage student interest. Direct democracy—which represents one of the major institutional differences between states—has been used by citizens to pass laws cutting taxes, increasing funding for public education, banning smoking in public places, prohibiting same-sex marriage, providing funding for stem cell research, and raising the minimum wage. Because of its increasing relevance to the lives of millions of Americans, we devote an entire chapter to the study of direct democracy in the American states and communities.

Plan of the Book

We try to convince students that state and local politics have important consequences for their own lives. The book begins with an introduction to some of the major questions asked when we study state and local politics and a discussion of some of the methods we use to answer such questions. The second chapter places states and localities in the larger context of the American federal system.

Subsequent chapters introduce students to various state and local political institutions, with a particular emphasis on how different institutions, in different places, may produce different outcomes. Chapter 3 examines rules that affect elections and participation, and Chapter 4 covers the unique institutions of direct democracy. Chapter 5 covers political parties and interest groups at the state and local levels. Chapters 6, 7, and 8 examine the core institutions of American state politics: legislatures, governors, and courts, respectively. Chapter 9 tackles issues facing various forms of municipal government, and Chapter 10 is devoted to state and local fiscal politics, including a discussion of how tax and spending political decisions affect public policy.

Special Features and Pedagogy

Boxed Features In order to emphasize further the book's theme that institutions matter, we have developed boxed features for each chapter that highlight the effects of institutions. These boxes provide thought-provoking, concrete examples of the kinds of problems and issues faced at the state and local levels so that students understand how institutions and systems affect actual individuals in real-life situations. Specifically, the boxes examine the way institutions influence outcomes and consider such topics as the impact that the threat of launching a ballot initiative has in spurring legislative action on an issue, Alaska's use of the mixed primary system, and the proliferation of "teen courts."

Design Vivid tables, maps, graphs, and photographs throughout the book provide the visual tools students need to process detailed comparative data on the states.

Endpapers The inside front and back covers of the book provide basic information on state and local governments for convenient reference.

Other Pedagogical Features Each chapter includes a full set of study aids, including a chapter outline, a chapter summary, and key terms. The chapter outlines list the major sections of the material presented so students can get a general sense of the topics to be covered, and the summaries provide a recap of the most important ideas of the chapters. The key terms and definitions provide an opportunity for students to check their mastery of the terminology. For those students who wish to further explore a topic, the companion website provides a list of suggested readings and a list of annotated websites for each chapter.

Instructor Resources

The PowerLecture for *State and Local Politics: The Essentials* CD-ROM contains the following:

- A test bank in Microsoft Word® and ExamView® computerized testing, created by the authors of the book, offers a large array of well-crafted multiple-choice and essay questions, along with their answers, page references, and learning objectives.

- PowerPoint® lectures bring together text-specific outlines, tables, and figures from the book for each chapter.

- An Instructor's Manual with chapter summaries, learning objectives, discussion questions, suggestions for stimulating class activities and projects, and tips on integrating media into your class, including step-by-step instructions on how to create your own podcasts.

Student Resources

- A companion website for *State and Local Politics: The Essentials* gives students access to tutorial quizzes, learning objectives, web links, suggested readings, and more. Visit http://www.cengage.com/politicalscience/donovan/stateandlocalpoliticsessentials1e.

This book, which condenses our fuller study of state and local politics, represents the tangible expression of the work of dozens of people. Fortunately for us, we have the honor of putting our names on the spine. We would like to express our deepest gratitude to all those who offered countless hours of their valuable time to help us in our efforts on this project. First, some of the nation's top political scientists gave us detailed feedback on early drafts of the chapters in their areas of expertise: Thad Beyle (University of North Carolina at Chapel Hill), Chris Bonneau (University of Pittsburgh), Tom Carsey (University of North Carolina at Chapel Hill), Susan Clarke (University of Colorado–Boulder), Richard Clucas (Portland State University), Chris Cooper (Western Carolina University), Peter Eisinger (New York University), Margaret Ferguson (Indiana University at Indianapolis), Peter Francia (Eastern Carolina University), Don Haider-Markel (University of Kansas), Zoltan Hajnal (University of California, San Diego), Melinda Gann Hall (Michigan State University), Jennifer Jensen (State University of New York at Binghamton), Lael Keiser (University of Missouri–Columbia), Gary Moncrief (Boise State University), Karen Mossberger (University of Illinois at Chicago), Dometrius Nelson (Texas Tech University), Adam Newmark (Appalachian State University), Steve Nicholson (University of California, Merced), Tony Nownes (University of Tennessee), Elizabeth Oldmixon (North Texas University), David Paul (Ohio State University–Newark), Marvin Overby (University of Missouri–Columbia), Eric Plutzer (Penn State University), Mark Rom (Georgetown University), Beth Rosenson (University of Florida), Richard Scher (University of Florida), Joe Soss (University of Wisconsin–Madison), Don Studlar (West Virginia University), Ray Tatalovich (Loyola University, Chicago), Bob Turner (Skidmore College), Craig Volden (Ohio State University), Carol Weissert (Florida State University), Dick Winters (Dartmouth College), Gerald Wright (Indiana University at Bloomington), and Joseph Zimmerman (State University of New York at Albany).

We would also like to thank those scholars and teachers whom Cengage recruited to review the entire manuscript as it moved closer toward its final form:

Robert Alexander	Ohio Northern University
Ross C. Alexander	North Georgia College and State University
David Bartley	Indiana Wesleyan University
Jack M. Bernardo	County College of Morris
Scott E. Buchanan	Columbus State University
Thomas M. Carsey	University of North Carolina at Chapel Hill
Nelson Dometrius	Texas Tech University
Donald P. Haider-Markel	University of Kansas
Amy E. Hendricks	Brevard Community College
Paula M. Hoene	Walla Walla Community College, Clarkston
Pressley Martin Johnson	University of California, Riverside
Andrew Karch	University of Texas at Austin
Christine Kelleher	Villanova University
Kenneth Kickham	University of Central Oklahoma

Junius Koonce	Edgecombe Community College
Adam Newmark	Appalachian State University
Anne Peterson	University of Washington, Bothell
Sherri Thompson Raney	Oklahoma Baptist University
John David Rausch, Jr.	West Texas A&M University
Scott Robinson	University of Texas at Dallas
David L. Schecter	California State University, Fresno
John A. Straayer	Colorado State University
Paul Teske	UCDHSC, Graduate School of Public Affairs
Caroline Tolbert	University of Iowa
Susan Peterson Thomas	Kansas State University
Jeff Worsham	West Virginia University

We would like to send out special appreciation to three scholars who helped us by testing an early draft of the book in their state and local government courses, giving us thoughtful and detailed comments about the manuscript and their students' reactions to it: Caroline Tolbert (Kent State University and University of Iowa), Carolyn Cocca (State University of New York at Old Westbury), and Richard Scher (University of Florida). For their invaluable (and frank) feedback, we also thank their students, including Kathryn N. Domanico, Numan Imtiaz, Jason Von Buttgereit, Thomas Mastrocinque, and Michele Ricero as well as many others who preferred to remain anonymous. Three scholars helped us by providing some of the data we have included herein: Tim Storey (National Conference of State Legislatures), Laura Langer (University of Arizona), and Barbara Van Dyke-Brown (University of Illinois at Springfield). Several of our own students helped us copyedit the manuscript and worked on the ancillaries, including Brian Bartoz (University of Illinois at Springfield) and Brittany Rouille, Leah Rose Cheli, and Aaron Retteen (University of Florida). We would also like to thank those wonderful people at Cengage who helped us turn the manuscript into this book and get it into your hands: Carolyn Merrill, executive editor; Rebecca Green, development editor; Amy Whitaker, marketing manager; and Katie Hayes, assistant editor. Finally, we would like to give a special thanks to Caroline Tolbert, not only for her extensive and valuable comments on the manuscript at various points in its development but also for her tremendous support, encouragement, and friendship from the beginning of this project to the end.

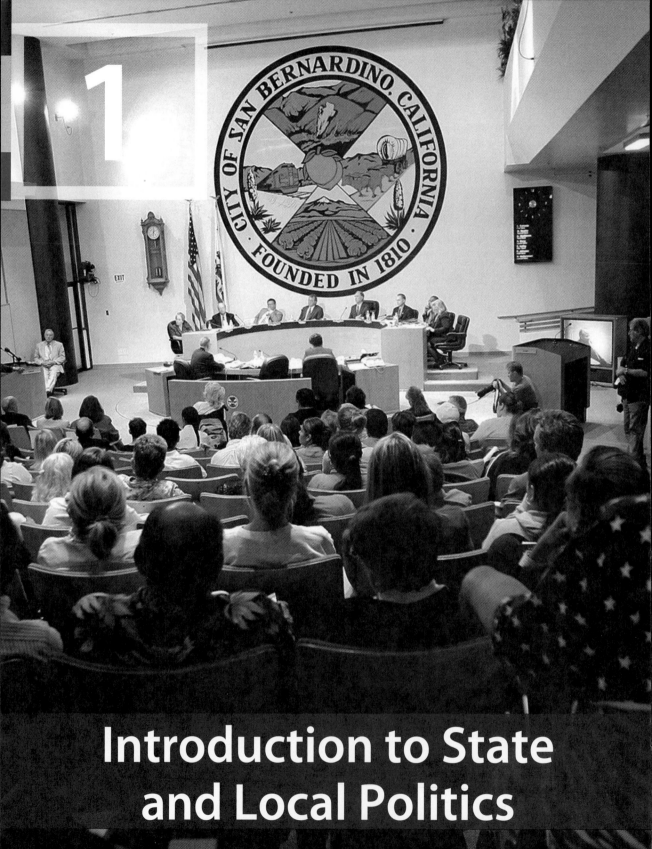

1

CITY OF SAN BERNARDINO, CALIFORNIA · FOUNDED IN 1810

Introduction to State and Local Politics

INTRODUCTION

Welcome to the study of the most important thing you never thought much about before—state and local government in the United States. In every chapter of this book, we focus on four important points that we hope will not only enlighten you about state and local government but also show you how the study of this aspect of American government will help you think and learn about politics and people more generally.

Our first point is that state and local governments are important to Americans in countless ways. And these governments are not just important to things like "governance" and "the economy," concepts that may seem rather vague and general to you. No, these governments are deeply important to you personally, in dozens of ways every day, from the moment you wake up until you turn off your light to go to sleep. Even while you are sleeping, state and local governments are busy affecting the quality of your life and the choices you can make the next day, the next year, and for the rest of your life. In fact, state and local governments have a far greater impact on your daily life than does the federal government—unless you happen to be a member of the U.S. armed forces. On virtually every page of this book, you will see in one way after another just how state and local governments affect you and everyone you know every day.

Our second point is that **political institutions** matter. Political institutions are the rules, laws, and organizations through which and by which government functions. Institutions are enduring mechanisms designed to translate the principles and values of public policy into reality. They set up consequences for policy makers' and citizens' choices, encouraging some and discouraging others. For example, the initiative is an institution that allows citizens to vote directly on public policy questions (Chapter 4). In the 1990s, 21 states adopted restrictions on how long state legislators could serve; that is, state legislative term limits (Chapter 6).[1] Not coincidentally, 19 of these 21 states did so using the initiative; of the 24 states whose constitutions allow the initiative, all but four passed term limits. In other words, although citizens are eager to adopt term limits when their political institutions give them a chance to do so, state legislators are loath to restrict their own careers. In short, the institutions with which we organize government have important, complex, and not always intended consequences.

[1] As you will see in Chapter 6, because of various court decisions and legislative action in six of these states, only 15 states have state legislative term limits today.

Reform is the third theme of this book. Political institutions are especially important because they are among the significant forces affecting people's lives that government can change most readily. That is, these institutions can be reformed by the actions of citizens and their government. There are many other social forces influencing peoples' lives that government can't easily change. A state or community's political culture, demographic composition, and economy have major political and personal impacts, but the government can't do much about these in the short term, even if it wanted to do so. But political institutions are relatively easy to change. For example, state legislative term limits was a significant institutional reform, the effects of which are only now becoming apparent. States and communities are constantly tinkering with their institutions. Throughout this book, we will discuss both the causes and effects of such reform.

Finally, perhaps our most obvious point is that state and local governments differ from one another. They differ in how they are organized, the policies they pursue, the institutions they establish, and the effects they have on their citizens. Thus, it matters in which state and city you live, whether as a student, a parent, a consumer, a businessperson, a retiree, or any other role in which you might find yourself throughout your life. For many people, this diversity can be baffling and, at times, frustrating. For example, you may know someone who attends another state college where the tuition is much higher or lower than yours—why is this the case? Other differences can be equally confusing and troubling to other types of people. Why must truckers slow down from 70 miles per hour to 55 mph when they cross the border from Indiana to Illinois on I-72 at Danville? Why do people in Vancouver, Washington, pay no state income tax, while those just across the Columbia River in Portland, Oregon, pay no sales tax? Why do

some states—and even some school districts in the same state—educate their children better than others? Why are rivers cleaner in some states than in others? And on it goes.

While these questions may cause some people to scratch their heads or pound the table, students of politics and policy look at them as wonderful opportunities to learn more about how people work together to help their communities survive and thrive. As such, the study of state and local politics and government not only raises important and interesting questions but it also offers us an extraordinary means to answer them—the comparative method. For example, if we want to know why some governments provide more services for their poor than others do, we can identify state and local governments that help their impoverished residents differently and *compare* them on other characteristics to look for clues to explain this difference. Perhaps governments that provide better services for their poor are wealthier, have more diverse economies, or have a more liberal political culture than those governments that provide the poor with fewer services. Even more interestingly, perhaps these factors have a more subtle and complex relationship than this.[2] With so many state and local governments in the United States (over 87,000 at last count),[3] political scientists have a vast and rich laboratory in which to study politics and policy, using the comparative method to tease out and demonstrate often quite intricate patterns of relationships.

In this chapter, we lay out our case for studying American state and local government, and we explain our approach to doing so. We hope that by the time you have finished this book, you will not be able to read the newspaper or watch the TV news without asking yourself why your government has done what it has done to deal with a particular problem, what other governments have done about that problem, why these governments

---

[2] Charles Barrilleaux, Thomas Holbrook, and Laura Langer, "Electoral Competition, Legislative Balance, and American State Welfare Policy," *American Journal of Political Science* 46 (2002): 415–27.

[3] U.S. Census Bureau, *Census of Governments*, GC02-1(P) (Washington, D.C.: U.S. Government Printing Office, 2002).

have adopted these different approaches to solving that problem, and which approach is better. In this way, you will become an amateur political scientist and a better and more intellectually active citizen with the tools to understand politics and government more deeply at all levels.

State and Local Government: Everywhere, All the Time

It may be impossible to overstate the importance of state and local government in your life. Just walk through your day and see how they affect you. Your alarm clock rings—the state government determines whether you will fall back and spring forward for daylight-saving time (residents of Arizona and Hawaii do not change their clocks).[4] You hit the light switch—electricity is generated according to an extraordinarily complicated set of state and local regulations to make it safe, affordable, and not unduly damaging to the environment. You may even live in one of those communities— such as Springfield, Illinois, and Orlando, Florida—where the local government actually generates and sells its own electricity. You have breakfast—the organic milk on your cereal is regulated and inspected by state officials. You take a shower—the water is probably provided by your local public utility. You drive to school—the roads are built and maintained by state, county, and local employees, and they are made safe by police officers from these same governments. You sit down in class—if you are a student at a college or university run by a state or local government (as most American college students are), everything about your education is controlled by officials and employees of these governments. Admissions requirements, tuition and fees, the degree requirements, which classes are offered, the topics that are covered

in each class—even the fact that you have been assigned to read this book—are all determined by state or local government officials. State and local governments also have a great deal of influence over what happens in private colleges, through various laws and regulations, monetary incentives, and so forth.

Beyond college, your life is affected by state and local government in innumerable other ways. They make sure your life is safer by regulating restaurants, doctors, teachers, dentists, accountants, lawyers, and undertakers—and even hair, fingernail, and tanning salons. Do you want to smoke a cigarette? State and local governments tax you heavily for the privilege and then tell you where and when you can do it. Do you want to use a gun? State and local governments closely regulate where and when you can buy that firearm and where and when you can shoot it. Do you want to go to a dance club? State and local laws regulate how loud the music can be, how much tax you pay on your food and beverage, who can serve you, and how late the club can stay open. Do you want to build a house or start a business? Buy insurance or drive a car? Get married or get divorced? Yes, these and many more of life's regular activities are regulated, encouraged, deterred, modified, or monitored by state and local government.

You get the idea. State and local governments are deeply involved in your life every day, all day, whether you know it or not. Although this may sound like something out of George Orwell's *1984*, in fact, almost all these government activities have been demanded by some group of citizens or businesses. We want government to do many things for us—to educate us well; to build good roads; to keep us safe from crime; to ensure that the various industries and professions we rely on are safe, reliable, and honest; and so forth. In a modern society, we need government to be involved in our lives both to encourage the things we want and to discourage those things that are unsafe or undesirable. Throughout

---

[4] Daylight-saving time was a highly controversial political issue in Indiana before it was settled in 2005. See Joseph Popiolkowski, "Daylight-Savings Time Dawns in Indiana," *Stateline.org*, online ed., September 20, 2005.

the United States' history, we have turned to state and local governments first for help. The national government in Washington, D.C., is far away from most of us, both physically and psychologically. State and local governments are literally as close as the street in front of our house, the school down the block, and the cop on the corner. In fact, aside from international relations and national defense (no small things, of course), the national government has very little to do with the public services you receive every day. State and local governments control virtually all domestic government policy in the United States. They are where the action is.

What Are Government, Politics, and Public Policy?

Before we get too far along, let's clarify three basic concepts that we will be discussing throughout this book: government, politics, and public policy. Although everyone has some idea of what these mean, we want to discuss them explicitly here so that we can have a common understanding as we move forward.

Government

Government is the authoritative apparatus by which a group of people organize themselves to achieve goals that they share with one another. People working together can do much more than they can do alone. Alone, nobody could build a dam, use stem cells to develop a cure for diabetes, or protect the environment from toxic waste dumping. Some common tasks can be accomplished by people working together voluntarily, usually out of an economic motivation. General Motors was organized to make cars so that its stockholders and workers could make a profit; United Airlines was organized to make money by flying people from place to place. But it is very difficult to gain immediate monetary

benefit from building a dam, studying stem cells, or monitoring the amount of waste that companies produce. Certainly, the community as a whole, and even some individuals, may benefit enormously from these things—towns are protected from floods, people are cured of disease, and the environment is improved. But no person or company would take the initiative to complete such projects alone because the benefits are widely dispersed, often noneconomic, and received over a very long time. In short, when people and firms cannot reap an immediate monetary profit, they rarely work together voluntarily—the Red Cross and Doctors Without Borders notwithstanding.

These are the kinds of tasks that government can do best: those with widely dispersed, long-term benefits where the potential for short-term, private profit is limited. By paying taxes, we collectively pitch in to undertake these tasks that help the community but that no one would or could do alone. Government, then, is the people who are hired and the institutions that are established to accomplish these common tasks that help us all.

Politics

Politics is the process by which we as a community determine what our government ought to do. Through politics, we decide which **public goods** our government should provide and how it should do so and who should benefit from these public goods and who should pay for them. Politics are the elections, the campaigns, the lobbying, the legislative process, and much else that we see daily in our newspapers and the TV news, all of them revolving around making these decisions. For example, in a race for governor, one candidate wants to encourage industry to come into the state, while the other wants to control growth and preserve the environment. The candidates present their arguments in their campaigns, and people vote based on which things they think the government should do and how they think the government should do them.

Politics also works in a less direct way when groups of citizens and businesses contact mayors, governors, and state and local legislators to present their arguments about what government ought to do. These elected officials then consider these citizens' and groups' values and information, weighing it against their own knowledge and judgment, and then make policy decisions. This is politics too, but it is a different kind than what you see in campaign commercials and debates on TV.

Public Policy

Public policy consists of the decisions that government makes and the actions that it undertakes to accomplish the common goals decided upon in the political process. These are the institutions, laws, regulations, norms, and traditions that define what government officials do. Anything that government or government officials do routinely and officially is policy. And every policy has, at its root and no matter how hard it may sometimes be to discern, a role in accomplishing some common goal of the **jurisdiction** that that government serves. For example, something as simple as police checking the speed limit of cars coming into a small town from the highway is public policy. What is the common goal that this policy is meant to help accomplish? To keep the town's streets safe for bicyclists, pedestrians, and other drivers.

Sometimes, a government worker's action may not seem like a public policy, and sometimes, the common goal of a policy may be hard to figure out. For example, maybe professors at a state university are required to give a final exam in every class. This is a public policy because it is a regulation established by a government official, such as the college dean or the university provost (who are both state workers). What is the common goal behind this policy? Perhaps it is meant to enhance students' education by (1) motivating them to study, (2) forcing professors to evaluate their students and thereby give them that motivation, and (3) forcing professors to teach well (because poor teaching may translate

into poor performance on the exams). Each of these is in some way a public good that the university is charged with helping to produce.

You may disagree with a public policy either because you think government should not pursue that common goal or because you don't think that that policy will help reach that goal. For example, many state lotteries advertise on TV. That ad campaign represents a public policy, the goal of which is to generate money for the state to spend on other activities, like education and prisons. You might object to that policy either because you don't think government ought to encourage people to gamble or because you think that the ads are so bad that they won't persuade anyone to buy a lottery ticket. Public policy is constantly evolving and changing through the process of political reform as different common goals are pursued and different approaches to meeting those goals are tried.

Taken together, government, politics, and public policy are all about how different groups of people work together to accomplish that which they could not accomplish alone. In this book, we explore how government, politics, and policy interact with the various social and economic conditions that exist in different parts of the United States to give us the marvelous mosaic of public life we find in the states and communities of this country.

Differences in Government, Politics, and Public Policy across the Country

American states and communities vary dramatically in a multitude of ways, including in their governments, politics, and public policy. Political scientists can use this variation to help explain why governments and people behave as they do in the political realm. You will read about many of these differences throughout this book, but here are three examples to whet your appetite.

Differences in Government: Women in State Legislatures

Women are much underrepresented in elective office in the United States, but as we discuss in various chapters of this book, this representation both has improved dramatically in recent years and varies greatly across the country. For example, in 2007, almost a quarter of all state legislators were women, up from less than 5 percent in 1970. Yet, even today, women are considerably better represented in some legislatures than others. As Figure 1.1 shows, in 12 states, women held over 30 percent of the legislative seats, whereas in other states, they held considerably fewer. In South Carolina, less than 10 percent of state legislators were women. Why is women's representation in state legislatures so different among the states?

One explanation for why women win legislative elections more frequently in some states than in others is simply differences in the bias against women serving in elective office, a holdover from the prefeminist era (Chapter 6). For example, political scientists have shown that when a state's electorate and party leaders hold more traditional attitudes toward religion and gender roles, women are less well-represented in its legislature.[5] Studies

---

Figure 1.1

Percentage of State Legislators Who Are Women, 2007

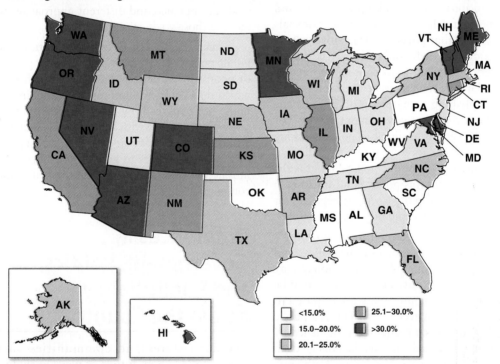

Note: This map shows the percentage of all state legislators (both house and senate) who are women. These figures reflect the results of the 2006 general election and were correct as of January 15, 2007.

Source: "Women in State Legislatures 2007," Center for American Women and Politics, Rutgers University, "Women in State Legislatures 2007," (http://www.cawp.rutgers.edu/Facts/Officeholders/stleg.pdf).

[5] John F. Camobreco and Michelle A. Barnello, "Postmaterialism and Post-Industrialism: Cultural Influences on Female Representation in State Legislatures," *State Politics and Policy Quarterly* 3 (2003): 117–38; Kevin Arceneaux, "The 'Gender Gap' in State Legislative Representation: New Data to Tackle an Old Question," *Political Research Quarterly* 54 (2001): 143–60; and Kira Sanbonmatsu, *Where Women Run: Gender and Party in the American States* (Ann Arbor: University of Michigan Press, 2006).

have also found that state legislatures that pay their members more, have longer sessions, and have districts with only one legislator tend to have fewer women members.[6] One explanation for this pattern supports the *bias against women theory*, in that voters may be less likely to vote for women to fill those positions that are somehow more valuable (for example, they pay better and require longer work commitments). Another explanation for this pattern is that because seats in these more professionalized legislatures generate more electoral competition and because women are more hesitant to enter political races than men of equal qualifications,[7] women run for these seats less often. Whether this greater reluctance to run for office is caused by some internalized social bias or something else remains to be explained. But note how studying the variation in women's representation in state legislatures not only helps us explain that intrinsically interesting phenomenon but also sheds light on the greater social forces surrounding women's role in American society.

Differences in Politics: Voting, Party Labels, and State Governors

Political parties in the United States are not nearly as ideological or well-organized as those in most other democracies, but they still serve as important labels for political candidates (Chapter 5).[8] Stepping into the voting booth, voters usually know little about what the numerous candidates on the ballot believe or even what their backgrounds and professional experiences are. But in most cases, they do know the political party that each candidate represents. In general elections, this allows voters to differentiate between the candidates

and, thus, cast a meaningful vote. In this way, political party labels provide information for citizens to make voting decisions. This is very limited information, to be sure, but it is usually better than no information at all.

A party label is most useful in voting for races where voters have less candidate information; this includes many races for state and local office. In presidential elections, the party label is less important because voters know a good deal about the candidates, everything from their military service to who their spouses and children are to their views on foreign policy. In state legislative elections, where most voters know virtually nothing about the candidates, voters typically cast their ballots based on their normal predisposition toward a candidate's party (Chapter 6).

Gubernatorial candidates fall in between presidential and state legislative candidates in terms of voter knowledge (Chapter 7). Although being governor is a very important job and he or she is typically the most visible public official in the state, many Americans still pay little attention to their governor. Thus, although the outcome of a gubernatorial race is influenced by the partisan leanings of a state's voters, a candidate of the state's minority party certainly can win with a well-funded, well-run campaign and a personality and set of political positions that appeal to voters. For example, all things being equal, Democratic gubernatorial candidates have the advantage in California, but with his celebrity status, large campaign war chest, and moderate political positions, Republican Arnold Schwarzenegger was elected governor of the Golden State in 2003. Gubernatorial candidates of a state's minority party are especially likely to win when the underlying values and ideology of the state's voters are

[6] James D. King, "Single-Member Districts and the Representation of Women in American State Legislatures: The Effects of Electoral System Change," *State Politics and Policy Quarterly* 2 (2002): 161–75; and Peverill Squire, "Legislative Professionalization and Membership Diversity in State Legislatures," *Legislative Studies Quarterly* 17 (1992): 69–79.

[7] Richard L. Fox and Jennifer L. Lawless, "Entering the Arena? Gender and the Decision to Run for Office," *American Journal of Political Science* 48 (2004): 264–80.

[8] Malcolm E. Jewell and Sarah M. Morehouse, *Political Parties and Elections in American States*, 4th ed. (Washington, D.C.: CQ Press, 2001).

less in line with those of the dominant party's national base. So, although the states of the Deep South were solidly Democratic in congressional and state legislative elections for over a century after the Civil War, they began electing Republican governors in the 1960s and 1970s, as that party's gubernatorial candidates articulated the party's conservative positions, showing that they fit well with the values of many Southern voters. And today, although Massachusetts is one of the most Democratic states in the nation, it is not necessarily the most liberal. This helps explain why four of the last five Bay State governors have been Republicans. Figure 1.2 shows the current distribution of Democratic and Republican governors across the country.

Differences in Public Policy: Funding Higher Education

Since government and politics vary so much across the country, it should be no surprise that the resulting public policy also varies tremendously. For example, Figure 1.3 shows something of the state-to-state variation on per capita spending on higher education.[9] Whereas New Hampshire spent only $87.74 per person on its colleges and universities in 2006, Wyoming was far more generous, spending $628.97 per person. The policy decisions that led to these spending levels affect people directly; for example, a full-time undergraduate state resident at the University of Wyoming paid as little as $2,700 in fees and tuition in 2006, while a comparable student at the University of

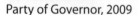

Figure 1.2

Party of Governor, 2009

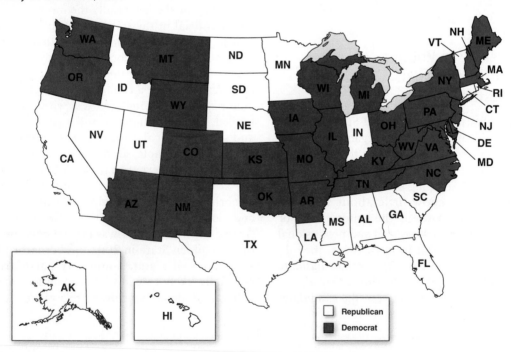

Source: National Governors Association, http://www.nga.org.

[9] Because states vary so greatly in population size, the only fair way to compare state spending is with per capita measures; that is, the amount spent per person living in a state.

Figure 1.3

Ranking on Per Capita Spending on Higher Education, 2006

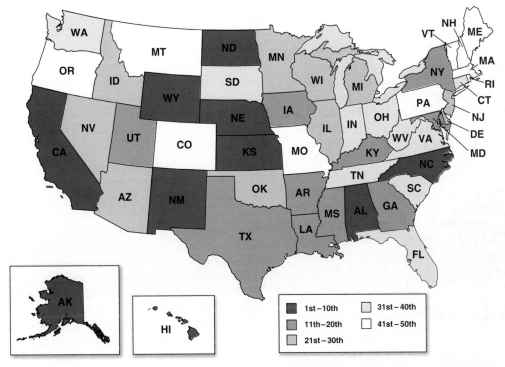

Note: The states are ranked based on their per capita spending on higher education in 2006.

Source: National Center for Higher Education Management Systems' Information Center, http://www.higheredinfo.org.

New Hampshire paid more than $10,000. This enormous difference in tuition is not because students at UNH get an education that is four times better than the education that students at UW receive. It is because policy makers in New Hampshire and Wyoming value public higher education differently.

Of course, the price of tuition is not the only policy choice behind a state's higher education financing system. For example, some states keep tuition low by skimping on financial aid. This helps middle-class families, but it may mean that fewer poor students are able to attend college. Alternatively, some states raise overall tuition but provide significant aid for the most needy. This can put pressure on middle-class families' finances while helping the poor. Then again, some states give financial aid based more on merit than on need, which tends to benefit more well-off students because they can afford

to attend better schools and take SAT–ACT prep courses and such, and they would not qualify for need-based aid.

Higher education spending is just one of a multitude of policy decisions that state and local policy makers make every year. In doing so, they work within their state's or community's political institutions, consider its politics, and weigh the often-competing values of its citizens.

Other Differences across the States and Communities

As anyone knows who has ever traveled more than 20 miles from home, American states and communities differ from one another in many ways besides their governments, politics, and public policy. The United States is so heterogeneous in so many ways that its diversity in government, politics, and public policy is not only less noticeable but also perhaps even less significant than its diversity in other ways. In fact, the variation in the social, economic, and even geographical characteristics of this country goes a long way toward explaining some of the political and policy differences we find. Just what are these other forces that affect our politics and policy so greatly? We do not have space to describe all the countless ways in which this country is diverse, but let us consider some of them, many of which you will already be very familiar with. As we describe these characteristics, think about how they can help explain why different states and communities pursue different public policies and have different politics.

Geography and History

The roots of many of the differences among the American states and communities are old. Even the very geography of the country affects our politics and policy. For example, tourists flock to Florida's sunshine and beaches, so that state relies heavily on the sales tax to funds its government because those tourists pay much of that tax (Chapter 10). Likewise, Alaska and Texas get outsiders to pay for some of their public services by taxing the extraction of oil and natural gas in their states. And any area's geography strongly affects its economy, which in turn has a big effect on its politics and public policy. For example, New England's many rivers gave it the power needed to develop the first manufacturing economy in the country in the 19th century, which led to urban living, labor unions, and political machines. The climate and soil of the Southeast were especially

suited for cotton and tobacco farming, which led to big plantations, slavery, Jim Crow laws, and conservative politics. Even within a single state, geographic variation can define politics and policy. For example, political conflict in Tennessee often divides those who live in its eastern mountains from those who live in the midstate farming belt and those who live along the Mississippi River. Many states' internal politics are defined by conflict between their coastal and inland areas or their mountainous and plains regions.

More recent history can also explain much of the variation in politics and policy around the country. During the Civil War, 11 states seceded from the country,[10] and the politics of these states still have unique qualities that can be traced back to that war and its aftermath.[11] For example, residual resentment for the humiliations of Union occupation during the Reconstruction era has instilled in these states a special antagonism for national government intervention into their affairs. And states in the West bear the marks of their years as frontier territory, such as women being more likely to be elected to office there than in most states in the East (see Figure 1.1). During the 19th and early 20th centuries, these states simply needed to attract women, and one way they did so was by empowering them politically. For example, women could vote in Wyoming in 1869, 50 years before the 19th Amendment to the U.S. Constitution gave them that right throughout the country.

Social Forces

States and communities also differ on a whole host of social characteristics that can affect their politics and policy. As a country of immigrants, an important set of social characteristics has to do with people's country of origin and how

---

[10] The 11 states that made up the Confederacy were Virginia, North Carolina, South Carolina, Georgia, Florida, Tennessee, Alabama, Mississippi, Louisiana, Arkansas, and Texas. Missouri, Kentucky, Delaware, and Maryland were known as border states. Although many of their citizens were sympathetic to the Confederacy, they never seceded from the Union. Also, West Virginia was a section of Virginia at the beginning of the war, but in 1863, in a move that rankled Virginia for over 100 years, it split off to become a separate state supporting the Union.

[11] V. O. Key Jr., *Southern Politics* (New York: Knopf, 1949).

they are distributed around the United States. Immigrants from the same place tend to enter the country at the same place and stay near there for a generation or two, at least before the mid-20th century, when travel became cheaper and easier. Thus, the big cities of the Northeast and Midwest have many people of eastern and southern European descent, whose ancestors arrived there in the late 19th and early 20th centuries. The South has a higher percentage of African Americans than other parts of the country because it was largely to those states that their ancestors were brought by force and enslaved until 1865. Many Latinos (or their ancestors) came to the United States from or through Mexico, so Texas, Arizona, and California have many Spanish-speaking residents within their borders. The ancestors of Asian Americans arrived in the West, so Washington, Oregon, and California have many residents of Asian descent.

As generations passed, certain characteristic migratory patterns developed within the country, shaping the patterns of ethnic and racial settlement that we see today. For example, as political oppression and the mechanization of agriculture forced many African Americans to leave the South, many of them moved north to work in the big manufacturing cities like Chicago, Detroit, and New York, especially during the two World Wars. So African Americans in the Northeast and Midwest are more concentrated in urban areas than are those who live in the South. More recently, Latinos also have moved north. But even though many Latinos are also attracted to the big cities, they are settling more frequently than blacks did in smaller towns and rural areas in the Midwest, where many have found jobs in food production. And in a unique settlement pattern, Arizona, Colorado, Utah,

and even Arkansas have pockets of Japanese Americans whose ancestors were forced there from the West Coast to live in concentration camps during World War II.

A state's or community's racial and ethnic composition can affect its politics and policy. For example, despite their lower percentage of the population in the Midwest and Northeast, African Americans began to be elected to political office earlier there than in the South. This is because in these northern states, they were concentrated in the cities, where they made up majorities in political districts more often than in the South, where they were dispersed in rural areas. Of course, their underrepresentation in political offices in the South before the end of the 20th century was also caused by the institutionalized racism in those states that routinely denied blacks their political rights.

Other aspects of a state's or community's social structure can also have a significant, if complex, impact on its politics and public policy.[12] For example, one in-depth study found that homogeneous states (like Minnesota and Vermont) populated mainly by whites who do not identify with an ethnic group tend to be quite liberal on a range of health, education, and welfare policies, whereas states with a higher percentage of people from racial or white-ethnic minority groups (like Mississippi and Illinois) had much less generous social policies.[13] But interestingly, when the impacts of these policies are broken down along racial and ethnic lines, members of minority groups living in more homogeneous states were worse off than those living in less homogeneous states. So, for example, whereas overall incarceration and child poverty rates are lower in Minnesota than in Mississippi, the incarceration and child poverty rates for African Americans

---

[12] Rodney E. Hero, *Faces of Inequality: Social Diversity in American Politics* (Oxford: Oxford University Press, 1998); Rodney E. Hero and Caroline J. Tolbert, "A Racial/Ethnic Diversity Interpretation of Politics and Policy in the States of the U.S.," *American Journal of Political Science* 40 (1996): 851–71; and Kenneth Meier, Joseph Stewart Jr., and Robert England, *Race, Class, and Education: The Politics of Second Generation Discrimination* (Madison: University of Wisconsin Press, 1989).

[13] Hero, *Faces of Inequality*.

are lower in Mississippi than in Minnesota.[14] This suggests that interest group politics and political representation, rather than **political ideology** or racism, are behind differences in how minorities are treated by public policy in this country. This is another example of how studying the states and communities can help us understand politics and policy making more generally.

The states and communities differ along many other social characteristics that can have political consequences. Some places have a higher percentage of elderly people living in them than others, whether because of retirees moving there (Florida and Arizona) or younger people moving away (Iowa and West Virginia). A political difference that this causes? Among other things, states and communities with more retirees spend more money on health care and other senior services, whereas places with fewer older people spend more on education but have a harder time generating the tax revenue to do so. Population density—the number of people per square mile of land—varies greatly not only between rural and urban areas within a state but also between states. Densely populated places tend to have more crime and poverty and be more economically diverse. A political difference that this causes? In cities and densely populated states (New Jersey and Connecticut), transportation policy is more about mass transit, whereas in small towns and sparsely populated states (Wyoming and Nebraska), transportation policy means highways. States and communities also differ in the extent to which people move in and out of them; that is, their mobility. In some places, people tend to stay put for generations (small towns and rural areas), whereas in others, those who have lived in their houses for five years are considered old-timers (suburban and urban areas). A political difference that this causes? Political participation tends to be higher in places with low mobility because people feel

more attached to the community and have more information about the candidates and issues. These social and economic characteristics—and countless others—have important political and policy consequences, some of which become apparent with only a little thought and some of which political scientists are still working to figure out.

Economic Characteristics

The geographic, historical, and social characteristics of a state or community help determine the way that people there earn their living and the types of businesses and industries that exist there. But a place's economy can also have significant independent effects on its government, politics, and public policy. For example, Michigan's economy has long been dominated by the automobile manufacturing industry, so private sector unions play a more powerful role in its politics than in Idaho, with its more agricultural economy. Furthermore, in today's global economy, a manufacturing economy can be unstable, with layoffs and rehirings happening frequently, so public budgets in Michigan can see more radical swings than those in Idaho.

Another economic characteristic of a state or community that has wide-ranging political effects is simply its wealth. Of course, places with more money can afford to provide better public services to their citizens. Less obviously but ironically, wealthy places need to tax their citizens at a lower rate than poorer places. This is because they have more wealth to tax, so doing so at a lower rate yields plenty of money. For example, 10 percent of $100 is the same as 1 percent of $1,000. And to add insult to injury, wealthy states and communities may actually tax their residents less overall because well-off people need many government services (like social welfare programs, police

---

[14] Hero, *Faces of Inequality.*

and fire protection, and so forth) less than poor people. This is why people find that their property taxes sometimes go down when they move to the suburbs from the city, even though their schools and other services are sometimes better (Chapter 10). On the other hand, people with more money often demand higher-quality government services and are willing to pay for them. For instance, they may be willing to pay higher taxes for high schools that offer several foreign languages and have a swimming pool, whereas these may be luxuries that a poor community simply cannot afford, no matter how much they may want them.

Besides differing in total wealth, the states and communities also differ in how that wealth is distributed among the people who live there.[15] Consider two states, each having an average annual household income of $75,000. If every household in one state earns $75,000, whereas in the other state, half of the households make $25,000 and the other half make $125,000, the states have very different economies. This difference can have a variety of political effects. For example, all things being equal, the more diverse state may have more distinct political parties and more political conflict because the poor and rich each find common cause and align their groups squarely against one another. This may lead the diverse state to spend more on law enforcement and less on public education, among other things. In the state with a more even wealth distribution, the lack of distinct wealth groups may reduce conflicts of interest and, thereby, reduce political conflict. The tax structures of these states will also probably be very different because of both the political dynamics involved and the available resources.

These are just a few examples of a multitude of aspects of a state's or community's economy that can have significant effects on its government, politics, and public policy. As you read through this book, you will see many more.

Political Values

Finally, there is one more potential explanation for the differences in the politics and policies of the states and communities that is probably what most of us think should be determining these things in a democracy—the thoughts, ideas, and values of the people who live there. First, consider people's most deep-seated ideas and values about politics and other people generally, including their attitudes about the proper role of government, their religious values, what they think is socially and morally valuable and should be encouraged, and what they think is harmful and should be discouraged. These attitudes and beliefs do not change easily over time, either for a person or for a community, and they are not evenly distributed around the country. Although Americans hold many attitudes and beliefs in common, there are some important differences from place to place in this country. And research has shown time and again that people's basic political and social values closely parallel the policies that their states and communities adopt, as most of us would hope and expect.[16]

The most common way Americans think about political values is along a one-dimensional continuum of political ideology—liberal versus conservative. Although most Americans—and even political scientists—would be hard-pressed to define these terms clearly, most people have a general understanding about what they mean and are willing to tell a pollster whether they are more or less liberal or conservative. More important for our purposes, different parts of

[15] Laura Langer, "Measuring Income Distribution across Space and Time in the American States," *Social Science Quarterly* 80 (1999): 55–67.

[16] Robert S. Erikson, Gerald C. Wright, and John P. McIver, *Statehouse Democracy: Public Opinion and Policy in the American States* (New York: Cambridge University Press, 1993); and Robert S. Erikson, Gerald C. Wright, and John P. McIver, "Public Opinion in the States: A Quarter Century of Change and Stability," in *Public Opinion in State Politics,* ed. Jeffrey E. Cohen (Stanford, Calif.: Stanford University Press, 2006).

Figure 1.4

Ranking from Most to Least Conservative Public Opinion

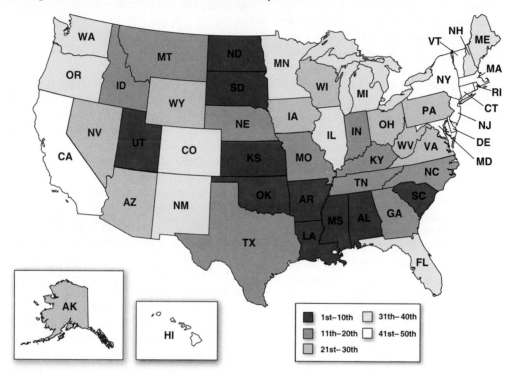

■ 1st–10th	□ 31th–40th
■ 11th–20th	□ 41st–50th
■ 21st–30th	

Note: These data consolidate and average hundreds of public opinion polls undertaken from 1996 to 2003. In this map, the darker the state, the more conservative are its residents.

Source: Adapted from Robert S. Erikson, Gerald C. Wright, and John P. McIver, "Public Opinion in the States: A Quarter Century of Change and Stability," in *Public Opinion in State Politics*, ed. Jeffrey E. Cohen (Stanford, Calif.: Stanford University Press, 2006).

the country tend to be more or less liberal or conservative (see Figure 1.4). Political scientists Robert Erikson, Gerald Wright, and John McIver compiled hundreds of newspaper polls from around the country for several decades and documented the state-to-state variation in **political ideology**.[17] These researchers have also shown that this ideology has important political impacts. Not surprisingly, those places that tend

to be conservative tend to vote Republican, and those that tend to be liberal tend to vote for Democrats, at least in recent years. Furthermore, those more conservative, more Republican states tend to have policies that we associate with that ideology and that party, such as stricter abortion and gambling regulations, less spending on education and welfare, more punitive criminal laws, and tax rates that are

[17] Erikson, Wright, and McIver, *Statehouse Democracy*; and Erikson, Wright, and McIver, "Public Opinion in the States." The role of ideology is so important in many political theories that several groups of political scientists have tried to measure it in the states in a variety of ways. For examples, see William D. Berry, Evan J. Ringquist, Richard C. Fording, and Russell L. Hanson, "Measuring Citizen and Government Ideology in the American States, 1960–93," *American Journal of Political Science* 41 (1998): 327–48; Paul Brace, Kevin Arceneaux, Martin Johnson, and Stacy Ulbig, "Does State Political Ideology Change over Time?" *Political Research Quarterly* 57 (2004): 529–40; Paul Brace, Kellie Sims-Butler, Kevin Arceneaux, and Martin Johnson, "Public Opinion in the American States: New Perspectives Using National Survey Data," *American Journal of Political Science* 46 (2002): 173–89; Ronald E. Weber and William R. Shaffer, "Public Opinion and American State Policy Making," *Midwest Journal of Political Science* 16 (1972): 633–49; William D. Berry, Evan J. Ringquist, Richard C. Fording, and Russell L. Hanson, "The Measurement and Stability of State Citizen Ideology," *State Politics and Policy Quarterly* 7 (2007): 111–32; and Cohen, *Public Opinion in State Politics*.

harder on the poor.[18] And we find a similar correlation between policy, party, and ideology in the more liberal and Democratic places around the country. Although this may not surprise you, it has only been relatively recently that scholars have been able to find real evidence that, in fact, Americans' values are translated pretty accurately through political parties into public policy.[19]

Reform and Political Institutions: The Rules of the Game Have Consequences

Thus, the United States is a vast and diverse country. High-speed communications, the Internet, and low-cost travel have homogenized this country to some degree, but Nevada is still not Pennsylvania, and Chicago is still not Key West. And you have already seen how some of the fundamental differences among people and places can go a long way toward explaining some of the differences we see in politics and policy around the country. But just as people's lives are not completely determined by the basic conditions into which they were born (for example, their race, their parents' income, and where they live), people in the states and communities can make choices about the ways in which they organize themselves that can affect their politics and policy for good or ill. That is, we can establish the political institutions that we want, and these institutions can affect the way we live and how our government works.

Just as with their histories, social forces, economics, and political values, the differences among the political institutions of American states and local governments can help us better explain the variations we see in politics and

public policy across the country. But perhaps more important, if we want to change our policies or politics, we need to concentrate on the aspects of civil society that we are able to *change.* For example, someone who wants to ban abortion can't just suddenly make her state more conservative. Nor can someone who wants to spend more money on state universities easily make his state wealthier. But people can reform their state's political institutions to make it easier to enact the policies that they desire. Therefore, political institutions take on a special importance in the study and explanation of the political differences among the states and communities.

An overarching theme of this book is that *politics and public policy are influenced by political institutions.*[20] As anyone who has ever played a sport or a video game knows, a game's rules have a significant impact on who succeeds in it; it is no different in government and politics. Political institutions are the rules that define how the game of government and politics is played; the end product of that game is public policy. Some political institutions are somewhat familiar to everyone, such as the governor's office, the city council, and the state's Department of Motor Vehicles. These institutions have buildings and staff with official titles, some of whom even wear uniforms. These really *look* like institutions. But some political institutions exist simply as sets of rules without any kind of physical edifice. For example, there is no building that we can point to and say, "That is direct democracy," but direct democracy is a political institution that is both very important in some states and varies from state to state (Chapter 4). Political parties and interest groups (Chapter 5) are also institutions in this sense.

More important than any outward trappings, each political institution has its own elaborate set of rules, some of which are

---

[18] Erikson, Wright, and McIver, *Statehouse Democracy*; and Erikson, Wright, and McIver, "Public Opinion in the States."

[19] Barrilleaux, Holbrook, and Langer, "Electoral Competition."

[20] E. E. Schattschneider, *The Semisovereign People* (New York: Harcourt Brace Jovanovich, 1960).

INSTITUTIONS MATTER

Political institutions are the rules, laws, and organizations through which and by which governments function. People establish political institutions for a particular purpose and with a permanence that goes beyond the people who created them. They require, prohibit, encourage, or discourage certain behavior. Because they are human-made, they can be changed when those with the authority decide to do so. Political institutions can be large, complex, and well-known, like your state legislature or your university. Political institutions can also be relatively narrow and have simple rules or laws that channel people and resources, like the type of primary election system your state uses. Political institutions can be established formally and backed by the force of law, like your state court system, or they can be processes and organizations developed voluntarily by people outside of government to engage in politics and influence policy making, like political parties and interest groups. Throughout this book, we discuss the various impacts that state and local political institutions have on politics and public policy in this country and on Americans' lives. In each chapter, we include a sidebar such as this with an example of these impacts.

laws, some of which are official regulations, and some merely procedures and customs. Such rules determine, for example, what powers the governor has, who can speak in the city council, when the sheriff's department can incarcerate a person, how someone becomes a judge, who can vote, and how your taxes are calculated. The rules that define and empower political institutions in U.S. states and communities are almost countless and are incredibly diverse, even in a single state or community.

But just as important for our purposes, these institutions can be quite different from jurisdiction to jurisdiction. For example, the mayor's offices in Atlanta and Milwaukee are very different institutions because the rules that define their powers are very different. Judges in Alabama and California are selected in different ways, and their courts are organized differently. Rules can even vary within a single institution; for example, New Hampshire's Senate has very different powers and election rules than its House of Representatives. These differences in political institutions can lead to a whole gamut of political and policy differences between these jurisdictions.

Those who work in and around politics and government understand very well the importance of institutions and institutional reform. State and local governments are constantly tinkering with their rules about elected officials' powers, how people can vote, who pays taxes, how property can be used, and every other government function and political activity you can think of. Rule changes—reforms—take up much of the time of policy makers and those trying to influence them. Throughout this book, we describe a wide range of political institutions and show how they affect who gets what from government and what happens when you change them.

Why Do They Tax Dogs in West Virginia? Using the Comparative Method of Political Analysis

As you have no doubt already noticed, another organizing theme of this book is our use of the **comparative method** of political analysis to *help explain patterns in politics and public policy*. We take advantage of the rich diversity found in the states and communities to pose general **hypotheses** and test general theories of political behavior and policy making. For example, one of us once wrote about how local governments put a tax on dogs in West Virginia, but they don't do this in New Jersey.[21] Why are these states' local government revenue policies distinctive in this way? Is it because West Virginia is not as wealthy as New Jersey and, therefore, simply needs more money? Is it because West Virginia is more rural and considers a dog to be an economic asset? Is it because of some difference in political culture or history? Other, perhaps more far-reaching differences in government, politics, and public policy may already have occurred to you, and you may already have posed hypotheses to answer them. For example, why do Democrats usually win state legislative elections in Massachusetts, whereas Republicans tend to win them in Idaho? Are there social or economic reasons for this difference? Why do governors in 48 states serve four-year terms, whereas those in New Hampshire and Vermont have only two-year terms? Is there a historical explanation for this or is it due to something special in the politics of these two neighboring states? Why does Texas execute a dozen or more murderers every year, while Wisconsin didn't even execute serial killer Jeffrey Dahmer? Is this perhaps due to political ideology?

The comparative method of explaining such differences is straightforward in principle. First, identify something you are interested in that varies in a general way from place to place, such as party success in state legislative elections, the length of gubernatorial terms, or the execution rate of convicted murderers. Second, hypothesize what might have caused this variation. A **hypothesis** is simply a potential answer to a research question that we derive from a theory.[22] For example, we might ask, "Why do some states elect mostly Democrats to their state legislatures, whereas others tend to elect Republicans?" Then, we might hypothesize that people living in cities tend to elect Democrats, while those in small towns and rural areas tend to elect more Republicans. Why would we expect this relationship? What theory of political behavior is behind this hypothesis? Our theory might be that city dwellers demand more government services, such as mass transit, police protection, sewer, and water, and, therefore, these people tend to support the party that believes most strongly in the value of government—the Democrats. Finally, we could test this hypothesis, not just by looking at the states where we originally noticed this difference—Idaho and Massachusetts—but also by gathering data on state legislative partisanship and place of residence for all 50 states. If we find that the pattern holds—that rural states tend to have more Republicans in their state legislatures than do urban states—then our hypothesis and theory are supported.

Although this hypothesis and theory probably do not surprise you, this story is a simple example of using the comparative method to suggest and then test an explanation for political differences among the states. And in doing so, we have not only explained this variation in state legislative elections but also tested the general theory of political behavior that was behind the hypothesis—that people elect members of a political party whose philosophy of government fits with their own self-interest. This ability to use the states and communities to help make general statements

---

[21] Christopher Z. Mooney, "'Why Do They Tax Dogs in West Virginia?' Teaching Political Science through Comparative State Politics," *PS: Political Science & Politics* 31 (1998): 199–203.

[22] Janet Buttolph Johnson and H. T. Reynolds, *Political Science Research Methods*, 6th ed. (Washington, D.C.: CQ Press, 2008), 70–77.

about political behavior is an important contribution to political science.

In this book, we are particularly interested in using the comparative method to *evaluate the effects of political institutions on politics and public policy*. Reformers who promote institutional change are essentially posing a hypothesis. For example, advocates of the initiative and referendum hypothesized that if people could vote directly on public policy, they would be energized and educated politically, leading to policy that was more in line with their values and beliefs than policy made through the traditional legislative process.[23] By using the comparative method, we can see whether this and other forms of tinkering with state and local government institutions have had the effects that these reformers had hypothesized. We can also see if these reforms have had any of the undesirable effects that their opponents had hypothesized or even if there were effects that no one

predicted. At root, the comparative method not only allows us to develop and test theory about political behavior but also helps us assess which policies and institutions have the best outcomes so that they can be implemented in other states and communities.

And why does West Virginia allow its counties to assess a tax on dogs? It comes down to a quirk of history. The Mountaineer State follows the old English tradition of taxing personal property, just as Virginia and a few other states do. In addition to taxing real estate, as most local governments do, these states tax things like cars, boats, livestock, and—sometimes—dogs. New Jersey developed its taxation system from different traditions. What lessons can we learn from this difference between these states? Perhaps that the reform of public policy is often slow and that history and inertia can't be overlooked as explanations for sometimes odd political institutions and policies.

Summary

State and local governments are deeply and broadly important to your everyday life. All day, in dozens of different ways, these governments affect your pocketbook, your quality of life, your family, and your future. And the more you know about state and local government, the more control you can take over your own life.

Throughout this book, we build on the three themes we have laid out in this chapter:

- *Comparisons* among the states and communities can help us understand them better.
- *Political institutions* can have important impacts on politics and public policy.

- Our public policies and political institutions can be *reformed*.

First, American states and communities differ from one another in myriad ways, including their histories, social structures, economics, values, politics, policies, and governments. We use the cause-and-effect relationships among these characteristics to understand our political world better. Second, political institutions—the rules, laws, and organizations through which and by which government functions—are enduring mechanisms designed to translate the principles and values of public policy into reality. We use the variation of these

---

[23] Daniel A. Smith and Caroline Tolbert, *Educated by Initiative: The Effects of Direct Democracy on Citizens and Political Organizations* (Ann Arbor: University of Michigan Press, 2004).

institutions around the country both to test and to demonstrate how the ways in which we choose to organize ourselves and our governments can have real impacts on politics and policies. And third, we examine the various efforts to reform our policies and institutions, considering why they have developed, what they have accomplished, and what the impacts of these efforts have been.

Key Terms

Comparative method	Jurisdiction	Political institutions
Hypothesis	Political ideology	Public goods

2

Federalism: State Politics within a Federal System

INTRODUCTION

Notice anything different about your new driver's license? Perhaps it has a digitized photograph, a hologram, a tamperproof casing, or a barcode on the backside? In January 2005, former President George W. Bush signed into law the National Intelligence Reform Act, known as the "Real ID" law. In addition to several other provisions that reorganized national security agencies in response to the 9/11 terrorist attacks, the Republican-sponsored law created national standards for the issuance of state driver's licenses.

Why does the U.S. Congress have the power to mandate how the states must issue their driver's licenses? Shouldn't this be a function retained by each of the 50 states? The Real ID law is but one of many examples of how Congress is able to expand its power into what traditionally has been the realm of state governments. The federal government's rapid response following the terrorist attacks of September 11, 2001, not only restructured the internal workings of the federal government but also altered the balance of power between the federal government and the states. Once again, the federal government—specifically Congress—exerted its power over the states, elevating the stature of the powerbrokers operating in the national capital, Washington, D.C. As we shall see, the cycle of centralization and devolution of power between the federal government and the states is a hallmark of the American federal system.

In this chapter, we examine the dynamic relationship between the federal and state governments. The ambiguity in the demarcation of state and national (or federal) institutional powers inherent in the U.S. Constitution has defined the way Americans have thought about government and politics and how we have designed our government institutions. After defining federalism and placing the American federal system in a broader comparative context, we investigate the ambiguities inherent in the U.S. Constitution. In discussing the historical trajectory and evolution of American federalism, we discuss the roles that Congress and the federal courts have played in delineating the relative powers of the national and state governments. We conclude by discussing how power has become more centralized in Washington following 9/11. What should become apparent in this story of American intergovernmental relations is the gradual, if at times punctuated, expansion of federal powers over the past century.

What Is Federalism?

The 50 American state governments constitute semisovereign political systems. Governmental powers in the United States are split geographically between national, state, and local governments. **Federalism** is the structural (or constitutional) relationship between a national government and its constitutive states. **Intergovernmental relations,** on the other hand, are the interactions among the federal government, state governments, and local governments. A federalist system of intergovernmental relations conjoins a national government with semiautonomous subnational governments but allows each to retain, to some degree, its "own identity and distinctiveness."[1] Although maintaining separate and autonomous powers, each layer of government is responsible for providing for the social and economic welfare of the populations living within its jurisdiction.[2] As we discuss below, the structure of a federalist system is different from those of unitary and confederal systems of governance.

How does a federalist system work? In theory, federalism combines the unifying powers of the national government with the diversity of subnational governments. The American states are not mere administrative appendages or extensions of the national government. Rather, they have discrete powers that are derived from the federal Constitution as well as their own constitutions and laws. Each layer of government has some autonomy, but there is much overlap in the powers held by the national and state governments.[3]

Sovereignty and State Variation in a Federalist System

In theory, under federalism, states retain a broad swath of sovereign powers, subject to the will of their own citizens. "In establishing this system," writes the historian Samuel Beer, "the governmental functions are apportioned so that, in the words of Founding Father James Madison[,] American people authorized and empowered two sets of governments: a general government for the whole, and state governments of the parts."[4] Such is a system of **dual federalism,** whereby the states are "no more subject within their respective spheres to the general authority than the general authority is subject to them within its own sphere"[5] (see Figure 2.1). Although sometimes pictured as a "layer cake," dual federalism does not necessarily imply that the national and state governments never encroach upon each other's territory. Rather, if a confectionary metaphor is to be used, the American system might be more aptly described as a "marble cake."[6]

Federalism and State Diversity

Because the national government does not have monopoly power in the American system, **decentralization** leads to tremendous diversity in the kinds of constitutions and laws the states have adopted over time. For example, the constitutions of the states vary considerably. Most state constitutions are longer than the U.S. Constitution, which has roughly 8,700 words (including its 27 amendments). State constitutions average 26,000 words; Alabama's

---

[1] Ronald Watts, "Federalism, Federal Political Systems, and Federations," *Annual Review of Political Science* 1 (1998): 117–37.

[2] Paul Peterson, *City Limits* (Chicago: University of Chicago Press, 1981), 67.

[3] David Walker, *The Rebirth of Federalism* (Chatham, N.J.: Chatham House, 1995).

[4] Samuel Beer, *To Make a Nation: The Rediscovery of American Federalism* (Cambridge, Mass.: Harvard University Press, 1993), 1–2.

[5] James Madison, "The Federalist No. 39: Conformity of the Plan to Republican Principles," *Independent Journal*, Wednesday, January 16, 1788, http://www. constitution.org/fed/federa39.htm.

[6] Morton Grodzins, "The American System," in *A Nation of States*, ed. Robert Goldwin (Chicago: Rand McNally, 1969); and Morton Grodzins, *The American System* (Chicago: Rand McNally, 1966).

Figure 2.1

Models of Federalism

Figure 2.1

Models of Federalism

Models of Federalism

Dual Federalism

National Government

No Interactions Between Layers

State Government

Cooperative Federalism

National Government

Multiple Interactions

State Government

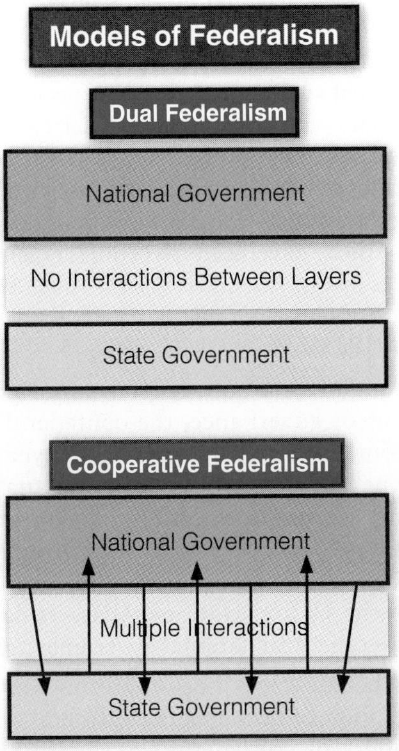

weighs in at 310,000 words and has more than 700 amendments. Vermont's, by contrast, is shorter than the U.S. Constitution. A handful of states still have their original constitutions, including Massachusetts (1780), Maine (1820), Wisconsin (1848), Minnesota (1858), Oregon (1859), Nevada (1864), Colorado (1876), Washington (1889), North Dakota (1889), South Dakota (1889), Wyoming (1890), Utah (1896), Oklahoma (1907), New Mexico (1912), Arizona (1912), Alaska (1959), and Hawaii (1959). Although Massachusetts still operates under its first constitution, hundreds of amendments have been added to it over the years. Georgia, by comparison, is on its tenth constitution, with citizens adopting the most recent one in 1983.[7] As we discuss in Chapter 7, some state constitutions permit their citizens

to vote for an array of statewide elected officials, including the offices of lieutenant governor, attorney general, secretary of state, commissioner of education, secretary of education, and even secretary of agriculture; in other states, the governor appoints these cabinet-level offices. The institutional diversity among the states is striking.

Unitary Systems: Centralized Power

In contrast to a federalist system of governance, some countries have *unitary* systems of governance, with all governmental power vested in the national government. As Figure 2.2 shows, a **unitary system** has a strong central government that controls virtually all aspects of its constitutive subnational governments (be they regional, territorial, state, or local units). Unitary systems, such as those in France, Israel, the Philippines, Sweden, China, and Kenya, consolidate all constitutional authority in the national government. In a sense, subnational divisions of the country are mere administrative appendages of the national government; that is, policy is made at the national level, and the subnational units simply carry out that policy.

There is far less regional diversity in terms of subnational electoral systems, governance structure, and public policy in countries with unitary systems of governance. The central governments in unitary systems are simply able to control the policy making that takes place at the subnational levels of government. By contrast, in the United States, policy decisions concerning criminal justice, public education, social welfare, health care, and transportation are often left to the states.

Confederal Systems: Decentralized Power

In terms of a spectrum of the balance of power between the national and subnational levels of government, a **confederal system** is located

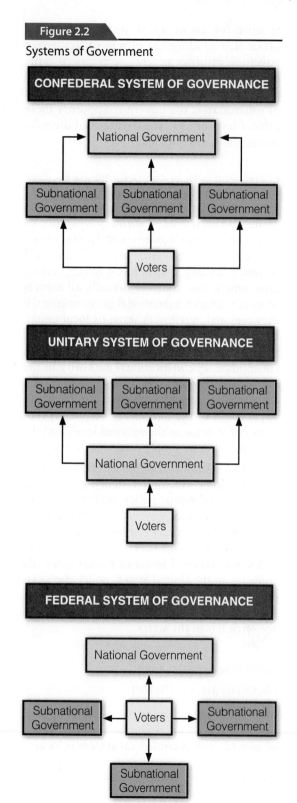

Figure 2.2

Systems of Government

CONFEDERAL SYSTEM OF GOVERNANCE

UNITARY SYSTEM OF GOVERNANCE

FEDERAL SYSTEM OF GOVERNANCE

at the opposite pole from a unitary system. A confederacy, as Figure 2.2 shows, is a system of governance whereby the national government is subject to the control of subnational, autonomous governments. In a confederacy, the constituent subnational governments enter into a covenant with one another and derive the bulk of their sovereign powers not from the central government but from their own constitutions.[8] As we discuss below, in the history of the United States, there have been two confederacies: the *Articles of Confederation* (1781–1889) and the Civil War–era *Confederate States of America* (1861–1865).

Compared to both federalist and unitary systems of governance, the confederal form has come under criticism over the years for its apparent instability and ineffectualness. The most prominent, and for some the most infamous, confederal governance structure in the world is headquartered in New York City—the United Nations (UN). Today, no purely confederal national government exists.

Although wary of decentralizing authority to the point of becoming a confederal system, defenders of confederal systems of shared governance argue that there are advantages when governmental powers are devolved to subnational units. First, because they are closer to and more familiar with the interests and needs of their constituents, locally elected officials are able to better represent the wants and needs of citizens. Second, decentralized decision making encourages policy experimentation and pluralistic solutions to local problems. Third, because there are more avenues for expressing opinions, democratic participation among the citizenry increases when government is decentralized. Fourth, policy responsiveness is enhanced when political authority is dispersed among subnational units. Finally, subnational units are able to provide and manage governmental services more efficiently than if they were carried out by the central government.

[8] Daniel Elazar, *American Federalism: A View from the States*, 3rd ed. (New York: Harper & Row, 1984); and Daniel Elazar, "Contrasting Unitary and Federal Systems," *International Political Science Review* 18 (1997): 237–52.

Why Federalism? America's Founding

One of the most fundamental struggles in American political history has been the turf battle for political power waged between the states and the national (or, as mentioned, federal) government. The cyclical ebb and flow of this tension between the national and state governments has been continuous for over two centuries and is rooted in the founding of the country. As Martha Derthick writes, "American federalism was born in ambiguity, it institutionalizes ambiguity in our form of government, and changes in it tend to be ambiguous too."[9] The inherent, ambiguous tensions of the American federalist system can be traced back to the late 18th century. In developing a federalist system, the founders had no working model on which to draw.[10] So, why did the United States end up adopting a federalist system of governance?

The Articles of Confederation

The United States has not always had a federalist system. The American colonies were originally chartered as independent settlements, under the control of European colonial powers. Settlers identified themselves not as Americans but as subjects of a colonial power. By the late 18th century, though, citizens of several of the original 13 colonies—frustrated by the dictates of the British Parliament and the monarchy of King George III—began challenging the consolidated power of Great Britain.[11] Rebellious leaders of the colonies convened in September 1774 to establish the First Continental Congress. Proposed jointly by the Massachusetts and Virginia legislatures, 12 of the 13 colonies sent delegates to Philadelphia for the proceedings; only Georgia did not immediately send representatives. The Continental Congress was weak, though, as the states retained the authority to reject or alter its wishes.

After the signing of the Declaration of Independence in 1776, it became apparent to many leaders of the fledging states that they needed a stronger central government, albeit one that would not undermine the sovereignty of the states. In 1777, the Second Continental Congress approved the **Articles of Confederation**, the country's first constitution, and sent it to the states for ratification.[12] As a confederal system, the document delimited the separation of powers between two layers of governments in an effort to make one nation out of 13 independent sovereign entities. Under the Articles, Congress was granted the authority to declare war and make peace, enter treaties and alliances, coin or borrow money, and regulate trade with Native Americans, but it could not levy requisite taxes or adequately enforce its commerce and trade regulations among the states. Members of the Continental Congress, who served one-year terms and were chosen by their state legislatures, acted typically as delegates of their state legislatures. Beholden to the states, the federal government—which lacked an executive branch to enforce laws passed by Congress—was wholly reliant on the states for its operating expenses.

The Federalists

Many founders were appalled by the ineffectualness of the federal government under the Articles. General George Washington, for

---

[9] Martha Derthick, "American Federalism: Half-Full or Half-Empty," *Brookings Review* 18 (2000): 24–27.

[10] Jack Rakove, *Original Meanings: Politics and Ideas in the Making of the Constitution* (New York: Knopf, 1997), 168.

[11] Over a span of a few years, a series of parliamentary acts were handed down from London, including the 1765 Stamp Act, which required the colonies to place revenue stamps on all official documents; the 1767 Townshend Acts, which placed duties on colonial imports; and the 1773 Tea Act, which granted the East India Company a monopoly over the export of tea from Britain.

[12] The Articles effectively served for nearly 12 years as the country's first constitution, despite the fact that it was not ratified until March 1781. Merrill Jensen, *The New Nation: A History of the United States during the Confederation: 1781–1789* (New York: Vintage, 1950), 18–27.

one, was "mortified beyond expression" that the federal government under the Articles was so emasculated that it could not even defend its citizens from relatively minor internal threats.[13] Tensions between rival sovereigns—the 13 states and Congress—were mounting. In May 1787, Congress called for a Constitutional Convention to amend the U.S. Constitution. Over that summer, delegates to the Constitutional Convention would decide to scrap the Articles, replacing them with a federalist system. In addition to restructuring the federal government's institutional design, the proposed constitution would alter the relationship between the federal government and the states, having each share power and the representation of their respective constituencies.[14]

Federalists who supported the new constitution argued in favor of a strong central government. But they made it clear that the central government's authority would be checked by the separation of powers among the legislative, executive, and judicial branches as well as through the division of sovereignty between the states and the federal government.[15] Writing in 1788 under the pseudonym "Publius," James Madison, Alexander Hamilton, and John Jay authored a series of pamphlets that collectively became known as the *Federalist Papers*. As part of a public relations campaign to generate popular support for the ratification of the Constitution, the authors claimed the new constitution would provide for internal checks and balances in the fledgling nation and would structurally limit the supremacy of the national government by creating competitive (sometimes rival, sometimes cooperative) state governments.[16]

The U.S. Constitution and the Historical Development of Federalism

Following Congress's submission of the U.S. Constitution to the states in 1787 and its subsequent ratification, a vexing question continued to linger: Which had more authority, the Union or the states?[17] Federalist sympathizers tried to downplay the power of the federal government in the proposed Constitution. Temporally and territorially, of course, the states clearly preceded the Union. Yet, compared with the failed Articles, the U.S. Constitution laid out clear powers for the federal government. Figure 2.3 displays some of the basic powers held in principle by the national and state governments when the Constitution was first adopted. As we discuss later in this chapter, the division of powers between the states and the federal government today hardly resembles the allocation in the 1790s. The continual fluctuation in the relative authority of the states and the federal government has cumulated in a slow expansion of federal power over time.

Federal Powers under the U.S. Constitution

There are several provisions found in the U.S. Constitution that enhance the power of the federal government and specifically the authority of Congress. The document grants

---

[13] Letter from George Washington to David Humphreys, October 22, 1786, George Washington Papers at the Library of Congress, 1741–1799, http://lcweb2.loc.gov/cgi-bin/query/r?ammem/mgw: @field(DOCID+@lit(gw290023)).

[14] David Brian Robertson, "Madison's Opponents and Constitutional Design," *American Political Science Review* 99 (2005): 225–43.

[15] Joseph Ellis, *Founding Brothers: The Revolutionary Generation* (New York: Knopf, 2001).

[16] David Epstein, *The Political Theory of the Federalist* (Chicago: University of Chicago Press), 1984; and Frederic Stimson, *The American Constitution as It Protects Private Rights* (New York: Charles Scribner's Sons, 1923).

[17] Rakove, *Original Meanings*.

Figure 2.3

Original Constitutional Powers of National and State Governments

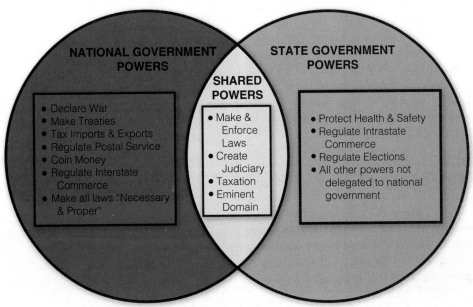

NATIONAL GOVERNMENT POWERS
- Declare War
- Make Treaties
- Tax Imports & Exports
- Regulate Postal Service
- Coin Money
- Regulate Interstate Commerce
- Make all laws "Necessary & Proper"

SHARED POWERS
- Make & Enforce Laws
- Create Judiciary
- Taxation
- Eminent Domain

STATE GOVERNMENT POWERS
- Protect Health & Safety
- Regulate Intrastate Commerce
- Regulate Elections
- All other powers not delegated to national government

Congress, the bicameral legislative arm of the national government, several explicit powers. These include the right to declare war; provide for the common defense; lay and collect taxes, duties, imposts, and excises; regulate commerce with foreign nations, among the several states, and with the Indian tribes; establish post offices and post roads; and provide for the general welfare of the United States. These "expressed" or "enumerated" powers of Congress, found in Article I, Section 8, Clauses 1–17 of the Constitution, especially the Commerce Clause, expand Congress's reach.

The National Supremacy Clause Article VI, Section 2, known as the **National Supremacy Clause**, stipulates that the U.S. Constitution and national laws and treaties "shall be the supreme law of the land . . . anything in the Constitution or Laws of any State to the Contrary notwithstanding." This means that the federal Constitution and federal laws trump any conflicting state constitutional provisions or laws. Thus, when there is no

clear delineation of which level of government is to have the dominant role in policy making or when there is a conflict in national and state public policies, federal laws are superior to state laws, and state laws are superior to local ordinances. As we discuss in Chapter 9, there is no mention of local governments in the U.S. Constitution. Powers of local governments are largely determined by states through the creation of municipal charters.

State and local governments, for example, are not permitted to enter into treaties with American Indian tribal nations without authorization from the federal government. Indian nations, which exist in 34 states, are "domestic dependent nations," a term coined by the U.S. Supreme Court in its 1831 decision *Cherokee Nation v. Georgia*. According to the high court's ruling in *Worcester v. Georgia*, which was handed down the following year, the national government has the authority to enter into agreements with sovereign Indian tribes. However, the federal government occasionally grants states the power to negotiate certain compacts with the tribes located within their boundaries.

One of the most common negotiation areas between the states and Indian tribes has to do with casino gambling. Congress in 1988 passed the Indian Gaming Regulatory Act, which requires tribes to enter compacts with their state governments specifying the types of gaming that are permitted on reservation lands and any compensation that should be made to the state governments. In 2000, for example, California voters approved a constitutional amendment allowing Nevada-style gambling on Indian reservations; in return, more than 60 Indian tribes, which generate over $5 billion in gambling revenue each year, agreed to allow unions to organize in their casinos, provide more than $1 million in aid to nongaming tribes, and make quarterly payments to the state to offset gambling addiction programs and other costs associated with the increased economic development and social pressures stemming from gaming.[18]

The Commerce Clause The **Commerce Clause** is the third clause in Article I, Section 8 of the U.S. Constitution. The clause gives Congress the power "[t]o regulate Commerce with foreign Nations, and among the several States, and with the Indian Tribes." As we discuss at length below, Congress has interpreted the 16-word clause broadly, greatly expanding its legislative power to intervene in a wide number of facets of the national economy. Beginning in 1824, with its decision *Gibbons v. Ogden*, the U.S. Supreme Court has generally granted Congress broad powers to pass laws dealing with issues only indirectly related to interstate commerce, such as civil rights, environmental regulations, possession of firearms and drugs, and Internet transactions. Congress's broad definition of interstate commerce has even been used to regulate Internet sales, racial segregation in restaurants and hotels, and the production of subsistence wheat crops in Kansas. Today,

with the increased interconnectivity of human activity, most economic activities extend beyond a state's borders and thus may fall prey to congressional regulations.

The Necessary and Proper Clause Unlike the *Articles of Confederation*, the Constitution also grants Congress wide discretion in its interpretation of its powers in Article I, Section 8. Clause 18 of Article I, Section 8, known as the **Necessary and Proper Clause** or the **Elastic Clause**, has been a key component in the centralization of power by Congress over time. The clause enables Congress to interpret and expand upon the 17 preceding substantive clauses in Article I, Section 8. Congress's implied powers give the national legislative body authority to make all laws that shall be "necessary and proper for carrying into execution the foregoing powers."

The Full Faith and Credit Clause Enshrined in Article IV, Section 1, the **Full Faith and Credit Clause** stipulates that the states must mutually accept one another's public acts, records, and judicial proceedings. Congress is given the authority to oversee the manner and effect of the reciprocity among the states. Today, the Full Faith and Credit Clause has regained prominence in the controversy over the acceptance of gay marriage in Massachusetts and California. In 1996, Congress passed and President Bill Clinton signed into law the Defense of Marriage Act. The act gave states the power to not legally recognize marriages between gay and lesbian couples performed in another state. Still, some social conservatives contend that if the U.S. Constitution is not amended, gay rights activists may be able to use the clause to force states that have outlawed gay marriage to recognize legal same-sex marriages sanctioned in other states, such as in Massachusetts and California.

Privileges and Immunities Clauses: Article IV and the 14th Amendment Article IV, Section 2 of the Constitution, the

---

[18] Institute of Governmental Studies, "Indian Gaming in California," University of California, Berkeley, 2006, http://www.igs.berkeley.edu/library/htIndianGaming.htm.

Privileges and Immunities Clause, ensures that residents of one state cannot be discriminated against by another state when it comes to fundamental matters, such as pursuing one's professional occupation, access to the courts, or equality in taxation.[19] Because of the Privileges and Immunities Clause, a state, for example, may not bar citizens from other states from practicing law in the state, assuming they pass the state's bar exam.

Section 2 of Article IV also includes a provision that was upheld by the U.S. Supreme Court's rather infamous 1857 decision *Dred Scott v. Sanford*. Before it was stricken by the 13th Amendment in 1865, the third clause of Article IV permitted states to maintain the institution of slavery and required fugitive slaves who had fled to free states to be forcibly returned to their legal slaveholders. The clause continues to be invoked by states wishing to preserve states' rights. In 1978, the high court struck down the "Alaska Hire Law," which had restricted the occupational opportunities of nonresidents interested in working in the state's oil industry. The Court, though, continues to permit what some view as a discriminatory practice: allowing public universities to charge higher tuition for out-of-state students.

State Powers under the U.S. Constitution

Federalists such as Alexander Hamilton, James Madison, and their fellow delegates who supported a strong national government during the proceedings of the 1787 Constitutional Convention in Philadelphia did not prevail on all fronts. Anti-Federalists, as they were known, expressed their discontent over the increased powers of the federal government. The Constitution was unfinished, they contended, as it failed to enshrine the rights of the states. "The Constitution did settle many questions, and it established a lasting structure of rules

and principle," writes Herbert Storing. "But it did not settle *everything*; it did not finish the task of making the American polity."[20] With the ratification of the U.S. Constitution, the political dialogue was just beginning, as Anti-Federalist concerns and principles became central to the ongoing debate.

The Bill of Rights Joining Thomas Jefferson and George Mason of Virginia, James Madison would eventually moderate his strong defense of the national government, also insisting that a **Bill of Rights** be appended to the Constitution upon its ratification. In December 1791, three-quarters of the states ratified the first ten proposed amendments to the Constitution. A major goal of the Bill of Rights was to ensure the protection of individuals from the national government. But it also protects the autonomy of the states. The Ninth and Tenth Amendments guaranteed that states were not deprived by the federal government of any rights not explicitly expressed in the Constitution. As many people in the states quickly discovered, though, the Bill of Rights did not immediately prevent state governments from depriving their residents of rights.

The Tenth Amendment The Tenth Amendment explicitly limits the powers of national government vis-à-vis the states. Also known as the Reserve Clause, it gives the states broad authority, stipulating, "The powers not delegated to the United States by the Constitution, nor prohibited by it to the States, are reserved to the States respectively, or to the people." Because there is no mention in the U.S. Constitution of numerous substantive issues, such as those dealing with education, public health, the environment, or criminal justice, it was widely understood by the founders that these policy domains would be left to the states. Despite the centralization of power brought about by the ratification of the U.S. Constitution in 1788, the Bill of Rights

---

[19] David Bogen, *Privileges and Immunities: A Reference Guide to the United States Constitution* (Westport, CT: Praeger, 2003).

[20] Herbert Storing, ed., *The Anti-Federalist: Writings by the Opponents of the Constitution* (Chicago: University of Chicago Press, 1985), 1.

infused the states with more sovereign powers. Because of the Tenth Amendment, in theory at least, the states are not administrative arms of the national government but rather constituent parts that retain their autonomy from the central government.

Federalism Today

As discussed previously, there are numerous provisions in the U.S. Constitution granting authority to the national government. Through the various powers granted by the U.S. Constitution, Congress has often asserted its authority over the states, preempting state laws. **Federal preemption** occurs when the federal government takes regulatory action that overrides state laws. Advocates of federal preemption claim that it is necessary to create a uniformity of laws and regulations so as to avoid a confusing and inconsistent patchwork of standards across the states. But preemptive legislation by Congress has created an ongoing tussle between the federal government and the states.[21] According to one count, between 1789 and 2005, Congress passed 529 preemption statutes.[22] Since the mid-1990s alone, Congress has preempted, and thus partially or completely curtailed, state regulatory authority in numerous areas, including food safety, health care, telecommunications, international trade, and financial services. Critics of federal preemption claim that it leads to less flexibility in regulations and the delivery of public services, hurts the ability of states to experiment with and develop best practices, limits the ability of states to coordinate their economic development priorities with their regulatory policies, and diminishes the protections that states are able to craft for their citizens.[23]

The Ebb and Flow (and Gradual Erosion) of Federalism

In 1908, future President Woodrow Wilson wrote, "The question of the relations of the states and the federal government is the cardinal question" of the American political system.[24] The fluidity as well as the inherent tension existing between the national and subnational levels of government comprise the defining characteristic of American federalism. The ebb and flow between the states and the national government, which were codified by the ratification of the U.S. Constitution in 1788 and the Bill of Rights in 1791, are a recurrent theme in the study of American politics. Competition or even disharmony between the national and state levels of government, then, is to be expected, with disagreements between the two layers of government being interpreted as a healthy sign that the division of powers is working.[25]

The Shifting Sands of Federalism

Since the country's founding, the locus of political power in the United States has flowed from the federal government to the states and back again to the federal government. These tidal shifts, though, have not been equal in force. Although at any given moment the relative level of power between the states and the national government is refreshingly and predictably fluid,[26] with each wave, the federal government has slowly eroded the sovereignty of the states. Many waves of federal encroachment on state power have been the result of crises—from the

---

[21] Joseph Zimmerman, *Contemporary American Federalism* (Westport, CT: Praeger, 1992).

[22] Joseph Zimmerman, *Congressional Preemption: Regulatory Federalism* (Albany: State University of New York Press, 2005).

[23] Raymond Scheppach, "Federal Preemption: A Serious Threat," *Stateline*, August 17, 2004, http://www.Stateline.org.

[24] Quoted in Kenneth Vines, "The Federal Setting of State Politics," in *Politics in the American States*, 3rd ed., ed. Herbert Jacob and Kenneth Vines (Boston: Little, Brown, 1976).

[25] Thomas Dye, *American Federalism: Competition among Governments* (Lexington, MA: Lexington Books Heath, 1990); and D. Kenyon and John Kincaid, eds., *Competition among States and Local Governments: Efficiency and Equity in American Federalism* (Washington, D.C.: Urban Institute, 1991). See also William Riker, *The Development of American Federalism* (Boston: Kluwer Academic, 1987).

[26] Zimmerman, *Contemporary American Federalism*.

INSTITUTIONS MATTER

JOHN C. CALHOUN'S COMPACT THEORY OF FEDERALISM

States' rights under the dual federalist system were taken to their logical extreme by John C. Calhoun during the first half of the 19th century. Calhoun, who served as vice president of the United States under the administrations of Presidents John Quincy Adams and Andrew Jackson, forcefully advanced what he called a compact theory of federalism. Interpreting the U.S. Constitution in the same vein as the Articles of Confederation, Calhoun argued the Constitution was confederal, binding together informally the several sovereign states. He contended that the enumerated powers of the federal government were severely circumscribed, being derived wholly from the powers of the states. Calhoun's

defense of states' rights included the concept of **nullification,** which held that a state was justified in rejecting national legislation and could render federal laws void and unenforceable if it refused to accept them. If federal laws were to be enforceable, such as a protective tariff placed on imported goods that was passed by Congress in 1828, they would need concurrent majorities, whereby the laws were consented to by a majority of citizens at both the national and state levels. If citizens in a state took a national law to be objectionable, a state had the right to nullify the law, making it invalid within the state's borders. Calhoun went so far as to declare that states had the right to secede, removing themselves from the Union.[a]

[a] Irving Bartlett, *John C. Calhoun: A Biography* (New York: Norton, 1993); and John Niven, *John C. Calhoun and the Price of the Union* (Baton Rouge: Louisiana State University Press, 1988).

Civil War, to World War I, to the Depression and the New Deal, to the War on Poverty in the 1960s, to 9/11. In the aftermath of each of these tidal storms, the states did not become mere appendages of the national government, but they did successively lose ground to the federal government.

The reason for this constant shifting and gradual expansion of the power of the federal government stems from the fact that the authority of the federal and state governments is not clearly demarcated in the U.S. Constitution. Because of the ambiguities of national and state powers, logical arguments have been made equally forcibly in defense of states' rights or for more centralized power. For example, at one extreme of the spectrum, Vice President John C. Calhoun of South Carolina in the mid-19th century advocated the theory of nullification, arguing that the states held veto power over the actions of the federal government, which included the right to permit slavery and reject national trade agreements. At the other extreme,

Alexander Hamilton argued that the United States had the right to establish a national bank that could assist the federal government in meeting its financial obligations and that the national government could impose tariffs and duties to protect nascent industries that were central to the national interest. Over the long haul, Hamilton's view of a stronger, more centralized federal government has prevailed.

Centralization and Devolution

The American federal system continually cycles through periods of centralization and devolution. **Devolution** is the decentralization of power and authority from a central government to state or local governments; **centralization** reverses the flow, empowering a national governing authority with unitary control and authority. Writing in the 1830s, the French observer Alexis de Tocqueville noted that devolution not only had positive administrative effects but also had beneficial political effects, in that it enhanced the civic values and opportunities of citizens.[27]

In the American context, centralization and **devolution** are relative terms, denoting the distribution of power and the level of policy-making responsibility taken on by the national or state governments. Besides the role of the federal courts, the level of centralization or devolution present in the American federalist system is dependent on a host of outside factors. In times of war and national crises, such as the aftermath of 9/11, an increasing amount of power tends to become centralized in Washington, D.C. Centralization also occurs when people call to redistribute the nation's wealth in an effort to create greater equity in society, perceive a need to establish national standards or policy goals, and make efforts to create more efficiencies in the implementation of public policy. Power tends to flow back to the states when citizens clamor for public policies that are better tailored to fit their specific needs or when there is growing distrust of nationally elected officials. Although at times political power devolves to the states, rarely does it completely offset any preceding periods of centralization.

Creeping Centralization: The Political Evolution of Federal Power

Abetted by the power vested in Congress by the federal courts, the authority of the federal government relative to the states grew considerably during the late 19th and 20th centuries.[28] During the mid-19th century, Congress passed several laws that slowly expanded the power of the federal government.

For example, in 1862, in the midst of the Civil War, the federal government cleared the way for westward expansion by passing the Pacific Railroad Act, giving charters to companies building a transcontinental railroad. That same year, Congress passed the Morrill Act, which provided territory to establish public schools and land grant universities, and the Homestead Act, which allowed citizens or persons intending to become citizens to acquire 160 acres of public land and then purchase it after five years for a nominal fee.[29] Following the Civil War, with the Union Army's defeat of the Confederate Army, advocates of states' rights were momentarily silenced, setting the foundation for a stronger federal government and the development of a national grants-in-aid system. In 1913, with the ratification of the 16th Amendment permitting the federal government to tax incomes, the powers of the federal government were dramatically enhanced.

The New Deal, World War II, and Cooperative Federalism

The relative sovereignty of the 50 states was altered during three notable high points of federal governmental power in the 20th century: the New Deal, World War II, and the Great Society programs of the 1960s.[30] Although there has been much rhetoric about the devolution of power to state and local governments, much of the political power initially grabbed by the federal government vis-à-vis the states during these time periods remains in Washington, D.C.

The New Deal programs of the 1930s advanced by the administration of President Franklin Delano Roosevelt forcefully inserted the administration of the federal government

---

[27] Alexis de Tocqueville, *Democracy in America*, bk. 1, chapter 5, http://xroads.virginia.edu/~HYPER/DETOC/home.html.

[28] See Stephen Skowronek, *Building a New American State: The Expansion of National Administrative Capacities, 1877–1920* (Cambridge: Cambridge University Press, 1982).

[29] Daniel J. Elazar, *The American Partnership: Intergovernmental Co-operation in the Nineteenth-Century United States* (Chicago: University of Chicago Press, 1962).

[30] Martha Derthick, "Wither Federalism?" *Urban Institute* 2 (1996): http://www.urban.org/UploadedPDF/derthick.pdf.

into the national economy as never before. In 1933, in an effort to mitigate the Great Depression, Congress passed the Agricultural Adjustment Act, which created educational programs and protected farmers by providing crop subsidies. The same year, Congress created the Civil Works Administration, which created public works jobs for millions of the unemployed, and also established the Civilian Conservation Corps, which sent a quarter of a million men to work camps around the country to help reforest and conserve the land. The Works Progress Administration, created by Congress in 1935, employed more than 8 million workers in construction and other jobs.[31] In 1936, Congress passed legislation creating a joint federal-state entitlement program, Aid to Families with Dependent Children (AFDC), which provided direct aid to families falling below the poverty line. Although these and other unprecedented incursions by Congress into policy areas previously controlled by the states were found to be constitutional, the U.S. Supreme Court struck down several other New Deal programs, including the National Recovery Administration and the Agricultural Adjustment Act, because of the congressional encroachment on the states.

The entry in 1941 of the United States into World War II gave rise to greater federal powers. In addition to asking Americans to make sacrifices for the war effort, the federal government commanded control of several aspects of the economy, rationing foodstuffs and consumer goods and even nationalizing some factories for wartime production. In addition to the dramatic increase in the number of military personnel, the number of civilian employees working in the federal bureaucracy skyrocketed, rising nearly fourfold to almost 4 million workers by 1945.

At the same time, as we discuss in Chapter 10 when examining the fiscal effects of federalism, annual spending by the federal government rose tenfold during the war, from $9 billion to more than $98 billion. By the end of the war, political power rested squarely in the hands of the president and the U.S. Congress.

The efforts of the Roosevelt administration, with the blessing and support of the Democrat-controlled Congress, to insert the federal government into the economy by way of the states are often characterized as **cooperative federalism**.[32] In such an arrangement, responsibilities for virtually all functions of government are interdependent, shared between the federal, state, and local governments. National and subnational officials act primarily as colleagues, not adversaries.[33] Although traces of such interlevel cooperation existed prior to the New Deal, the collaboration between various layers of government blossomed during the 1930s, with Congress utilizing **categorical grants** to entice the state governments to cooperate.

The Great Society and Coercive Federalism

In the 1960s, Congress further expanded the scope of the federal government by using **block grants** to spread a wide swath of programs across the nation. Following the assassination of President John F. Kennedy, President Lyndon B. Johnson urged Congress to create a "Great Society," one that would bring about many of the social and economic changes unrealized during his predecessor's truncated term in office. Many political observers questioned the ability, as well as the will, of many state officials to provide equal protection of the law and social services to all their citizens. Political scientist John Kincaid has

---

[31] William E. Leuchtenberg, *Franklin D. Roosevelt and the New Deal, 1932–1940* (Princeton, N.J.: Princeton University Press, 1963); and Alan Brinkley, *The End of Reform: New Deal Liberalism in Recession and War* (New York: Knopf, 1995).

[32] Elazar, *The American Partnership.*

[33] Walker, *The Rebirth of Federalism.*

characterized this period of expanding national growth and attendant federal programs, which some scholars date from 1960 to 1972, as **coercive federalism**.[34] With the federal government spearheading and funding several new programs in its war on poverty, some scholars have referred euphemistically to this period as creative federalism.[35] Congress sought to relieve growing social pressures found across the American states by expanding social welfare programs, including those intended to reduce urban and rural poverty and eradicate public school inequalities. In many instances, the federal government completely bypassed the states, funneling grant-in-aid directly to local governments.

In the 1960s, building on the U.S. Housing Act of 1937, Congress established an array of federal programs to aid citizens in policy areas traditionally left to the states. With the approval of the Economic Opportunity Act of 1964, Congress created an Office of Economic Opportunity that was in charge of administering numerous local antipoverty programs. The following year, Congress established the Department of Housing and Urban Development, which was charged with improving public housing and urban life. In addition, Congress passed the 1964 Civil Rights Act—which enforced the right to vote, extended federal protection against discrimination in public accommodations, and outlawed job discrimination—and the 1965 Voting Rights Act, which guaranteed the right to vote to African Americans. In the mid-1960s, Congress passed legislation creating Medicare, which created a national health insurance program for the elderly, and Medicaid, a joint federal–state-funded health care program for poor people. Each and every one of these programs increased the relative power of the federal government vis-à-vis the states.

The Continued Expansion of Federal Powers during the 1970s

Although many of the programs established during the Great Society era have been either mothballed or transferred in part by Congress to the states, many still exist. The list of programs created by the federal government during the 1960s and early 1970s is impressive and expansive. In each case, state sovereignty over these policy areas was slowly eroded. Created in the 1960s, the Head Start public education program continues to prepare disadvantaged poor children for their first years of school; similarly, the Food Stamps program provides sustenance to those falling below the poverty line. Medicare and Medicaid, two of the largest domestic federal programs today, provide millions of Americans with medical insurance and health care. In addition to continuing to regulate auto emissions and the use of toxic chemicals, the Environmental Protection Agency, created by Congress in 1970, enforces the cleanup of hazardous waste, monitors the ozone layer, and enforces clean air and water laws.

In the early 1970s, the Richard Nixon administration pushed for more block grants and changes to the way federal grants were administered. The president also pushed for **General Revenue Sharing (GRS)**, a grant-in-aid program whereby the federal government provides financial aid to subnational units but does not prescribe how those units are to allocate the funding. Congress, however, abandoned the grant-in-aid scheme, as lawmakers were unable to claim credit for projects that the federal government paid for but that were implemented by subnational officials.[36]

All these social welfare programs have undergone restructuring since their creation. Yet, they are very much essential components

---

[34] John Kincaid, "From Dual to Coercive Federalism in American Intergovernmental Relations," in *Globalization and Decentralization*, ed. John Jun and Deil Wright (Washington, D.C.: Georgetown University Press, 1996), 29–47.

[35] Walker, *The Rebirth of Federalism*, 25.

[36] Timothy Conlan, *New Federalism: Intergovernmental Reform from Nixon to Reagan* (Washington, D.C.: Brookings Institution Press, 1988).

of the social welfare system expanded by the federal government during the 1960s.[37] Indeed, Great Society programs have had lasting effects on reducing malnutrition, infant mortality, and inequality in obtaining medical services as well as improving affordable housing, job training, and environmental cleanup efforts.[38]

New Federalism During the Reagan Era

In the 1980s, many scholars observed how power seemed to be devolving back to the states. They pointed to the rise of entrepreneurial activities of the American states, with the state governments taking on new responsibilities to energize their economies by creating new jobs and economic opportunities.[39] The creative, self-directed activities of state and local governments conformed to the dominant political ideology of the time, decentralization, advanced most prominently by Republican President Ronald Reagan. In his first inauguration in 1981, Reagan famously pronounced, "Government is not the solution to our problem; government is the problem." To many states' rights proponents, they had a champion in the White House.

During the Reagan years (1981–1989), Congress aggressively consolidated categorical grants into block grants, cutting or eliminating entirely the funding of existing federal programs in the process. This wholesale transformation occurred despite the fact that the administration never outlined a clear set of principles regarding the proper delineation of federal and state powers. In 1982, the administration went so far as to propose what would become known as the "Big Swap," whereby the federal government would turn over to the states the responsibility to provide for education, social services, transportation, and cash public assistance programs in exchange for taking over the provision of health services for the poor. To offset their increased costs, the states would receive a portion of the federal tax revenue. Congress rejected the proposal, as members were leery that the state and local governments would be unable to shoulder the financial costs of their new policy responsibilities.[40] As one longtime observer of American federalism noted, the Reagan administration's zeal to lessen the capacity of the federal government was not so much driven by devolution as by an "antigovernmental imperative" of "individualism."[41] Reagan and his top officials calculated that if federal dollars to states and localities were reduced, those governments would necessarily cut back on social programs. But rather than cutting programs, many state and local governments used their own funds to continue the programs. This was not the first time in American history that arguments over federalism were used to try to conceal or advance other political agendas.

The Political Expediency of Federalism

Despite Reagan's pronouncements that power should be devolved to the states, the federal government continued to exert its authority vis-à-vis the states during the 1980s and 1990s. It is often the case that federal officials will spout the devolution line, but when push

---

[37] Michael Katz, *The Undeserving Poor: From the War on Poverty to the War on Welfare* (New York: Pantheon, 1989); and James Patterson, *America's Struggle against Poverty, 1900–1980* (Cambridge, Mass.: Harvard University Press, 1981).

[38] John Schwarz, *America's Hidden Success: A Reassessment of Public Policy from Kennedy to Reagan*, rev. ed. (New York: Norton, 1988), 68–69.

[39] Peter K. Eisinger, *The Rise of the Entrepreneurial States* (Madison: University of Wisconsin Press, 1988); and David Osborne, *Laboratories of Democracy* (Boston: Harvard Business School Press, 1988).

[40] Alice Rivlin, "The Federal Government in a Federal System: Current Intergovernmental Programs and Options for Change," Congressional Budget Office, August 1983, http://www.cbo.gov/showdoc.cfm?index=5067&sequence=0.

[41] Beer, *To Make a Nation*, xiii.

comes to shove, they usually—if not always—back off.[42] Many actions taken by Congress in the 1980s were driven by political expediency as much as any ideological commitment to the Reagan doctrine of "New Federalism." Take, for instance, the passage of the Anti Drug Abuse Act of 1988, which came exactly four years after the passage of the Comprehensive Crime Control Act of 1984. The bills, which created mandatory sentences for federal crimes and revised bail and forfeiture procedures, came just a few weeks prior to the 1984 and 1988 general elections, respectively. Both pieces of legislation were largely the result of Democrats and Republicans trying to outbid each other to look tough on crime at election time.

With the Anti Drug Abuse Act of 1988, Congress felt it needed to respond to the tragic death of Boston Celtics first-round draft pick Len Bias. Bias was a collegiate star at the University of Maryland who died of a cocaine overdose. Then-speaker of the U.S. House of Representatives, Democrat Tip O'Neill from Boston, worked with Republican leaders to pass mandatory five-year federal sentences for possession of small amounts of illegal drugs favored by the poor (five grams of crack cocaine and 10 grams of methamphetamines or PCP) and of larger amounts favored by the wealthy (500 grams of powered cocaine). The law, which required employers receiving federal aid to provide a "drug-free workplace" or risk suspension or termination of a grant or contract, was adopted without hearings, debate, or expert testimony.

Expanding National Power: Setting National Standards

In the early 1990s, Congress passed numerous laws encroaching on the power of the states. In 1990, Republican President George H. W. Bush signed into law a bill (the Gun Free School Zones Act of 1990) passed by a Democratic-controlled Congress making the possession of guns in or near schools a federal crime. In 1994, President Clinton signed into law bills making domestic violence (the Violence against Women Act of 1994) and failure to run background checks before the sale of weapons (the Brady Bill of 1994) federal crimes. (Both laws were later struck down by the U.S. Supreme Court.) By 1994, Congress had created 50 new crimes that could be prosecuted in federal court, many with possible death sentences.[43] With its "Three Strikes You're Out" legislation, Congress federalized penalties for the possession of marijuana, created mandatory minimum sentence guidelines for federal judges, and allowed the death penalty for certain drug-related crimes. Prior to 1994, many of these crimes were prosecuted in state courts, at the discretion of state prosecutors. With all these laws, Democrats joined Republicans to ensure that their party would not be demonized come election time as being soft on crime.

The Devolution Revolution?

After Republicans took over the U.S. House and Senate in 1994, under the leadership of House Speaker Newt Gingrich, a more conservative Congress did try to tackle the centralization of power in Washington, D.C. Led by Gingrich, Republicans pushed forth their Contract with America, which, among other policy goals, called for devolution of power to the states. One of the only pieces of legislation packaged as part of the Contract with America to become law was the Unfunded Mandate Reform Act of 1995. In an effort to mitigate criticism among state and local government officials for the encroachment of the federal government on state powers, Congress agreed to restrict bills containing unfunded mandates. An **unfunded mandate**

[42] Timothy Conlan, *From New Federalism to Devolution: Twenty-Five Years of Intergovernmental Reform* (Washington, D.C.: Brookings Institution Press, 1998).

[43] American Bar Association Report, "The Federalization of Criminal Law," February 16, 1999, http://www.abanet.org/crimjust/fedreport.html.

is a public policy that requires a subnational government to pay for an activity or project established by the federal government. Many state and local governments were upset with regulations handed down by Congress in the 1980s and 1990s with no money with which to implement the legislation. With its 1995 act, Congress must now include a cost estimate for any program including a mandate costing state or local governments at least $50 million. In addition, any mandate costing state or local governments more than $50 million a year can be stopped by a point-of-order objection raised on either the House or Senate floor. A majority of the membership in either chamber is allowed to override the point of order and pass the mandate, but the objection affords the chamber an opportunity for debate.

Despite the flurry of rhetoric urging the decentralization of power to the states since the Republican Party took control of Congress in the mid-1990s, Congress has taken few concrete steps to actually transfer policy responsibilities to the states. As has been the case since the United States' founding, philosophical and ideological arguments over federalism have been trumped by quests for political power. Most notably, Congress passed legislation to "end welfare as we know it" by altering the long-standing joint federal-state social welfare entitlement program, AFDC. The New Deal program was replaced by the Personal Responsibility and Work Opportunity Reconciliation Act (PRWORA), which created a block grant program, Temporary Assistance for Needy Families (TANF), signed into law by President Clinton in 1996. The new law required eligible recipients to work in exchange for time-limited assistance but gave the states wide latitude in determining both the work requirements and the levels of cash and in-kind assistance that recipients could receive.

Despite the rhetoric of devolution, the actions of the Republican-controlled Congress

and the administration of George W. Bush only increased the powers of the federal government. Following the complications of the 2000 presidential election, in 2002, Congress passed the Help America Vote Act, a grant-in-aid program that required the states to establish federal standards for voting. Earlier that same year, Congress passed the No Child Left Behind Act, which mandated that public schools make "adequate yearly progress" or risk losing federal support. In 2004 alone, the federal Department of Education placed more than 26,000 of the nation's 91,400 public schools on probation because they failed to make "adequate yearly progress." With each of these new laws, the Republican-controlled Congress greatly expanded its reach into what are traditionally the domains of state or local government.

When Does the Federal Government Become Stronger?

There has been little systematic research investigating the distribution of political power between the American states and the federal government over time. Using a measure of the level of policy centralization between 1947 and 1998, one recent study finds that the authority of the national government in the United States has gradually increased since World War II, diminishing the power of the state governments. The authors do not find, however, any patterns of stable growth in federal authority during the five-decade period. Rather, the growth in the authority of the national government has come in fits and starts. More significantly, perhaps, efforts to devolve power to the states during the presidential administrations of Republicans Richard Nixon and Ronald Reagan—contrary to their rhetoric of devolving power to the states—did not lead to the states having increased policy-making authority.[44]

[44] Ann Bowman and George Krause, "Power Shift: Measuring Policy Centralization in U.S. Intergovernmental Relations, 1947–1998," *American Politics Research* 31 (2005): 301–25.

Umpiring Federalism: The U.S. Supreme Court

Given the inherent ambiguity in the interpretation and implementation of American federalism, who determines whether the state governments or the federal government has the constitutional authority to make laws? Soon after the founding of the United States, the federal courts assumed the role of adjudicating disputes between the federal and state governments. As umpire, the federal courts determine who is in the right when disputes between the national and subnational levels of government arise. In particular, the U.S. Supreme Court serves as the ultimate arbiter of the tension existing between the federal government and the states, with the highest state courts deciding the constitutionality of state laws under state constitutions. However, as we witnessed in 2001 with the U.S. Supreme Court's controversial *Bush v. Gore* decision that tipped the presidential contest, its decisions on questions of federalism are not always consistent or grounded in historical precedence.[45] In its hasty decision, five conservative members on the bench ruled against the precedence of states' rights, overturning the Florida Supreme Court's ruling that ordered a manual recount of all undervoted ballots in the state.

Judicial Review of the Power of the Federal Government

In 1819, 16 years after the U.S. Supreme Court ruled that it had the final word on determining whether laws were in conflict with the U.S. Constitution, the high court put the question of national government broadly usurping state power to the test in the case *McCulloch v. Maryland*. The State of Maryland had imposed a tax on transactions, including those of the Second Bank of the United States, on all banks that were not chartered in the state.

The Supreme Court, under the direction of Chief Justice John Marshall, ruled that although it was not explicitly granted the right, Congress with its implied powers had the authority to establish a national bank. Under the Commerce Clause, found in Article I, Section 8 of the Constitution, the Court ruled that Congress had the power to lay and collect taxes, borrow money, and regulate commerce. Therefore, the Court ruled that the national bank was a "necessary and proper" outgrowth of the federal government's powers. Furthermore, the Court ruled that the State of Maryland had no constitutional authority to tax the national bank. The ruling, in tandem with *Gibbons v. Ogden* (1824), which permitted Congress to regulate interstate navigation, solidified the supremacy of the federal government over the state governments. In particular, the Court's rulings greatly empowered the federal government's hold over questions of dealing with interstate commerce.

The Supreme Court and Dual Federalism

For much of American history, not all individuals have been protected equally by the U.S. Constitution's Bill of Rights. Irrespective of one's race, ethnicity, or creed, a person's civil liberties have largely depended on where that person resided. Although perhaps difficult to comprehend today, the civil liberties found in the first eight amendments to the U.S. Constitution did not automatically apply to all citizens. Rather, from the late 18th and into the 20th century (1789–1913), the United States was characterized by a system of **dual federalism**. In theory, under dual federalism, citizens are essentially governed by two separate legal spheres. Every eligible person is a citizen of the national government and, separately, a citizen of the state in which he or she resides.

In a series of early rulings, the U.S. Supreme Court interpreted the Bill of Rights as being

[45] E. J. Dionne and William Kristol, *Bush v. Gore: The Court Cases and the Commentary* (Washington, D.C.: Brookings Institution Press, 2001).

applicable only to the actions of the federal government, not the states. In its 1833 decision *Barron v. Mayor and City Council of Baltimore*, the Court ruled that these federal civil liberties provided "security against the apprehended encroachments of the general government—not against those of local governments." The Court ruled that the Fifth Amendment to the U.S. Constitution—which limits the taking of private property for public use without just compensation—did not apply to the states, as "each state established a constitution for itself, and in that constitution, provided such limitations and restrictions on the powers of its particular government, as its judgment dictated."[46]

Unless specifically limited by their own state constitutions, states were not bound by the restrictions that the Bill of Rights placed on the federal government. Indeed, the states were not obliged to take positive (or affirmative) action to protect their citizens from governmental actions, even those of other citizens. For example, several states in the early 19th century had established official state religions; Congregationalism, for example, was Connecticut's official religion until 1818, and until 1833, every man in Massachusetts was required by state law to belong to a church. Other states limited the freedom of their citizens to openly criticize the government.

The Civil War and National Unity

Prior to the Civil War (1861–1865), the American system of dual federalism permitted the states certain latitude to determine their own social and economic relations. In the mid-19th century, there were clear regional divisions in the United States. In addition to deep cultural differences, there were profound disagreements among the states on how to best manage and regulate the national economy, including most notably the question of slavery. Undergirding these questions of human rights

and the economy, though, was the ever-present issue of federalism; namely, states' rights.

The Civil War fundamentally changed American federalism. In early 1861, following the election of Republican Abraham Lincoln, seven Southern states seceded from the Union. In February, these states, led by South Carolina, created a new government, the Confederate States of America. The state governments seized property—including forts—of the federal government. Soon thereafter, in April 1861, the American Civil War began. Eventually, 11 Southern states would secede from the Union; by the end of the war, over 620,000 Union and Confederate soldiers were killed. With the end of the war came the opportunity for the victorious national government to reshape the contours of American federalism.

Incorporating the 14th Amendment into the States

The end of the Civil War fundamentally altered the American system of dual federalism. Most notably, the ratification of the 14th Amendment in 1868 provided for a single national citizenship. In part, the 14th Amendment states:

> No State shall make or enforce any law which shall abridge the privileges or immunities of citizens of the US; nor shall any state deprive any person of life, liberty, or property without due process of law; nor deny to any person within its jurisdiction the equal protection of the laws.

In extending federal rights through the Due Process Clause and "Equal Protection of the Laws" Clause of the 14th Amendment, the Supreme Court has slowly incorporated the Bill of Rights into the states. The **incorporation of the Bill of Rights** has been gradual, taking place through a series of U.S. Supreme Court decisions. For example, it was not until 1925, when the

---

[46] Harry Scheiber, "Federalism and the American Economic Order, 1789–1910," *Law & Society Review* 10 (1975): 57–118.

Court ruled in *Gitlow v. New York*, that the 14th Amendment made the First Amendment's protection of freedom of speech applicable to the states. Subsequent rulings by the Court slowly began incorporating other amendments of the U.S. Constitution that protect the civil liberties of Americans into the states.[47] Although this process of incorporation was slow, many states adopted new state constitutions that provided greater rights than the federal Constitution.

Establishing Minimum Standards for the States

Through a series of rulings during the 1950s and 1960s, the U.S. Supreme Court aggressively drew upon the 14th Amendment to greatly expand the scope of powers held by Congress to enforce the amendment's guarantees. Under the guidance of Chief Justice Earl Warren, a former Republican governor of California who was appointed to the Court by President Dwight D. Eisenhower in 1953, the Court ruled that state and local governments were required to affirm the equal protection of their citizens. In the landmark decision *Brown v. Board of Education* (1954), the Court overturned the long-standing practice of "separate but equal" racial segregation of public schools. The Court also invalidated discriminatory electoral practices in several states with a series of decisions anchored by *Baker v. Carr* (1962), which granted the federal courts jurisdiction to hear reapportionment cases dealing with the malapportionment of legislative seats and required that state legislatures be apportioned on the basis of population.[48]

The Court under Earl Warren, as well as his successor Chief Justice Warren Burger, also enshrined a broad array of due process rights afforded to individuals under the 14th Amendment. In its 1963 decision *Gideon v. Wainwright*, the Court struck down a criminal procedural statute in Florida that criminal suspects did not have the right to consult with an attorney. In *Griswold v. Connecticut*, which the Court decided in 1965, the Warren Court struck down a Connecticut law that forbade married couples from using contraception after Estelle Griswold was arrested and convicted for distributing birth control products from her clinic. In its 1973 *Roe v. Wade* decision, the Court ruled that states, such as Texas where the case unfolded, were not permitted to criminalize or wholly thwart abortions, as such actions would violate a woman's right to privacy afforded to her under the 14th Amendment, although in subsequent abortion-related decisions, such as *Webster v. Reproductive Health Services* (1989), the Court gave the states considerably more room to regulate the procedure.[49]

In each of these decisions, the high court established minimal standards—a floor—in terms of incorporating the protections of civil rights and liberties afforded by the federal Bill of Rights and 14th Amendment. In this era of "new judicial federalism," the Court did not curtail the right of the states to go beyond these minimal standards. Indeed, many states have public policies—for example, minimum or living wage laws, environmental regulations, and antidiscrimination laws—that far exceed the standards set by the federal government.[50] Most notably, in 1985, the high court ruled in *Garcia v. San Antonio Metropolitan Transit Authority* that federal wage and hour standards (set by Congress in 1974) were applicable to employees of state and local governments. In other words, the Court agreed that Congress had the authority over the supposedly

[47] Carl Swidorski, "The Courts, the Labor Movement and the Struggle for Freedom of Expression and Association, 1919–1940," *Labor History* 45 (2004): 61–84.

[48] Gerald Rosenberg, *The Hollow Hope: Can Courts Bring about Social Change?* (Chicago: University of Chicago Press, 1991).

[49] Jean Cohen, "Democracy, Difference and the Right of Privacy," in *Democracy and Difference: Contesting the Boundaries of the Political*, ed. Seyla Benhabib (Princeton, N.J.: Princeton University Press), 187–217.

[50] John Kincaid, "The State and Federal Bills of Rights: Partners and Rivals in Liberty," *Intergovernmental Perspective* 17 (1991): 31–34.

"sovereign" states regarding how much they had to pay their workers.[51]

Expanding States' Rights

With its ever-evolving interpretations of the Constitution, the U.S. Supreme Court recently has made decisions that have tried to return some authority back to the states. Leading the charge to rein in the powers of the federal government, former Chief Justice William H. Rehnquist, who died in 2005, took a much narrower view of the scope of the 14th Amendment. With Rehnquist at the helm of a deeply divided bench, the Supreme Court began to crack down on the national encroachment on state government prerogatives, especially those enhanced by an expansive reading of the Interstate Commerce Clause. In *United States v. Lopez* (1995), the Court found that Congress had overstepped its authority when in 1990, it passed the Gun-Free School Zones Act, which made it a federal crime to carry a firearm in a designated school zone. A high school senior, Alfonso Lopez Jr., was charged by the federal government after he brought a concealed handgun to school. Lopez was subsequently found guilty and sentenced to prison for six months. In its narrow 5–4 decision, the Court ruled that Congress did not have the authority to craft a criminal statute under the guise of regulating a supposed economic activity as permitted under the jurisdiction of the Commerce Clause. Rehnquist's majority opinion reasoned that because the activity did not directly affect interstate commerce (there was no evidence that the gun in question traveled across state lines), Congress did not have the authority to criminalize the possession of a gun in a school zone. It was the first decision in over 50 years in which the Court abrogated Congress's power to regulate an

activity by using the Commerce Clause for cover.[52]

Two years later, in 1997, the high court ruled again to limit the reach of Congress. In *Printz v. United States*, the Court reaffirmed the principle that the Necessary and Proper Clause does not give Congress the power to compel local law enforcement agents, such as Montana's Ravalli County Sheriff Jay Printz, the plaintiff in the case, to conduct background checks on individuals wishing to buy a handgun. In a 5–4 decision, the Court ruled that Congress stretched the Necessary and Proper Clause too far when it passed the Brady Handgun Violence Prevention Act in 1993. The Court ruled that Congress could not use the Necessary and Proper Clause to regulate handgun sales. Then, in 2000, the Court ruled in *United States v. Morrison* that the Violence against Women Act that Congress passed in 1994 was unconstitutional, as it did not deal with an activity that substantially affected interstate commerce. Time and again under the leadership of Rehnquist, the high court limited Congress's authority to invoke the Commerce Clause to regulate in areas that have only an insignificant connection with interstate commerce.[53]

The States' Rights Legacy of the Rehnquist Court?

Following a string of decisions granting more power to the federal government, Linda Greenhouse, the *New York Times*' celebrated chronicler of the Supreme Court, asked rhetorically, "Will the Rehnquist Court's federalism revolution outlast the Rehnquist Court?" Greenhouse asked if the Court's effort to protect states' rights was more "a revolution of convenience" than driven by some deep

[51] John Pittenger, "Garcia and the Political Safeguards of Federalism: Is There a Better Solution to the Conundrum of the Tenth Amendment?" *Publius* 22 (1992): 1–19.

[52] Cornell Clayton and Howard Gillman, eds., *Supreme Court Decision-Making: New Institutional Approaches* (Chicago: University of Chicago Press, 1999).

[53] Mark Tushnet, *Taking the Constitution Away from the Courts* (Princeton, N.J.: Princeton University Press, 1999).

ideological commitment.[54] With the appointment of John Roberts as the new chief justice in 2005, it appears that the effort to bolster states' rights has begun to fade.

Some cracks in the Court's bulwark to protect states' rights were already appearing in the waning days of the Rehnquist Court. Prior to retiring from the bench in 2005, Chief Justice Rehnquist was on the losing side in the case *Gonzales v. Raich*, when the Court ruled that federal law enforcement officials have the authority to enforce a congressional act prohibiting the cultivation and possession of marijuana, even for physician-approved uses. Since the mid-1990s, ten mostly Western states had passed statutory ballot initiatives permitting physicians to prescribe medical marijuana to patients to relieve their pain and suffering. The Court's majority allowed Congress to preempt state medical marijuana laws, meaning that the more than 100,000 patients receiving the herbal doses are now subject to federal arrest and prosecution. The chief justice was one of only three justices who voted in the minority, arguing that on grounds of states' rights, California should be allowed to regulate homegrown "medical marijuana." With the decision, some Supreme Court watchers, such as Michael Greve of the conservative-leaning American Enterprise Institute, claim that "the federalism boomlet" that devolved responsibilities to the states "has fizzled," as "the court never reached a stable equilibrium" to enable decentralization to take hold for good.[55]

Yet, in 2006, the newly constituted Roberts Court ruled 6–3 to uphold an Oregon law allowing physician-assisted suicide and to strike down the federal government's effort in 2001 to punish any doctor prescribing a lethal dose of a federally controlled drug in an effort to terminate a patient's life. The Court's majority in *Gonzales v. Oregon* found that the Department of Justice did not have the authority to use the 1971 Controlled Substances Act to override the Oregon law, which was passed via a citizen initiative in 1994 and then reaffirmed in a 1997 statewide referendum.[56] Rather, the Court ruled that the states—not the federal government—were responsible for the regulation of their own medical practices. The Court's ruling, with Roberts notably joining a dissenting opinion, provided the first evidence that the new leader of the high court was ready to retreat from Rehnquist's states' rights agenda, although some of his fellow justices were perhaps not yet ready to follow.[57]

Because of the inherent ambiguity in the U.S. Constitution, the Supreme Court has a tremendous amount of power in settling interpretive differences between the federal government and the state governments. In one sense, federalism is what five judges with lifetime tenure say it is, and the Court's interpretation evolves as its members come and go. As the recent spate of rulings on federalism suggests—with the Court deciding that Congress has the power to criminalize the cultivation of marijuana for medical use even though a state allows it, but that Congress does not have the power to criminalize the possession of a handgun near a school or prevent a state from allowing certain citizens to take their own lives—there is some truth to this somewhat cynical interpretation of how federalism plays out in practice. Whether this drastic or not, the American federalist system has been undoubtedly affected by the legal reasoning, political ideology, and personal preferences of the nine justices on the high court.

[54] Linda Greenhouse, "The Rehnquist Court and Its Imperiled States' Right Legacy," *New York Times*, June 13, 2005, p. A3.

[55] Greenhouse, "The Rehnquist Court."

[56] Charles Lane, "Court Hears Case on Suicide Law," *Washington Post*, October 6, 2005, p. A4.

[57] Charles Lane, "Justices Uphold Oregon Assisted-Suicide Law," *Washington Post*, January 18, 2006, p. A1.

Federalism in an Age of Terror

As mentioned earlier, the national government's response to the terrorist attacks of September 11, 2001, as well as to subsequent threats to the security of the nation, has created a new set of challenges for the 87,000-plus local and 50 state governments. A hallmark of the "war on terror" waged by the administration of George W. Bush was the centralization of political power in Washington, D.C. Yet, much of former President Bush's war on terror was conducted on the ground at the state and local levels. As such, many state and local governments became severely affected, and in some cases constrained, by the crush of new federal laws and administrative rulings stemming—however indirectly—from 9/11.

9/11 and Federal Powers

During the first term of George W. Bush, the Republican-controlled Congress passed numerous laws impinging on the authority of the states. The USA PATRIOT Act, passed in 2001 just 45 days after the 9/11 attacks, expanded the federal government's police powers, including the right to access medical and tax records, book purchases, and the borrowing of library books as well as conduct secret home searches. President Bush even authorized the National Security Agency to monitor—without preclearance from a judge—phone calls and e-mails of U.S. citizens. In response, nearly 400 local governments and a handful of states passed resolutions denouncing the PATRIOT Act. Some of these nonbinding resolutions urge local law enforcement officials to refuse requests made by federal officials that may violate an individual's civil rights under the U.S. Constitution.[58]

Reverberations from 9/11 also touched upon substantive policy areas that at first blush seem to have little to do with homeland security. Besides concerns voiced by civil libertarians that much of the new federal legislation has curtailed the civil liberties of American citizens, Congress passed legislation increasing federal control over state and local governments in a host of policy arenas. The federal crackdown on foreign threats has impinged directly on areas normally under the control of state and local governments, enabling the federal government to reign supreme over the states. Under the ever-expansive umbrella of homeland security, federal laws regulating public health care facilities, restricting the importation of prescription drugs, nationalizing K–12 education policies, and standardizing state driver's licenses have all encroached upon policy areas traditionally delegated to the states.

The War on Terror and State Militias

One of the areas greatly affected by the post-9/11 landscape concerns the National Guard. According to Article 1, Section 8, of the U.S. Constitution, the National Guard is commanded directly by governors during times of peace. Unlike federal troops, which may not enforce civilian laws unless authorized by Congress, the National Guard is permitted to enforce state laws. Immediately following 9/11, many governors called up members of the National Guard to protect potentially vulnerable airports, nuclear power plants, water treatment facilities, and bridges in their states. In the past, governors have activated the National Guard to deal with natural disasters and civil unrest in their states—providing flood relief to Iowa residents in 2001 and securing South Central Los Angeles in 1992 after rioters killed 55 people and destroyed more than $1 billion worth of property following the acquittal of police officers on trial for the beating of motorist Rodney King.[59]

[58] Bill of Rights Defense Committee, "Resolutions Passed and Efforts Underway, by State," 2005, http://www.bordc.org/index.php.

[59] Robert Preiss, "The National Guard and Homeland Defense," *Joint Forces Quarterly* 36 (2005): 72–78, http://www.ngb.army.mil/media/transcripts/Preiss_JFQ_36_article.pdf.

Because of the war in Iraq, there are fewer National Guard troops available to governors to assist in emergency situations. Since September 2001, over 430,000 National Guardsmen and -women (along with other "reservists") have been "involuntarily activated"—that is, called into federal service by the Pentagon.[60] Because these erstwhile "weekend warriors" may serve up to two years of active duty overseas, governors have fewer troops to deploy when a natural disaster strikes. In September 2005, when Hurricane Katrina hit the northern Gulf of Mexico coast, search-and-rescue and disaster relief efforts were hampered in Alabama, Florida, Louisiana, and Mississippi due to the lack of National Guard troops available. Kathleen Blanco, the Democratic governor of Louisiana at the time, was so disappointed with the slow response by the federal government that she initially refused a White House request to turn over control of the National Guard to the president. In response to the chaotic response in the aftermath of Hurricane Katrina, Congress in 2006 modified a 200-year-old law, the Insurrection Act of 1807, to empower the president to take control of National Guard troops not only to put down rebellions but also for natural disasters and other public emergencies.[61]

Crises and Opportunistic Federalism

The centralization of power in Washington, D.C., that followed 9/11 was not unexpected. After every other national crisis—the Civil War, the Great Depression, and World War II—the federal government has asserted greater authority over states and localities. For over 200 years, in the aftermath of a national tragedy, the national government has tried to usurp political power, preempting the authority of subnational state and local governments.[62] The pattern simply reasserted itself after 9/11, as wave after wave of federal power has washed away much of the authority of the American states.

Due to the shock of 9/11 and the public outcry to secure the nation's homeland, President Bush increased the role of the federal government in the name of defending the homeland, and Congress obligingly followed his lead. Some, though, have questioned the increased role (and spending) of the federal government. For example, in 2005, the Republican-controlled Congress appropriated $825 million in Urban Area Security Initiative grants to the nation's cities. Congress decreased the total amount it spent on the program in 2006, but many of the new grants to combat terrorism were disbursed to cities not typically considered high-risk areas, as Figure 2.4 documents. Ironically, many members of Congress, who once heralded the downsizing of the federal government when President Reagan was in office, eagerly supported increasing the powers and spending of the federal government, especially if those dollars were for homeland security programs or newly created federal jobs in their own states. Indeed, after a decade of downsizing the personnel of the federal bureaucracy, with more than 350,000 federal jobs cut during the eight years of the administration of President Clinton, the federal government created more than 100,000 new public sector jobs during Bush's first term in office.[63]

Both Republicans and Democrats use centralization arguments when they advance their policy goals and political opportunism.

[60] Lawrence Kapp, "Reserve Component Personnel Issues: Questions and Answers," Congressional Research Service, Library of Congress, January 10, 2005, http://us.gallerywatch.com/docs/php/US/CRS/RL30802.pdf.

[61] Kavan Peterson, "Governors Lose in Power Struggle over National Guard," *Stateline*, January 12, 2007, http://www.stateline.org/live/details/story?contentId=170453.

[62] Joseph Zimmerman, "Federal Preemption under Reagan's New Federalism," *Publius* 21 (1991): 7–28.

[63] U.S. Office of Management and Budget, "The Budget of the United States Government, Fiscal Year 2006, Historical Tables," http://www.gpoaccess.gov/usbudget/fy06/pdf/hist.pdf.

Figure 2.4

Homeland Security Urban Security Initiative Grants, 2006

HOMELAND SECURITY LOSERS AND WINNERS

Urban Area Security Initiative grants, intended to provide additional money to high-risk areas, declined to $711 million in 2006 from $825 million last year. New York and Washington were among the biggest losers.

URBAN AREA	PERCENTAGE CHANGE, 2005-06	ACTUAL CHANGE (MILLIONS)	URBAN AREA	PERCENTAGE CHANGE, 2005-06	ACTUAL CHANGE (MILLIONS)
Phoenix	-60.8%	$ -6.1	Jersey City/Newark	+44.1%	$ +15.2
Denver	-49.8	-4.3	Louisville, Ky.	+41.2	+3.5
New Orleans	-49.8	-4.6	Charlotte, N.C.	+39.0	+3.5
Pittsburgh	-49.8	-4.8	Omaha	+38.3	+3.2
Buffalo	-48.8	-3.5	Atlanta	+29.6	+5.5
San Diego	-46.0	-6.8	Jacksonville, Fla.	+26.0	+2.4
Columbus, Ohio	-42.9	-3.3	Milwaukee	+25.9	+2.2
District of Columbia	-40.2	-31.0	St. Loius	+23.7	+2.2
New York City	-40.1	-83.1	Sacramento	+17.3	+1.3
Anaheim/Santa Ana, Calif.	-39.4	-7.8	Chicago	+13.8	+7.3

Note: Three cities received grants in 2006 that had not in 2005: Fort Lauderdale, Fla. ($10 million), Orlando ($9.4 million), and Memphis ($4.2 million)

Source: Department of Homeland Security

The New York Times

Source: *New York Times,* from Department of Homeland Security data, http://www.nytimes.com/2006/06/01/washington/01security.html.

Backlashes against centralized policy making in the nation's capital—from the abandonment of the First Bank of the United States in 1811, to the collapse of Reconstruction in the 1870s, to the Great Society programs of the 1960s—are as predictable as the cycles of the moon. Indeed, there are growing indications that subnational resistance to contemporary federal policies and the co-optation of power by those inside the Beltway is already taking root. Somewhat hypocritically, it is now the Democrats—who since the 1930s, and especially during the Great Society years of the 1960s, called on the federal government to override states' rights—who are leading the charge to downsize the federal government's reach in many policy realms, especially in areas concerning public education and homeland security. With the American federalist system, ideological visions of federalism are readily trumped by political considerations.

Summary

In his landmark dissent in *New State Ice Co. v. Liebmann* (1932), Louis Brandeis, an associate justice of the U.S. Supreme Court, coined the phrase "laboratories of democracy." Brandeis wrote, "It is one of the happy incidents of the federal system that a single courageous State may, if its citizens choose, serve as a laboratory; and try novel social and economic experiments without risk to the rest of the country." Many commentators have lauded Brandeis's minority ruling, as it highlights the genius of the United States' federal system. With the premium the system places on state and local experimentation as well as competition, in theory, the responsibilities for policy making are often devolved to the states.

Despite the gradual erosion of authority caused by wave after wave of federal government power crashing on their shores, the states have retained much policy-making discretion. The states have been at the forefront of experimentation in education, social welfare, political economy, criminal justice, and regulatory policies and are often in competition with one another in crafting and implementing public policies. As Justice Brandeis indicated, competition among the states, as well as between the states and the federal government, encourages policy experimentation and diffusion among the states.[64] In the American system, the states not only do battle with the federal government but are also perennially challenging one another over how to implement domestic public policies being handed down from Washington.

Since at least the turn of the 20th century to the present day, the states have had to struggle to maintain their autonomy from the federal government. In addition, states have had to go it alone when the federal government has opted not to become involved in making public policy. Recently, for example, California voters approved a $3 billion bond measure, placed on the ballot via an initiative, for stem cell research. The effort to fund such research was precipitated by cutbacks by the federal government to fund stem cell research. With the State of California functioning within a competitive market, taxpayers there are willing to finance research that will in all likelihood benefit the state's economy.

In this sense, the "quiet revolution" in the states, which Carl Van Horn observed in the 1980s, is still occurring.[65] However, as states have gradually become more powerful actors, increasing their state capacities and becoming more professionalized, so too has the federal government. State governments, with their ambiguous constitutional autonomy, continue to be relegated as semisovereign units in the system of American federalism. The following chapters compare many of the institutional differences found across the states and their localities.

[64] Karen Mossberger, *The Politics of Ideas and the Spread of Enterprise Zones* (Washington, D.C.: Georgetown University Press, 2000).

[65] Karl Van Horn, *The State of the States* (Washington, D.C.: CQ Press, 1989).

Key Terms

Articles of Confederation

Bill of Rights

Block grants

Categorical grants

Centralization

Coercive federalism

Commerce Clause

Confederal system

Cooperative federalism

Decentralization

Devolution

Dual federalism

Federalism

Federal preemption

Full Faith and Credit Clause

General Revenue Sharing (GRS)

Incorporation of the Bill of Rights

Intergovernmental relations

National Supremacy Clause

Necessary and Proper Clause

Nullification

Privileges and Immunities Clause

Unfunded mandate

Unitary system

3

Participation, Elections, and Representation

INTRODUCTION

Thomas Jefferson, who served as a legislator in colonial Virginia, suggested that a healthy democracy depends on having ordinary citizens engaged with local politics.[1] Jefferson's sentiments were shared by Alexis de Tocqueville, an early observer of American democracy. Jefferson and de Tocqueville stressed that people could best learn how to govern themselves and remain true citizens by participating in local politics.[2] Today, many perceive that access to elected officials in Washington, D.C., depends on large campaign contributions, whereas state and local officials are a short drive or bus ride away. One might assume that because state and local officials are fairly easy to contact and because state and local politics are immediately accessible and visible to citizens, more people would participate in local than national politics. Clearly, political participation must be easier, and more common, closer to home.

By one key measure, the opposite is true. The average person is far more likely to vote in national elections than in his or her state and local contests. This chapter examines this paradox of participation: Despite the fact that state and local governments are closest to people, Americans participate more in national elections than state and local elections.[3] Despite many attempts to increase voter participation in the United States, turnout at state and local elections remains low. The decline in participation, furthermore, has been most dramatic in the United States' central cities.[4]

[1] See Thomas Jefferson, *Notes on the State of Virginia* (1785); see also John Winthrop, "A Model of Christian Charity" (1630).

[2] See Alexis de Tocqueville, *Democracy in America*, 2 vols. (1835–1840). See also Robert Dahl, "The City and the Future of Democracy," *American Political Science Review* 61 (1967).

[3] Participation in local elections is also lower than in national elections elsewhere. For Britain, see Collin Rallings and Michael Thrasher, "Local Electoral Participation in Britain," *Parliamentary Affairs* 65 (2003): 700–15. In the Netherlands, see Henl van de Kolk, "Turnout in Local Elections: Explanations of Individual and Municipal Turnout Differences" (paper presented at the European Consortium for Political Research Joint Workshops, 2003).

[4] Esther Fuchs, Robert Shapiro, and Lorraine Minnite (2001) "Social Capital, Political Participation and the Urban Community" in S. Sargent, J. P. Thmpson and M. Marrenn (eds.) *Social Capital and Poor Communities*. New York: Russell Sage Foundation.

Forms of Political Participation

Citizens interact with their government in many ways—the most visible is electing their representatives and instructing them on how to behave. Elections are by no means the only manner through which people participate in the political process. Voting and elections are often given disproportionate attention because of their capacity to alter who controls government and to grant legitimacy for those who serve as elected officials. Low rates of participation in elections, then, may be a cause for concern. At some point, turnout at elections might be so low that the actions of elected officials lack legitimacy in the eyes of those who did not participate. But how low is too low? Most Americans over age 18 did not vote in recent presidential elections. Using this as a benchmark for "normal" levels of participation, the norm seems to be that most people don't participate.[5] As Table 3.1 illustrates, fewer vote in "odd-year" (that is, not during the year of a presidential election) state elections and even fewer in local elections.

Scholars and democratic theorists offer us limited guidance about how much public participation can shrink before the legitimacy of a democratic government evaporates. It seems clear, however, that fewer are participating now than in previous decades and that there are growing differences between those who do participate and those who do not.[6] If participating citizens were largely similar to nonparticipating citizens, low levels of political participation might not be such a worry. As we see below, however, there is clear evidence of **participation bias**—or differences between those citizens who participate and those who do not.[7]

Table 3.1

Levels of Voter Participation in the United States in Different Races

Voting-Age Population Participating	%
2008 presidential race	56.6
2007 gubernatorial races	38.1 (LA, KY, and MS)
2006 congressional race	37.0
2000 California local races	30.0

Source: Federal Election Commission; Zoltan Hanjal and Paul Lewis, "Municipal Institutions and Voter Turnout in Local Elections," *Urban Affairs Quarterly* 38, no. 5 (2003): 654–68; Louisiana, Kentucky, and Mississippi secretaries of state; and United States Elections Project, http://elections.gmu.edu.

Participation Is Much More than Voting

Voting involves electing representatives, and in many places that use direct democracy (see Chapter 4), voting also involves public decisions to approve or reject policy proposals. There are many other ways, in addition to voting, that Americans are engaged politically. Some of these other forms of political participation may be seen as attempts to instruct elected officials on how to act after elections are held. Indeed, all of what governments do—the laws, policies, rules, and regulations they pass—takes place between elections, after we have voted. People participate by joining groups, **lobbying** (that is, by making their case to elected representatives and other public officials), attending meetings, and writing letters, among other activities.

Why Bother? The Stakes Are High   Although most Americans do not usually vote in their state and local elections, political engagement

---

[5] In 2004, turnout was 56 percent of voting-age population and 60 percent of voting-eligible population. This was the highest level of participation in the United States since 1992.

[6] Stephen Macedo et al., *Democracy at Risk: How Political Choices Undermine Citizen Participation, and What We Can Do about It* (Washington, D.C.: Brookings Institution, 2005).

[7] See, for example, Sidney Verba, Kay Schlozman, and Henry E. Brady, *Voice and Equality: Civic Voluntarism in American Politics* (Cambridge, Mass.: Harvard University Press, 1995).

at the local level is relatively impressive when compared with the public's engagement with national political campaigns and presidential elections. If public opinion surveys are to be believed, many (and occasionally most) adult Americans show up to vote in presidential elections once every four years, but they spend little time actively engaged in working on national political issues. More Americans say that they spend their time working on issues that face their schools and their communities rather than spend time involved with high-profile presidential elections. This makes some sense, given the stakes. In the previous chapter, we discussed the scope of what state and local governments do. Most critically, state and local governments spend about 17 cents of every dollar generated by the American economy (far more than that spent by the federal government). The U.S. Supreme Court has given states wide latitude over many areas of policy. Cities and counties control nearly all aspects of land-use decisions, and state and local courts administer the vast majority of civil and criminal cases. Furthermore, over 95 percent of all elected positions in the United States are at the local level.

Participation at state and local levels, then, is likely to have a substantial impact on what government does. Americans are actually relatively optimistic about their ability to accomplish things at the local level. As Table 3.2 illustrates, nearly three-quarters believed that "people like you" can have a moderate or big impact in making their communities better places to live. Table 3.3 illustrates that although Americans are fairly cynical about politics generally, and many distrust government at any level, they are more trusting of their local governments and less likely to believe that they have "no say" at the local level compared to the national level.

Yet, the effect of political participation might be understood in terms of the cliché "The squeaky wheel gets the grease." That is, if we assume that governments respond mostly to those who participate and less to those who do not, we can understand who

Table 3.2

Local Political Efficacy (N = 3,003)

Overall, How Much Impact Do You Think People Like You Can Have in Making Your Community a Better Place to Live?	%
No impact at all	4
A small impact	19
A moderate impact	42
A big impact	35

Source: Social Capital Benchmark Survey, 2000.

Table 3.3

Public Trust and Efficacy in Local and National Government (N = 3,003)

Trust Local or National Government to Do What Is Right	Local (%)	National (%)
Always or most of the time	42	29
Some of the time	46	53
Hardly ever	11	18

Source: Social Capital Benchmark Survey, 2000.

People Like Me Have No Say in What Local or National Government Does[a]	Local (%)	National (%)
Agree	35	41
Disagree	62	50

[a] Question to respondents was as follows: "Do you agree or disagree that 'people like me have no say in what the [federal] government does' and 'people running my community don't really care much about what happens to me'?"

Source: National Election Study, 2000; and Social Capital Benchmark Survey, 2000.

gets what from government, at least in part, by considering who participates.

Who Participates? Who Does Not? Political participation in nearly all forms—voting, attending meetings, contacting public officials, and contributing to political candidates—is not behavior that is randomly distributed across the population. Depending upon the form of participation we are examining,

Table 3.4

Levels of Local Participation in the United States (N = 3,003)

In the Last 12 Months, Did You . . .	Overall (%)	Poor (%)	Wealthy (%)
Attend a public meeting to discuss school or town affairs?	45	31	63
Work on a community project?	38	23	60
Attend a PTA or school group meeting?	24	14	34
Participate in a neighborhood or homeowner association?	22	12	41
Participate in a group that took action for local reform?	18	9	30

Note: Poor = household income is $20,000 or less; wealthy = $100,000 or more.

Source: Social Capital Benchmark Survey, 2000.

there may be substantial differences between those who participate and those who do not. Consider the forms of participation listed in Table 3.4. There are striking differences across income groups. The wealthy tend to be overrepresented relative to average people and less wealthy people in several forms of local-level political participation. Most wealthy people say they go to public meetings and work on community projects. Most of the least affluent people do not. It is important to note, however, that wealth itself and education alone are not what cause people to participate in politics. Education and wealth lower the costs of becoming engaged with politics.

By "costs," we mean such things as time and the difficulty of collecting and processing political information.

Voting

When we consider voting, there are clear differences between who votes and who does not. One study found that although 55 percent of all American adults earned lower- to middle-level incomes, this majority group represented only 46 percent of voters in national elections, 43 percent of campaign hours volunteered, and just 16 percent of campaign dollars provided to candidates.[8] This participation gap between the affluent and less wealthy may be even greater in state and local elections that have lower levels of citizen participation. The voting population tends to overrepresent the affluent, older voters, people from white-collar professions, people with higher levels of education, and those who have jobs.[9] That said, voters are probably more representative of the general citizenry than other types of participants, such as campaign contributors and members of organized political groups.[10]

Voter turnout in local elections is also significantly higher in cities with a higher-social-status population and in places with more voters who are over 65 years old.[11] Public opinion surveys suggest that homeownership may have no impact on whether someone votes in national elections,[12] but the incentives to vote that come with homeownership—being concerned about property values and property taxes—are more likely to be felt in local elections. Records of actual votes cast in a nonpartisan Atlanta mayoral race, for example, demonstrated

[8] Verba, Schlozman, and Brady, *Voice and Equality*.

[9] Jan Leighley and Jonathan Nagler, "Socioeconomic Class Bias in Turnout, 1964–1988: The Voters Remain the Same," *American Political Science Review* 86, no. 3 (1992): 725–36; and Jan Leighley and Jonathan Nagler, "Individual and Systemic Influences on Turnout: Who Votes?" *Journal of Politics* 54, no. 3 (1992): 718–40.

[10] Verba, Schlozman, and Brady, *Voice and Equality*.

[11] Zoltan Hanjal and Paul Lewis, "Municipal Institutions and Voter Turnout in Local Elections," *Urban Affairs Quarterly* 38, no. 5 (2003): 654–68.

[12] Eric Plutzer, "Voter Turnout and the Life Cycle: A Latent Growth Curve Analysis" (paper presented at the Midwest Political Science Association meeting, 1997).

that homeowners are more likely to vote than renters. The stimulating effect of property tax issues on voter turnout was famously seen in California in 1978, where more people voted on a property tax cut measure (Proposition 13) than voted in the gubernatorial race on the same ballot.

Contacting and Contributing

The participation gap between rich and poor is even more striking when we look at the "activists"—people who donate their time and money to candidates and who contact government officials. Sixty percent of all reported "contacts" with public officials came from the top 45 percent of income earners.[13] Studies of people who contact local officials suggest that contacting increases with social status and income, although contacts based on needing help from the government may be related to having less income.[14] It's not just income alone that causes contacting. In addition, wealth corresponds with education, with political skills, and with efficacy—the sense that political involvement can actually make a difference.

Attending Meetings

State and local politics differ from national politics in that the actions of government are more accessible locally. Many aspects of state and local government require open public meetings that provide for public comment. Individual citizens and people representing organized groups may attend without having to bear substantial travel costs. Mandates that government provide open meetings do not necessarily ensure that officials give full consideration to all citizen comments.

Interest Group Activity

In addition to contributing to groups, citizens join and serve on boards of homeowners' associations, school groups, and many different voluntary political and social groups that work to shape their states and communities. An influential theory of interest group activity, collective action theory, predicts that groups seeking economic benefits from governments (such as tax breaks and public subsidies) are more likely to remain organized and well funded than groups seeking "public" benefits, such as parks and consumer protections.[15] Records detailing which political groups register to lobby the federal government are consistent with this theory. Nearly two-thirds of political action committees (PACs)—including those spending the most on lobbying—are affiliated with corporations, trade groups, professional associations, and the health care industry. Only 22 percent were "nonconnected" ideological and public interest groups, and 10 percent were labor groups.[16]

At the local level, the presence of organized suburban neighborhood associations may have an upper-status bias, reflecting that affluent suburbanites have resources to organize and work collectively to protect themselves (and their property values) from unwanted development.[17] Survey data reported in Table 3.4 also show large differences across income groups in who gets involved with local political groups. Compared to those from households in the bottom one-fifth of all incomes, people in the top fifth of all incomes were twice as likely to be involved with Parent-Teacher Association (PTA) groups and other school groups. They were three times more likely to be involved with neighborhood

---

[13] Verba, Schlozman, and Brady, *Voice and Equality.*

[14] Elaine Sharp, "Citizen Initiated Contacting of Local Officials and Socio-Economic Status," *American Political Science Review* 76 (1982): 109–15; but see Rodney Hero, "Explaining Citizen-Initiated Contacting of Government Officials," *Social Science Quarterly* 67 (1986): 626–35; and Michael Hirlinger, "Citizen-Initiated Contacting of Local Officials," *Journal of Politics* 54 (1992): 553–64.

[15] Mancur Olson, *The Logic of Collective Action* (1965).

[16] As of January 2000. See Federal Elections Commission, http://www.fec.gov/press/pacchart.htm.

[17] John Logan and Gordana Rabrenovic, "Neighborhood Associations: Their Issues, Their Allies," *Urban Affairs Quarterly* (1990): 2668–94.

groups and almost four times more likely to be involved with a local political reform group.

Group activity can have important effects on the policies that states and cities adopt. In the early part of the 20th century, the work of women's groups accelerated state adoption of "mothers' pension benefits"—a forerunner to the federal Aid to Families with Dependent Children (AFDC) program.[18] When American women were largely shut out of the voting arena, middle-class and upper-status women formed a million-member General Federation of Women's Clubs that lobbied effectively for mothers' pensions and consumer protections.[19]

Grassroots Political Activity

Many interest groups function by collecting contributions from members to pay for the work of full-time staff. Groups with a broader base

of support may rely on rank-and-file members or on the general public to bring attention to their issue. As examples, neighborhood groups may attempt to pack city council hearings with residents worried about the impact of proposed developments or to promote neighborhood interests. Crime and environmental degradation have prompted grassroots activism at the local level. Grassroots neighborhood groups also organize to fight poverty, promote quality housing, and resist urban renewal. Prominent figures supported by grassroots neighborhood groups have been elected mayor in cities such as Boston; Cleveland; Portland, Oregon; and Santa Monica, California.

Social Movements and Protest

In addition to joining formal groups, people participate in larger, broad-based

Peter Pettus, Library of Congress Prints and Photographs Division, Washington, D.C. [LC-US262-133090]

Participants in the 1965 civil rights march from Selma, Alabama, to Montgomery, the state capital. This march and others brought attention to barriers that kept blacks from voting. Participants were attacked and beaten by police before they reached Montgomery.

[18] Theda Skocpol, Christopher Howard, and Susan Goodrich Lehmann, "Women's Associations and the Enactment of Mothers' Pensions in the United States," *American Political Science Review* 87, no. 3 (1993): 686–701.

[19] Ada Davis, "The Evolution of the Institutions of Mothers Pensions in the United States," *American Journal of Sociology* 35 (1937): 573–87.

social movements. Social movements may comprise many loosely affiliated groups that share a common purpose of sustained, mass-based participation throughout a large number of communities in order to mobilize public opinion and change public policy. Formal channels of participation in social movements are sometimes difficult to define but may include the forms discussed above as well as lawful protest, public demonstrations, and peaceful civil disobedience.

The American Civil Rights Movement serves as a classic example of a broad, mass-based social movement working in many communities to change the nation's perceptions of racial segregation and voting rights abuses.

How Many Citizens Participate?

Records show low levels of voting at the state and local levels, yet many American adults are politically active at the local level. Between elections, these politically active citizens try to shape policy by attending meetings and testifying at public hearings. In 2000, 45 percent of Americans reported that they had attended at least one meeting in the last 12 months to discuss affairs related to their town or schools. Another 20 percent said they attended at least two such meetings in the previous year. Significant numbers also reported working on community projects and working with groups that promoted social and political change in their communities.[20] Political participation can also take forms such as circulating petitions, attending protests, contacting elected officials, writing letters, and the like. Over 50,000,000 Americans belong to homeowners' associations, with over 1 million serving on boards and committees. Although these numbers are impressive, local political participation seems to be declining. By 1990, half as many people reported voting in local elections than did in 1967.[21]

Barriers to Participation at the State and Local Levels

As Figure 3.1 illustrates, there is substantial variation in voter participation across the 50 states, just as there is across American towns and cities. Minnesota and Maine lead the nation in the percentage of adults over 18 who voted in the 2008 presidential election, with over 70 percent of their **voting-age population** having participated. Hawaii, Texas, and Arizona rank lowest, with less than half of the adults in these states voting. These vastly different participation rates are a result of many factors. States like Minnesota have far more people with traits known to correspond with interest in politics. A higher proportion of Minnesotans have college degrees and higher income levels than people in states like Texas. Maine and Minnesota also have far fewer noncitizens than Texas and Arizona. Only U.S. citizens can vote in presidential elections, which means we should also think of voter turnout as a percentage of a state's **voting-eligible population**—that is, the proportion of citizens who vote who are not disenfranchised by felony convictions. States differ as to the rules they use to define which citizens are eligible to participate in elections, and they use different rules about when (or if) a person must register to vote prior to an election.

Race- and Gender-Based Barriers

States set many rules that affect who votes and who does not. Although the 15th Amendment to the U.S. Constitution (1870) says that the right to vote cannot be denied "on account of race or color," the amendment was substantially meaningless for nearly a century. In the later half of the 19th century, many states erected substantial barriers to the voting

---

[20] 2000 Social Benchmark Survey.

[21] Verba, Schlozman, and Brady, *Voice and Equality*, 72.

Figure 3.1

Voter Participation in the 2008 Presidential Election, by State Percentage of all state residents 18 years of age or over voting in the November 2008 general election.

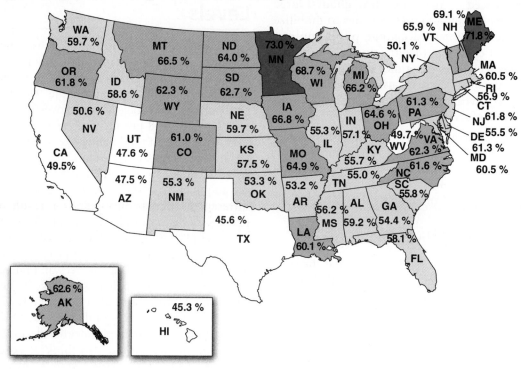

process in order to prevent African Americans from voting. Some rules requiring that voters register far in advance of elections were often adopted in response to the perception that corrupt party machines (see Chapter 5) had their supporters "vote early, and vote often." Other barriers were racially motivated, such as **racial gerrymandering** (drawing districts to ensure low minority representation), closing polling places, not allowing voters to register, implementing literacy tests and poll taxes (discussed below), and establishing **grandfather clauses** that allowed whites to vote regardless of whether they paid a poll tax or passed a literacy test. Such rules were used to reverse

the expansion of African-American voting rights that occurred after the Civil War.[22]

Prior to 1920, states could also deny women the right to vote, and most did. Utah and Washington allowed women to vote briefly in the 1880s, and the Territory of Wyoming gave women the vote in 1869. Idaho (1896), Washington (1910), and California (1911) were the first states to extend voting rights to women. After the 19th Amendment (1920) was adopted, women won the right to vote in any state, but racially motivated barriers to voting persisted.

Prior to the Civil Rights Movement and the Voting Rights Act of 1965, local election

---

[22] See Alexander Keyssar, *The Right to Vote: The Contested History of Democracy in the United States* (New York: Basic Books, 2000).

officials had the discretion to apply these barriers selectively, in order to disenfranchise blacks but not whites.[23] In some places, blacks who attempted to register faced economic reprisals, physical violence, and even death. In 1964, for example, only 7 percent of blacks in Mississippi were registered to vote, compared to 70 percent of whites. In Alabama, 19 percent of blacks were registered in 1965, compared to 70 percent of whites.[24] At the time the Voting Rights Act was adopted, several southern states required people to pass subjective **literacy tests** in order to register, and four southern states required voters to pay a tax (called a **poll tax**) to vote in state elections.[25] The **Voting Rights Act of 1965** applied to states, counties, and cities that had low minority voter participation. It gave the federal government the authority to enforce the right to register and vote and allowed federal observers to monitor elections. It gave federal authorities the power to review and "preclear" any changes to voter registration and election rules in jurisdictions covered by the act in order to restore voting rights. It also ended literacy tests in six southern states with low registration levels (Alabama, Georgia, Louisiana, Mississippi, Virginia, and much of North Carolina).

As late as 1970, 18 states still had literacy tests that prospective voters were required to pass in order to register (these were finally banned in 1975 due to their history of discriminatory application).[26] In 1972, the U.S. Supreme Court moved to end state laws requiring that a person reside in a jurisdiction at least one year prior to registering to vote.

In 1975, the act was amended to apply to states and counties with low registration levels and large non-English-speaking populations (all of Alaska, Arizona, and Texas and many areas in other states). The act was also amended to give plaintiffs greater latitude to challenge election practices—including at-large plans—that can be shown to dilute minority representation.

Despite Civil War–era amendments to the U.S. Constitution extending voting rights regardless of race, it took well over a century for the U.S. Congress and the U.S. Supreme Court to strike down the most overt prohibitions on voting.[27] But the gap between white and black registration levels in southern states covered by the Voting Rights Act was nearly eliminated by 1988 as a result of the Voting Rights Act. This does not mean that all barriers were eliminated by the act. Some state and local governments responded to increased minority participation by changing how they conducted their elections in order to dilute the influence of minority voters. The act is still used to guard against such practices and its key provisions were reauthorized for 25 years in 2006. Whether racially motivated or not, state policies that make it difficult to register and vote are still more likely to be present in states with greater racial diversity.[28] Mississippi, Louisiana, and South Carolina— which have some of the highest proportions of black residents in the United States—had the longest requirements for preregistration before elections (30 days in 2008). Polls were open for 14 or 15 hours in Connecticut, Rhode Island, Maine, and New Hampshire on

[23] U.S. Department of Justice, http://www.usdoj.gov/crt/voting/intro/introc.htm.

[24] Bernard Grofman, Lisa Handley, and Richard G. Niemi, *Minority Representation and the Quest for Voting Equality* (New York: Cambridge Press, 1992).

[25] Chandler Davidson, "The Evolution of Voting Rights Law," in Grofman, Handley, and Niemi, *Minority Representation*.

[26] In *Oregon v. Mitchell* (1970), the U.S. Supreme Court upheld a temporary five-year federal ban on the tests. The ban was made permanent in 1975.

[27] Chandler Davidson and Bernard Grofman, eds., *Quiet Revolution in the South: The Impact of Voting Rights Act 1965–1990* (Princeton, N.J.: Princeton University Press, 1994).

[28] Kim Q. Hill and Jan Leighley, "Racial Diversity, Voter Turnout, and Mobilizing Institutions in the United States," *American Politics Quarterly* 27, no. 3 (1999): 275–95; and Shaun Bowler and Todd Donovan, "State-Level Barriers to Participation" (paper presented at the American Political Science Association meeting, September 2005).

INSTITUTIONS MATTER

DIFFERENT WAYS TO DRAW DISTRICTS

The practice of drawing electoral boundaries for a jurisdiction is known as districting, or redistricting. Because so many voters support whatever candidate their party nominates for an office, the location of boundaries for a district can have huge implications for which party wins the district. A district where 60 percent of the voters are Democrats will almost certainly elect a Democrat. Likewise, a district that is 60 percent Republican will almost certainly elect a Republican. People drawing boundaries for districts have knowledge of where each party's voters live.

This raises the question, then, about who should draw district boundaries. Although the process varies considerably from state to state, in most states, the legislature has the final say over what the boundaries for state legislative and congressional districts will look like. This means that a party having a majority in the legislature, with a sympathetic governor, can largely draw maps as it sees fit: It can maximize the number of districts that the majority party is likely to win, it can create "safe" seats for incumbents, or both. The majority party may also try to spread the opposition party's supporters thinly across as many districts as possible to dilute their power. If control of government is divided between both major parties, incumbents of both parties might see fit to agree that most districts should be safe for one or the other party.[a] These "bipartisan" plans may protect incumbents from having a serious threat in any reelection campaign.

Several states place control of drawing district maps in the hands of an appointed commission or with the courts. Commissions and courts may have partisan interests but not as strong as the partisan interests affecting legislators. One study of state districting plans found that elections were more competitive when districting plans were produced by courts and commissions than when produced by incumbent politicians.[b]

[a] Bruce Cain, "Assessing the Partisan Effects of Redistricting," *American Political Science Review* (1985): 320–33.
[b] Jamie Carson and Michael Crespin, "The Effect of State Redistricting Methods on Electoral Competition in United States House Races," *State Politics and Policy Quarterly* 4 (2004): 455–69.

Election Day in 2008 but for just 12 hours in racially diverse Florida, Georgia, Mississippi, South Carolina, and Texas.

Registration Barriers

Although many of the most egregious barriers to voting are now gone, there are still important differences in registration laws across the states. In 1995, the National Voter Registration Act (also called the "Motor Voter" Act) went into effect, requiring that states accept mail-in registrations for federal elections if postmarked 30 days prior to an election and requiring that public agencies provide voter registration forms.

States continue to have discretion to allow voter registration on the same day of the election or to have waiting periods of up to 30 days. States also have the discretion to adopt laws that make it easier (or harder) to vote by mail. As of 2005, states with higher proportions of African-American residents continued to have more barriers to registration and easy voting.[29]

Having registration offices open for shorter hours and having closing dates for registration further from the election can depress turnout.[30] Conversely, states that allow registration on the day of the election rank highest in voter participation. As of 2006, there were six

[29] Bowler and Donovan, "State-Level Barriers to Participation."

[30] Leighley and Nagler, "Socioeconomic Class Bias in Turnout," 1964–1988; Leighley and Nagler, "Individual and Systemic Influences on Turnout"; and Steven Rosenstone and Raymond Wolfinger, "The Effect of Registration Laws on Voter Turnout," *American Political Science Review* 72 (1978): 22–45.

states with Election Day registration at local polling places (Idaho, Maine, Minnesota, New Hampshire, Wisconsin, and Wyoming). North Dakota does not require voter registration, and Montana allows Election Day registration at a county clerk's office. In nearly every state, however, it is the citizen's responsibility to remember to register ahead of time and to seek out a public agency in order to do this. In many other nations with higher voter turnout, the government assumes the responsibility for finding citizens and making sure they are properly registered to vote (just as the U.S. Census Bureau attempts to find everyone once a decade).

Districting Barriers

A larger institutional barrier to voting may be found in the nature of American elections themselves. Elections for nearly every seat in the U.S. House of Representatives, most state legislatures, and many city and county councils are conducted in single-member districts under **winner-take-all** rules. This means that the single candidate winning the most votes represents a specific geographical area. Winner-take-all election rules tend to produce two-party systems. That is, because there is nothing to be won for candidates from parties that always place third or fourth, people fear wasting their vote on such parties, and only the largest parties survive.[31] Winner-take-all elections are the main reason that the U.S. Congress, every state legislature, and nearly every local partisan council are dominated by representatives of just one or two political parties.

District boundaries used to elect representatives must be redrawn on occasion, or redistricted, to account for shifts in population. Critics of the redistricting process note that incumbents can have too much influence over how their district lines are drawn, such that elected officials are picking their voters rather than voters picking the officials. Democrat incumbents have incentives to make sure that their districts' boundaries include as many loyal Democratic voters as possible, whereas Republican incumbents have incentives to pack their districts with as many Republican voters as possible.[32] In many states, partisan elected officials have near total control over how these districts are drawn. In other states, legislators pick "bipartisan" commissions to make district maps or have the courts settle the issues. Parties keep detailed records of block-by-block voting trends and use sophisticated computer mapping programs to design their preferred districts.

When elections are one-sided, there is less campaign activity. When elections are contested by just one major party, there may be no campaign. Without campaigns, voters are probably less likely to notice that an election is being held. Turnout decline in American elections since 1960 corresponds with a decline in competitive elections, as more districts are drawn to be safe for just one party or the other. Congressional and state legislative races are often uncontested by one of the major parties because they have no chance to win. In recent years, over one-third of all state legislative races have not been contested by one of the major parties.[33] When fewer races are contested, fewer candidates campaign, and fewer citizens are likely to be engaged by the election.[34]

Who Is Ineligible?

State governments set rules about who is eligible to vote in their state and local elections.

---

[31] William Riker, "The Two-Party System and Duverger's Law: An Essay on the History of Political Science," *American Political Science Review* 76, no. 4 (1982): 753–66.

[32] Rob Ritchie, *Monopoly Politics*. Takoma Park, MD: Center for Voting and Democracy, 2000.

[33] National Conference of State Legislatures data. Archived at: http://www.ncsl.org/programs/press/2004/unopposed_2004.htm. Accessed August 18 2008.

[34] Todd Donovan and Shaun Bowler, *Reforming the Republic: Democratic Institutions for the New America* (Upper Saddle River, N.J.: Prentice Hall, 2004).

They have the power to decide if certain groups of people may vote or not in state and local elections (federal law regulates who may vote in federal contests). Depending on the state, people found to be "mentally incompetent," convicted felons who served their time, people in prison, people on parole, and legal immigrant noncitizens may be banned from voting. Or depending on the state's laws, they may be permitted to vote.

California, Nevada, New Jersey, and Florida had more noncitizens per capita in 2005 than any other states. Noncitizens typically cannot vote. Florida, Texas, and Mississippi also have far more inmates, parolees, felons, and ex-felons than the average state and do not allow many of them to vote.[35] Felon-voting bans were adopted by states in the late 1860s and 1870s as the 15th Amendment was extending voting rights to African Americans.[36] States with larger nonwhite prison populations were more likely to ban convicted felons from voting than states where more whites were in the prison population. States with more white prisoners in the 20th century were subsequently more likely to soften or repeal these laws than states with higher African-American prison populations.[37] Southern states have been significantly less likely to repeal laws that prevent ex-felons from ever voting again. One of the largest sources in the decline in voter turnout in recent years is the steep increase in the proportion of citizens who are losing their voting rights due to felony convictions, often for drug possession.[38]

Where Are the Greatest Barriers?

Restrictions on voting include requiring that voters register at least 20 days in advance, not allowing polling place registration, not allowing parolees or felons to vote, having shorter than average polling place hours, allowing no early voting, placing restrictions on "no-excuse" absentee voting, and other similar rules.

The state with the most of these in 2007 was Mississippi, followed by several other southern states, including Kentucky, Virginia, Alabama, Maryland, Florida, Georgia, and Texas. Nevada, New York, and Pennsylvania also score high. North Dakota placed the least restrictions on voting, with Vermont, Oregon, and Maine also having few restrictions. Other things being equal, states with more of these barriers had lower voter participation.[39]

Party System Barriers

Local political party organizations traditionally played a large role in mobilizing voters and getting them to participate in politics. Local party "machines" once relied heavily on large numbers of loyal workers to get their supporters to the polls. Some party workers could be rewarded with municipal jobs in exchange for their work on behalf of the party's electoral efforts. Party workers checked the sign-in sheets at polling places to track who had not yet voted, tracked down those who had not yet voted, gave people rides to polling places, and called on neighbors to remind them to vote. It helped if local elections were contested under party labels and held in sync with high-profile national races. Party labels and local party organizations lowered the "cost" that voters faced when voting. Party labels—usually Democrat or Republican—told voters a lot about relatively unknown candidates seeking state and local offices.

---

[35] Over 1 percent of the Texas adult population are felons or ex-felons. The U.S. average is 0.67 percent. See Michael McDonald, Voter Turnout Project, George Mason University, Fairfax, Va. Ex-felons may vote in Texas, but parolees, inmates, and probationers may not. Mississippi and Florida also prevent ex-felons from voting.

[36] See Jeff Manza and Christopher Uggen, *Locked Out: Felon Disenfranchisement and American Democracy* (New York: Oxford University Press, 2005).

[37] Angela Behrens, Christopher Uggen, and Jeff Manza, "Ballot Manipulation and the 'Menace of Negro Domination': Racial Threat and Felon Disenfranchisement in the United States, 1850–2002," *American Journal of Sociology* 109 (2003): 559–605.

[38] Michael P. McDonald and Sam Popkin, "The Myth of the Vanishing Voter," *American Political Science Review* 95 (2000): 963–74.

[39] Analysis from Bowler and Donovan, "State-Level Barriers to Participation."

Decades of antiparty reform laws passed by state legislatures have changed the role of parties in many states.[40] Civil service reforms make it difficult—if not illegal—for parties to reward their supporters with public sector jobs. Nowadays, nearly 75 percent of local elections are nonpartisan. Nearly all local elections (95 percent) in western states are nonpartisan, whereas most local contests in the northeastern states remain partisan.[41] Turnout remains higher today in local partisan elections. Many places also have their nonpartisan local elections in "off years," out of sync with higher-profile contests—further depressing turnout.

Historians demonstrate that many of these antiparty reforms were adopted at the start of the 20th century to "depoliticize" local politics and ensure that the influence of working-class people and racial and ethnic minorities would be diluted in favor of people who wanted to improve the business climate in their cities.[42] The drop in party mobilization of voters has been found to be one of the largest factors behind low turnout in the United States.[43] With the decline of parties, Americans may now be less likely to have someone knock on their door to encourage them to vote. However, experiments in cities like Columbus, Ohio, and Raleigh, North Carolina, demonstrate that face-to-face visits with voters before a local election can increase participation by about 10 percent.[44] However, few organizations have the resources to mount large-scale, door-to-door canvassing drives.

Noncompetitive Elections

Local elections may be less competitive than in previous decades. This means elections have less ability to get people's attention or provide them with information about local affairs. One study estimated that the number of candidates seeking local office dropped by 15 percent from 1974 to 1994.[45] Another study found that 17 percent of mayoral candidates ran unopposed in California in 2003 and found that seven California cities cancelled their elections that year due to lack of competition.[46]

State laws determine how local elections will be conducted. In many local elections, candidates run at large (that is, citywide). At-large elections were another antiparty, **Progressive era** reform designed to weaken the influence of political parties and the lower-status voters, often recent immigrants, whom they relied upon for support. The Progressive era of the early 1900s was a period of much experimentation with election rules. At-large elections were sold as a "good government" reform, in part, for their ability to get working-class ethnics, blacks, and Socialists off of city councils.[47] Because minorities and the poor are often concentrated in specific neighborhoods and because most white voters usually vote for white candidates,[48] racial and ethnic minority

---

[40] Walter Dean Burnham, *Critical Elections and the Mainsprings of American Politics* (New York: Norton, 1970), chs. 4–5.

[41] Tari Renner, "The Municipal Election Process: The Impact on Minority Representation," in *The Municipal Yearbook*, ed. International City Managers Association (Washington, D.C.: International City Managers Association, 2005).

[42] Amy Bridges, *Morning Glories* (Princeton, N.J.: Princeton University Press, 1999); and Burnham, *Critical Elections*.

[43] Steven Rosenstone and John Mark Hansen, *Mobilization, Participation and Democracy in America* (New York: Longman, 2003).

[44] Alan S. Gerber and Donald P. Green, "The Effects of Personal Canvassing, Telephone Calls and Direct Mail on Voter Turnout: A Field Experiment," *American Political Science Review* 94, no. 3 (1993): 658.

[45] Robert Putnam, *Bowling Alone* (New York: Simon & Schuster, 2000).

[46] New York Times, 21 September 2003. p. 30.

[47] Bridges, *Morning Glories*; Samuel P. Hays, "The Politics of Municipal Reform in the Progressive Era," *Pacific Northwest Quarterly* (1961): 157–69; and Chandler Davidson and George Korbel, "At-Large Elections and Minority Group Representation," *Journal of Politics* 43 (1981): 982–1005.

[48] Paul Kleppner, *Chicago Divided: The Making of a Black Mayor* (DeKalb: Northern Illinois Press, 1985). For a thorough review of the literature and critical analysis of this proposition, see Keith Reeves, *Voting Hopes or Fears: White Voters, Black Candidates and Racial Politics in America* (New York: Oxford University Press, 1997).

President Lyndon Johnson giving Dr. Martin Luther King Jr. a pen used to sign the Voting Rights Act of 1965.

candidates often have a better chance of being elected from small districts rather than at large when they run for a citywide office.[49] Districted contests facilitate the election of minority candidates, but if districts are drawn to be heavily homogeneous (that is, safe for a minority group), districted elections may also limit competition.

The Effect of Place

People who live in smaller communities tend to participate more. Across a wide range of American towns and cities, people are more likely to contact public officials and attend board meetings, for example, if they live in a place with a smaller population.[50] Voter turnout in local elections is also higher in places with a lower population, even after accounting for things such as levels of income and the racial-ethnic composition of the cities.[51] People in Vermont are more likely to attend town meetings if they live in less populous communities.[52]

A sense of place, or a sense of community, seems to increase political participation. Many people develop the social skills and networks—the **social capital**—they use in political activity by volunteering with local service clubs and social, fraternal, and religious groups.[53] For example, by organizing a bake sale for a church or an auction to raise money for a soccer team, one might build social networks and learn fundraising skills that carry over to political activity. Where there is more social capital, then, there is likely to be more political participation. Social capital seems to coexist with trusting other people, and residents of smaller places

[49] Davidson and Grofman, *Quiet Revolution in the South*; and Richard Engstrom and Michael D. McDonald, "The Election of Blacks to City Councils," *American Political Science Review* 75 (1981): 344–54.

[50] Eric Oliver, "City Size and Civic Involvement in Metropolitan America," *American Political Science Review* 94, no. 2 (2000): 362–63; also see Robert Dahl and Edward Tufte, *Size and Democracy* (1973).

[51] Hanjal and Lewis, "Municipal Institutions and Voter Turnout." Also see Stephen Hansen, Thomas Palfrey, and Howard Rosenthal, "The Downsian Model of Electoral Participation: Formal Theory and Empirical Analysis of the Constituency Size Effect," *Public Choice* 52 (1987): 15–33.

[52] Frank Bryan, *Real Democracy: The New England Town Meeting and How It Works* (Chicago: University of Chicago Press, 2003).

[53] James Coleman, *Foundations of Social Theory* (Cambridge, Mass.: Belknap, 1990); and Putnam, *Bowling Alone*.

tend to trust other people more than residents of larger places do.[54] A prominent investigation of social capital found that people in smaller places were much more likely to volunteer in their communities, to work on community projects, and to give to charity.[55]

Personal Barriers

When Americans are asked about the barriers to local participation, lack of information is the barrier most frequently cited as being a serious impediment. As Table 3.5 illustrates, over one-third of Americans agree that not knowing where to begin or not having enough information is a serious barrier to becoming involved in local politics. People with no education beyond high school, African Americans, and Hispanics were significantly more likely to share these sentiments.[56] People who work in congested urban areas a few miles from their neighborhood polling places may also be less likely to vote.[57]

Table 3.5	

Public Attitudes as Barriers to Participation in Local Politics

Public Attitudes	%
Lack of information or don't know how to begin	35
Feel unable to make a difference	26
Work schedule (too busy)	25
Poor transportation	20
Feel unwelcome	22
Safety concerns	28

Source: Social Capital Benchmark Survey, 2000.

Breaking Down Barriers to Voter Participation

One of the ironies about low rates of political participation in the United States is that for the last several decades, serious efforts have been made to remove barriers to voting and political participation—but participation remains low. Congress passed the Voting Rights Act in 1965, empowering the federal government to take control of local voter registration agencies away from racist state and local governments. Federal antipoverty "community action" programs of the 1960s also included requirements for the "maximum feasible participation" of community residents in implementing the programs.[58] The participatory elements of community action programs were soon abandoned as being ineffective, but the Voting Rights Act had the dramatic effect of bringing voter participation rates among African Americans to levels equal with those of whites.[59]

Subsequent efforts to boost participation have been less effective. In the 1980s, political parties spent millions on Get Out the Vote (GOTV) drives. In the 1990s, Congress also passed the Motor Voter Act to make registration easier. MTV's Rock the Vote encouraged young people to register and vote. These efforts may have increased registrations, but they seem to have had little effect on getting newly registered voters to actually vote. The hotly contested Bush versus Kerry 2004 presidential race, in contrast, was associated with an increase in voting.

State-Level Reform Efforts

In the past decade, several states have also attempted to make it easier for people to vote.

---

[54] Wendy Rahn and Thomas Rudolph, "A Tale of Political Trust in American Cities," *Public Opinion Quarterly* 69 (2005): 530–60.

[55] Putman, *Bowling Alone*.

[56] Social Capital Benchmark Survey; and author's calculations.

[57] James Gimpel and J. E. Schuknecht, "Political Participation and the Accessibility of the Ballot Box," *Political Geography* 22 (2003): 471–88.

[58] Daniel Patrick Moynihan, *Maximum Feasible Misunderstanding: Community Action in the War on Poverty* (New York: Basic Books, 1969).

[59] When the effects of income and education on participation are accounted for, African Americans vote at higher rates than whites. Leighley and Nagler, "Individual and Systemic Influences on Turnout."

On the West Coast and in a few states in other areas, for example, many people now take advantage of less restrictive rules about absentee voting. These rules allow them to vote permanently by mail without having to provide any reason. Oregon adopted all-mail elections in 1998, and 34 of 39 counties in Washington held all elections by mail as of 2007. Texas and other states implemented "early voting" and set up polling places days before elections to make voting easier. Some states have experimented with Internet voting, particularly for overseas military personnel.

Effect of Reforms on Voter Participation

Despite these efforts, participation in American elections remains low compared to elections in most other established democracies. There is some evidence that reforms such as voting by mail might slightly increase turnout, and liberal absentee laws were found to increase turnout among students.[60] Studies suggest that the increased turnout associated with making voting more convenient might exacerbate social bias in the electorate by increasing turnout among white, wealthy, and better-educated voters at a greater rate than turnout among minorities and the less affluent.[61]

Interest Matters

It probably comes as little surprise that participation in state and local politics is largely the domain of those who are most interested in politics. It may be less obvious that having an interest in politics often has

a distinct class bias and that some reforms designed to increase turnout might, ironically, magnify this bias. Efforts to increase participation by making it easier to vote can increase turnout but do not make elections any more interesting. As noted above, lack of information is the primary reason that people mention when citing barriers to participation—particularly the less affluent, the less educated, and racial and ethnic minorities. Competitive elections, increased campaign activity, and active political parties may increase interest and information about elections. Most current reform efforts focus on making it more convenient for people to vote. The people who take advantage of increased convenience tend to be people who already have some engagement with politics—those with education and higher incomes.[62]

Increasing Citizen Engagement with Competitive Elections

This is not to say that reforms can't increase participation across the board. Increased electoral competition and more information about candidates and issues may significantly increase participation in state and local politics. Partisan local elections, multiparty politics, and even "semiproportional" nonpartisan elections have each been shown to be associated with higher levels of participation.[63]

Eliminating partisan gerrymandering in the design of electoral districts might also help boost interest in state politics by making more state legislative contests competitive. In presidential, gubernatorial, congressional, and state legislative races, voter participation is

---

[60] Jeffrey Karp and Susan Banducci, "Absentee Voting, Participation, and Mobilization," *American Politics Research* 29 (2001): 183–95.

[61] J. Eric Oliver, "The Effects of Eligibility Restrictions and Party Activity on Absentee Voting and Overall Turnout," *American Journal of Political Science* 40 (1996): 498–513; and Jeff Karp and Susan Banducci, "Going Postal: How All Mail Elections Influence Turnout," *Political Behavior* 22 (2000): 223–39. On Internet voting, see R. Michael Alvarez and Jonathan Nagler, "The Likely Consequences of Internet Voting for Political Representation," *Loyola of Los Angeles Law Review* 34 (2001): 1115–52.

[62] A full extension of this argument can be found in Adam Berinsky, "The Perverse Consequences of Electoral Reform in the United States," *American Politics Research* 33, no. 4 (2005): 471–91.

[63] Andre Blais and Ken Carty, "Does Proportional Representation Foster Voter Turnout?" *European Journal of Political Research* 18 (1990): 167–81; and Shaun Bowler, Todd Donovan, and David Brockington, *Election Reform and Minority Representation* Columbus, OH: Ohio State University Press (2003).

greater in places where the vote gap between the winning and losing candidates narrows. People tend to participate more when elections are close than when they are uncompetitive. Some suggest that voters are more likely to calculate that their participation will be decisive in close races—causing turnout to increase.[64] We suggest that close, competitive elections increase participation, as these races generate more campaign activity and information. Others contend that close elections force party leaders and political groups to mobilize more voters.[65] However, if every district was drawn so that either party had a chance to win, a relatively small shift in votes in each district from one party to another could result in dramatic changes in how many seats a party holds in the legislature.

Experiments with Alternative Local Election Systems

Different types of local election systems can also encourage more candidates to run, which increases campaign activity and, as a result, increases participation. Unique experiments with "semiproportional" local election systems in Texas, Alabama, and a few other states demonstrated that cumulative voting systems offer minority candidates more opportunities to win than standard at-large elections. There are different forms of **at-large elections**. Under standard at-large elections, if there are five city council seats, each seat is elected separately by all voters in the city. Cities using standard at-large elections often narrow the field of candidates with a primary contest that determines the two candidates who will contest each position in the general election. The candidate with a majority wins, and if there is a cohesive citywide majority, it sweeps every seat. This means minority-supported candidates have little chance to win. **Cumulative voting**

modifies the at-large system by allowing voters to cast multiple votes for one or more candidates running citywide. This allows some candidates with less than a majority to win and causes minority candidates to run active campaigns. Cumulative voting has been found to increase turnout in local elections by about 5 percent and to increase campaign activity.[66]

E-Government

City and state governments have also tried to stimulate citizen interest and participation by making it easier for people to follow government through electronic media from the convenience of their own homes. Many states and cities maintain public access cable TV stations to broadcast hearings and meetings and maintain ever-improving websites designed to make it easier to contact public officials.

Voter Choice in State and Local Elections

When people vote in partisan state and local elections, their decision-making process is somewhat similar to the process they use when voting in national elections. Voters who identify with a political party have a very strong inclination to pick candidates from their party. Party labels—Democrat, Republican, Libertarian, and so on—act as a cue as to the policies the candidate might pursue. If people know nothing about a candidate except the candidate's party label— as is often the case—the inclination to vote based on party labels may even be stronger because voters have little more to guide their choices. Voters also tend to give incumbents the benefit of the doubt and may also reward or punish candidates for state offices based on

---

[64] For a discussion, see Gary Cox and Michael Munger, "Closeness, Expenditures and Turnout in the 1982 US House Election," *American Political Science Review* 83 (1989): 217–31.

[65] V. O. Key Jr., *Southern Politics: In the State and Nation* (New York: Knopf, 1949).

[66] Bowler, Donovan, and Brockington, *Election Reform and Minority Representation*.

the health of the economy.[67] They may also be more likely to punish a governor for the health of the state economy than the national economy.[68] Despite these factors, a voter's party affiliation is the main thing driving voter choice in partisan contests.

If candidates must run for office without party labels on the ballot, however, the voter's decision-making process is different. In nonpartisan elections, which are quite common at the local level, voters may be more likely to rely on endorsements of slating groups. These groups mimic the role of parties by recruiting and publicizing candidates sympathetic to the goals of the group. Pro-business slating groups have been found to have important influence in low-turnout local elections.[69] In smaller communities, the absence of parties and slating groups may cause voters to look for familiar-sounding names (incumbents) or look for friends and neighbors who might be running.[70] Even in primary election contests in California (where all candidates are from the same party), candidates for less visible "down-ballot" offices collect more votes near their hometowns, where they are better known.[71]

Effects of Voter Participation on Public Policy

Levels of participation in state and local politics are affected by state laws that regulate voter registration, polling place hours, absentee voting rules, representation, and many other factors. As we have shown above, these rules can make it easier or harder to vote and can make elections more or less interesting by limiting or increasing electoral competition, information, and representation. It is important to stress that the effects of these rules are not neutral; many of them filter out minorities and the less affluent or increase participation by the wealthy. In this section, we consider how rules might affect who participates and how this affects who gets represented and who gets what from government.

High-Voter-Participation Election Rules

Under one condition, state law could allow cities to have partisan local elections, with state and local contests held in conjunction with an "even-year" general election. By holding state and local contests in sync with presidential contests, more people would probably vote in state and local races. New voters could be allowed to register at the polls and vote on the day of the election. If a state used highly competitive districts to elect its legislature, more candidates would campaign, further increasing interest. Ex-felons and legal immigrant noncitizens could be allowed to vote in state and local races. Some elections could also be awarded by proportional representation, further encouraging different candidates to campaign. It is unlikely these sorts of reforms would be adopted without massive public pressure, as incumbent politicians of both major parties typically resist changing the rules that existed when they were elected.[72]

Low-Voter-Participation Election Rules

Under a second condition, state law could require local elections to be nonpartisan—a rule that limits the information available

[67] Lonna Atkeson and Randal Partin, "Economic and Referendum Voting," *American Political Science Review* 89 (1995): 99–107.

[68] Robert Stein, "Economic Voting for Governor and US Senator," *Journal of Politics* 52 (1990): 29–53.

[69] Chandler Davidson and Luis Fraga, "Slating Groups as Parties in a 'Nonpartisan' Setting," *Western Political Quarterly* 41 (1988): 373–90.

[70] Key, *Southern Politics*.

[71] Shaun Bowler, Todd Donovan, and Joseph Snipp, "Local Sources of Information and Voter Choice in State Elections: Micro-Level Foundations of the Friends and Neighbors Effect," *American Politics Quarterly* 21 (1993): 473–89.

[72] Shaun Bowler, Todd Donovan, and Jeffrey Karp, "Why Politicians Like Electoral Institutions: Self-Interest, Values or Ideology," *Journal of Politics* 68, no. 2 (2006): 454.

to the voters. State and local contests could be allowed only in "odd years" when no important federal contests are on the ballot. Voters would have to register at least 30 days in advance, and only citizens without felony convictions could vote. State legislative districts could be gerrymandered to ensure that parties didn't have to compete against each other in a single district, and local council races could be by single-member districts, leaving many incumbents without opposition.

Our point is not that more voter participation is always better but that participation is, in part, a function of laws that are under state control. State legislatures can make it harder or easier for people to participate, and state laws can make elections more or less competitive. State laws affect not only who can vote but also if the elections will generate interest sufficient to stimulate the participation of a wide range of people. Rules thus shape the composition of the electorate; that is, they determine who ends up making demands on government.

The scope of the differences between participants and nonparticipants is likely to vary across states and is due to state laws as well as the demographic profile of the state's residents. In California, for example, surveys estimate that 75 percent of likely voters in the 2004 election were white, yet only 49 percent of the state's adult population was white.[73] Part of these differences stems from lower participation rates among young voters and Latinos and the fact that many Latino citizens have not registered to vote. States with larger proportions of recent immigrants have similar gaps between participants and nonparticipants. An estimated 20 million legal, tax-paying immigrant noncitizens—1.3 million in New York City alone—are prohibited from voting in the United States. In a few communities, however, they are allowed to vote in local elections.[74]

Public Policy and Public Opinion

Representation means that elected officials, to some degree, produce laws and policies that their constituents want. Evidence from the 50 states demonstrates that citizens' preferences for public policy generally correspond with the policies that states adopt. States where more people identified themselves as liberals had more liberal public policies, and states where more people identified themselves as conservatives had more conservative policies.[75] Something must be working to connect public preferences to policy. Elected representatives may reflect the public in response to those citizens who participate in politics, and those who participate may be fairly representative of the public opinion of the state's larger population. That is, representatives may respond to pressure from voters and constituents and do what the voters want. Or politicians may simply anticipate what people want, regardless of whether people participate or not. This distinction presents an important question for democracy: Does active political participation make the actions of government better represent what citizens want? Put differently, does more participation—or less social bias in participation—make state and local policy more representative of public opinion?

Does Participation Make State and Local Policy More Representative?

It is possible for elected officials to be perfectly representative of the public, even if most people don't participate in politics. This would require that representatives have a keen sense of what everyone wanted and strong incentives to give people what they want. More realistically,

---

[73] National Association of Latino Elected and Appointed Officials, "Voter and Party Profile," June 2004, http://www.naleo.org/press_releases/CA_Profile_02–04_fin.pdf.

[74] Alexandra Marks, "Should Non Citizens Vote?" *Christian Science Monitor*, 27 April 2004.

[75] Robert Erikson, Gerald Wright, and John P. McIver, *Statehouse Democracy: Public Opinion and Policy in the American States* (New York: Cambridge University Press, 1993).

representatives may do things that reflect what the general public wants when there is more pressure on them to do so.

As examples, states with just one dominant political party (such as the U.S. South through most of the 20th century) had policies less representative of what the public probably wanted than states where two parties compete for voter support. Competition between parties is expected to force legislators to try to attract support by passing popular policies—including things that are popular with the poor.[76] Primary election systems (discussed in Chapter 5) that allow more people to participate also produce representatives who are more likely to share their constituents' opinions on policy.[77] States with direct democracy (Chapter 4) also adopt some public policies, such as death penalty laws as well as laws requiring parental notification for abortions, that are closer to the state's public opinion than policies adopted in states that lack the pressure of direct democracy.[78]

Participation Bias

As we illustrated earlier in this chapter, people who participate in politics are different than nonparticipants. But does this mean that nonparticipants want different things from their governments than participants do or that by responding mainly to those who participate, governments are not very representative of the general public? Scholars are divided on this question. A study of a national sample of public opinion in 1972 and another from 1988 found that voters and nonvoters had largely similar policy preferences.[79] These results have been used to support the idea that American governments are largely representative of all citizens, even those who do not vote. If government responds only (or mostly) to those who vote or contribute, participation bias (the overrepresentation of the wealthy) might mean that state and local policies are not representative of the population. Recent studies of national opinion have found that nonvoters are more liberal on social welfare issues than voters.[80]

Participation is relatively high in national elections, however. Far fewer vote in state and local contests. Given this fact, and given the increased information demands associated with state and local elections, it is possible that there are greater gaps in policy preferences between participants and nonparticipants in local elections than in national contests. If participants are different than nonparticipants, what are the policy consequences of this participation bias?

Effects of Participation Bias

Several scholars provide evidence that the turnout decline in American elections has produced an overrepresentation of upper-middle-class and upper-class people and an underrepresentation of lower- and middle-class citizens.[81] One way to assess if participation bias matters is to look at how differences in state policies across the 50 states correspond with differences in who participates.

---

[76] Key, *Southern Politics*, ch. 14, 307. Evidence from the contemporary era suggests the poor get more when Democrats are in power rather than when the Democrats are losing in close competition against Republicans.

[77] Elisabeth Gerber and Rebecca Morton, "Primary Election Systems and Representation," *Journal of Law, Economics and Organizations* 14, no. 2 (1998): 304–24.

[78] Elisabeth Gerber, *The Populist Paradox* (Princeton, N.J.: Princeton University Press, 1999); also see John Matsusaka, *For the Many or the Few: The Initiative, Public Policy, and American Democracy* (Chicago: University of Chicago Press, 2004).

[79] Raymond Wolfinger and Steven Rosenstone, *Who Votes* (New Haven, Conn.: Yale University Press, 1980); and Sidney Verba, Kay Schlozman, Henry Brady, and Norman Nie, "Citizen Activity: Who Participates? What Do They Say?" *American Political Science Review* (1993): 303–18.

[80] Adam Berinsky, "Silent Voices: Opinion Polls, Social Welfare Policy and Political Equality in America," *American Journal of Political Science* 46 (2002): 276–87.

[81] Frances Fox Piven and Richard A. Cloward, *Why Americans Don't Vote* (New York: Pantheon, 1989); and Walter Dean Burnham, "The Turnout Problem," in *Elections American Style*, ed. A. James Reichley (Washington, D.C.: Brookings Institution Press 1987).

Effects on State Policies The magnitude of this "class bias"—the overrepresentation of the wealthy—is larger in some states and smaller in others. A study of the 1980s found the inequality in participation was highest in Kentucky, New Mexico, Texas, Georgia, and Arkansas. These are states with high minority populations—most with legacies of erecting barriers to voter participation. States with the most balanced representation between the rich and poor were New Jersey, Minnesota, Louisiana, Illinois, and Nebraska.[82] The study found that state-level class bias in participation during the 1980s was strongly related to lower state welfare (AFDC) spending. States where the poor were underrepresented among participating voters spent less per person on welfare than states where the poor were better represented. A study of state spending from 1978 to 1990 found similar results, with welfare spending higher where there was higher lower-status-voter turnout.[83]

If bias in participation affects which candidates end up winning elections, then it may also affect what governments do. Despite claims by third-party presidential candidates Ralph Nader (in 2000) and George Wallace (in 1968) that there is no difference between the Democratic and Republican parties, there are clear policy differences at the state level related to which party has more control over the state government. Republican control at the state level means less Medicaid spending; Democrats spend more.[84] Republicans may tax less[85] and use a different mix of taxes and expenditures than Democrats[86] (see Chapter 10).

Elections and Representation

Elections can be thought of as a tool for translating votes into "seats." When a group or party has seats in a state legislature or on a city or county council, it has a form of representation. Election rules have a great effect on which parties or groups have representation. The rules used to conduct elections, like many things examined in this book, are not always (if ever) neutral. They can affect who wins and who loses, who gets more seats—and, in short, who ends up being represented.

Number of Representatives per District

The number of representatives elected inside a district's boundaries may affect who is represented in a legislature. Most states now elect their state legislators from single-member districts (SMDs)—but it hasn't always been this way. In single-member districts, the winning candidate is whoever has the most support—a simple plurality. Some states have more than one representative per district (just as each U.S. state has two U.S. senators per statewide district). The number of representatives for a specific geographic area is referred to as **district magnitude**.

In the middle of the 20th century, about half of all American state legislative seats were elected by **multimember districts** (MMDs), where two or more candidates are elected to represent each district.[87] Many of these older

[82] Kim Q. Hill and Jan Leighley, "The Policy Consequences of Class Bias in State Electorates," *American Journal of Political Science* 36, no. 2 (1992): 351–65.

[83] Kim Q. Hill, Jan Leighley, and Angela Hinton-Andersson, "Lower-Class Mobilization and Policy Linkages in the U.S. States," *American Journal of Political Science* 39, no. 1 (1998): 75–86.

[84] Coleen Grogan, "Political-Economic Factors Influencing State Medicaid Policy," *Political Research Quarterly* 47, no. 3 (1994): 589–623.

[85] Brian Knight, "Supermajority Vote Requirements for Tax Increases: Evidence from the States," *Journal of Public Economics* 67, no. 1 (2000): 41–67.

[86] D. L. Rogers and J. H. Rogers. "Political Competition and State Government Size," *Public Choice*, 105, no 1–2 (2000): 1 - 21; and Timothy Besley and Anne Case, "Political Institutions and Policy Choices: Evidence from the United States," *Journal of Economic Literature* 41, no. 1 (2002): 7–73.

[87] Maurice Klain, "A New Look at the Constituencies: The Need for a Recount and Reappraisal," *American Political Science Review* 49 (1955): 1105–19.

MMDs overrepresented rural areas. A series of U.S. Supreme Court rulings required that states apportion legislative districts equally according to population.[88] Since the 1950s, many states have abandoned their MMD systems, often as part of their plans to equally apportion districts by population. Those that now use MMDs can no longer give extra representation to rural areas.

There are important differences in how states use MMDs to elect their legislatures. In Washington and Idaho, lower-house districts elect two representatives, but candidates run for two separate positions. These elections are largely identical to those held in SMDs because voters can't vote for more than one candidate per position. In Arizona, however, voters cast two votes to select two representatives from a single list of candidates who will represent their district. The top two candidates win. In Vermont, if there are three representatives per district, voters cast three votes across a single list, and the top three win. Illinois used three-member districts with a semiproportional representation system known as cumulative voting for decades, ending the system in 1980. In MMD systems such as those used in Arizona, Vermont, or Illinois (until 1980), candidates can win a seat with less than a majority and even with less than a plurality. The winning candidates are the first-, second-, and third-place finishers—depending on how many seats are elected from the district. New Jersey, North Dakota, and South Dakota also use MMDs to elect their lower house.

Effects of Multimember Districts on Minority Representation MMD elections can produce different patterns of representation than SMD elections. Some suggest that MMDs hurt the chances of minority candidates, especially in areas where minority vote strength is geographically concentrated—places where a heavily minority SMD might be drawn.[89] Others note that evidence showing MMDs giving advantages to white candidates is dated. Because MMDs allow candidates to win with a relatively low vote share, MMDs might help minority candidates get elected. Recent studies suggest these systems may have produced more racial and ethnic minority representation in state legislatures from 1980 to 2003 than found under SMDs. African Americans appeared particularly advantaged but Latinos less so.[90]

There is clear evidence that traditional "at-large" MMDs disadvantage minority candidates in local elections.[91] In these systems, candidates file for one position out of several in a district, and only the first-place candidate for each position can win a seat. In *Gingles v. Thornberg* (1986), the U.S. Supreme Court ruled that local MMD at-large elections may be an unconstitutional "dilution" of minority vote influence if the minority group is geographically compact and politically cohesive and there is a history of "bloc voting" by whites that leads to the defeat of minority candidates. If these conditions exist, a judge may order the jurisdiction to switch to SMD elections or some alternative that will allow the minority group to elect a representative of their choice. However, in *Shaw v. Reno* (1993), a 5–4 Court decision also ruled that it would not tolerate district maps that maximize minority representation by drawing **majority-minority districts** based exclusively on where minority voters live.

[88] *Baker v. Carr*, 1962; *Reynolds v. Sims*, 1964; and *Wesberry v. Sanders*, 1964.

[89] Malcolm E. Jewell, *Representation in State Legislatures* (Lexington: University of Kentucky Press, 1982); and Gary Moncrief and Joel Thompson, "Electoral Structure and State Legislative Representation," *Journal of Politics* 54 (1992): 246–56.

[90] Lilliard Richardson and Christopher Cooper, "The Mismeasure of MMD: Reassessing the Impact of Multi-Member Districts on the Representation on Descriptive Representation in the United States" (2003) Manuscript, Truman School of Public Affairs, University of Missouri.

[91] Engstrom and McDonald, "The Election of Blacks to City Councils."

Campaign Spending

Politicians campaign to tell voters about themselves (and their opponents). These campaigns cost money, and politicians spend a significant amount of their time raising campaign funds.[92] Money clearly matters at all levels of American politics: Candidates who spend more in state and local races typically do better in elections than those who spend less.[93] Campaign spending may be particularly important for candidates challenging incumbents. Because challengers are less well-known than incumbents, challenger spending may produce more "bang for the buck" than incumbent spending. Challenger spending disseminates information about a lesser-known candidate, so any dollar spent can increase information about the candidate. Incumbents may be so well-known prior to an election that their spending may have less effect on their vote share.[94]

Spending on campaigns transmits information to citizens—through TV, radio, direct mail, and other modes of advertising. Because the information is meant to cast candidates in a good light (and their opponents in a bad light), the quality of this information may be dubious. A survey of voters in one state found that 81 percent believed campaign advertising was "misleading." A slightly higher proportion of politicians in the state agreed.[95] Nonetheless, voters use the information they get from political ads. People are more likely to be aware of state-level elections as spending increases,[96] and spending may cause skeptical voters to seek out additional information. Spending may also cause increased media coverage. Although turnout in elections is mostly structured by larger socioeconomic and institutional forces already discussed in this chapter, higher levels of spending in state-level races can also increase voter turnout.[97] One study of spending in state legislative races concluded that for every dollar spent per eligible voter, turnout increased by 1.2 percent.[98]

Finance Regulations State laws also determine who can contribute to state and local candidates; how much individuals, groups, or political parties may give; and how contributions must be disclosed to the public. Some states, such as Massachusetts and Oregon, have a broad range of restrictions on contributions. Others, like Idaho, Texas, and Virginia, have minimal regulations.[99] Defenders of these regulations note that they give the public more information about who the candidates might be beholden to and that these rules limit the influence of money in politics. Critics argue that limits on spending might make it harder for lesser-known challengers to unseat

[92] Peter Francia and Paul Herrnson, "Begging for Bucks," *Campaigns and Elections*, April 2001.

[93] Kedron Bardwell, "Campaign Finance Laws and the Competition for Spending in Gubernatorial Elections," *Social Science Quarterly* 84, no. 4 (2003): 811–25; and Robert K. Goidel, Donald A. Gross, and Todd G. Shields, *Money Matters: Consequences of Campaign Finance Reform in U.S. House Elections* (Lanham, Md.: Rowman & Littlefield, 1999).

[94] Gary Jacobson, "The Effects of Campaign Spending in House Elections: New Evidence for Old Arguments," *American Journal of Political Science* 34 (1990): 334–62; and Donald Philip Green and Jonathan S. Krasno, "Rebuttal to Jacobson's 'New Evidence for Old Arguments,'" *American Journal of Political Science* 34 (1990): 363–72.

[95] Todd Donovan, Shaun Bowler, and David McCuan, "Political Consultants and the Initiative Industrial Complex," in *Dangerous Democracy?* ed. Larry Sabato, Howard Ernst, and Bruce Larson (Lanham, Md.: Rowman & Littlefield, 2001), 127.

[96] Shaun Bowler and Todd Donovan, *Demanding Choices* (Ann Arbor: University of Michigan Press, 1998), 152.

[97] Robert Hogan, "Campaign and Contextual Influences on Voter Participation in State Legislative Elections," *American Politics Review* 27, no. 4 (1999): 403–33.

[98] Francia and Herrnson, "Begging for Bucks."

[99] John Pippen, Shaun Bowler, and Todd Donovan, "Election Reform and Direct Democracy: Campaign Finance Regulation in the American States," *American Politics Quarterly* 30, no. 6 (2002): 559–82.

incumbents and that spending limits may make elections less competitive. There is some evidence that these rules do reduce spending in state races and that they might also limit electoral competition if limits are set too low.[100]

Clean Money A handful of states provide full public financing for state legislative campaigns in exchange for candidates promising to reject all private contributions. Maine and Arizona became the first states to do this in 2000. Vermont, Massachusetts, New Mexico, and North Carolina have also adopted **clean money and public financing of campaigns** programs, and other states, such as Minnesota, provide partial public funding of candidate campaigns in exchange for candidates limiting the total amount that they raise from private sources.

One major idea behind these clean money laws is to make sure candidates are not beholden to their donors. Advocates of publicly financed campaigns also hope it will broaden the pool of people who seek office and cut down the amount of time politicians spend raising money. One study found that state legislative candidates spend less time raising money in states with public financing of campaigns.[101]

Representation of Parties

Nearly every partisan office in the United States is elected on a winner-take-all basis. Second-, third-, and lower-placing candidates win nothing. If a party rarely does better than second place in most contests, it will win few offices and likely disappear.

Despite this, third-party and independent candidates have had more success in state and local elections than in congressional and federal

races over the last several decades. Since 1990, a few were elected as governor (Angus King in Maine, Jesse Ventura in Minnesota, and Lowell Weicker in Connecticut).[102] As of 2007, minor parties and independent candidates held just 19 seats in state legislatures (out of 7,382 positions in 50 states).[103] Almost half of these minor-party and independent candidates served in Vermont (which uses MMD elections and clean money for campaign finance). Minor-party and independent candidates have also won seats in Arizona and Massachusetts under clean money rules.

Representation of Women

States differ substantially in terms of the number of women who are elected to office. As of 2008, 23.7 percent of state legislators were women—far more than in the U.S. Congress and double the levels of women in state legislatures back in 1981. Although this is still modest representation given that most of the population is female, the growth of representation of women in the past 25 years has important implications. The growing number of women in state-level posts means that the pool of women with elected experience who seek higher-level positions has grown.

In six states (Arizona, Colorado, Minnesota, New Hampshire, Vermont, and Washington), one-third of all state legislators were women as of 2008. States with the lowest rates of women representation were South Carolina (9 percent), Oklahoma (12 percent), Alabama (13 percent), and Kentucky (13 percent). Why do some states have three times more representation of women than others? Some have noted that three of the states with the most women in their legislatures (Arizona, Vermont, and Washington) use

[100] Donald Gross, Robert Goidel, and Todd Shields, "State Campaign Finance Regulations and Electoral Competition," *American Politics Research* 30, no. 2 (2002): 143–65.

[101] Peter Francia and Paul S. Herrnson, "The Impact of Public Finance Laws on State Legislative Elections," *American Politics Research* 31, no. 5 (2003): 520–39.

[102] Howard J. Gold, "Explaining Third-Party Success in Gubernatorial Elections," *Social Science Journal* 42 (2005): 523–40.

[103] National Conference of State Legislatures, "2006 Partisan Composition of State Legislatures," http://www.ncsl.org/statevote/partycomptable2007.htm.

MMD elections.[104] One problem with this logic, however, is that Washington does not use "pure" MMD elections; candidates actually run for individual positions, where the winner takes all. Other explanations for the differences in levels of women's representation emphasize the role of political parties and regional (or cultural) effects. Some parties have made greater efforts to recruit candidates to seek office.[105] There are clear regional differences. Women are less represented in the South and more represented in the West and New England.

Representation of Racial and Ethnic Minorities

African Americans, Latinos, Asians, and Native Americans are underrepresented in state legislatures relative to their share of U.S. population, as illustrated in Table 3.6. The pattern for minority representation at the local level is similar. Although 11 percent of all state legislative seats are held by minorities, some groups are better represented than others. Minority populations are not evenly distributed across the nation or within states such as Hawaii, California, and New Mexico, where various minority groups combine to form a majority of the state's population. This means that there are great differences across the United States in minority representation at the state and local levels.

Hawaii (67 percent "minority" legislators), California (27 percent), Texas (25 percent), Mississippi (25 percent), Alabama (25 percent), New Mexico (23 percent), and Louisiana (22 percent) have the highest levels of minority representation in their states' legislatures. States with few minorities, not surprisingly, elect few minorities. The Idaho legislature, for example, was 100 percent white in 2005. Yet, even relatively high levels of minority representation in places like California and New Mexico are deceptive. These states, along with Arizona, lead the nation in the gap between the proportion of state residents who are minority and the proportion of their representatives who are. In contrast, minorities in Mississippi and Alabama, although still underrepresented, are much more represented relative to their share of the population than minorities in California, Texas, and Arizona.[106]

Why are large populations of minorities better represented in some places than others? The answers are race and single-member districting. In state and local elections, African Americans benefit from the use of majority-minority districts drawn with boundaries that ensure the district's population is heavily African American. This guarantees that the district will elect an African American, and it has led to near proportional representation of African Americans in many local elections. It also explains relatively high levels of

Table 3.6

Minority Representation in U.S. State Legislatures

	White (%)	African American (%)	Latino (%)	Asian or Pacific Islander (%)	Native American (%)
U.S. population	69	12	13	4	1
All state legislators	89	8	2	1	0.5

Source: Samantha Sanchez, *Money and Diversity in State Legislatures, 2003* (Helena, Mont.: Institute on Money in State Politics, 2005).

[104] Wilma Rule and Joseph F. Zimmerman, *United States Electoral Systems: Their Impact on Women and Minorities* (Westport, Conn.: Greenwood Press, 1992).

[105] Miki Caul, "Women's Representation in Parliament: The Role of Political Parties," *Party Politics* 5 (1999): 79–98.

[106] Samantha Sanchez, *Money and Diversity in State Legislatures, 2003* (Helena, Mont.: Institute on Money in State Politics, 2005).

minority representation in Deep South states, where African Americans are the predominant minority group.[107] In western and southwestern states, however, the largest minority group is Latinos. Latinos turn out at lower rates than African Americans and are not as segregated as African Americans in the South.[108] Latinos, moreover, are a less ethnically cohesive group than African Americans. All these factors combine to make it more difficult to design districts at the state or local level that are certain to produce Latino representation.[109] At the local level, Latinos win more seats via SMDs than they do under "at-large" arrangements,[110] but they may not win as many seats as African Americans.

Majority-minority districts present a paradox. They clearly increase the number of minorities holding state and local offices, and they offer people **descriptive representation**; that is, the ability to see people like themselves serving as their representative. When minority candidates win seats, moreover, they are able to affect the substance of public policy in ways that benefit their constituents and affect whether minorities are hired to implement policies approved by cities and school boards.[111] Descriptive representation of minorities at the local and congressional

level may also increase minority trust and participation and reduce political alienation among minority citizens.[112]

Some suggest that there may be a trade-off between descriptive representation and the substantive representation of minority interests. By packing large proportions of a minority group into one safe district, the group may have less overall influence in a legislature than they may have had if they were a swing group electing representatives across a larger number of districts.[113] Almost 95 percent of minority state legislators were Democrats in 2005, so we might assume that people in these districts find their substantive policy interests advanced by Democrats more than Republicans. A majority-minority district can help elect a minority Democrat representative, but this may also weaken other Democrats' chances of winning in surrounding districts. The minority district gains descriptive Democratic representation locally, but Democrats may elect fewer seats statewide, making it more difficult to advance the substantive policy goals of minority voters in the majority-minority district. Another potential consequence of majority-minority districts is a loss of electoral competitiveness. Minority legislators are much more likely to run unopposed than white legislators.[114]

---

[107] Engstrom and McDonald, "The Election of Blacks to City Councils."

[108] Douglas Massey and Nancy Denton, "Trends in Residential Segregation of Blacks, Hispanics and Asians," *American Sociological Review* 52 (1987): 802–25.

[109] Jerry Polinard, Robert Wrinkle, and Tomas Longoria, "The Impact of District Elections on the Mexican American Community," *Social Science Quarterly* 17, no. 3 (1991): 608–14; Delbert Taebel, "Minority Representation on City Councils: The Impact of Structure on Blacks and Hispanics," *Social Science Quarterly* 59 (1978): 142–52; and A. Velditz and C. Johnson, "Community Segregation, Electoral Structure and Minority Representation," *Social Science Quarterly* 67 (1982): 729–36.

[110] David Leal, Ken Meier, and Valerie Martinez-Ebers, "The Politics of Latino Education: The Biases of At-Large Elections," *Journal of Politics* 66, no. 4 (2004): 1224.

[111] J. L. Polinard, Robert Wrinkle, Tomas Longoria, and Norman Binder, *Electoral Structure and Urban Policy: The Impact of Mexican American Communities* (New York: M. E. Sharpe, 1994); and Kenneth J. Meier, Eric Gonzalez Juenke, Robert Wrinkle, and J. L. Polinard, "Structural Choices and Representation Biases: The Post-Election Color of Representation," *American Journal of Political Science* 49, no. 4 (2005): 748–749.

[112] Lawrence Bobo and Frank Gilliam Jr., "Race, Sociopolitical Participation and Black Empowerment," *American Political Science Review* (1990): 377–93; Adrian Pantoja and Gary Segura, "Does Ethnicity Matter? Descriptive Representation in Legislatures," *Social Science Quarterly* 84 (2003): 441–60; and Susan Banducci, Todd Donovan, and Jeffrey Karp, "Minority Representation, Empowerment and Participation," *Journal of Politics* 66 (2004): 534.

[113] David Lublin, *The Paradox of Representation: Racial Gerrymandering and Minority Interests in Congress* (Princeton, N.J.: Princeton University Press, 1997).

[114] Sanchez, "Money and Diversity in State Legislatures, 2003," 6.

Summary

A healthy democracy depends, at least in part, on having citizens who are engaged with each other and with politics. Participation in local voluntary groups is one way that people learn the skills required to be citizens. As important as local democracy is, this chapter illustrates that there are substantial barriers to participation at the state and local levels. Elections are often designed to be uncompetitive, a situation that may serve only incumbents well. Nonpartisan races, uncompetitive elections, and other barriers may depress interest in state and local politics.

But this need not be the case. One theme of this book is that institutions matter and institutions can change. Race-based barriers to voting have been reduced substantially over the last 100 years. This is evidence that the rules can change and that political participation can become more inclusive.

Key Terms

At-large elections

Clean money and public
  financing of campaigns

Cumulative voting

Descriptive representation

District magnitude

Efficacy

Grandfather clause

Literacy tests

Lobbying

Majority-minority district

Multimember district

Participation bias

Poll tax

Progressive era

Racial gerrymandering

Social capital

Voting-age population

Voting-eligible population

Voting Rights Act of 1965

Winner-take-all

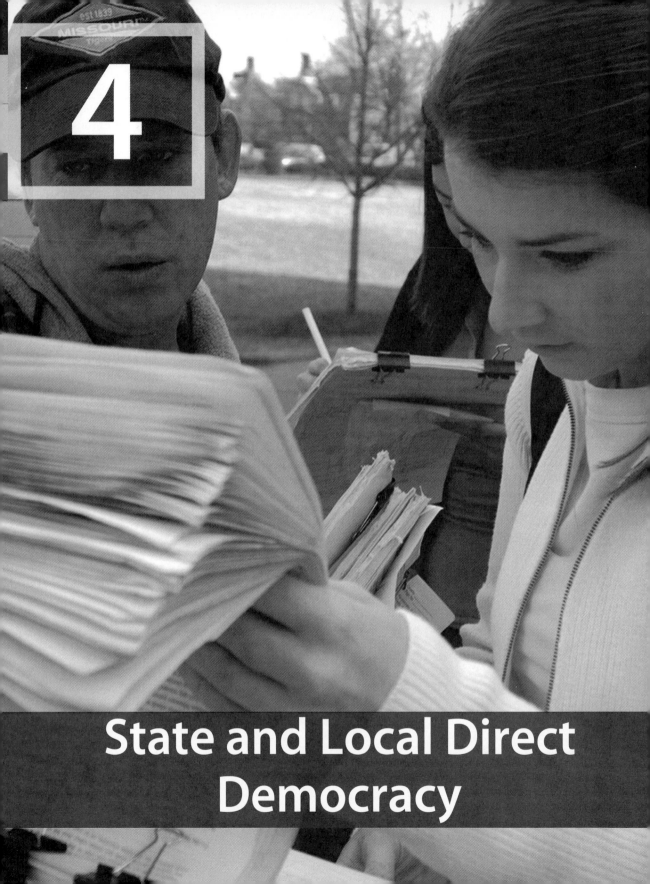

4

State and Local Direct Democracy

INTRODUCTION

The link between citizens and their government can be quite different at the state and local levels than at the national level. State legislators and local governments regularly refer matters to voters for their approval; in fact, most states require that amendments to state constitutions ultimately be approved by voters. In nearly half the states, people can draft their own legislation and petition to have a public vote to approve or reject it. Additionally, many local governments, including those in states that do not allow the usage of direct democracy at the state level, permit this process. Some of our biggest cities—including Baltimore, Columbus, Dallas, Denver, Detroit, Houston, Jacksonville, Los Angeles, Miami, Milwaukee, New York, Phoenix, Portland, San Antonio, San Diego, San Francisco, Seattle, and Washington, D.C.—permit citizens to propose charter amendments to be placed on the ballot for fellow citizens to either adopt or reject. In fact, a majority of Americans reside in cities and towns where they can vote directly on matters of public policy.[1] Processes of direct democracy can leave elected representatives with limited influence over public policy. It is difficult to understand state and local politics in much of the nation without considering the effects of direct democracy.

In many American states and communities, citizens have more ability to affect what their governments do than other people in almost any other political system in the world. Apart from areas in Switzerland, no other places with such freewheeling democratic arrangements exist. In its most extreme form, direct democracy gives people outside the corridors of power the potential to cut taxes, propose tax hikes or new spending programs, veto most laws passed by elected representatives, and even remove elected officials from office. This contrasts dramatically with how American citizens participate in national politics. Although the United States is one of the few advanced democracies to have never put a question of national policy or constitutional design up for a public vote, these questions are commonly decided by voters at the state and local levels. Americans regularly decide on matters such as local school funding, land-use rules, social policy, or how much their state should borrow for specific long-term projects. The scope of direct democracy varies widely across the states and thus provides one of the key features distinguishing politics in some states and cities from that in other places. In this chapter, we consider American direct democracy as a grand democratic experiment that allows us to consider, in effect, whether more democracy is "better." That is, does democratic politics work "better" when citizens are given more direct control over their government? As we shall see, no consensus exists among political observers, pundits, journalists, scholars, or politicians about these questions. We also illustrate that each state has a unique set of rules defining how direct democracy works, and these rules affect how much the process is used. Politics and policies can be fundamentally different in states with freewheeling forms of direct democracy.

[1] John Matsusaka, *For the Many or the Few: The Initiative, Public Policy, and American Democracy*

Institutions of Direct Democracy

Three main features of direct democracy are the referendum, the initiative, and the recall. Almost every state uses some form of referendum. As Figure 4.1 reveals, 24 states have some form of a statewide initiative, 24 allow a statewide popular referendum (most of which also provide the initiative), and 18 states have provisions for the recall of state officials.

Referendum

A referendum is a public vote on a statute or a constitutional amendment that has already been considered by a state legislature or local government. The most widely used instrument of direct democracy in the American states (and localities) is the legislative referendum. In the case of the **legislative referendum,** elected officials have control over the question that voters will consider, although legislators are often bound to place certain items on state ballots. Use of legislative referendums at the national level is quite widespread, with nearly every advanced democratic nation other than the United States using the process.[2] Every American state has some provision for a legislative referendum— particularly for state constitutional matters. Most state constitutions require that voters approve constitutional amendments via referendum, and some require that voters approve when a state issues debt. Legislators may also choose to defer to the wisdom of voters and allow them to have the final say over controversial issues, such as tax increases.

Figure 4.1

States with Statewide Initiatives, Popular Referendums, and Recalls

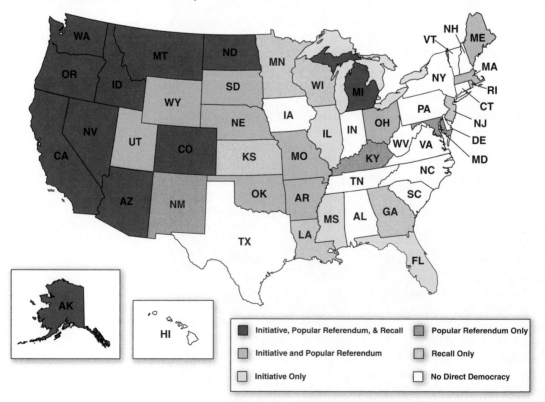

Legend:
- Initiative, Popular Referendum, & Recall
- Initiative and Popular Referendum
- Initiative Only
- Popular Referendum Only
- Recall Only
- No Direct Democracy

[2] David Butler and Austin Ranney, eds., *Referendums around the World: The Growing Use of Direct Democracy* (Washington, D.C.: AEI Press, 1994).

The **popular referendum**, by way of contrast, allows a person or group to file a petition to have a public vote on a bill that the legislature has already approved. Every state with the initiative process (except Florida, Illinois, and Mississippi) also allows citizens to propose popular referendums.[3] The popular referendum is effectively a public veto of a law. Proponents may qualify popular referendums for the ballot by collecting a certain percentage of signatures in a set amount of time following the passage of the legislation in question.

Initiative

The two types of initiative process in the United States are the direct initiative and indirect initiative. The **direct initiative** allows a person or group to file a proposed bill with a state office and then collect signatures from voters to qualify the measure for a spot on the state ballot. If the initiative qualifies, voters have a direct say on approving or rejecting the proposal. If voters approve the measure, it becomes law.[4] An **indirect initiative** functions as a petition to have the legislature consider a bill proposed by citizens. This is similar to the Swiss system. If the indirect initiative qualifies by its proponents collecting enough signatures, the legislature can adopt or reject the bill. If it is rejected by the legislature, it must be placed on the ballot to give voters a chance to approve or reject the proposal.

Direct and indirect initiatives appear on the ballot if sufficient signatures are collected. Rules for qualifying initiatives vary across the states, but the number of signatures on petitions required to qualify is typically set as a fixed percentage of votes cast in a previous election or as a fixed percentage of all registered voters. Most states with any sort of initiative process only have direct initiatives; however, a few (Alaska, Maine, Massachusetts, and Wyoming) have indirect

initiatives only. Five additional states (Michigan, Nevada, Ohio, Utah, and Washington) allow both direct and indirect initiatives. Depending on the state, a legislature may submit to voters an indirect initiative that it rejected, along with its own alternative proposal; alternatively, the legislature may simply take no action.

Recall

The **recall** allows a person or group to file a petition for a public vote to remove an elected official from office prior to when the official's term expires. The first place in the United States to adopt the recall was Los Angeles in 1903. Many cities and 18 states now have rules allowing for the recall of elected officials, although the process is rarely used at the state level. Only two governors have been recalled: Lynn Fraiser of North Dakota in 1921 and Gray Davis of California in 2003. A gubernatorial recall in Arizona came close to being successful, but before the process was completed, Governor Fife Symington was forced to resign in 1997 after being convicted of bank fraud by a federal jury. Previous efforts in Arizona in 1987 to recall then Governor Evan Mecham were also unsuccessful, although the effort pressured Mecham to resign. There have been numerous successful recall efforts of state legislators and local elected officials, however.[5]

In most states that allow the recall process, the signature requirement for qualification is much greater than that required for the initiative and referendum.[6] Some states require that proponents of either a state or local recall establish compelling grounds to have a vote to remove an elected official (such as criminal misconduct), whereas other states' rules are less restrictive or have no formal requirement that substantial misconduct be established in order to proceed with a recall. States also differ in how recalls are conducted. In some situations, voters

[3] David Magleby, *Direct Legislation: Voting on Ballot Propositions in the United States* (Baltimore: Johns Hopkins University Press, 1984).

[4] A simple majority is usually required for approval, although some states require more. See Richard Ellis, *Democratic Delusions: The Initiative Process in America* (Lawrence: University Press of Kansas, 2002).

[5] Shaun Bowler and Bruce Cain, eds., *Clicker Politics: Essays on the California Recall* (Englewood Cliffs, N.J.: Prentice Hall, 2005).

[6] Magleby, *Direct Legislation*.

are given two choices on one ballot: first, they decide if the official should be removed; then they may decide who should replace the official. This was the case with the California recall, where, after deciding on Governor Davis's fate, voters then had 135 candidates to choose from (including actor Arnold Schwarzenegger, porn publisher Larry Flynt, ex–child actor Gary Coleman, and at least two adult "entertainers," Angelyne and Mary Carey; see Figure 4.2).

Figure 4.2

California Recall Ballot

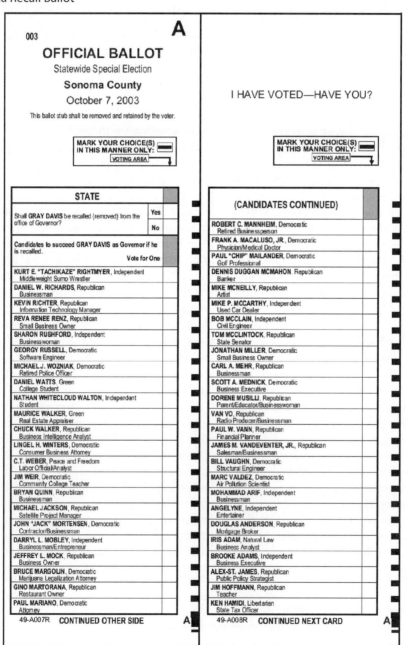

In other cases, voters are only asked the question about the recall. In these cases, the office is left vacant until the next election, a replacement is appointed, or a special election is conducted later to fill the vacancy.

More Responsible and More Representative Government?

Part of the difficulty in assessing the merits and pitfalls of direct democracy lies in how we define what a "better" democratic system might look like. One way to consider this task is to ask if direct democracy in the states makes politics more responsible and more representative.[7] Early advocates of direct democracy claimed that it could do both.

The Promise of Direct Democracy

Direct democracy has its roots in the Populist and Progressive movements of the late 19th century and early 20th century, respectively. In the early 1900s, campaign contributions were largely unregulated, and bribery and graft were not uncommon in state legislatures. State and local elected officials were paid poorly, and, with few laws regulating political corruption, they were subject to influence

INSTITUTIONS MATTER

"THE GUN BEHIND THE DOOR"

In 2006, state legislatures across the country were evidently feeling the "heat" being packed by various groups, as the threat of the citizen initiative impelled them into action. According to the Ballot Initiative Strategy Center (http://www.ballot.org), a nonprofit group that tracks ballot initiatives, several state legislatures took up bills they had previously ignored (or opposed) because potential ballot issues resonated strongly with citizens.

In the spring of 2006, a citizens' group in Oregon collected signatures for an initiative to rein in the runaway interest rates that payday loan companies foist on borrowers. The measure was polling like gangbusters. It was so popular that the Oregon legislature decided to convene a special session in April to pass legislation nearly identical to the initiative. Not only that, but the sponsor of the bill was also the same woman who the previous year had killed legislation that would have accomplished the same ends— and all because of the threat of an initiative.

In Michigan, the Republican-controlled legislature realized in March 2006 there was a good chance a popular minimum wage initiative would be on the November ballot. The GOP leadership, fearful of having their candidates running in an election with such a popular issue, wisely decided to push through the legislature a languishing Democratic bill to raise the state's minimum wage. Democratic governor Jennifer Granholm signed the bill into law. The initiative campaign, which was organized by organized labor, promptly shuttered its doors.

Using the initiative process as a lever to pry stubborn legislation out of the recesses of a legislature is nothing new. Democratic presidential candidate Woodrow Wilson argued in 1911 that it could be used by citizens to apply tacit pressure on capricious state legislatures, forcing them to abide by the will of the people. By way of analogy, Wilson understood the practice of citizen lawmaking as the "gun behind the door—for use only in case of emergency, but [a] mighty good persuader, nevertheless."[a]

---

[a] Ballot Initiative Strategy Center, "Oregon: Another Initiative 'Pays' Off," 21 April 2006, http://ballotblog.typepad.com/ballotblog/2006/04/oregon_another_.html.

[7] Todd Donovan and Shaun Bowler, "Responsible and Representative?" in *Citizens as Legislators: Direct Democracy in the United States*, ed. Shaun Bowler, Todd Donovan, and Caroline Tolbert (Columbus: Ohio State University Press, 1998).

by firms seeking favorable treatment from government. As one observer of the 1880s Oregon legislature noted, it consisted of "briefless lawyers, farmless farmers, business failures, bar-room loafers, Fourth-of-July orators [and] political thugs."[8] Many elected officials had little enthusiasm for social, economic, and political reforms that may have had widespread support among the general public.

To Populist and Progressive reformers of that era, representative government alone could not be trusted to serve the public interest. Their goal was to give the public greater influence over the behavior of elected officials. Reformers were suspicious of the power that wealthy economic interests had over elected representatives. In this context, then, reformers argued that by giving people the ability to write their own laws and veto unpopular laws passed by legislators, public policy would be more representative of public opinion. Likewise, it was assumed, then, that elected officials would often work to protect powerful economic interests by doing such things as granting monopolies, giving away public resources, blocking health and safety regulations, and blocking anticorruption laws. If the public could use direct democracy as an end run around these elected officials, reformers assumed that public policy would become more responsible.

This was, in part, the promise of direct democracy 100 years ago. In considering how direct democracy works in American states and communities today, it is important to consider the adoption of direct democracy in its historic context. We assess how it might make politics more representative of public opinion and consider whether it makes policy more responsible. The latter quality, of course, is much more difficult to assess.

Populist Origins of Direct Democracy

Although states in New England have practice with town meeting forms of local government that provide for direct citizen voting on policy questions, direct democracy did not exist at the state level prior to the late 1890s. Eighteen of the 24 states that currently have the initiative process adopted it between 1898 and 1914. Many of the early initiatives reflected the agenda of groups that agitated for the adoption of direct democracy. Issues such as woman suffrage, prohibition, labor laws, and electoral reforms were common in the first decade that direct democracy was in use.

The initiative process at the state level was first adopted in South Dakota in 1898, but it was first used statewide in Oregon in 1904. Several political movements that included organized labor, disaffected farmers, proponents of the so-called single tax, Prohibitionists, and women's suffrage advocates pressed their states to adopt the initiative, recall, and referendum. These direct democracy tools were part of a larger set of reforms advocated by the **Populist Party** in the 1890s, including direct election of U.S. senators, direct election of the president, direct voter control candidate nominations, direct primary elections, and the income tax.[9] Recall that Figure 4.1 illustrates how direct democracy is more common in the West, in part because minority parties had greater political influence there and because some of these states were just forming their first constitutions when Populists and Progressives were most influential.[10]

The Ebb and Flow of Ballot Initiatives

From the 1930s to the 1960s, as legislatures became more professional and anticorruption

[8] David Schuman, "The Origin of State Constitutional Direct Democracy: William Simon Uren and the Oregon System," *Temple Law Review* 67 (1994): 947–63, 949.

[9] Shaun Bowler, Todd Donovan, and Eric D. Lawrence, "Introducing Direct Democracy" (paper presented at the annual meeting of the American Political Science Association, Washington, D.C., August 2005).

[10] Daniel A. Smith and Dustin Fridkin, "Delegating Direct Democracy: Interparty Legislative Competition and the Adoption of the Initiative in the American States," *American Political Science Review* 102 (2008): 333–50.

laws took hold, direct democracy was used less. It made a comeback, however, as groups again began to use the initiative process to promote public votes on policy questions. There has been a steady increase in the number of statewide ballot measures that have qualified since the 1960s. The use of initiatives reached a new peak in the 1990s, when there were nearly 400 initiatives on statewide ballots—far more than in any other decade.[11] The annual use of initiatives remained relatively high by historic standards after 2000. It is important to remember that roughly 60 percent of all initiatives that qualify for state ballots are rejected by voters;[12] however, measures that pass can have a powerful effect on the design of state political institutions and on the political agenda.

Studies find a large degree of stability in terms of the subjects of ballot measures on which voters have been asked to decide over most of the last 100 years. The most common initiatives since 1980 have been governmental reform measures, such as term limits and campaign finance regulation (23 percent) and taxation questions (22 percent). Social and moral issues (17 percent) and environmental measures (11 percent) are the next most common questions.[13] Some attribute the revival of direct democracy in recent decades to a new generation of citizens who demand more say in politics but who are less interested in traditional forms of participation via representation by political parties.[14] Others note that the rise of initiative use in the United States corresponded with the proliferation of new interest groups[15] and with the maturation of a sophisticated industry of campaign professionals promoting the use of initiatives.[16]

The Explosion Continues

In the 2008 general election, there were 59 initiatives and two popular referendums on the statewide ballots of 35 states. There were also hundreds more local referendums and initiatives on the ballots of all 50 states. Substantively, ballot propositions cover a remarkable range of issues; some of the issues involved are complex, whereas others are relatively straightforward. Some measures make national headlines; others remain obscure in terms of public or media attention. Voters have cast ballots dealing with issues as diverse as banning gay marriage, punishing negligent doctors, prohibiting the confinement of pregnant pigs, limiting the taxation and spending powers of state governments, funding stem cell research, and ending affirmative action programs and social welfare benefits to illegal immigrants. In many states, virtually no subject matter is off-limits.

Looking just at the November 2004 ballot, six states featured initiatives banning same-sex marriage, whereas another five had legislative referrals on the same topic. Four states had measures dealing with tort reform and medical malpractice, with voters in Florida and Nevada being faced with competing proposals authored by dueling doctors and trial lawyers. Floridians and Nevadans also voted to raise the minimum wage. Coloradoans approved a measure mandating utility companies to

---

[11] Ellis, *Democratic Delusions*.

[12] David Magleby, "Direct Legislation in America," in Butler and Ranney, *Referendums around the World*.

[13] Caroline J. Tolbert, "Cycles of Democracy: Direct Democracy and Institutional Realignment in the American States," *Political Science Quarterly* 118 (2003): 467–89.

[14] Russell Dalton, Wilhelm Burklin, and Andrew Drummond, "Public Attitudes toward Direct Democracy," *Journal of Democracy* 12 (2001): 141–53; and Ian Budge, "Political Parties in Direct Democracy," in *Referendum Democracy: Citizens, Elites and Deliberation in Referendum Campaigns*, ed. Matthew Mendelsohn and Andrew Parkin (New York: Palgrave, 2002).

[15] Magleby, "Direct Legislation in America."

[16] David Broder, *Democracy Derailed: Initiative Campaigns and the Power of Money* (New York: Harcourt Brace, 2000); and Larry Sabato, Bruce Larson, and Howard Ernst, *Dangerous Democracy?* (Lanham, Md.: Rowman & Littlefield, 2001).

develop alternative energy sources and raised taxes on tobacco but rejected a proposal calling for the proportional allocation of electors for the Electoral College. Voters in Montana approved legalizing marijuana use for medicinal purposes. Californians voted on 16 statewide measures, including 11 initiatives and one popular referendum; one of the five initiated measures approved on Election Day was a proposition authorizing the state to issue $3 billion in state bonds over ten years to finance embryonic stem cell research. As voters in Florida, Nebraska, and Oklahoma all voted to expand gambling operations in 2004, their counterparts in Michigan and California opted to rein in gambling operations by Native American tribes, and voters in Washington nixed the expansion of slot machines in current gaming establishments.[17]

Differences across Initiative States

States differ with regard to how directly democratic their direct democracy processes are in practice. In most of the United States, direct democracy is limited to legislative referendums used at both the state and local levels. Most western states that adopted the initiative early have rules that allow citizens to draft **constitutional initiatives** as well as **statutory initiatives**. Statutory initiatives are more readily amended or repealed by the legislature in some states (such as Colorado, Maine, Idaho, and Missouri), whereas others require waiting periods, supermajorities, or both before a statutory initiative may be amended. California is the only state where the legislature may neither amend nor repeal an initiative statute.

In states where rules for direct democracy were put in place when Populists and Progressives were still influential (such as Arizona, California, Colorado, and Oregon), provisions for the initiative and popular referendum are more radically democratic than what exists in states that adopted the initiative process later in the 20th century. States that adopted the direct initiative and popular referendum in the early 1900s have rules that make it relatively easy to qualify for the ballot. Most early-adopting states have a relatively low threshold of signatures required to qualify initiatives as well as other requirements to qualify ballot measures.[18]

Using the Initiative

As Figure 4.3 reveals, Oregon and California—two early adopters—lead the pack in initiative use, with both states averaging 6.4 initiatives per each two-year election cycle. Over 300 initiatives have appeared on Oregon and California statewide ballots since those states adopted direct democracy. The six states with the most frequent use of initiatives (Arizona, California, Colorado, North Dakota, Oregon, and Washington) have averaged more than three initiatives per general election since the Progressive era.[19] Roughly 60 percent of all initiative activity has taken place in these six states.[20] Few states, however, look like California or Oregon in terms of the ease of qualifying initiatives for the ballot and the difficulty that legislatures face when it comes to amending voter-approved initiatives.

The handful of states that adopted direct democracy long after the demise of the Populists and Progressives have much more restrictive rules on how it can be used. Alaska included the initiative in its constitution when

---

[17] Ballot Initiative Strategy Center, "Election Results 2004," December 2004, http://www.ballot.org.

[18] Shaun Bowler and Todd Donovan, "Measuring the Effect of Direct Democracy on State Policy: Not All Initiatives Are Created Equal," *State Politics and Policy Quarterly* 4 (2004): 345–63.

[19] Caroline Tolbert, Daniel Lowenstein, and Todd Donovan, "Election Law and Rules for Using Initiatives," in Bowler, Donovan, and Tolbert, *Citizens as Legislators*.

[20] Ballot Initiative Strategy Center, "Election Results 2004."

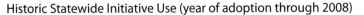

Figure 4.3

Historic Statewide Initiative Use (year of adoption through 2008)

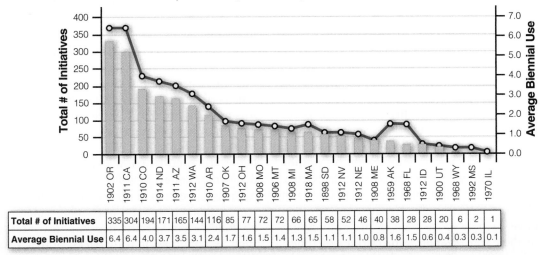

Total # of Initiatives	335	304	194	171	165	144	116	85	77	72	72	66	65	58	52	46	40	38	28	28	20	6	2	1
Average Biennial Use	6.4	6.4	4.0	3.7	3.5	3.1	2.4	1.7	1.6	1.5	1.4	1.3	1.5	1.1	1.1	1.0	0.8	1.6	1.5	0.6	0.4	0.3	0.3	0.1

Note: Bars represent the total number of initiatives that qualified in a state since its adoption of direct democracy, with values plotted along the left-side axis. The line represents the average number of initiatives in a state every two years, with values plotted on the right-side axis.

it was admitted to the union (1959), but only Florida and Wyoming (1968), Illinois (1970), and Mississippi (1992) have adopted the initiative process since that time. Three of these states (Florida, Illinois, and Mississippi) only allow constitutional initiatives. Illinois and Mississippi place severe restrictions on the subject matter that may appear on the ballot, and both states have strict provisions for qualification. As such, initiatives are rarely used in these two states—only one initiative has ever appeared on the Illinois ballot, and only two have qualified in Mississippi.[21]

Limits on Initiative Content

Generally speaking, any topic is a potential initiative subject. A few states, however, prohibit measures dealing with the judiciary, bills of rights, or tax questions. The major constraints on initiatives are constitutionality and single-subject laws, both of which are

typically evaluated by state courts after a measure has been approved by voters. Some states allow elected officials or courts to amend or revise the language of propositions without the proponent's consent. Of the 24 states, only six have much of a preelection review at all. Four states—Colorado, Idaho, Montana, and Washington—have an advisory preelection certification process.

Half of the initiative states have rules that limit initiatives to one subject. Most state courts have been fairly tolerant of individual proposals with sweeping breadth, as long as their component parts could be seen as reasonably germane to one subject. State legislatures originally adopted the **single-subject rule** to ban egregious attempts at building coalitions of supporters by rolling many attractive features into a single measure in the hopes of expanding potential support for it. One famous yet unsuccessful initiative proposal from California linked the regulation

[21] National Conference of State Legislatures, "Initiative and Referendum in the 21st Century: Final Report and Recommendations of the NCSL I&R Task Force," Denver, Colo., 2000, http://www.ncsl.org/programs/legman/irtaskfc/landR_report.pdf.

of margarine, voting rights for Native Americans, gambling, fishing, mining, and apportionment of the state senate into a single initiative question.[22] This sort of "log-rolling" proposal is prohibited by single-subject laws. Only Florida's State Supreme Court has been known to regularly nullify initiatives on single-subject grounds, even after proponents have collected hundreds of thousands of valid signatures to qualify their measures for the ballot. The Florida State Supreme Court is also the only court to overtly declare that single-subject evaluations should be applied more rigorously to initiatives than legislative bills.[23] Since 2000, however, state courts in California, Colorado, Nevada, and Oregon have become more rigid in the application of their state's single-subject rule. At times, this has meant that a single initiative must be split into several questions that are put before voters simultaneously.[24]

Qualifying for the Ballot

Initiatives and referendums, when they qualify for the ballot, are usually placed on a ballot whenever the next regularly scheduled general election occurs. This means direct democracy votes typically occur in even-numbered years. Some states (including Maine, Ohio, and Washington) have initiative votes annually in November, and a few (such as California) place initiatives and referendums on general and primary ballots every two years, so voters decide on an array of initiatives and referendums at least twice a year in even years. California and a handful of other states also allow either the governor or the legislature to schedule special statewide elections in odd years for votes on initiatives and referendums.

States that allow the initiative have considerable variation regarding how easy it is for citizens to use the process. Most states share four basic steps.[25] First, the proposal is drafted by proponents. Next, it is forwarded to a state office that issues an official title and summary of the measure. Proponents may then circulate petitions—usually within a fixed time period, often 90 or 180 days—for voters to sign. Finally, the state verifies whether a valid number of signatures were collected. If so, the proposal is placed on the ballot. Rules for qualification vary across direct democracy states. In some states, petitioners have less time than in others. Some states also require that a certain proportion of signatures be collected in specific geographical areas, such as congressional districts. States also differ in the proportion of voters' signatures required to qualify for the ballot. Differences in these rules and in the population of a state affect how costly it is to get on a ballot. The difficulty of collecting hundreds of thousands of signatures means that many proponents hire people to collect signatures. Qualification is more difficult, and more costly (see Table 4.1), when a higher proportion of signatures must be collected in a shorter time period.[26]

Amateurs or Professionals?

In many states, it is difficult to place a measure on the ballot unless professional petition firms are paid to collect some or all the signatures required for qualification. In large states like California and Florida, where more than 600,000 valid signatures are routinely required to qualify a constitutional amendment initiative, few measures reach the ballot without proponents resorting to hiring

---

[22] Winston Crouch, *The Initiative and Referendum in California* (Los Angeles: Haynes Foundation, 1950).

[23] Daniel Lowenstein, *Election Law: Cases and Materials* (Durham, N.C.: Carolina Academic Press, 1995), 282.

[24] Ellis, *Democratic Delusions*, 144–46.

[25] For a more detailed discussion of California's initiative process, see California Secretary of State, http://www.ss.ca.gov/elections/elections.htm.

[26] Susan Banducci, "Direct Legislation: When Is It Used and When Does It Pass?" in Bowler, Donovan, and Tolbert, *Citizens as Legislators*.

Table 4.1

Ease of Qualifying Ballot Initiatives Index

State	Qualification Difficulty Index
Oregon	0
California	1
Colorado	1
North Dakota	1
Arkansas	2
Ohio	2
Michigan	2
South Dakota	2
Idaho	2
Arizona	3
Washington	3
Oklahoma	3
Montana	3
Missouri	3
Massachusetts	3
Utah	3
Nebraska	4
Maine	4
Nevada	4
Florida	4
Illinois	4
Alaska	5
Mississippi	5
Wyoming	6

Note: Higher scores indicate more difficulty; states with lower scores have the easiest rules for qualification.

Source: Shaun Bowler and Todd Donovan, "Measuring the Effect of Direct Democracy on State Policy: Not All Initiatives Are Created Equal," *State Politics and Policy Quarterly* 4 (2004): 345–63.

firms that use paid petition gatherers to collect signatures. Some of these signature-gathering firms will have their subcontractors carry multiple petitions for the various groups that have hired them to gather signatures. In states that have fewer voters, it is easier to collect the required signatures. In Colorado, for example, less than 70,000 valid signatures are needed to qualify either a statutory or constitutional amendment initiative.

Today, few citizen-based groups have the resources to collect signatures equal to 12, 8, or even 5 percent of a state's voting population. The use of paid signature gatherers and professional campaign staff has been part of the process in some states since early in the 20th century.[27] In the early 1900s, paid petition gatherers in some states were earning upward of $0.03 a signature.[28] As the raw number of signatures required to qualify has increased, fewer voluntary, "grassroots" measures appear on state ballots.[29] In California, for example, volunteer petition campaigns are rarely successful. Those who wish to get a constitutional initiative amendment onto the ballot have to gather signatures equivalent to 8 percent of the number of votes for governor. This means gathering close to 1 million signatures in just 150 days, as a large percentage of signatures will surely be found to be invalid. Petition management firms in the state offer proponents a guarantee of qualification but at a price that runs close to $2 million for each initiative to be qualified. Paid signature gatherers in California have been known to earn up to $5 per valid signature, although the $1 to $2 range is more typical. In less populous states, the cost to qualify an initiative ranges anywhere between $50,000 and $400,000.

[27] Charles Beard and Birl Shultz, eds., *Documents on the State-Wide Initiative, Referendum and Recall* (New York: Macmillan, 1912); and David McCuan, Shaun Bowler, Todd Donovan, and Ken Fernandez, "California's Political Warriors: Campaign Professionals and the Initiative Process," in Bowler, Donovan, and Tolbert, *Citizens as Legislators*.

[28] Daniel A. Smith and Joseph Lubinski, "Direct Democracy during the Progressive Era: A Crack in the Populist Veneer?" *Journal of Policy History* 14 (2002): 349–83.

[29] Broder, *Democracy Derailed*; Peter Schrag, *Paradise Lost: California's Experience, America's Future* (New York: New Press, 1998); John Haskell, *Direct Democracy or Representative Government? Dispelling the Populist Myth* (Boulder, Colo.: Westview, 2001); and Ellis, *Democratic Delusions*.

Champions of direct democracy have long argued that if the process is to combat the power of wealthy established interests, petition efforts should rely on volunteers only. In this spirit, several states passed laws banning the use of paid signature gathering. In the early 1900s, several states, including Ohio, South Dakota, and Washington, passed laws banning paid petition gatherers. In the 1930s and 1940s, Oregon and Colorado also passed laws banning the practice, with Idaho and Nebraska following suit in the late 1980s.[30] The U.S. Supreme Court eventually overturned these laws in **Meyer v. Grant** in 1988, reasoning that the First Amendment protected paid petitioning, as it was a form of political speech.[31] This ruling, and the difficulties of qualifying measures, means that wealthy groups (unions, corporations, business organizations, professional associations, and trade groups) and wealthy individuals play a prominent, if not dominant, role in affecting what gets put to a public vote. Roughly a dozen states have responded by passing laws requiring circulators to disclose if they are being paid or not, and Oregon and North Dakota prohibit paid signature gathers from being compensated on a per-signature basis, requiring them instead to be paid a fixed salary or an hourly wage.[32]

Millionaires' Amusement?

Wealthy individuals, such as Microsoft cofounder Paul Allen, Hollywood actor-director Rob Reiner, billionaire financier George Soros, tech-industry businessman Ron Unz, and even actor Arnold Schwarzenegger (in his pregovernor, *Terminator* days) have all bankrolled the qualification of successful ballot initiatives. For his part, Allen convinced taxpayers to subsidize a new stadium for his then-mediocre football team, the Seattle Seahawks, but Washington voters rejected the school reform initiative he funded. In 1998, Reiner sponsored an initiative to create early childhood development programs, and in 2006, he sponsored a tax on wealthy individuals to expand preschool education. In the 1990s, Soros, along with a couple of other wealthy individuals, helped finance nearly a dozen initiatives legalizing the medical use of marijuana. Unz used his money to bankroll measures to repeal bilingual education programs in California, Arizona, Colorado, and Massachusetts. In 2002, Schwarzenegger funded an initiative that bulked up spending on his state's afterschool programs (and helped to burnish his image as a budding policy wonk).[33]

The Financing of Direct Democracy Campaigns

The large sums of money spent on ballot measure campaigns gave rise to concerns about the presence of an "initiative industrial complex."[34] From this perspective, paid political consultants are seen not just as "guns for hire" but also as actors who create the demand for their services by advocating their own proposals for ballot measures. Their services include signature gathering, polling, crafting TV ads, and purchasing airtime for ads.

[30] National Conference of State Legislatures, "Initiative and Referendum in the 21st Century."

[31] *Meyer v. Grant*, 486 U.S. 414 (1988).

[32] Todd Donovan and Daniel A. Smith, "Identifying and Preventing Signature Fraud on Ballot Measure Petitions," in Election Fraud: Detecting and Deterring Electoral Manipulation, Michael Alvarez, Thad E. Hall, and Susan D. Hyde, eds.,(Washington, D.C.: Brookings, 2008).

[33] Elizabeth Garrett, "Democracy in the Wake of the California Recall," *University of Pennsylvania Law Review* 153 (2004): 239–84; Daniel A. Smith, "Initiatives and Referendums: The Effects of Direct Democracy on Candidate Elections," in *The Electoral Challenge: Theory Meets Practice*, ed. Steven Craig (Washington, D.C.: CQ Press, 2006); and Richard Hasen, "Rethinking the Unconstitutionality of Contribution and Expenditure Limits in Ballot Measure Campaigns," *Southern California Law Review* 78 (2005): 885–926.

[34] Schrag, *Paradise Lost;* and David Magleby and Kelly Patterson, "Consultants and Direct Democracy," *PS: Political Science and Politics* 31 (1998): 160–62.

The public clearly has concerns about the campaign side of direct democracy. Despite being overwhelmingly in favor of the initiative process, people claim that initiative campaigns are misleading, that campaigns are too expensive, and that "special interests" dominate the process.[35] Writing in 2003, the *Los Angeles Times*, a longtime and persistent critic of the initiative process, editorialized, "Direct democracy is running amok" in California. Critics in other states agree, such as the former president of the Florida Senate, who has warned of the potential "Californication" of Florida resulting from the rash of expensive initiative campaigns.[36]

One critical question about direct democracy is whether consultants are driving the process more than citizens.[37] Some note that consulting and initiative marketing firms "sometimes test market issues for their feasibility . . . and then shop for a group to back them" and that petition firms may try to drum up business after pitching issues to potential sponsors.[38] However, few examples of this have occurred in California or elsewhere. The claim is likely overreaching, as one is hard-pressed to find evidence of this type of practice, save for a single campaign professional promoting a lottery initiative in 1988.[39]

Nonetheless, the amount of money spent on initiative politics can be staggering. In 2006, nearly $525 million was spent on 73 ballot initiative campaigns in 18 states. In several states, more money was spent on ballot initiative campaigns than for all other races for political office combined. In California alone, proponents and opponents of eight initiatives on the November ballot spent more than $300 million in an effort to qualify the measures and sway voters of the merits of their arguments. Two years earlier, in 2004, expenditures across initiative states nearly topped $400 million on just 59 statewide measures, double the amount spent on 117 ballot measures (both initiatives and referendums) on the ballot in 2002. Ballot measure committees squaring off in 2004 in just four states—California, Florida, Michigan, and Oregon—spent more than $338 million, accounting for 85 percent of the total expenditures on ballot initiative campaigns that year.[40]

Direct Democracy Campaigns and the Supreme Court

These enormous expenditures are possible because the U.S. Supreme Court views initiative campaigns differently than candidate contests. The Court recognizes that large contributions to candidates may create either the appearance or the actuality that a candidate for office may become corrupted.[41] This ruling has allowed Congress and state legislatures some limited ability to regulate the size of contributions given to candidates. Contributions to initiative campaigns, in contrast, are seen as attempts at direct communication with voters rather than attempts to influence elected officials. In *Bellotti v. First National Bank of Boston*, the Court reasoned in 1978 that there was no possibility of corruption or appearance of corruption because a ballot measure can't provide any illicit political favors to a donor of a campaign. In its *Bellotti* decision, the Court

---

[35] Shaun Bowler, Todd Donovan, Max Neiman, and Johnny Peel, "Institutional Threat and Partisan Outcomes: Legislative Candidates' Attitudes toward Direct Democracy," *State Politics & Policy Quarterly* 1 (2001): 364–79.

[36] Smith, "Initiatives and Referendums."

[37] Magleby and Patterson, "Consultants and Direct Democracy."

[38] Schrag, *Paradise Lost,* 16.

[39] Todd Donovan, Shaun Bowler, and Dave McCuan, "Political Consultants and the Initiative Industrial Complex," in Bowler, Donovan, and Tolbert, *Citizens as Legislators.*

[40] Daniel A. Smith, "Money Talks: Ballot Initiative Spending in 2004," Ballot Initiative Strategy Center Foundation, Washington, D.C., May 2006, http://www.ballot.org.

[41] *Buckley v. Valeo,* 424 U.S. 1 (1976).

reasoned that states thus have no compelling reason to limit the First Amendment right of donors contributing to initiative campaigns.[42] The 1978 decision was also the Court's first effort to explicitly extend free speech rights to corporations.[43] Simply put, no limits exist on what sources can be used, or the amount spent, in ballot initiative campaigns.

"Special" Interests and Initiative Campaigns

As noted above, one common critique of direct democracy is that well-financed campaigns trick voters into passing policies that they actually do not prefer. The argument that "special" interests dominate the initiative process is a plausible one. After all, if it can take up to $1 million to simply ensure a proposal gets on the ballot, playing initiative politics obviously requires significant resources. Ordinary citizens are likely to lack such funds, but established, well-funded groups are not so disadvantaged. Powerful special interests, the argument goes, can afford to get any issues they want onto the ballot, and once the initiative is on the ballot, they buy enough spin doctors, campaign managers, and TV ads to get voters to vote for things they do not want or for things that harm the public interest.[44]

We can assess this argument by breaking it into two questions: first, do "special" economic interests dominate the initiative process (as opposed to broad-based, citizen concerns); and second, are voters readily swayed by expensive TV campaigns? One way to assess these questions is to ask whether narrowly focused economic interests (for example, banks, trade and industry groups, corporations, and professional associations) outspend other, broader-based kinds of citizens' groups. Another way is to ask whether these economic groups tend to win the initiative contests they finance.

Which Groups Dominate Direct Democracy? One major study of the role that interest groups play in the initiative process defines economic groups as those whose members and donors are almost exclusively business firms and professional organizations rather than individual citizens. Examples include the Missouri Forest Products Association, the California Beer and Wine Wholesalers, the Washington Software Association, and businesses such as casino operators and tobacco giant Philip Morris.[45] This study of eight states found that 68 percent of campaign contributions came from such narrowly based economic groups. It also found that ballot measures with more financial backing from economic interests were more likely to fail.[46] A similar study found that wealthy economic interests in California regularly outspent broadly based "citizen" groups, and 80 percent of campaign spending by these economic groups was directed against citizen group proposals that threatened business interests. However, when economic interest groups spend in favor of their own initiatives, they usually lose.[47]

In short, most of the big money in direct democracy comes from "special" interests

[42] *First National Bank of Boston v. Bellotti*, 435 U.S. 765 (1978); and Daniel A. Smith, "Campaign Financing of Ballot Initiatives in the American States," in Sabato, Larson, and Ernst, *Dangerous Democracy?*

[43] Tolbert, Lowenstein, and Donovan, "Election Law and Rules for Using Initiatives."

[44] For variants of this argument, see David Broder, *Democracy Derailed;* Schrag, *Paradise Lost;* and Daniel A. Smith, *Tax Crusaders and the Politics of Direct Democracy* (New York: Routledge).

[45] Elisabeth Gerber, *The Populist Paradox: Interest Group Influence and the Promise of Direct Legislation* (Princeton, N.J.: Princeton University Press, 1999), 69–71.

[46] Gerber, *The Populist Paradox*, 110.

[47] Elisabeth Gerber, "Interest Group Influence in the California Initiative Process," *Public Policy Institute of California Report,* November 1998, http://www.ppic.org/content/pubs/R_1198EGR.pdf.

defending themselves or, as with the case of the malpractice initiatives in Florida, fighting each other. A battle over a 1988 automobile insurance regulation in California provides an extreme example: Insurance companies and trial lawyers' groups spent over $82 million promoting four competing initiatives and spending heavily against a fifth proposal placed on the ballot by Ralph Nader's consumer group. Voters rejected all four well-financed initiatives but approved the fifth insurance measure (the one endorsed by consumer activist Nader).[48]

Does Money Matter in Initiative Campaigns?

Money spent to defeat initiatives tends to be quite effective. Some research shows that a dollar spent by the "No" campaign has almost twice as much impact on the eventual vote share than a dollar spent by the "Yes" side.[49] Other studies suggest that spending by proponents is less effective or has no effect when compared to spending against ballot measures. This may explain why narrow economic groups regularly defeat initiatives such as environmental regulations or consumer protections that enjoy substantial majority support in preelection polls.[50] Despite this, measures supported by broad-based and grassroots citizens' groups pass at rates a bit higher than average.[51]

Although exceptions do exist, wealthy economic interests aren't usually successful at using initiatives to "buy" public policy, but they are often successful in blocking many proposals—such as health care requirements and environmental regulations—that directly affect them. Most initiatives that do pass can be seen, for better or worse, as tapping into the preferences and concerns of the broader public, including social and moral questions.[52] Many measures that pass, such as tougher criminal-sentencing laws, animal protection laws regulating hunting, or even somewhat peculiar measures—such as a 1998 California initiative that banned the slaughter of horses for human consumption and a 2002 Florida initiative that amended the state's constitution to prohibit the confinement of gestating pigs in crates—pass despite having relatively little campaign spending by the proponents.

Dumber than Chimps? Voting on Ballot Questions

A voter's ability to make reasonably informed choices on ballot measures depends on what sort of information is available. Few suggest that voters study the details of the laws they are voting on. Rather than using exhaustive research, they decide on the basis of information shortcuts that are easily available.[53] Information about who is in favor of or against a proposal may be the primary shortcut many people use.[54] Partisanship is one of the most reliable predictors of voting on ballot measures.[55] If, for example, voters see a prominent Democrat support a proposition,

---

[48] Arthur Lupia, "Shortcuts versus Encyclopedias: Information and Voting Behavior in California Insurance Reform Elections," *American Political Science Review* 88 (1994): 63–76.

[49] Banducci, "Direct Legislation."

[50] Magleby, *Direct Legislation*; and Bowler and Donovan, *Demanding Choices*.

[51] Gerber, *The Populist Paradox*, 18–19; and Donovan, Bowler, McCuan, and Fernandez, "Contending Players and Strategies," 90.

[52] Bowler and Donovan, *Demanding Choices*.

[53] Arthur Lupia, "Dumber than Chimps? An Assessment of Direct Democracy Voters," in Sabato, Larson, and Ernst, *Dangerous Democracy*?

[54] Arthur Lupia and Mathew McCubbins, *The Democratic Dilemma: Can Citizens Learn What They Need to Know*? (New York: Cambridge University Press, 1998); Lupia, "Shortcuts versus Encyclopedias"; and Bowler and Donovan, *Demanding Choices*.

[55] Smith and Tolbert, "The Initiative to Party"; and Regina Branton, "Examining Individual-Level Voting Behavior on State Ballot Propositions," *Political Research Quarterly* 56 (2003): 367–77.

then loyal Democratic voters are likely to support the proposition and Republicans oppose it.

Where do voters find these cues to help them make informed decisions on ballot questions? In many states, an official state agency mails every registered voter a pamphlet that lists each ballot proposal and includes arguments for and against the proposition. Other sources include media coverage and paid ads. The availability of information shortcuts may explain why so few examples of initiatives pass that are later found to be unpopular with the voters who approved them.

Does Direct Democracy Deceive Voters?

Because voters may not know much about the subjects of ballot initiatives and may not have partisan cues when voting, there may be room for campaign ads to determine which initiatives voters approve. It is unclear, however, how much effect paid ads have on voter choices. Most people believe that initiative campaign ads are attempts to mislead.[56] Despite the expenditure of tremendous sums of money, voters claim to discount the usefulness of political ads. One survey found people had multiple sources of information to consider when deciding on initiatives, and most reported that they didn't rely much on information from paid ads. Most voters claimed that neutral information provided by the state and information from the news media was most important to

them when figuring out how to vote on initiatives.[57]

Perhaps surprisingly, TV ads may actually provide useful cues to voters. One study of initiative campaign TV ads from several states found the ads often provide cues, such as names of sponsors or opponents, as well as name prominent groups, newspapers, and politicians who have taken positions on the measure.[58] High levels of spending on initiative TV ads probably increase public awareness of initiatives and may increase public attention to campaign issues. This may explain higher levels of general knowledge about politics in states with prominent initiative campaigns.[59] Relatedly, another study found voters more likely to have heard about initiatives when more was spent on the campaigns and found that more citizens voted on initiatives that had higher campaign spending.[60]

Direct Democracy and Electoral Politics

Initiative and referendum campaigns can alter a state's political context. Several examples of ballot measures affect the agenda and tone of candidate elections.[61] In 1998, for example, Republican Party operatives in Colorado tried to link Democratic candidates to positions on state ballot initiatives that Republicans expected voters to find unpopular. Democrats did the same and ran campaign ads linking the Republican

---

[56] Bowler, Donovan, Neiman, and Peel, "Institutional Threat and Partisan Outcomes," 370.

[57] Shaun Bowler and Todd Donovan, "Do Voters Have a Cue? TV Ads as a Source of Information in Referendum Voting," *European Journal of Political Research* 41 (2002): 777–93.

[58] Bowler and Donovan, "Do Voters Have a Cue?"

[59] Mark Smith, "Ballot Initiatives and the Democratic Citizen," *Journal of Politics* 64 (2002): 892–903.

[60] Bowler and Donovan, *Demanding Choices*.

[61] Steven P. Nicholson, *Voting the Agenda: Candidates Elections and Ballot Propositions* (Princeton, N.J.: Princeton University Press, 2005); Todd Donovan, Caroline Tolbert, and Daniel Smith, "Priming Presidential Votes by Direct Democracy," *Journal of Politics* 70 (2008): 1217–31; Sunshine Hillygus and Todd Shields, "Moral Issues and Voter Decision Making in the 2004 Presidential Election," *PS: Political Science and Politics* 38 (2005): 201–10; Daniel A. Smith, Matthew DeSantis, and Jason Kassel, "Same-Sex Marriage Ballot Measures and the 2004 Presidential Election," *State and Local Government Review* 38 (2006): 78-91; Barry Burden, "An Alternative Account of the 2004 Presidential Election," *The Forum* 2 (2004): Article 2, http://www.bepress.com/forum/vol2/iss4/art2.

gubernatorial candidate to two antiabortion measures. The Republican had been trying to distance himself from social conservatives.[62] During their 2004 Florida campaign, the rival U.S. Senate candidates attempted to craft their campaign themes to fit with initiatives on the state's ballot. Republican nominee Mel Martinez, for example, worked several ballot issues into his standard campaign speech and at candidate debates.[63] And in California, numerous candidates for governor, including Arnold Schwarzenegger, have sponsored initiatives to promote their candidacies.

Political party organizations also use initiatives to promote **wedge issues**—issues they hope will divide the opposing party's

Governor Arnold Schwarzenegger's voter guide. These were mailed to thousands of homes in 2005 with instructions on how to support his positions on ballot measures. All of the governor's proposals were defeated.

candidates and weaken the opposition's base of support. Major examples of wedge issues from the past decade are affirmative action and immigration initiatives. Republicans promoted a California initiative to restrict affirmative action (Proposition 209) and another measure restricting services to illegal immigrants (Proposition 187), hoping that Democrats across the nation would be forced to adopt policy positions that would harm their chances for reelection. Republican governor Pete Wilson of California as well as Democratic candidate John Van de Kamp both raised money to put several policy questions on the ballot when they sought office.[64]

Anecdotes and academic studies also suggest that different ballot measures can mobilize different elements of the electorate at different times.[65] A classic example is the 1982 California gubernatorial election. The Democratic mayor of Los Angeles, Tom Bradley, led narrowly in polls conducted immediately prior to the November vote, but Bradley ended up losing to Republican George Deukmejian. In this case, polls may have had difficulty estimating how an initiative would shape the participating electorate. The same ballot included a highly contested gun control measure, Proposition 15, which the National Rifle Association (NRA) opposed. The NRA spent over $5 million against the measure and rallied progun voters to the polls.[66] Deukmejian probably benefited from these voters being drawn to the polls.

The Effects of Direct Democracy on Turnout

Statewide ballot initiatives may also affect the electoral landscape by bringing voters to the polls. In 1978, more Californians cast votes for a critical antitax measure (**Proposition 13**) than cast votes for the governor's race on the

[62] Smith and Tolbert, *Educated by Initiative.*

[63] Smith, "Initiatives and Referendums."

[64] Smith and Tolbert, "The Initiative to Party."

[65] Caroline J. Tolbert, John Grummel, and Daniel A. Smith, "The Effect of Ballot Initiatives on Voter Turnout in the American States," *American Politics Research* 29 (2001): 625–48.

[66] John Allswang, *The Initiative and Referendum in California, 1898–1998* (Stanford, Calif.: Stanford University Press, 2000), 125–26.

same ballot. Studies of voting prior to the 1990s concluded that ballot measures did not affect voter turnout. Political scientist David Magleby concluded in 1984 that "turnout is not increased by direct legislation," although occasionally, a highly salient measure, such as California's Proposition 13 in 1978, "might encourage" higher turnout.[67]

Recent studies of initiative use, however, have produced evidence that initiatives can increase turnout by nearly 2 percent per initiative in midterm elections and nearly 1 percent in presidential elections, all else being equal.[68] Initiatives receiving substantial media attention have the greatest effect on turnout, particularly in "off-year" (non–presidential election year) state elections.[69] In municipal races, evidence has shown that at the local level, cities that use the initiative process have higher voter turnout than cities that don't allow their citizens to place measures directly on the ballot.[70]

The Effects of Direct Democracy on Citizens

The presence of highly visible initiatives and frequent voting on ballot measures may make people feel more as if they "have a say" in politics.[71] Evidence shows that people in states with initiatives have higher levels of political engagement and political participation than people in noninitiative states, although it is difficult to establish if this is due to the effects of direct democracy or due to something else that is unique to these states. One study found that people have higher levels of factual knowledge about politics in states where initiatives are used more frequently, perhaps because initiatives stimulate media attention and because voting on initiatives requires that they acquire information to make decisions.[72] Another found that people in initiative states are more likely to engage in political discussion, have greater political knowledge, and contribute to interest groups.[73] Some evidence indicates that frequent use of initiatives causes voters to feel more competent when participating in politics, more likely to think that they have a say, and more likely to think that public officials care about what they think.[74] Similar results have been found in Swiss cantons.[75]

Direct Democracy and Minorities

As noted above, one of the original concerns about direct democracy is the potential it has to allow a majority of voters to trample the rights of minorities. Many still worry that the process can be used to harm gays and lesbians as well as ethnic, linguistic, and religious minorities.[76] Those who worry about repressive majorities point to a series of antiminority

---

[67] Magleby, *Direct Legislation*, 197.

[68] Tolbert, Grummel, and Smith, "The Effect of Ballot Initiatives on Voter Turnout in the American States."

[69] Mark Smith, "The Contingent Effects of Ballot Initiatives and Candidate Races on Turnout," *American Journal of Political Science* 45 (2001): 700–6.

[70] Zoltan Hajnal and Paul Lewis, "Municipal Institutions and Voter Turnout in Local Elections," *Urban Affairs Review* 35 (2003): 645–68.

[71] Smith and Tolbert, *Educated by Initiative*.

[72] Smith, "Ballot Initiatives and the Democratic Citizen."

[73] Caroline J. Tolbert, Ramona McNeal, and Daniel A. Smith, "Enhancing Civic Engagement: The Effect of Direct Democracy on Political Participation and Knowledge," *State Politics and Policy Quarterly* 3 (2003): 23–41.

[74] Shaun Bowler and Todd Donovan, "Democracy, Institutions, and Attitudes about Citizen Influence on Government," *British Journal of Political Science* 32 (2002): 371–90.

[75] Bruno Frey and L. Goette, "Does the Popular Vote Destroy Civil Rights?" *American Journal of Political Science* 41 (1998): 245–69; and Matthias Benz and Alois Stutzer, "Are Voters Better Informed When They Have a Larger Say in Politics?" *Public Choice* 119 (2004): 31–59.

[76] See, for example, Lydia Chavez, *The Color Bind: California's Battle to End Affirmative Action* (Berkeley: University of California Press, 1998); Barbara Gamble, "Putting Civil Rights to a Popular Vote," *American Journal of Political Science* 41 (1998): 245–69; Rodney Hero and Caroline Tolbert, "A Racial/Ethnic Diversity Interpretation of Politics and Policy in the States of the U.S.," *American Journal of Political Science* 40 (1996): 851–71; and Donald P. Haider-Markel, Alana Querze, and Kara Lindaman, "'Win, Lose or Draw?' A Reexamination of Direct Democracy and Minority Rights," *Political Research Quarterly* 60 (2007): 304–14.

measures approved by voters. A majority of voters have supported initiatives repealing affirmative action in California, Michigan, Washington, Colorado, and Nebraska. Battles over immigration has been a perennial issue on the ballot in Arizona. Voters have approved propositions repealing bilingual education in Arizona, California, and Massachusetts (although voters rejected such an initiative in Colorado). Initiatives declaring English an "official language" have been approved in numerous states.[77] Scores of measures dealing with gay rights and gay marriage have appeared on state and local ballots,[78] and many cities have held referendums on whether to abolish low-income housing.[79] This presents a critical question: Does direct democracy harm minorities?

Evidence shows that the initiative process "is sometimes prone to produce laws that disadvantage relatively powerless minorities—and probably is more likely than legislatures to do so."[80] State and local ballot initiatives have been used to undo policies—such as school desegregation, protections against job and housing discrimination, and affirmative action—that minorities have secured from legislatures where they are included in the bargaining process. But most initiatives probably do not produce divisions between majorities of white voters and minority voters. Studies of support for ballot initiatives across different groups of voters show that minority voters were no more likely to support the losing side in an initiative contest than white voters. This may reflect that most initiatives do not pit the interests of racial and ethnic minorities against those of the majority or perhaps that minorities and whites have similar issues and concerns addressed by the initiative process. It is important to note, however, that on issues dealing with racial and ethnic matters, studies show that racial and ethnic minorities do end up more on the losing side of the popular vote.[81]

The issue of gay rights has been one of the more contentious areas of initiative politics where minority interests are frequently put to a vote. Majorities have, in some cases, voted to restrict the extension of some civil rights to gays and lesbians. Until recently, with the rash of anti–gay marriage amendments on statewide ballots, voters in a number of states had refused to pass most measures that would deny gays and lesbians protections against discrimination. A 1992 antigay measure in Colorado, Amendment 2, which changed the state constitution to expressly prohibit local laws aimed at protecting gays and lesbians against discrimination, was a major exception.[82] The Colorado measure was eventually overturned by the U.S. Supreme Court in 1996 for being an unconstitutional denial of equal protection before the law.[83] Voters have, however, been much less tolerant of granting equal marriage rights to gays. Citizens in more than two dozen states have voted on whether to ban same-sex marriages, and voters in every state (except Arizona in 2006) have supported the ban.

---

[77] Jack Citrin, Beth Reingold, Evelyn Walters, and Donald Green, "The 'Official English' Movement and the Symbolic Politics of Language in the United States," *Western Political Quarterly* 43 (1990): 535–60.

[78] Donald Haider-Markel, "AIDS and Gay Civil Rights: Politics and Policy at the Ballot Box," *American Review of Politics* 20 (1999): 349–75; and Todd Donovan, James Wenzel, and Shaun Bowler, "Direct Democracy Initiatives after *Romer*," in *The Politics of Gay Rights*, ed. Craig Zimmerman, Ken Wald, and Clyde Wilcox (Chicago: University of Chicago Press, 2000).

[79] Roger Caves, *Land Use Planning: The Ballot Box Revolution* (Newbury Park, Calif.: Sage, 1992).

[80] Cain and Miller, "The Populist Legacy," in Sabato, Larson, and Ernst, *Dangerous Democracy?* 52.

[81] Zoltan Hajnal, Elisabeth Gerber, and H. Louch, "Minorities and Direct Legislation: Evidence from California Ballot Proposition Elections," *Journal of Politics* 64 (2002): 154–77.

[82] Donovan, Wenzel, and Bowler, "Direct Democracy Initiatives after *Romer*."

[83] *Romer v. Evans*, 517 U.S. 620 (1996).

The record of direct democracy for minority interests is a mixed bag, then. Racial and ethnic minorities may agree with majority voters on most ballot measures, but there have been some critical initiatives where minority rights have been lost when put to a public vote. Yet, in nearly every instance where the initiative process has been used to limit minority rights to fair housing, desegregated schools, public services, and protections against discrimination, courts have stepped in to overturn initiatives and uphold minority rights.[84] But regardless of whether antiminority ballot measures pass or fail, they may still have effects on people they target. By targeting a minority group with an initiative, for example, public attitudes about the group (or about policies that benefit the group) can be changed, with mass opinion becoming less tolerant of the targeted minority group.[85]

The Effects of Direct Democracy on Public Policy

By this point, it should be clear that there are many reasons to expect that direct democracy can make a state's political environment and its public policies different than if there were no initiative process. When voters are allowed to make direct choices on policies, they sometimes make decisions that their elected representatives would not. An obvious example of this is term limits. Voters in many states have placed limits on time their representatives may serve. Absent the initiative process, elected representatives rarely, if ever, adopt such a policy.[86] But besides term limits and some forms of campaign finance reform, states that use the initiative are no

November 2006: Antigay marriage activists rally in front of the Massachusetts State House, demanding that the marriage question be put to a popular vote.

---

[84] Kenneth Miller, "Constraining Populism: The Real Challenge of Initiative Reform," *Santa Clara Law Review* 41 (2001): 1037–84; and Bowler and Donovan, *Demanding Choices*.

[85] Donovan, Wenzel, and Bowler, "Direct Democracy and Minorities."

[86] The exception is Louisiana. Caroline Tolbert, "Changing Rules for State Legislatures: Direct Democracy and Governance Policies," in Bowler, Donovan, and Tolbert, *Citizens as Legislators;* and Bowler and Donovan, "Measuring the Effect of Direct Democracy on State Policy."

more likely than states without the process to adopt ethics and lobbying reform measures.[87] It is unclear, then, whether or not direct democracy systematically makes policy more representative of what people want or if it leads to "better" public policy.

Some scholars and practitioners have proposed that the mere presence of the initiative process can affect public policy by changing how legislators behave. If legislators anticipate that there is a threat that someone might pass a law by initiative, legislators may have greater incentives to pass some version of the law so they can maintain influence over what the final law looks like.[88] Initiatives can also send signals about the sort of policies the public wants.[89] Several studies show that certain public policies—including abortion regulations, death penalty laws, some civil rights policies, and spending on some state programs—more closely match public opinion in states with initiatives than in states without initiatives.[90] As an example, states with liberal public opinion and initiatives may have relatively liberal abortion rules, whereas states with conservative opinions and initiatives may have conservative policies. Absent the initiative, policies may be less likely to reflect the state's opinion climate. Studies that examine a wide range of state policies, however, find no such effects; some initiatives may make policy more reflective of public opinion with some policies but not others.[91]

The biggest effects of direct democracy on policy may be in the realm of what Caroline Tolbert calls "governance policy"—policies that set the rules about how government can function. Voters in initiative states can and do pass measures that amend rules that structure the political system itself. These include initiatives that may run counter to the interests of elected officials. States with the initiative process are more likely to have adopted term limits and tougher rules for adopting new taxes and increasing spending[92] and were quicker to adopt some campaign finance regulations.[93] Examples of tax limitation measures include California's Proposition 13 of 1978, Oregon's Measure 5 in 1990, and Colorado's Taxpayers Bill of Rights (TABOR) amendment of 1992. If given a chance via direct democracy, voters often place constraints on what their representatives can do, especially when it comes to fiscal matters.

Long-Term Effects of Direct Democracy

Direct democracy can alter state policy directly by providing an additional point of access for citizens and interest groups. Advocates of decriminalization of drugs, campaign finance reforms, physician-assisted suicide, and many other policies have successfully used direct democracy to do an "end run" around state legislatures that did not turn their ideas into policy. As noted above, some suggest this threat

---

[87] Daniel A. Smith, "Direct Democracy and Election and Ethics Laws," in *Democracy in the States: Experiments in Elections Reform*, eds., Bruce Cain, Todd Donovan, and Caroline Tolbert (Washington, D.C.: Brookings, 2008).

[88] Gerber, *The Populist Paradox*.

[89] Thomas Romer and Howard Rosenthal, "Bureaucrats versus Voters: On the Political Economy of Resource Allocation by Direct Democracy," *Quarterly Journal of Economics* 93 (1979): 563–87.

[90] Kevin Arceneaux, "Direct Democracy and the Link between Public Opinion and State Abortion Policy," *State Politics and Policy Quarterly* 2 (2002): 372–87; Elisabeth Gerber, "Legislative Response to the Threat of Popular Initiatives," *American Journal of Political Science* 40 (1996): 99–128; Gerber, *The Populist Paradox*; Matsusaka, *For the Many or the Few*; and Bowler and Donovan, "Measuring the Effect of Direct Democracy on State Policy."

[91] Michael Hagen, Edward Lascher, and John Camobreco, "Response to Matsusaka: Estimating the Effect of Ballot Initiatives on Policy Responsiveness," *Journal of Politics* 63 (2001): 1257–63; and John Camobreco, "Preferences, Fiscal Policies, and the Initiative Process," *Journal of Politics* 60 (1998): 819–29.

[92] Tolbert, "Changing Rules for State Legislatures."

[93] John Pippen, Shaun Bowler, and Todd Donovan, "Election Reform and Direct Democracy: The Case of Campaign Finance Regulations in the American States," *American Politics Research* 30 (2002): 559–82.

of the "gun behind the door" makes state policy more representative of state opinion. But what are the major long-term consequences of direct democracy on state policy?

In addition to promoting specific policy ideas, the initiative process allows those outside the legislature, and those outside the traditional corridors of power, the ability to permanently change rules that define institutions of government. As examples, initiatives have been used to rewrite state rules about how judges sentence criminals, how much a state may collect via existing taxes, and how much the legislature may spend in a given year. Initiatives have been used to change rules about future tax increases and have placed limits on how often legislators may run for reelection.

There are reasons, though, to expect that the long-range effects of direct democracy are not that dramatic. Once an initiative is approved by voters, proponents often do not have the resources or political clout to maintain pressure on legislators over time to ensure that their law is implemented as the proponents would like. Elected officials can eventually rewrite rules, amend what voters approved (in most states), or stall implementation. The end result may be that "the policy impact of most initiatives reflects a compromise between what electoral majorities and government actors want."[94] This means that governing is quite different in initiative states, yet direct democracy has not replaced the role of the legislature.

Majority Tyranny and Judicial Review

The potential effects of initiatives on policy are further muted when we consider judicial review. Initiatives, like any other law, must be consistent with the U.S. Constitution and state constitutions and must abide by a state's regulations on the initiative process, such as subject matter constraints. State and federal courts tend to treat initiative laws just like laws passed by legislatures, regardless of how popular they may have been with voters. Courts have been very willing to strike down voter-approved initiatives. One study of several states found that most state initiatives ended up being challenged in court, with 40 percent overturned in whole or in part.[95] People challenging voter-approved initiatives in court may increase their odds of success because they are able to "venue shop": They can file cases in different districts of either state or federal courts in order to find judges most likely to grant them a favorable ruling.

Assessments of Direct Democracy

When some of the most careful observers of American politics turn their attention to the process of direct democracy, their assessments of it are rather negative. Alan Rosenthal, a preeminent scholar of state legislatures, suggests that growing enthusiasm for direct democracy—in the form of the growing use of opinion polls that influence representatives as well as the use of initiative and referendum—has a corrosive effect on representative government. Rosenthal suggests that a demise of representative government has occurred in American states over recent decades, leaving legislators with less responsibility for government and leaving states more difficult to govern.[96] Some blame direct democracy for shattering the fiscal health of some states, then leaving elected officials to pick up the pieces. Initiatives are also blamed for promoting confrontational (and unconstitutional) policies that target minority groups, such as immigrants and gays and lesbians.

---

[94] Elisabeth Gerber, Arthur Lupia, Mathew McCubbins, and Roderick Kiewiet, *Stealing the Initiative* (Upper Saddle River, N.J.: Prentice Hall, 2001), 110.

[95] Miller, "Constraining Populism."

[96] Alan Rosenthal, *The Decline of Representative Government* (Washington D.C.: CQ Press, 1998).

Public Approval of Direct Democracy

As Figure 4.4 reveals, the public remains quite supportive of the initiative process in states where it is used rather frequently. The public looks at direct democracy quite differently, and more positively, than many political observers and elected officials do. Even voters who have experienced California's high-stakes, high-cost system of direct democracy remain supportive of the process.[97] In contrast, surveys of elected officials find much less enthusiasm about direct democracy. For their part, legislators in direct democracy states would like to change things so that they have more say over what ends up going to a public vote and also have more ability to amend laws after voters approve them.[98]

The Case for and against Direct Democracy

To its defenders, direct democracy is seen as a tool that would empower the "grassroots" and weaken the influence that special interests had over elected representatives. Direct democracy could "level the playing field" by giving more political value to individual voters, as opposed to those who finance political campaigns. Proponents of direct democracy have also argued that the process can build better citizens. Participating in meaningful policy choice may lead citizens to seek out more information. Voting directly on policy might also encourage citizens to have more interest in politics and feel more engaged with their government.[99]

From the start, critics of direct democracy raised several objections to the process. It may

---

Figure 4.4

Public Opinion about Direct Democracy in California and Washington

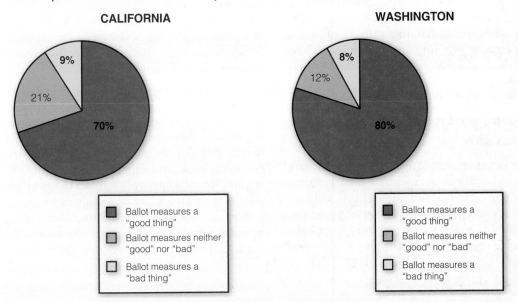

Source: Shaun Bowler, Todd Donovan, Max Neiman, and Johnny Peel, "Institutional Threat and Partisan Outcomes: Legislative Candidates' Attitudes toward Direct Democracy," *State Politics & Policy Quarterly* 1 (2001): 364–79.

[97] Shaun Bowler and Todd Donovan, "Reasoning about Institutional Change: Winners, Losers and Support for Electoral Reform," *British Journal of Political Science* 37 (2007): 455–76.

[98] Bowler, Donovan, Neiman, and Peel, "Institutional Threat and Partisan Outcomes."

[99] For a summary of these arguments, see Smith and Tolbert, *Educated by Initiative.*

be difficult, they claimed, for the average voter to understand the nuances of difficult public policy questions, as many people simply pay no attention to politics. Elected officials have time to deliberate about issues and reach compromises that might accommodate rival positions. Initiative proposals, in contrast, can be framed by a proponent as an all-or-nothing choice, which is then decided upon by a relatively ill-informed electorate. A more enduring critique focuses on the potential for tyranny of the majority. American representative government involves many checks and balances and veto points. Direct democracy, in contrast, allows voters to pass laws hostile to minority interests or pass laws repealing hard-fought victories that minorities achieved via representative government.[100] A modern criticism of the process is that it now costs $1 million or more to qualify measures for the ballot in a large state—leaving the process well beyond the reach of average citizens. Peter Schrag, an astute and longtime observer of politics in the Golden State, described in his scathing book on direct democracy how the initiative process encourages the "embracing and demagoguing [of] hot-button issues" by candidates who hope to "showcase" their credentials.[101]

The Future of American Direct Democracy

As we noted above, many critics describe state and local direct democracy as a kind of "faux populism."[102] Instead of making politics more representative or more responsible, modern direct democracy may no longer have room for regular, grassroots citizen activists.

Criticism of modern direct democracy has led to the introduction of scores of proposals to reform the process. Each year, legislators in initiative states propose legislation to alter how the initiative process works. Few of these have been approved, but they illustrate how some elected officials view what the future of direct democracy should be.

Restricting the Use of the Initiative Process Surveys of legislators reveal support for direct democracy as a concept, coupled with a desire to get elected representatives more involved with laws that voters might approve.[103] Many reform proposals introduced by state legislatures are designed to make it more difficult to qualify measures for the ballot.[104] These include proposals to raise the number of signatures required or shorten the time period to collect signatures. Other proposals of this sort include rules requiring that a certain proportion of signatures be collected across all regions of a state (counties or congressional districts) and rules making it more difficult to pay people to collect signatures.[105] In the wake of California's recall of Governor Davis, there were also calls to make future use of recall petitions more difficult.

Even if these proposals were to enjoy majority support among legislators, barriers exist to discourage the passage of such regulations. Major structural rules governing direct democracy are embedded in state constitutions, and constitutional changes require voter approval. Politicians may be reluctant to attack the mechanisms of direct democracy, fearing a populist backlash. Public opinion surveys demonstrate that voters do not want to limit their power over the initiative

[100] Gamble, "Putting Civil Rights to a Popular Vote."

[101] Schrag, *Paradise Lost*, 226.

[102] Smith, *Tax Crusaders and the Politics of Direct Democracy*.

[103] Bowler, Donovan, Neiman, and Peel, "Institutional Threat and Partisan Outcomes."

[104] Waters, *The Battle over Citizen Lawmaking*.

[105] Daniel A. Smith, "The Legislative Regulation of the Initiative," (paper presented at the annual meeting of the State Politics and Policy Association, Philadelphia, PA, May 2008).

process, so constitutional referendums proposing to do this are more than likely to be rejected (although Floridians in 2006 approved a legislative referendum requiring all subsequent ballot measures to receive at least 60 percent of the popular vote). Furthermore, federal courts have rejected overt attempts to ban the use of paying people to collect signatures and rules requiring that signatures be collected across all of a state's counties, regardless of the population of counties.[106]

The popular appeal of direct democracy remains deeply rooted. Another problem with proposals to reform the mechanisms of direct democracy is that most do nothing about campaign spending levels. Because ballot initiative campaign spending can't be limited according to the 1978 *Bellotti* decision, gross disparities in spending between proponents and opponents of an initiative can only be mitigated if public funds were used to maintain some minimum level of funding for both sides. Tougher qualification barriers, in contrast, are likely to make it more difficult to organize volunteers to qualify measures as well as increase the costs of paying petitioners to qualify something for the ballot. Rather than increasing the influence of "grassroots" citizens' groups, reforms that make it more difficult to qualify measures will probably increase any advantages that wealthy interests may already have. Ironically, if it becomes more difficult or costly to collect signatures, the need to pay people to collect signatures is likely to increase.

Expanding the Use of Direct Democracy At the same time as many incumbent state legislators are attempting to limit use of direct democracy in their states, there have been proposals in noninitiative states to introduce the initiative and referendum. The most visible of these proposals come from governors rather than legislators. Past governors of Louisiana (Mike Foster), Minnesota (Jesse Ventura), New York (George Pataki), and Rhode Island (Donald Carcieri) have made public their support of the process. There have also been several legislative attempts by minority parties to introduce the process.[107] Legislation considered, but ultimately rejected, by the New Jersey legislature in 2002, for example, would have given citizens the power of the indirect statutory initiative. That November, voters in Rhode Island easily approved an advisory referendum placed on the ballot by the governor asking whether the state should have an initiative process; lawmakers subsequently ignored the popular vote. More recently, the Minnesota and Alabama legislatures considered bills to create a scaled-down version of the initiative, but those efforts failed.

Despite this public enthusiasm and the support of some states' governors, voters have little reason to expect that direct democracy will expand to additional states in the near future. This is due to the fact that state legislators largely control whether their state will change rules to allow direct democracy. Legislators are reluctant to adopt rules that weaken their control over the political agenda.[108] Absent heightened interparty legislative competition and another social movement pushing for major political reform similar to the Populist and Progressive movements a century ago, elected representatives are unlikely to adopt or expand direct democracy.[109] Voters have probably even less reason to expect adoption of the initiative, referendum, or recall at the national level.

---

[106] *Meyer v. Grant*, 486 U.S. 414 (1988); Smith, "Campaign Financing of Ballot Initiatives in the American States."

[107] Craig Holman, "An Assessment of New Jersey's Proposed Limited Initiative Process," Brennan Center for Justice at New York University School of Law, 2002, http://www.iandrinstitute.org/New%20IRI%20Website%20Info/I&R%20Research%20and%20History/I&R%20Studies/Holman%20-%20Review%20of%20Proposed%20NJ%20Initiative%20Process%20IRI.pdf.

[108] Shaun Bowler, Todd Donovan, and Jeffrey Karp, "Why Politicians Like Electoral Institutions: Self-Interest, Values, or Ideology?" *Journal of Politics* 68 (2006): 434–46.

[109] Smith and Fridkin, "Delegating Direct Democracy."

Summary

Direct democracy is a curious American institution. It plays a large role in the politics of some states and communities but much less of a role in other places. The initiative, referendum, and recall were adopted in an era when overt corruption among state legislators and local elected officials was common. Rather than thwarting the political influence of wealthy interests, however, direct democracy may give powerful, established interests an additional tool they may use to shape public policy. It represents one of the major institutional differences between states like California and New York or between Arizona and Connecticut.

This chapter illustrates that direct democracy—specifically, the initiative process—has important effects where it is used. It can change the rules that affect how elected officials govern and may alter participation levels and the issues voters use when evaluating candidates. There is also some evidence that direct democracy may lead state policies to be more representative of what voters in a state prefer. Whether direct democracy makes politics better, though, is often left to the eye of the beholder.

Key Terms

Constitutional initiative

Direct initiative

Indirect initiative

Legislative referendum

Meyer v. Grant

Popular referendum

Populist Party

Proposition 13

Recall

Single-subject rule

Statutory initiative

Wedge issues

5

Political Parties
and Interest Groups

INTRODUCTION

Political parties and interest groups are critical players in the electoral process, governance, and policy making of the states. For two longtime observers of state politics, "the single most important factor in state politics is the political party."[1] You will get a sense in this chapter that not all parties at the state and local level are equally powerful. Parties come in all kinds of shapes, sizes, and political flavors, and their respective influence within a state varies widely. At their most rudimentary level, parties allow individuals to come together periodically to articulate a political viewpoint. Parties also help to cultivate and nurture the ambitions of political leaders, mobilize citizens to vote, organize governments, and formulate public policy.[2]

Interest groups, on the other hand, are often portrayed in the media as detriments to the common good or general welfare. "The popular perception," according to one interest group scholar, "is that interest groups are a cancer spreading unchecked throughout the body politic, making it gradually weaker, until they eventually kill it."[3] Like political parties, though, organized interests play an indispensable role in state politics. Organized interests not only help protect the interests of those who join them; belonging to an organization can help cultivate democratic values and enhance the capacities of individuals and the communities in which they live. As we shall see, both political parties and interest groups are essential political players in states and localities.

[1] Sarah Morehouse and Malcolm Jewell, *State Politics, Parties, and Policy*, 2nd ed. (Boulder, Colo.: Rowman & Littlefield, 2003), 15.
[2] David Hedge, *Governance and the Changing American States* (Boulder, Colo.: Westview, 1998); Joseph Schlesinger, "The New American Political Party," *American Political Science Review* 79 (1985): 1152–69; and John Aldrich, *Why Parties? The Origin and Transformation of Party Politics in America* (Chicago: University of Chicago Press, 1995).
[3] Jeffrey Berry, *The New Liberalism: The Rising Power of Citizen Groups* (Washington, D.C.: Brookings Institution Press, 1997), 19.

Alex Wong/Getty Images

Understanding Political Parties

Political parties serve multiple functions. Parties may be rightly understood as one of the principal agencies for "aggregating and mobilizing the interests of vast numbers of citizens, enhancing voters' capacity to hold public officials accountable, acting as agents of political socialization, and organizing the decision-making institutions of government."[4] Parties recruit candidates running for office, oversee the nominations of those candidates, and provide a durable link between citizens and their governments. Less clear is whether a party needs to be ideologically coherent or merely functional in order to truly be understood as a party.[5]

Some scholars view parties from a normative perspective, offering a prescriptive ideal of what parties ought to strive to become. According to this **responsible party model,** parties should be ideologically consistent, in that they should present to voters a clear platform and set of policies that are principled and distinctive. Voters are expected to choose a candidate based on whether they agree with the proposed programs and policies of that candidate's party. Once taking office, the candidate (and his or her party) is to be held responsible for implementing the party's program and policies.[6] However, because of institutional constraints (as discussed in

Chapter 3)—such as single-member, winner-take-all elections, direct and open primaries, and federalism—the two major political parties tend to operate as "big tents," allowing considerable disagreement over their principles and policies in an effort to win elections.[7]

Sometimes, though, it is quite rational for parties to try to broaden their coalitions in their search for the elusive median voter, even if it means compromising on their core convictions. After all, parties are self-interested organizations, striving to maximize votes for their candidates in order to win elections.[8] Emphasizing the pragmatic character of American parties, some scholars have advanced a **functional party model,** which defines a party as "any group, however loosely organized, seeking to elect governmental officeholders under a given label."[9] This functional definition captures the primary goal of parties in the United States: winning and maintaining control of political office.[10]

Regulating Parties as Quasi-Public Entities

Political parties are "quasi-public" entities, meaning that they are not only regulated by the states but also carry out official functions conferred upon them by the states. As such, they are more akin to public utilities than private associations.[11] Until the 1950s, for example, many Democratic parties in the

---

[4] John Bibby and Thomas Holbrook, "Parties and Elections," in *Politics in the American States: A Comparative Analysis,* 8th ed., ed. Virginia Gray and Russell Hanson (Washington, D.C.: CQ Press, 2004).

[5] John Coleman, "Responsible, Functional, or Both? American Political Parties and the APSA Report after Fifty Years," in *The State of the Parties: The Changing Role of Contemporary American Parties,* 4th ed., ed. John Green and Rick Farmer (Lanham, Md.: Rowman & Littlefield, 2003).

[6] Edmund Burke, *Select Works of Edmund Burke: A New Imprint of the Payne Edition,* vol. 1 (Indianapolis, Ind.: Liberty Fund, 1999), 150; and Richard Hofstadter, *The Idea of a Party System: The Rise of Legitimate Opposition in the United States, 1780–1840* (Berkeley: University of California Press, 1969).

[7] John Gerring, *Party Ideologies in America, 1828–1996* (Cambridge: Cambridge University Press, 2001); Geoffrey C. Layman, Thomas M. Carsey, and Juliana Menasce Horowitz, "Party Polarization in American Politics: Characteristics, Causes, and Consequences," *Annual Review of Political Science* 9 (June 2006): 67–81; and Gary Miller and Norman Schofield, "Activists and Partisan Realignment in the United States," *American Political Science Review* 97 (May 2003): 245–60.

[8] Anthony Downs, *An Economic Theory of Democracy* (New York: Harper, 1957), 25.

[9] Leon Epstein, *Political Parties in Western Democracies* (New York: Praeger, 1967).

[10] Leon Epstein, *Political Parties in the American Mold* (Madison: University of Wisconsin Press, 1986), 25.

[11] Epstein, *Political Parties in the American Mold,* 155–99.

South were permitted by state law to hold discriminatory "white-only" primaries that excluded blacks from participating in the party nomination process. These "Jim Crow" laws, which codified racial segregation far beyond electoral politics and were designed specifically to restrict black suffrage, included such barriers to voting as poll taxes, literacy tests, and an array of complex voter registration laws.[12] In 1964, the 24th Amendment was ratified, outlawing the poll tax in federal elections. The next year, Congress enacted the Voting Rights Act, outlawing state election laws that discriminated against minorities, immigrants, and the poor.

Today, party registration, party nomination, and ballot access laws vary greatly across the states. Although federal law establishes that the voting age is 18 and over, that federal elections are held on the first Tuesday after the first Monday in November, that there may be no poll taxes or literacy tests to determine voter eligibility, and that all polling places must be accessible to people with disabilities, within these broad parameters every state is permitted to establish its own set of laws that regulate voting and political party status.[13] As such, state regulations governing political parties differ considerably.

In a series of rulings, the U.S. Supreme Court has provided broad contours of what is permissible when it comes to the rights of political parties and their members as well as the kinds of regulations the states may place on political parties.[14] In general, the high court has upheld the associational rights of the major parties, but it has also reaffirmed the rights of states to regulate state parties in the name of maintaining and preserving political stability.[15]

Although hardly constitutive of a coherent jurisprudence, several important high court rulings concern the associational rights and state regulations of state political parties.[16]

Primaries and Caucuses

Parties have broad discretion in determining how candidates running on their party labels are to be nominated. By defining who may participate in their nomination process, the parties are essentially able to define who belongs as a party member. At the same time, state legislatures make the rules governing elections, including whether the state will have a primary election or a caucus in which the nominees running on party labels are determined. Primaries and caucuses are held weeks or months ahead of the general election to determine who will appear on the general election ballot. In a **direct primary** election, voters select one candidate affiliated with a political party for each elected office; the party nominees later face one another in a general election.

Caucus A few states use a party **caucus**, or even a series of party caucuses, to nominate candidates. At a caucus, party members informally meet, deliberate, and then cast votes for their preferred candidates. Party members not only discuss the candidates and the pressing issues but also elect delegates to the party's county conventions. These, in turn, elect delegates to the party's congressional and state conventions, which (in presidential election years) elect national convention delegates. In Iowa, for example, a caucus participant must be registered with a party as well as a resident of the precinct in which the caucus is being held (often in a school, a town hall, or even a private home). Iowa has

---

[12] V. O. Key, *Southern Politics in the State and Nation* (New York: Knopf, 1949).

[13] Bibby and Holbrook, "Parties and Elections."

[14] David Ryden, *The Constitution, Interest Groups, and Political Parties* (Albany: State University of New York Press, 1996).

[15] Sandy Maisel and John Bibby, "Power, Money, and Responsibility in the Major American Parties," in *Responsible Partisanship? The Evolution of American Political Parties since 1950*, ed. John Green and Paul Herrnson (Lawrence: University Press of Kansas, 2002).

[16] Lisa Disch, *The Tyranny of the Two-Party System* (New York: Columbia University Press, 2002).

no absentee voting, as the citizen must attend a caucus meeting to have his or her voice heard and counted.

Closed and Open Primaries A **closed primary** system is one in which voters must register with a political party prior to Election Day and can only vote for candidates of the party for which they are registered. Independent or unaffiliated voters may not vote in a party's primary. A **semiclosed primary** system allows those who are registered with the party or who are registered as independents to vote in a party's primary. In an **open primary**, by contrast, voters are not required to register their party affiliation with the state and may freely and secretly choose the ballot of any party's primary in which they wish to vote. Some states use a **semiopen primary**, which

permits registered voters to vote in any party's primary, but voters must publicly declare on Election Day the party primary in which they choose to vote.

Today, as Figure 5.1 displays, 27 states currently have closed or semiclosed primaries, 21 have open or semiopen systems, and two (Louisiana and Washington) have a top-two blanket primary. These categories are not definitive. A few states, most notably Alaska, permit a mix of primary systems, as state parties have chosen for themselves different types of primary elections. Until 2007, for example, West Virginia's Democratic primaries were closed, but its Republican primaries were semiopen, with independents allowed to cast ballots for GOP candidates. Now both parties have open primaries.

Figure 5.1

States with Closed Primaries, Open Primaries, and Nonpartisan Blanket Primaries

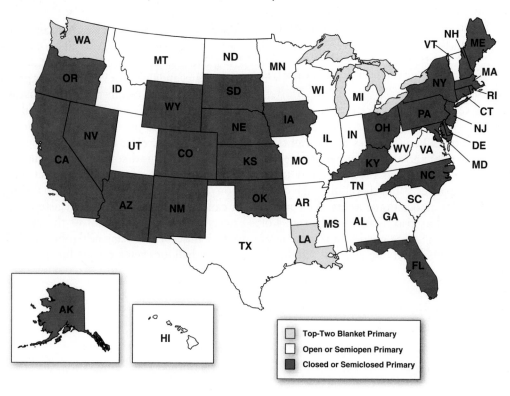

Legend:
- Top-Two Blanket Primary
- Open or Semiopen Primary
- Closed or Semiclosed Primary

Top-Two Blanket Primaries In 2008, the U.S. Supreme Court handed Republican and Democratic state political parties a defeat when it ruled that a successful 2004 ballot initiative in Washington calling for a top-two blanket primary system was constitutional. In its decision, *Washington State Grange v. Washington State Republican Party*, the court ruled that the top-two blanket primary, in which the two candidates for an office—regardless of their party affiliations—who receive the most votes in the primary are to face off in the general election, did not deprive state parties of their associational rights to choose their party nominees. A virtually identical system, called a **nonpartisan blanket primary**, is used in Louisiana. Primaries for state and local offices (but not federal offices) in the Bayou State are nonpartisan, with all candidates, regardless of their party label, facing off in a single primary. A candidate wins the election outright if he or she receives more than 50 percent of the vote in the primary. If no candidate wins a majority of votes, the top two candidates—irrespective of their party—run against one another in the general election. Often, this has meant that two Democrats face off against one another in the general election.

INSTITUTIONS MATTER

ALASKA'S OPTIONAL PRIMARY SYSTEM

In 2001, the Republican-controlled state legislature in Alaska adopted a restrictive closed primary system. In 2005, however, the Alaska Supreme Court invalidated the statute, ruling that such a primary system violated the state's constitutional guarantees of associational rights. As a result of the decision, Alaska now affords parties the option of holding the primary of their choosing. Two or more political parties may decide jointly to hold a primary, whereby all the candidates that have opted in are on the same ballot. The candidate from each party who wins the most votes advances to the general election. In contrast, a party may hold a semiclosed primary if it so desires. In 2006, as Figure 5.2 shows, the Democratic, Libertarian, Independence, and Green parties decided to hold a combined, semiopen primary, allowing any registered voter (including even Republicans) to vote for any one of their candidates running for office. In contrast, the Alaska Republican Party opted to hold a semiclosed primary, allowing registered Republicans as well as registered undeclared and nonpartisan voters to cast ballots for a slate of Republican candidates.

Figure 5.2

Alaska's 2006 Primary Election Ballot Choices

2006 Primary Election – Ballot Choices

There are three ballot types
Each Voter May Receive Only ONE Ballot Type

The party affiliation on the precinct register determines which candidate ballot a voter is eligible to vote.

Ballot Type	Political Party Candidates on Ballot	Who Can Vote This Ballot
Combined with **Ballot Measures**	Alaska Democratic Party Alaska Libertarian Party Alaskan Independence Party Green Party of Alaska	*Any registered voter* Party Affiliation Codes on Precinct Register: A – D – G – L – M – R – N – O – U – V
Republican with **Ballot Measures**	Alaska Republican Party	*Voters Registered as:* **Republican, Nonpartisan and Undeclared** Party Affiliation Codes on Precinct Register: R – U – N
Ballot Measures Only	No Candidates *This ballot is for voters who do not want to vote for any candidate*	*Any registered voter*

X01 (Rev. 5/30/06)

Source: Alaska- Lieutenant Governor, http://www.gov.state.ak.us/ltgov/elections/forms/x01_06.pdf

The Effect of Primary Systems on Representation Primaries vary with regard to how much voters are permitted to participate in the nomination process. In theory, open primaries should encourage more participation among the electorate, as all voters, even independents (sometimes referred to as unaffiliateds), may cast a ballot in the election. The costs associated with voting are much less in blanket and open primary systems than in closed systems. Yet, analyses of voter turnout levels across states with open versus closed primary systems do not reveal any significant differences in rates, as the mobilization of citizens goes well beyond the particularized costs or benefits of an individual's decision to vote. Because open primaries diminish the control that parties and candidates have over who participates in the nomination process, parties and candidates may have less incentive to bolster turnout.[17]

Party Fusion

States may prohibit the name of a candidate running for a political office from appearing more than once on a ballot, a practice known as **party fusion**. Fusion permits two or more parties to nominate the same candidate for office. In a 1997 ballot access case, *Timmons v. Twin Cities Area New Party*, the U.S. Supreme Court affirmed the regulatory power of state legislatures by affirming Minnesota's law banning fusion—the listing of a candidate on the ballot under two or more political parties. The Court ruled 6–3 that the state's antifusion law was constitutional, as it did not severely burden the associational rights of the members of the New Party. In the words of the majority decision, the ruling upheld the right of the states to avoid "voter confusion," protect political stability in the state, and protect the integrity of the ballot by prohibiting

candidates to be cross-listed as two or more parties' nominee for a given elective office.

Of the ten states (Arkansas, Connecticut, Delaware, Idaho, Mississippi, New York, South Carolina, South Dakota, Utah, and Vermont) that allow party fusion today, only minor parties in New York continue to use it with considerable frequency. The Conservative, Independence, and Working Families parties in New York (see Figure 5.3) are usually not strong enough to have their candidates win against Republicans or Democrats. Instead, these minor parties routinely cross-endorse Republican or Democratic candidates running for office. If the cross-endorsed candidate wins, the minor party can claim that it had a hand in the victory—pointing to the votes cast for the candidate on its minor party label.[18]

Party Ballot Access

States have been granted wide latitude by the U.S. Supreme Court to determine what parties and their candidates must do to qualify for the ballot. In some states, the rules are fairly restrictive; in others, they are less so. Democrats and Republicans are, by state law, usually given "major-party" status and are entitled to permanent space on the ballot. A minor party may have to collect a certain number of signatures or register some percentage of the state's voters with their minor party before being granted ballot access. A candidate wishing to run as an independent or as the nominee of a new political party usually has to collect thousands of signatures in order to qualify for the ballot. In other states, candidates wishing to run for office need only pay a nominal filing fee.[19] In most states, parties typically retain their ballot access as long as one of their candidates collects a minimum percentage of votes cast in a state election.

[17] Rebecca Morton, *Analyzing Elections* (New York: Norton, 2006).

[18] Joel Rodgers, "Pull the Plug," *Administrative Law Review* 52 (2000): 743–68; and David Dulio and James Thurber, "America's Two-Party System: Friend or Foe?" *Administrative Law Review* 52 (2000): 769–92.

[19] Richard Winger, "The Importance of Ballot Access," 1994, http://www.ballot-access.org/winger/iba.html.

Figure 5.3

New York Party Fusion Ballot, 2004

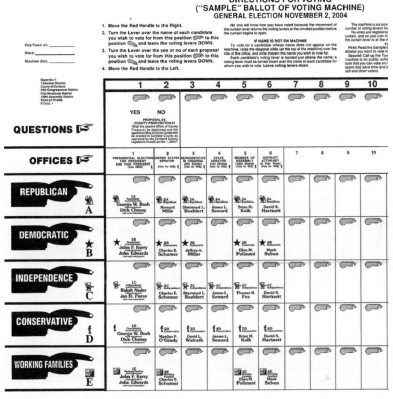

Source: Cortland County, New York, http://www.cortland-co.org/election/images/BallotSheets04/scan07.gif.

Many states continue to have very onerous ballot qualification standards. In the 1970s, for example, Arkansas lawmakers required minor parties to collect signatures equal to 7 percent of votes cast in the last election in order to qualify for the ballot. The U.S. Supreme Court subsequently ruled the requirement could not exceed 5 percent. In Virginia, candidates running as independents for statewide office are required to collect 10,000 signatures from registered voters to have their names placed on the ballot; at least 400 of those signatures must come from each of Virginia's congressional districts.[20]

Party-in-the-Electorate

Parties are often understood as tripartite social structures composed of three integrated components: party-in-the-electorate, party organization, and party-in-government.[21] Although somewhat limited and overly schematic, the three-pronged framework can serve as a heuristic, allowing us to isolate and appreciate the various dimensions of political parties.[22] We begin our discussion with party-in-the-electorate, which refers to ordinary citizens—eligible voters as well as

[20] Richard Winger, "What Are Ballots For?" 1988, http://www.ballot-access.org/winger/wabf.html.

[21] V. O. Key, *Politics, Parties, and Pressure Groups*, 5th ed. (New York: Thomas Y. Crowell, 1964), 163–65.

[22] J. P. Monroe, *The Political Party Matrix: The Resistance of Organization* (Albany: State University of New York Press, 2001).

nonvoters—who identify with and share some sense of loyalty to a particular party.

Partisan Identification

The strength of an individual's attachment to a political party is measured by **party identification** (PID). A person's PID usually forms early in adulthood and is largely conditioned by one's family. Party identification is a genuine form of social identity that is affected in part by sociopsychological influences; a person is often initially drawn to a political party because of his or her sense of belonging and allegiance.[23] As people age, though, they often make retrospective and prospective cognitive evaluations (or running tallies) of how the parties are doing.[24] Because some people are continually adjusting their PID in response to political and economic change, evidence at the macro level reveals that the average PID in some states has been slowly changing.[25] For example, in the 1980s, many white Southerners who were ideologically conservative but still loyal to the Democratic Party began identifying more with the Republican Party. As a result, southern states began turning redder as partisan identification became more Republican.

Political Ideology

Not all Democrats and Republicans have the same political ideology or a consistent and coherent belief system concerning the principles of political rule. When individual political ideologies are aggregated, political ideologies found across the states vary considerably. Cultural, economic, demographic, and sociological dissimilarities may lead states to have more liberal or more conservative electorates. Because national public opinion polls tend not to survey a representative number of respondents from all 50 states, there are relatively few direct measures of state-level political ideology. As such, scholars have tried to derive indirect measures of a state's political ideology by using election returns and interest groups' ratings of members of Congress from each state, by pooling data from newspaper public opinion polls, and by using data from national election surveys designed to study U.S. Senate races.[26] Regardless of the method, these studies show that southern states—such as Alabama, Arkansas, and Oklahoma—tend to be the most ideologically conservative, and northern states—such as Massachusetts, Maryland, and New York—tend to be the most liberal in the country.

Does a state's political ideology predict the kinds of public policies it adopts? Usually but not always. As discussed in Chapter 1, state policies tend to reflect the median ideological preferences of the states' citizens. However, Democratic-controlled legislatures, for example, tend to produce policies that are more conservative than their more liberal citizens.[27] The reason for this divergence between citizen ideology and public policy could be rational; parties often pursue public policies catering to the median voter in order to win future elections rather than passing public policies that are reflective of their ideology.[28]

[23] Donald Green, Bradley Palmquest, and Eric Schickler, *Partisan Hearts and Minds: Political Parties and the Social Identities of Voters* (New Haven, Conn.: Yale University Press, 2002).

[24] Morris Fiorina, *Retrospective Voting in American National Elections* (New Haven, Conn.: Yale University Press, 1981).

[25] Robert Erikson, Michael MacKuen, and James Stimson, *The Macro Polity* (New York: Cambridge University Press, 2002); and Alan Abramowitz and Kyle Saunders, "Ideological Realignment in the U.S. Electorate," *Journal of Politics* 60 (1998): 634–52.

[26] See William Berry et al., "Measuring Citizen and Government Ideology in the American States," *American Journal of Political Science* 42 (1998): 327–48; Gerald Wright, Robert Erikson, and John McIver, "Measuring State Partisanship and Ideology with Survey Data," *Journal of Politics* 47 (1985): 469–89; Barbara Norrander, "Measuring State Public Opinion with the Senate National Election Study," *State Politics and Policy Quarterly* 1 (2001): 111–25; Paul Brace et al., "Public Opinion in the American States: New Perspectives Using National Data," *American Journal of Political Science* 46 (2002): 173–89; and Thomas Carsey and Geoffrey Layman, "Party Polarization and 'Conflict Extension' in the American Electorate," *American Journal of Political Science* 46 (2002): 786–802.

[27] Wright, Erikson, and McIver, "Measuring State Partisanship and Ideology."

[28] Downs, *An Economic Theory of Democracy*; and Thomas Dye, "Party and Policy in the States," *Journal of Politics* 46 (1984): 1097–116.

Are a State's Partisan Identification and Political Ideology Related?

A state's partisan identification leanings and its political ideology are not always correlated, or linked together. States populated with citizens having strong Republican ties—Utah, South Dakota, Idaho, and Kansas, for example—are not inhabited solely by citizens who are ideologically conservative. Some states with heavy Republican PID are actually less ideologically conservative than states with high percentages of Democratic identifiers. Likewise, several states with strong Democratic PID are considerably more ideologically conservative than states with high proportions of Republican identifiers. Only a functional understanding of political parties can accommodate the tremendous diversity of political ideology and partisanship found across the American states.

For example, states with more ideologically liberal populations are not necessarily more Democratic, and states more ideologically conservative are not necessarily more Republican. Massachusetts, for instance, lives up to its reputation as being one of the most liberal states in the union. Yet, seven states, including Oklahoma, a state ranked as one of the most conservative in the country, have stronger levels of Democratic PID than the Bay State. According to one study, two of the most conservative states—Arkansas and Alabama—do not even register in the top 30 of Republican-leaning states with respect to their PID.[29]

From an institutional perspective, there are several reasons why a state's political ideology and partisanship are not always correlated. As mentioned in Chapter 3, states have differing registration laws, making it alternatively easier or more difficult for citizens to initially register with a political party or subsequently switch their party registration. Most states require voting-age citizens to register their party affiliation with

the state at least 30 days prior to an election, although under the National Voter Registration Act passed by Congress in 1993, all states must allow voters to register to vote by mail and when applying for a driver's license. Nine states (Idaho, Iowa, Maine, Minnesota, Montana, New Hampshire, North Carolina, Wisconsin, and Wyoming) have same-day registration, allowing eligible citizens to register to vote on Election Day. North Dakota has no voter registration requirements; all voting-age citizens living in the state may cast ballots. These differences can affect partisan identification, irrespective of political ideology. Residents in states with strict registration laws and a closed primary system, for example, might be more inclined to identify with a political party because they are required by state law to register with a party if they want to vote in a primary. Variations in state registration laws may also help to explain why the percentage of voters who are registered with a party in a state is not always a reliable indicator of the level of partisan identification within a state.

Party Organization

Over the years, state and local party organizations have shown their adaptability by responding to changing regulatory and electoral conditions. In the early 1970s, state and local political parties—along with their national brethren—were often given up for dead because they were seen as dinosaurs of a bygone era. Today, most state and many local political parties are vibrant organizations, carrying out essential campaign activities, such as mobilizing voters and raising campaign funds in support of their candidates. Party organization refers to the network of elected and appointed party officials; paid staffers; national, state, and local committees; and volunteer workers.[30] Some political scientists have reduced the organizational role of

---

[29] Norrander, "Measuring State Public Opinion with the Senate National Election Study."

[30] John Bibby, "Party Networks: National-State Integration, Allied Groups, and Issue Activists," in *The State of the Parties: The Changing Role of Contemporary Parties*, 3rd ed., ed. John Green and Daniel Shea (New York: Rowman & Littlefield, 1999).

parties to a single function—that of electing candidates. In today's "candidate-centered era," a party is designed primarily as a "party-in-service" to candidates.[31]

The level of party organization across the 50 states varies considerably. State parties are typically composed of a state central committee, congressional district committees, county committees, and ward or precinct committees. The structure of state parties, though, can be far more complex. The California Democratic Party, for example, has what can only be described as a Byzantine organizational flowchart. Each level of the state party has members who are either elected or appointed to their positions. Almost all party officials at the local level are volunteers, although most state parties now have permanent, paid staff at the central committee level.[32] Most state parties convene annual conventions that are attended by party delegates and the party's elected officials. Most states hold primaries to choose a party's nominee for the general election, but a few states use party conventions to vet and select party nominees.

At a minimum, if a party organization is to be successful, it must be able to overcome barriers to collective action. The organizational configuration a party selects, though, may be tight or loose. A functional definition of a political party accommodates variation in party organizations found across the country—from urban party machines, to well-financed and professionally staffed state party committees, to the underfinanced and disorganized bands of volunteers running some local party organizations. Recall that

a functional definition of parties is not concerned with a party's organizational hierarchy but rather its preoccupation with contesting elections. As rational actors, then, state and local parties have been able to adapt their organizational structures to the changing regulatory and electoral environment, thereby ensuring their continued relevance.[33]

The Rebirth of Party Organizations

For much of the 20th century, state and local political party organizations were mere shadows of their former selves. It was not until the 1970s that many state and local party organizations began to strengthen themselves organizationally, expanding their bureaucratic and programmatic capacities. Research conducted during the 1970s and 1980s highlighted the institutionalization of state parties, depicting the integration of new party professionals and the bureaucratization of what were once often parochial, unsophisticated organizations. Most state parties during that period began to establish permanent headquarters and hire specialized staff to raise contributions and direct campaigns.[34] The parties transformed themselves from provincial party machines into service vendors ready to recruit, train, and support candidates in their run for office.[35] Although the labor-intensive parties of the 19th century are in the past, state and local party organizations have reinvigorated themselves as service providers. By the turn of the millennium, scholars generally agreed that state political parties were as strong and fiscally sound as they were anytime in recent history.[36]

[31] Schlesinger, "The New American Political Party."

[32] Raymond La Raja, "State Political Parties after BCRA," in *Life after Reform*, ed. Michael Malbin (Boulder, Colo.: Rowman & Littlefield, 2003).

[33] Monroe, *The Political Party Matrix*.

[34] Cornelius Cotter, James L. Gibson, John F. Bibby, and Robert J. Huckshorn, *Party Organizations in American Politics* (New Brunswick, N.J.: Eagleton Institute of Politics, Rutgers University, 1984).

[35] Paul Herrnson, "Do Parties Make a Difference? The Role of Party Organizations in Congressional Elections," *Journal of Politics* 48 (1986): 589–613; and Xandra Kayden and Eddie Mahe, *The Party Goes On: The Persistence of the Two Party System in the United States* (New York: Basic Books, 1985).

[36] John Aldrich et al., "Challenges to the American Two-Party System: Evidence from the 1968, 1980, 1992, and 1996 Presidential Elections," *Political Research Quarterly* 53 (2000): 495–522; and Morehouse and Jewell, *State Politics, Parties, and Policy*.

Measuring Party Organizational Strength

There are several comparative studies of the 50 state organizations that measure party organizational strength. Unfortunately, the methodologies scholars have utilized to measure party organizational strength have varied widely, leading to some inconsistent findings.[37] Many of the studies gauging state party organization have measured the number of staff and other party assets. Party organizations, of course, are much more than their staff. They can also be understood as a complex web of political consultants and campaign specialists and elected officials in national, state, and local offices as well as their respective staff. A recent study finds that party organization strength influences the ideological tenor of the party, with more top-down, hierarchical structures being more moderate, and those with more open structures being more polarized.[38]

State Party Financing

As with any organization, the capacity and relative power of state party organizations are directly affected by their money-raising prowess. Considerable variation in state campaign finance laws exists across the states when it comes to restricting contributions and expenditures of political parties. A dozen states (Arkansas, Florida, Georgia, Idaho, Illinois, Maine, Missouri, Nebraska, New Mexico, Oregon, Utah, and Virginia) allow unlimited contributions from virtually any source to be made to state political parties. Roughly the same number have similarly lax contribution

regulations, except that they prohibit donations from corporations and labor unions; eight other states prohibit contributions from corporate entities but allow union donations.[39] Alabama, for instance, allows individuals, **political action committees** (PACs), labor unions, and national party committees to contribute unlimited sums to the state political parties but limits corporations to donations of only $500 per election. Campaign finance laws in Arizona and Texas are similar to Alabama's, except that unions may not make contributions to state parties with money drawn from their own treasuries. Connecticut, on the other hand, allows individuals to contribute up to $5,000 per year to state parties, but it completely bans corporations and unions from making contributions from their treasuries, permitting them to make only limited PAC contributions.

Many of these state campaign finance regulations are new. Between 1990 and 2000, over 30 states adopted campaign finance laws that directly or indirectly affected state parties. Going through state legislatures, but also circumventing politicians who were the beneficiaries of lax campaign finance restrictions, good government public interest groups placed more than two dozen initiatives on statewide ballots dealing with campaign finance issues during the decade.

The capacity of state parties to raise campaign contributions ranges tremendously. The disparity across states in party fundraising has less to do with the organizational strength of the Democratic or Republican Party within a state and more to do with the kind of campaign finance laws that are on the books.

---

[37] See, for example, James Gibson et al., "Assessing Party Organizational Strength," *American Journal of Political Science* 27 (1983): 193–222; James Gibson, John Frendreis, and Laura Vertz, "Party Dynamics in the 1980s: Changes in County Party Organizational Strength 1980–1984," *American Journal of Political Science* 33 (1989): 67–90; Robert Huckshorn et al., "Party Integration and Party Organizational Strength," *Journal of Politics* 48 (1986): 976–91; David Mayhew, *Placing Parties in American Politics: Organization, Electoral Settings, and Government Activity in the Twentieth Century* (Princeton, N.J.: Princeton University Press, 1986); and Sarah Morehouse, *The Governor as Party Leader: Campaigning and Governing* (Ann Arbor: University of Michigan Press, 1998).

[38] Daniel Coffey, "Measuring Gubernatorial Ideology: A Content Analysis of State of the State Speeches," *State Politics and Policy Quarterly* 5 (2005): 88–103. See also John Coleman, "Party Organizational Strength and Public Support for Parties," *American Journal of Political Science* 40 (1996): 805–24.

[39] Center for Responsive Government, "Contributions Limits on State Party Committees," 2002, http://www.publicintegrity.org/partylines/overview.aspx?act=cl.

Contribution levels are largely contingent on two factors: state campaign finance regulations and the competitiveness of state and federal elections. State parties raised a total of $621 million in the 2005–2006 election cycle. A handful of Democratic and Republican state parties raked in more than $20 million during the cycle, including those in California and Florida. The Republican Party of Florida topped all other state parties in total receipts for the two-year period, with a haul of nearly $68 million. The Republican Party of Georgia amassed more than $15 million during the cycle; in contrast, the Vermont Democratic Party raised only $88,000 and the Montana Republican Party raised only $19,000 during the period.[40]

Party-in-Government

Party-in-government refers to candidates running for elective office as well as officeholders at the local, state, and national levels who are elected under the party label. With the exception of Nebraska (because of its nonpartisan, unicameral legislature), Republicans and Democrats dominate the governmental structure of every state. As we discuss in Chapter 6, political parties structure state government, especially state legislatures. Of course, because of winner-take-all elections and restrictive ballot access laws, the two-party dominance of state legislatures and statewide elected officials exaggerates the level of popular support for the two parties in the electorate. Due to these structural barriers, it is difficult for citizens who are displeased with the two-party system to articulate their dissatisfaction with the status quo.[41]

Party Competition in State Legislatures

Although political parties may be inevitable, their mere existence is not sufficient to guarantee a democratic form of governance. Rather, competition *between* the parties is said to be essential for democracies to function. Competition forces the parties to become more internally cohesive and disciplined, giving citizens a real choice at the polls.[42]

Aggregate election results suggest that competition in state legislatures among the two main political parties is at an all-time high. Between 1950 and 2000, a clear majority of legislative seats across the states were held by Democrats; by 2000, though, the partisan split in legislative seats between the parties had become dead-even. Figure 5.4 displays legislative party control in 2009 of the 49 states with partisan legislatures. Following the 2008 general election, Democrats held 3,058 of the 5,411 (57 percent) state house seats in the 49 states (Nebraska only has an upper chamber), Republicans held 2,331 seats (43 percent), and independents and third parties held but 17 seats (with the balance being temporarily vacant). Of the 1,922 state senate seats (which excludes Nebraska's 49 nonpartisan seats), Democrats held a slim advantage of 1,024 seats (53 percent) to 888 seats (46 percent) for the Republicans, with just 3 seats held by independents and third-party candidates (with the balance remaining vacant).[43]

Figure 5.4 can be somewhat deceptive, as states vary considerably with respect to the degree of legislative party control. In addition, some states historically have had intense two-party competition, whereas others have had a tradition of single-party dominance.

---

[40] Raymond La Raja, Susan Orr, and Daniel Smith, "Surviving BCRA: State Party Finance in 2004," in *The State of the Parties*, 5th ed., ed. John Green and Daniel Coffey (Boulder, Colo.: Rowman & Littlefield, 2006); National Institute on Money in State Politics, "State Elections Overview, 2006," http://www.followthemoney.org/press/Reports/State_Overview_2006.pdf.

[41] Theodore Lowi and Joseph Romance, *A Republic of Parties? Debating the Two-Party System* (Lanham, Md.: Rowman & Littlefield, 1998).

[42] V. O. Key, The Responsible Electorate: Rationality in Presidential Voting, 1936–1960 (Cambridge, Mass.: Harvard University Press, 1966).

[43] National Conference of State Legislatures, "2008–2009 (Post-Election) Partisan Composition of State Legislatures," http://www.ncsl.org/statevote/partycomptable2009.htm.

Figure 5.4

Partisan Control of State Legislatures, 2009

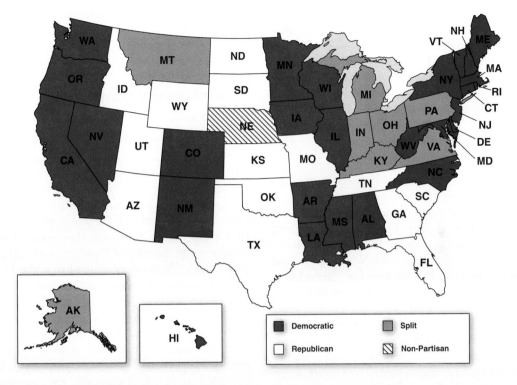

Source: National Conference of State Legislatures, http://www.ncsl.org/statevote/statevotemaps2008.htm.

Many of the social and economic conditions as well as numerous institutional rules that helped to ensure one-party dominance have eroded or have been eliminated, making two-party competition more common throughout the country. This is particularly true in the South, as the Republican Party over the past 30 years has become more competitive, and even dominant, in some states. Today, two-party competition exists in every state, although to different degrees.

Party Control and Interparty Competition

There are numerous ways to measure the party control and interparty competition of a state's party system. One of the most popular methods was first developed by Austin Ranney and has become known as the "Ranney Index."[44] The index averages four measures of party competition: the proportion of the gubernatorial vote won, the proportions of the state senate and state house seats won, and the proportion of time (over a given period) the governorship and the two legislative chambers are controlled by a party. Ranney's measure of state party control ranges from 0 (complete Republican control) to 100 (complete Democratic control), and his measure of interparty competition ranges from 50 (no party competition) to 100 (a perfectly competitive two-party system).

[44] Austin Ranney, "Parties in State Politics," in *Politics in the American States*, ed. Herbert Jacob and Kenneth N. Vines (Boston: Little, Brown, 1965). See also James King, "Inter-Party Competition in the American States: An Examination of Index Components," *Western Political Quarterly* 42 (1989): 83–92; and Thomas Holbrook and Emily Van Dunk, "Electoral Competition in the American States," *American Political Science Review* 87 (1993): 955–62.

In terms of party control, 19 states over a 20-year period (1980–2000) had solid Democratic control, and another 12 leaned Democratic. In contrast, there were only eight solidly Republican states, with another ten that leaned Republican. The most Democratic state during this period—in terms of the control of the governor's office and the state legislature—was Maryland (with a score of 80.8), followed closely by Arkansas and Hawaii. Utah, with a score of 25.1, was by far the most Republican state, with South Dakota and Idaho also solidly in the hands of the GOP.

Ranney's interparty competition scores give us a sense of where the battles between the two major parties were taking place over this time period. The states with the highest scores—Delaware (98.5), followed closely by Wisconsin, Michigan, and New York—had intense interparty competition. Maryland, with a score of 69.2 and dominated by the Democratic Party, was by far the least competitive state over the time frame. Utah, with the strongest Republican Party control score of any state, interestingly had a higher interparty competition score (75.1) than seven states controlled by the Democrats.

Increasing Interparty Competition

Since the 1970s, across a range of indicators, there has been a gradual increase in interparty competition in the American states. Much of this increase has occurred in the South, where there has been a wholesale transformation of solid Democratic Party control giving way to the rise of the Republican Party. Between 1980 and 2000, Democratic Party control declined precipitously as the 20th century came to a close. When comparing the averages of the last five years with those of the first five years

of the period, 40 states shifted from being less Democratic to being more Republican, and nearly all the states that were classified as Republican became even stronger under GOP control.[45] Figure 5.5 provides visual evidence of the level of interparty competition across the states.[46]

Why Interparty Competition Matters

State governments produce different kinds of public policies depending on the dynamics of party strength and interparty competition. Evidence shows that heightened interparty competition leads to public policies that are more representative of the whole population of a state rather than just its elites. In his classic work *Southern Politics in the State and Nation*, V. O. Key argued that the lack of party competition in southern states from the 1880s through the 1950s enabled the "haves" in society to run roughshod over the "have-nots," as the dominant Democratic Party had no fear of reprisal at the polls. Key argues that because they were unlikely to be defeated at the next election, the majority southern Democrats did not have to respond to the concerns and needs of all the people residing in their states. Others have formally tested Key's proposition that lack of party competition leads to worse redistributive policy outcomes, finding some support.[47] More recently, as interparty competition has increased across the country, scholars have found that increased party competition in a state tends to lead to the passage by state legislatures of more liberal public policies. Specifically, Democratic-controlled legislatures in states with tough electoral competition from Republicans tend to pass more liberal public policies, whereas the reverse holds for Republican-controlled state

---

[45] Morehouse and Jewell, *State Politics, Parties, and Policy*, 109.

[46] Bibby and Holbrook, "Parties and Elections."

[47] James Garand, "Partisan Change and Shifting Expenditure Priorities in the American States, 1945–1978," *American Politics Quarterly* (October 1985): 355–91; and Morehouse and Jewell, *State Politics, Parties, and Policy*, 50.

Figure 5.5

Interparty Competition, 1999–2006

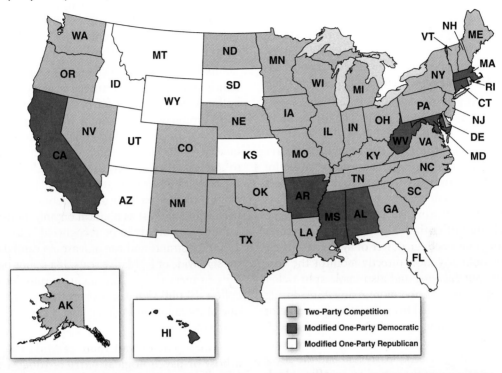

Two-Party Competition
Modified One-Party Democratic
Modified One-Party Republican

Source: John Bibby and Thomas Holbrook, "Parties and Elections," in *Politics in the American States,* 8th ed., eds. Virginia Gray and Russell Hanson (Washington, D.C.: CQ Press, 2004).

legislatures facing stiff Democratic electoral challenges.[48]

Evidence reveals that heightened interparty competition leads to greater levels of participation by citizens. General election voter turnout in the 11 southern states from 1960 to 1986 averaged less than 40 percent, well below the national average. With the decline of the Democratic Party's lock on state government and the advent of greater interparty competition, average turnout among these states increased to nearly 43 percent between 1990 and 1996. Comparing the two periods, Alabama had an 8-point increase, and Louisiana experienced a double-digit jump in turnout.[49]

Whither Third Parties?

Nearly every state is dominated by a two-party system. Over 99 percent of state legislative seats are held by either Democrats or Republicans. Although some scholars point to the historical or cultural bias for having two dominant parties in the states, the primary reason for

[48] Holbrook and Van Dunk, "Electoral Competition in the American States"; Charles Barrilleaux, "Party Strength, Party Change, and Policymaking in the American States," *Party Politics* 6 (2000): 61–73; Charles Barrilleaux, "A Test of the Independent Influences of Inter-Party Electoral Competition and Party Strength on State Policy," *American Journal of Political Science* 41 (1997): 1462–66; Charles Barrilleaux, Thomas Holbrook, and Laura Langer, "Electoral Competition, Legislative Balance, and American State Welfare Policy," *American Journal of Political Science* 46 (2002): 415–27; and James Alt and Robert Lowry, "Divided Government, Fiscal Institutions and Budget Deficits: Evidence from the States," *American Political Science Review* 88 (1994): 811–28.

[49] Calculations derived from Morehouse and Jewell, *State Politics, Parties, and Policy*, table 2.1.

the two-party duopoly is institutional. There are many constraints that limit the possible success of third parties. Some of these barriers are constitutional, such as the single-member district electoral systems used in most states. Other hurdles are statutory, such as ballot access restrictions, which are often very onerous for third parties and their candidates.[50]

Third parties at the state and local levels have not always been weak. The adoption in most states of the Australian ballot (or secret ballot) in the late 19th century initially gave a boost to third parties. The Australian ballot placed governments—rather than the parties themselves—in charge of printing ballots and administering elections, making voting a private rather than a public act. The secret ballot diminished the power of the **party bosses,** who could no longer directly monitor the vote choices of citizens, and also made split-ticket voting possible. Furthermore, many states during this period switched from a **party-column ballot** (sometimes known as the Indiana ballot), which listed all the candidates running for separate offices by their political party and had the effect of strengthening the parties, to an **office-block ballot,** which made split-ticket voting easier, thereby weakening the major parties.[51] Today, 17 states still use party-column ballots, which encourage straight-party voting (see Figure 5.6). With the push of a single button, voters are able to support all the candidates running for office of a given party.[52]

Third parties, such as the Libertarian, Green, and Natural Law parties, have been hampered by both the direct primary system and ballot access laws adopted by the states. The direct primary system of nominating congressional and state officials has hurt the prowess of state-level third parties in the states. Because party bosses no longer overtly control the nomination processes of the two major

parties, Republican and Democratic party dissidents are able to act as "outsiders" while remaining within the two parties. As such, the major parties are able to absorb dissidents and broader protest movements, which in the past often led to the rise of third parties.

Ballot access laws also ensure that the two major parties are guaranteed a place on the ballot, whereas minor parties—if they do not win a certain percentage of the vote in a previous election—are required to collect signatures to qualify for the ballot. In some states, this barrier to access is relatively easy to overcome. Colorado lawmakers in 1998 made it easier for minor parties to win recognition as actual political parties and not just as political organizations; all a third party needs to be recognized is to have 1,000 registrants and run at least ten candidates for statewide or legislative seats. If a minor party fails to meet this requirement, it must either collect 10,000 signatures on petitions or have one of its candidates win at least 5 percent of a statewide vote.

Third parties and their candidates face a host of psychological barriers too. At the individual level, citizens who vote regularly (likely voters) tend to have a strong allegiance to one of the two major parties. In addition, citizens who are alienated from the political system, and who therefore might be likely suspects to vote for a third-party candidate, are much less likely to vote. Because of the winner-take-all nature of most state and local elections, third parties often have a difficult time convincing contributors to give them money. Because candidates running on third-party tickets have little chance of winning, the media tend not to cover them. It becomes a self-fulfilling prophecy that because their candidates rarely win, third parties have a difficult time recruiting qualified candidates to run on their ticket.

---

[50] John Bibby and Sandy Maisel, *Two Parties—or More?* 2nd ed. (Boulder, Colo.: Westview, 2002).

[51] Richard Niemi and Paul Herrnson, "Beyond the Butterfly: The Complexity of U.S. Ballots," *Perspectives on Politics* 1 (2003): 317–26.

[52] David Kimball, Chris T. Owens, and Katherine M. Keeney, "Residual Votes and Political Representation," in *Counting Votes: Lessons from the 2000 Presidential Election in Florida,* ed. Robert Watson (Gainesville: University Press of Florida, 2004).

Figure 5.6

Party-Column and Office-Block Ballots

PART OF MASSACHUSETTS OFFICIAL BALLOT, NOVEMBER, 1908.

To vote for a Person, mark a Cross X in the Square at the right of the Party Name, or Political Designation. **X**

To vote for a Person, mark a Cross X in the Square at the right of the Party Name, or Political Designation. **X**

GOVERNOR	Mark ONE
JAMES F. CAREY — of Haverhill	Socialist
EBEN S. DRAPER — of Hopedale	Republican
WALTER J. HOAR — of Worcester	Socialist Labor
WILLIAM N. OSGOOD — of Lowell	Independence League
JAMES H. VAHEY — of Watertown	Democratic
WILLARD O. WYLIE — of Beverly	Prohibition

LIEUTENANT GOVERNOR	Mark ONE.
CHARLES J. BARTON — of Melrose	Democratic
JOAO CLAUDINO — of New Bedford	Socialist Labor
LOUIS A. FROTHINGHAM — of Boston	Republican
JOHN HALL, Jr. — of West Springfield	Socialist
ROBERT J. McCARTNEY — of Kingston	Independence League
FRANK N. RAND — of Haverhill	Prohibition

CONGRESSMAN — Tenth District	Mark ONE.
J. MITCHELL GALVIN — of Boston	Republican
CHARLES J. KIDNEY — of Boston	Independence League
JOSEPH F. O'CONNELL — of Boston	Democratic
HAZARD STEVENS — of Boston	Free Trader

COUNCILLOR — Second District	Mark ONE.
ALBION F. BEMIS — of Brookline	Republican
CHARLES G. KIDDER — of Taunton	Independence League

SENATOR — First Norfolk District	Mark ONE.
JAMES E. FOLEY — of Randolph	Democratic
JOHN J. GALLAGHER — of Hyde Park	Socialist
EUGENE C. HULTMAN — of Quincy	Republican

PART OF INDIANA STATE TICKET. NOVEMBER, 1908.

Democratic Ticket.

For Governor, THOMAS R. MARSHALL.

For Lieutenant-Governor, FRANK J. HALL.

For Secretary of State, JAMES F. COX.

For Auditor of State, MARION BAILEY.

For Treasurer of State, JOHN ISENBARGER.

Republican Ticket.

For Governor, JAMES E. WATSON.

For Lieutenant-Governor, FREMONT GOODWINE.

For Secretary of State, FRED A. SIMS.

For Auditor of State, JOHN C. BILLHEIMER.

For Treasurer of State, OSCAR HADLEY.

Prohibition Ticket.

For Governor, SUMNER W. HAYNES.

For Lieutenant-Governor, ABRAHAM HUNTSINGER.

For Secretary of State, WILLIAM H. HILL.

For Auditor of State, HENRY COONS.

For Treasurer of State, WILLIAM H. CROWDER.

People's Party Ticket.

For Governor, FRED J. S. ROBINSON.

For Lieutenant-Governor, ORLANDO L. ROSS.

For Secretary of State, RICHARD BONEWITZ.

For Auditor of State, JAMES S. REEVES.

For Treasurer of State, AARON McDONALD.

Source: Alex Peterman, Elements of Civil Government. New York: American Book Company, 1916, http://www.gutenberg.org/files/15018/15018-h/images/img-187.jpg and http://www.gutenberg.org/files/15018/15018-h/images/img-186.jpg.

Every blue moon, of course, third-party candidates do win elective office at the state or local level. A study of voting patterns for presidential candidates found three factors have motivated citizens to vote for third-party candidates: majority party deterioration, an influx of new voters with weak allegiance to the two major parties, and, most importantly, attractive third-party candidates who present viable alternatives to major nominees.[53] The same factors are often in place at the state level. Since 1930, eight third-party and independent candidates have been elected governor, including four since 1990. Most recently, in 1998 in Minnesota, former professional wrestler Jesse "The Body" Ventura, running as a Reform Party candidate, won with 37 percent of the vote.

Understanding Interest Groups

Like parties, interest groups are essential components of the democratic process. They serve a basic function of aggregating different points of view and pushing policy agendas in the public sphere. By linking the public to elected officials, interest groups encourage individuals to participate in state and local affairs, allowing their voices to be heard. Without a collective voice, citizens would have relatively little direct power over their elected officials. Casting ballots, after all, happens infrequently, every two years or so. And most people have limited access to their elected officials or political party operatives. If individuals are to be heard and represented by elected officials, they often require a vehicle to collectively convey their concerns. As countervailing forces, interest groups can apply pressure on public officials, educate them about the issues, and push them to adopt or defeat a public policy. They can even serve as **watchdogs**, monitoring government programs and sounding a public alarm if they uncover inefficient or mismanaged programs or corruption.

Of course, interest groups do not always promote the values and desires of the public interest; regularly, they attempt to promote their own agendas and sway public officials. Some groups have more clout—some might say too much—in state and local politics, influencing who governs.[54] It will also become apparent to you that interest groups are not randomly distributed throughout society but reflect an inherent upper-class bias, with corporate interests and wealthier individuals having greater representation in state and community interest group systems.[55]

Defining Interest Groups

What are interest groups, and how do they differ from merely having an interest? As you might expect, interest groups come in all shapes and sizes, advancing a seemingly infinite number of political causes. Nearly every one of you will belong to at least one—if not several—interest groups during your lifetime. An interest group is a formally organized body of individuals, organizations, or enterprises that shares common goals and joins in a collective attempt to influence the electoral and policy-making processes. Simply put, an interest group is any organization that attempts to influence the electoral process or governmental policy making. Unlike political parties, interest groups do not nominate or run a slate of candidates for political office and do not take over the reins of government. Many interest groups are heavily involved in the electoral process; others focus on lobbying elected officials and policy makers.

[53] Steven Rosenstone, Roy Behr, and Edward Lazarus, *Third Parties in America: Citizen Response to Major Party Failure*, 2nd ed. (Princeton, N.J.: Princeton University Press, 1996).

[54] Robert Dahl, *Who Governs?* (New Haven, Conn.: Yale University Press, 1961).

[55] Peter Bachrach and Morton S. Baratz, "Two Faces of Power," *American Political Science Review* 56 (1962): 947–52.

If we are to adhere strictly to this definition, "farmers," for example, would not constitute an interest group. Because different farmers have different interests, they fail to meet the definitional standard of sharing common goals. For example, dairy farmers in Wisconsin have interests that are quite dissimilar from those of alfalfa, soybean, and corn growers in Iowa and Illinois or even other dairy farmers in California and Vermont. Wisconsin dairy farmers want to keep down the cost of the feed for their herd, prevent California milk producers from expanding their agribusiness operations, and ensure a fair milk-pricing system. Some may want to increase state and federal subsidies to set aside land for conservation easements protecting wetlands; limit price supports for small, organic dairies in Vermont; and even allow the injection of bovine growth hormone into their cows to increase milk production. Indeed, there are even several competing interest groups representing milk producers in Wisconsin, including the National Milk Producers Federation, the Dairy Farmers of America, the Wisconsin Dairy Business Association, and the State Dairyman's Association. It is important to keep in mind that an interest is categorically different from an organization or a group. Individuals may (and often do) share common concerns with one another without ever belonging to a group.

Types of Interest Groups

The universe of interest groups is not limited to membership organizations, or groups of like-minded individuals sharing common social, economic, or political goals joining together to advance them. Membership organizations bring together individuals—such as the myriad farmer organizations mentioned above—to pursue their collective goals. Some well-known membership organizations with an active presence in the states include the Chamber of Commerce, the Sierra Club, the National Rifle Association, the American Federation of Teachers, Common Cause, and the American Association for Justice (formerly known as the Association of Trial Lawyers of America).

In addition to membership organizations, the definition also includes associations. Associations do not have individuals as members; rather, their members are composed of individual businesses, unions, or even other associations from the public and private spheres. The Texas Petroleum Marketers and Convenience Store Association, the Michigan Beer and Wine Wholesalers, and the Association of Washington Business are all examples of associations, which are also known as "peak associations."

Finally, under this broad definition of interest groups, enterprises—from corporate and family-owned banks to hospitals to insurance companies to colleges and universities—are also included. Enterprises are not membership-based and do not have individuals as members. Employees of an enterprise are usually not involved or even consulted when it pursues a policy or electoral outcome. Publicly traded corporations, for example, do not need to obtain shareholder approval before pursuing political and electoral goals. As such, an enterprise is permitted to support issues and candidates that may be at odds with the preferences of its employees or shareholders.

Madison's "The Federalist No. 10"

Interest groups are not new. Although the term did not become part of the political vernacular until the late 19th century, interest groups are rooted in the fabric of American political life and were heavily involved in the founding of the nation. Interest groups, or what Founder James Madison called "minority factions" in his classic essay "The Federalist No. 10" are inevitable in a free society. The causes of both majority and minority factions, Madison argued, are "sown into the nature of man." Although a "necessary evil," Madison realized that factions were essential to liberty. If citizens lacked the ability to form factions, they could potentially be tyrannized by government, squandering their fundamental liberties in the process. Madison's solution was to create an institutional framework of checks and balances to control the baneful effects of factions.[56]

Some scholars have been critical of Madison's solution, what political scientists often refer to as **pluralism**. Not all interests, they claim, can be organized, and some are structurally more advantaged than others. E. E. Schattschneider, for instance, argued that the pressure group system is limited to those groups that are private and that are organized. As a result, "The flaw in the pluralist heaven is that the heavenly chorus sings with a strong upper-class accent," in that the pluralist system has a **mobilization of bias** benefiting private, organized interests.[57] Because the distribution of interests participating in the interest group system is uneven and "far from isomorphic with the distribution of interests in society," for-profit and business organizations are likely to dominate.[58]

Interest Groups and Their Members

Why do people join interest groups, and how do they maintain themselves organizationally? Scholars have taken two very different approaches—one grounded in social dynamics and group theory and the other in microlevel economics—in an effort to gain some leverage on these questions.

How Do Interest Groups Form?

In the 1950s, David Truman advanced what has become known as **disturbance theory**.[59]

Focusing on macrolevel shifts that cause groups to emerge in response to a change in the status quo, Truman argued that voluntary associations would form naturally out of the desire of humans to satisfy their needs. Various interests, including even **potential interests**, would galvanize collectively, according to Truman, when their common interests were marginalized or threatened. When macrolevel societal or environmental disturbances in society occur—such as changes in demographic shifts, changes in the economy, advances in technology, or crises or societal disruptions, such as those resulting from plagues and disease, war, or even natural disasters like hurricanes or earthquakes—new patterns of interaction are created. With such occurrences, nascent groups will emerge in response to the change in the status quo. The resulting new groups help restore the larger "social equilibrium" of the interest group system. For Truman, it was rational for individuals to voluntarily join groups to further their own interests.

Barriers to Collective Action

Other social scientists were not so sure about the natural proclivity of individuals to voluntarily join groups. For some, disturbance theory seemed too easy. Problematizing the logic of collective action, economist Mancur Olson turned his attention to microlevel, transactional reasons why an individual may—or may not— choose to join a group. Olson began by tackling the **free-rider problem**; that is, the assumption that individuals will try to benefit from **public goods** without paying for them. Contra Truman, Olson contended that there are many costs associated with an individual joining a group. If given a choice, rational actors would

---

[56] James Madison, "The Federalist No. 10," 1788, http://www.constitution.org/fed/federa10.htm.

[57] E. E. Schattschneider, *The Semisovereign People* (New York: Holt, Rinehart & Winston, 1960).

[58] David Lowery and Virginia Gray, "Bias in the Heavenly Chorus: Interests in Society and before Government," *Journal of Theoretical Politics* 16 (2004): 5–30, 6.

[59] David Truman, *The Governmental Process* (New York: Alfred A. Knopf, 1951).

generally not join groups, choosing instead to benefit from the actions of the groups without bearing any of the attendant costs.[60]

Flipping many of the assumptions of pluralism on its head, Olson pointed out that individuals usually join groups for three reasons: peer pressure, coercion, or if they receive some type of **selective benefit**. By keeping itself small, a group can exert peer pressure on potential free-riders, embarrassing them to join the group. When small, it is easy for a group to determine who is benefiting from its actions without bearing the costs of membership. Individuals too have an easier way of calculating the costs and benefits of becoming a member when a group is small. People might also join groups when they are coerced to do so. For example, say you just graduated from law school and want to become a practicing attorney in the State of North Carolina. You first must pass the state bar exam. Once you do, you must pay annual dues to the North Carolina State Bar and complete mandatory continuing legal education course requirements every year.

For some, an important incentive to join a group is to receive a selective benefit that is only provided to members of the group. For example, some retirees join the American Association of Retired Persons (AARP) for the various benefits it provides to its 30 million–plus members, such as discounts on group health insurance, lower rates on hotels and car rentals, or price-reduced tickets to the theater and the movies. Like Truman's macrolevel perspective, Olson's rational choice microlevel framework does not provide a complete picture of group activity. Some people, of course, decide to join groups even if no overt peer pressure, coercion, or selective benefits exist. We do not necessarily think any worse of these people—call them altruistic—but Olson's rational choice framework sees them

largely as acting irrationally by not taking advantage of free-ridership.

Interest Group Techniques

In their concerted effort to represent their constituencies, interest groups use different tactics to shape public policies and elections. What do interest groups do, how do their techniques differ, and which groups are most active at the state and local levels? From classic insider techniques, such as lobbying policy makers, to outsider techniques, such as issue advocacy, electioneering, and litigation, interest groups are increasingly using multiple strategies to maximize their effectiveness.[61]

Although interest groups do not typically engage in every type of activity, there are many common patterns across the states and across interests. A 1990s study of some 301 state-level organizations surveyed in three states (California, South Carolina, and Wisconsin) revealed various insider and outsider techniques that groups use to shape public policy. Nearly all state-level interest organizations report using insider techniques, such as lobbying state legislators, testifying at legislative hearings, contacting government officials, helping to draft legislation, and meeting with government officials. Interest groups also use outsider tactics, including grassroots campaigns to mobilize supporters, letter-writing campaigns, and having influential constituents contact elected officials. Less than half report that they contribute money to candidates, and still fewer say they work on campaigns or endorse candidates. Two of every five organizations claim they use litigation as a strategy, but only one in five runs issue ads or engages in protest activities.[62] Although activities of interest

---

[60] Mancur Olson, *The Logic of Collective Action* (Cambridge, Mass.: Harvard University Press, 1965).

[61] Kay Lehman Schlozman and John Tierney, *Organized Interests and American Democracy* (New York: Harper & Row, 1986); Thomas Gais, *Improper Influence: Campaign Finance Law, Political Interest Groups, and the Problem of Equality* (Ann Arbor: University of Michigan Press, 1986); and Ken Kollman, *Outside Lobbying: Public Opinion and Interest Groups Strategies* (Princeton, N.J.: Princeton University Press, 1998).

[62] Anthony Nownes and Patricia Freeman, "Interest Group Activity in the States," *Journal of Politics* 60 (1998): 86–112.

groups operating at the local level are similar, because many community-based groups lack necessary resources, they tend to use more reactive—as opposed to proactive—strategies when trying to influence public policy.[63]

Lobbying

Lobbying is an integral part of the state and local policy-making process, as it is the systematic effort to influence public policy by pressuring governmental officials to make decisions that comport with the interests of the group pursuing the desired action. The advocacy community in every state capital now consists of hundreds or even thousands of people being paid to alter public policy. It should come as no surprise to you that lobbying is big business. In 2004, nearly $1 billion was spent on lobbying activities in the 42 states that require lobbying expenditure reports. In some states, lobbyists—not citizens—have become known sardonically as the "True Constituency."[64]

The growth of the lobbying industry is indicative of its importance. As one keen observer of state legislatures notes, "Any group that can be touched by state government cannot afford to be without representation. If groups do not realize the need for a lobbyist at the outset, they soon learn their lesson."[65] This was certainly the case regarding Native American tribes. Since the passage of the Indian Gaming Regulatory Act in 1988, which opened the way for casino-style gambling on tribal lands, the lobbying efforts of Indian tribes have skyrocketed, as they have used their newfound wealth to pursue traditional insider strategies.[66] As with other groups, the lobbying efforts of the tribes have helped ensure their collective voice is heard by state and local policy makers.

What Do Lobbyists Do? Lobbyists try to influence policy making by marshaling information and communicating it to policy makers.[67] Lobbyists regularly monitor pending legislation, communicating directly with policy makers and their staff about the potential substantive and political impacts of policy choices. Lobbyists need to know not only how but also when to communicate information and to whom. In addition to meeting with policy makers, lobbyists provide information to officials about issues and give testimony before committee hearings. In states with less professional legislatures, elected officials often do not have the resources to stay informed on every issue, so they take cues from lobbyists. Lobbyists even help draft legislation. Testimony provided by lobbyists, of course, is heavily biased, despite claims from the lobbying industry that they are simply providing impartial, objective information.

Types of Lobbyists Lobbying may be conducted by in-house, contract, government, or voluntary lobbyists. Roughly 40 percent of all the lobbying done in state capitals is conducted by **in-house lobbyists**, with individuals who are employees of a membership group, association, or institution representing their own organization. The Kentucky Distillers' Association, the Montana Mining Association, the Texas Association of Business, the California Nations Indian Gaming Association, the Iowa Corn Growers Association, and the Nevada State AFL-CIO all use in-house lobbyists to maintain a foot in the doors of state lawmakers and policy makers. According to one survey of interest

[63] Christopher Cooper and Anthony Nownes, "Citizen Groups in Big City Politics," *State and Local Government Review* 35 (2003): 102–11.

[64] Martin Dyckman, "It's Fla. Voters vs. the True Constituency," *St. Petersburg (Fla.) Times*, 3 April 2005.

[65] Alan Rosenthal, *The Third House: Lobbyists and Lobbying in the States* (Washington, D.C.: CQ Press, 1993), 5.

[66] Richard Witmer and Fredrick Boehmke, "American Indian Political Incorporation in the Post–Indian Gaming Regulatory Act Era," *Social Science Journal* 44 (2007): 127–45.

[67] Anthony Nownes, *Pressure and Power: Organized Interests in American Politics* (Boston: Houghton Mifflin, 2001).

Lobbyists and lawmakers crowd "The Rail" outside the Illinois House of Representatives chambers at the Illinois State Capitol in Springfield. While angry citizens were pleading for legislative help in 2007 because of soaring electric rates, dozens of lobbyists, many with key connections to decision makers, worked with Ameren and ComEd to fight a rate rollback and freeze.

group activity in the states, roughly 75 percent of in-house lobbyists are male.[68]

In contrast, **contract lobbyists** work either independently or for a lobbying firm. They typically work for multiple clients and charge their clients an hourly fee. Many contract lobbyists—who are predominantly male—are former legislators, elected or appointed state officials, or staff. Contract lobbyist extraordinaire Frank L. "Pancho" Hays (who sold his Colorado lobbying firm Hays Hays and Wilson in 2003 but remains a registered lobbyist) was legendary in Denver for his self-effacing, ever-professional demeanor. The son of a former lieutenant governor, Hays represented business interests as diverse as the Denver Broncos professional football team,

tobacco giant Philip Morris, the Wine and Spirits Wholesalers of Colorado, Colorado Ski Country USA, the Colorado Association of Realtors, and the Cherry Creek School District. Roughly 20 percent of the lobbying corps in state capitals is composed of contract lobbyists, depending on the professionalization of the state legislature.[69]

Lobbying done by government employees, who are sometimes referred to euphemistically as governmental relations personnel or legislative liaisons, is also quite common. Roughly 30 percent of all lobbyists in the states are government lobbyists, a figure that is difficult to exactly determine, as many states do not require government personnel to register when they lobby. Municipal, county,

[68] Clive Thomas and Ronald Hrebenar, "Interest Groups in the States," in Gray and Hanson, *Politics in the American States.*

[69] Nownes and Freeman, "Interest Group Activity in the States."

Photo by AP Photo/Seth Perlman

and regional governments as well as special districts, fire and police forces, and municipal and county hospitals and agencies all have business before the state.[70]

Finally, about 10 percent of state lobbying communities are composed of individuals who give their time and expertise without compensation.[71] These individuals are known as volunteers or, in some instances, as "hobbyists." Volunteer lobbyists tend to assist public interest groups—retirees helping out the League of Women Voters of Ohio or the Gray Panthers of Metro Detroit, college students interning with Colorado Common Cause or the Georgia Public Interest Research Group (GeorgiaPIRG), and high school students earning civic education credit by putting in ten hours a week working with Arizona Rock the Vote or a Maine chapter of Mothers Against Drunk Driving.[72]

The Rise of the Statehouse Lobbying Corps In the 1980s, the number of firms and individuals registered to lobby state governments skyrocketed. By 1990, the average number of interest groups in a state registered to lobby a state legislature was 587, up from an average of only 196 in 1975. The total number of registered lobbyists also increased exponentially over the time period. In 1990, there were nearly 29,352 lobbyists registered in the 50 states, up from just 15,064 in 1980. Since that time, the number of groups registered to lobby and the number of lobbyists in the states has continued to grow. In 1999, there were just under a total of 37,000 registered lobbyists; by 2006, there were more than 42,000.[73]

Today, state lawmakers are outnumbered by lobbyists on average by a ratio of five to one. In New York, there are nearly 4,000 lobbyists registered in Albany, enough for each lawmaker to have 18 lobbyists of his or her own. There are more than ten registered lobbyists for each lawmaker in Arizona, Colorado, Florida, Illinois, and Ohio. In contrast, only two states, Maine and New Hampshire, have more lawmakers than registered lobbyists.[74] Although the "old bulls"—large corporations—still tend to dominate the lobbying corps in state legislatures, much turnover occurs in the corridors of state capitols. The annual turnover of registered lobbyists working for businesses is actually higher than it is for those working for membership groups and associations.[75]

Regulating Lobbyists State ethics laws and registration requirements for lobbyists have been on the books for years.[76] New York instituted the first comprehensive governmental ethics law in 1954. Since that time, states have passed a patchwork of ethics legislation, resulting in a "Byzantine array of public integrity rules and regulations that vary tremendously from state to state."[77] As Figure 5.7 reveals, 12 states regulate only legislative lobbying, 20 regulate the lobbying of both legislative and executive officials, and 18 regulate the lobbying of all government officials.

Every state requires lobbyists to register with a state regulatory agency or the state legislature, although limitations and disclosure requirements on lobbying activities vary

---

[70] Thomas and Hrebenar, "Interest Groups in the States."

[71] Nownes and Freeman, "Interest Group Activity in the States."

[72] Center for Lobbying in the Public Interest, "Ten Immutable Paradoxes of Public Interest Lobbying," http://clpi.org/tips_facts.html#.

[73] Jennifer Anderson et al., "Mayflies and Old Bulls: Organization Persistence in State Interest Communities," *State Politics and Policy Quarterly* 4 (2004): 140–60; National Institute on Money in State Politics, "Lobbyist Link," http://www.followthemoney .org/database/graphs/lobbyistlink/.

[74] John Broder, "Amid Scandals, States Overhaul Lobbying Laws," *New York Times*, 24 January 2006.

[75] Anderson et al., "Mayflies and Old Bulls."

[76] Rosenthal, *The Third House*; and Beth Rosenson, "Against Their Apparent Self-Interest: The Authorization of Independent State Legislative Ethics Commissions, 1973–1996," *State Politics and Policy Quarterly* 3 (2003): 42–66.

[77] Peggy Kerns and Ginger Sampson, "Do Ethics Laws Work?" *State Legislatures*, July–August 2003, 40–43.

Figure 5.7

State Lobbying Laws

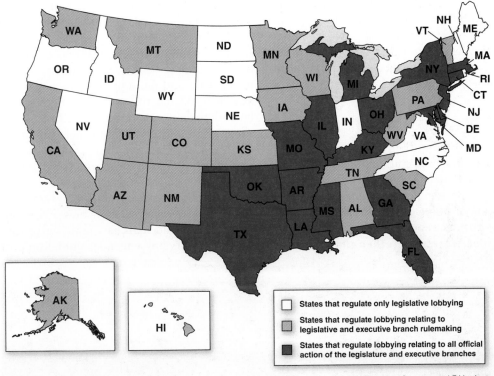

Source: Council on Governmental Ethics Laws

Source: State Legislatures, April 2005, http://www.ncsl.org/programs/pubs/slmag/2005/05SLApr_TandT.pdf.

considerably. According to one scholarly composite index of state lobbying regulations, South Carolina had the toughest laws in 2003, followed by Arkansas, Maine, Texas, Washington, California, and Kentucky. North Dakota had by far the most lax lobbying requirements of any state in 2003, although Wyoming, Virginia, Oklahoma, North Carolina, Illinois, and Arizona were not too far behind. The stringency of South Carolina's laws increased dramatically in the early 1990s. In 1990, its lobbying laws had been among the least restrictive of any state. Kentucky also increased from one of the lower tiers of regulation to the top. On the other hand, Virginia, and to a lesser degree Indiana, which in the early 1990s had some of the most rigorous lobbying restrictions, now rank near the bottom of the index.[78]

The relative effectiveness of lobbyists is conditioned by institutional constraints existing within a state. State lobbying restrictions on gifts to lawmakers and prohibitions on campaign finance activities by lobbyists can diminish the clout of lobbyists. Term limits on state legislators can affect the behavior and relative influence of lobbyists.[79] Term limits tend to weaken the long-standing ties and social networks that lobbyists work tirelessly to cultivate over time with government officials.

---

[78] Adam Newmark, "Measuring State Legislative Lobbying Regulation," *State Politics and Policy Quarterly* 5 (2005): 182–91.

[79] John Carey, Richard Niemi, and Lynda Powell, *Term Limits in State Legislatures* (Ann Arbor: University of Michigan Press, 2000); and Marjorie Sarbaugh-Thompson et al., *The Political and Institutional Effects of Term Limits* (New York: Palgrave Macmillan, 2004).

Studies have shown that states with term limits have more lobbyists who report having to work harder to do their jobs. Yet, term-limited states also have worse ethical behavior among lobbyists, which might be tied to lobbyists in these term-limited states wielding more influence in the legislative process than they do in states where incumbents may keep their office interminably.[80]

Issue Advocacy

Rather than having their lobbyists directly press lawmakers and public officials to take action that benefits their members, some interest groups use indirect tactics to influence the making of public policy. Although fewer interest groups report regularly engaging in outsider strategies rather than insider strategies, many groups do engage in issue advocacy. **Issue advocacy** is a form of political speech that mentions issues and the positions taken on those issues by elected officials or candidates but stops short of expressly advocating the support or defeat of those elected officials or candidates. Issue ads themselves may be articulated in any type of media—TV and radio broadcasts, newspaper ads, billboards, placards, banners strung behind airplanes, handbills, and fliers—with some costing millions and others just a few dollars. Each state regulates issue advocacy differently, although most take cues from the federal government's regulations.

Interest groups may employ several issue advocacy strategies, including boycotts, sit-ins, mass rallies, and marches, which give their issues visibility and engender public support.

Photo by Sacramento Bee/Brian Baer, http://www.sacbee.com/content/politics/story/12956253p-13803679c.html.

Union members protesting Governor Arnold Schwarzenegger's budget cut, in Sacramento, California, 2005.

[80] Christopher Mooney, "The Impact of State Legislative Term Limits on Lobbyists and Interest Groups" (paper presented at the Fifth Annual State Politics and Policy Conference, East Lansing, Mich., May 2005).

In May 2005, for instance, over 10,000 protestors congregated on the steps of the California state capitol building in Sacramento, donning T-shirts, carrying placards, and shouting the slogan "Schwarzenegger's got to go." With busloads of teachers, nurses, firefighters, prison guards, machinists, and hotel and service workers blanketing the capitol grounds, the protestors wanted to send Republican governor Arnold Schwarzenegger a clear message "that there are a lot of people who are really concerned about what he is doing to the state," as one elementary school teacher put it to a reporter. More specifically, the Alliance for a Better California, a coalition of unions, protested the governor's budget and proposed ballot measures, which included severe cuts in public education and health care and efforts to diminish the power of public sector unions.[81]

Other groups, most notably liberal- and conservative-leaning public interest groups and labor unions, provide their members (and the broader general public) with information about incumbents and candidates running for office. These educational efforts—the groups do not actually endorse candidates—are nevertheless quite political. Some groups produce scorecards reporting the voting records of incumbents. For example, New Yorkers against Gun Violence is a nonprofit advocacy group that publicizes the destructive effects of gun violence in New York and advocates gun legislation. The group regularly compiles and distributes a legislative voting scorecard detailing whether members of the legislature supported or opposed key bills dealing with guns.

Electioneering

Interest groups not only try to shape the public policy debate through their lobbying and issue advocacy. Organized interests can also actively participate in the electoral

process in a variety of ways. Many become engaged in candidate campaigns in an effort to influence who will be elected and thus have a hand in making public policy. The practice of explicitly supporting candidates or political parties is known as **electioneering**. Working on campaigns or financing candidates and parties helps to solidify the relationships that interest groups have with winning candidates and the parties in control of the state legislatures. Not all electioneering comes in the form of financial contributions. Some interest groups provide candidates and political parties with nonmonetary, in-kind contributions. Such contributions include sharing data from public opinion polls, giving out membership lists for fundraising, and lending staff and field operations for support during the campaign. Other groups will publicly endorse their support or opposition for candidates. Of course, many groups give monetary contributions directly to candidates and political parties. For these groups, state laws vary considerably with regard to what kinds of contributions they are permitted to give, how much they may give, and to whom they may give.

Regulating Campaign Contributions

Rulings by the U.S. Supreme Court have consistently struck down federal and state laws banning or limiting expenditures by interest groups that are made independently of candidates and parties, which are known as "independent expenditures." However, the Court has given wide latitude to state legislatures to regulate and limit the amount of money that interest groups may give directly to candidates and political parties.[82] Countless municipal and county governments, and all but 13 states, have passed laws that place restrictions on the amount of campaign contributions that can be made by interest

---

[81] Alexa Bluth, "Thousands Protest Governor's Plans," *Sacramento Bee*, 26 May 2005, http://www.sacbee.com/content/politics/v-pring/story/1295653p-13803679c.html.

[82] *Nixon v. Shrink Missouri Government PAC* (2000); but see the Supreme Court's decision *Vermont Republican State Committee, et al. v. William Sorrell, et al.* (2006) for limits on expenditures and how low states can regulate contributions to candidates.

groups to candidates and political parties. The effort by states to limit spending in candidate campaigns has largely stemmed from the perception that special interests—predominantly corporations and business associations—have had undue influence in candidate races.

Similar to the regulation of elections, there exists a tremendous amount of variation across the states in the amount of regulation in the campaign finance activities of interest groups. Nineteen states prohibit corporations from making contributions to state parties and candidates from their general treasuries; another dozen states ban unions from contributing to campaigns using their general treasury funds. Eighteen states permit state parties to receive unlimited contributions from political action committees (PACs), legal entities that allow like-minded individuals who belong to a corporation, labor union, or virtually any other organization to pool their money and contribute directly to candidates and political parties. Thirteen states allow interest groups to give directly from their corporate or union treasuries to candidates. Eleven states, including Florida, Illinois, and Virginia, permit any type of interest group to make unlimited contributions to state political parties.[83]

PAC Contributions PAC contributions made to candidates running for office depend largely on the type and ideology of the interest group that controls the PAC. Some interest groups give according to their principles; others have more pragmatic giving patterns. Liberal PACs affiliated with local and state chapters of unions such as the Service Employees International Union and the American Federation of Teachers as well as pro-choice groups, such as NARAL and Planned Parenthood, give nearly all their contributions to Democrats. Conservative PACs

affiliated with single issues, such as the National Rifle Association (NRA) and state affiliates of the National Right to Life, give nearly exclusively to Republicans. In contrast, many corporate-controlled PACs are equal-opportunity givers, writing checks to both Republican and Democratic candidates—as long as they are incumbents. Rather than ideology, these pragmatic PACs use their campaign donations as a means to purchase continued access to lawmakers and policy makers. According to one study, the energy industry—primarily oil and gas companies and their peak associations—pumped more than $134.7 million into candidate committees and state parties between 1990 and 2004. Nearly 70 percent of those contributions went to incumbents, irrespective of their political party.[84]

In the 2006 election cycle, state-level candidates (running for governor, legislatures, and state supreme courts) raised over $2.3 billion for their campaigns, much of it coming from special interest groups through their PACs. The combined financial, insurance, and real estate sector gave the most to state legislative candidates, contributing more than $70 million (with roughly $43 million going to Republican candidates). The health sector contributed more than $50 million to both parties, with Republicans getting a slightly larger share. Organized labor and interest groups representing trial lawyers each gave more than $50 million to state-level candidates, with most of it going to Democrats. Single-issue groups, which usually are more ideological, contributed slightly more than $10 million to candidates, with Democrats receiving the lion's share.[85]

Money, it is often said, is like water. It is hydraulic, leveling itself and circumventing any barriers placed in its way. It can swamp the democratic process. A survey conducted in

---

[83] Edward Feigenbaum and James Palmer, *Campaign Finance Law 2002* (Washington, D.C.: Federal Election Commission, 2003).

[84] Edwin Bender, "Energy Companies Build Power Base in Statehouses," Institute on Money in State Politics, http://www.followthemoney.org/press/Reports/200410061.pdf.

[85] National Institute on Money in State Politics, "State Elections Overview, 2006."

2002 of some 1,300 interest groups operating in 38 states found that state contribution limits affect the contribution strategies that groups make. States with laws severely restricting interest group contributions to candidates tend to increase groups' spending in other electioneering areas. Interest groups operating in those states tend to increase their expenditures on issue advertising and independent expenditures in candidate elections.[86]

Litigation

Some interest groups turn their attention to state and federal courts when doing battle. As interpreters of laws and constitutions, courts are important venues for interest groups if they have been stymied by policy makers or administrators charged with implementing a law. One survey of state organizations finds that roughly half of all interest groups report that they either often or sometimes use litigation, or legal action, as a tactic.[87] For some groups, a lawsuit may be easier, less expensive, and more effective than paying lobbyists to advance their cause through the

legislative process. This might be especially true for groups with small memberships, little political influence in the state or community, or less than stellar reputations.

When pursuing a litigation strategy, interest groups tend to use one of two tactics. Some groups will seek out laws that they view as unconstitutional and file what is known as a "test case" on behalf of an aggrieved individual. One of the best-known test cases is *Brown v. Board of Education of Topeka* (1954). The National Association for the Advancement of Colored People (NAACP) had filed a suit on behalf of the parents of an eight-year-old elementary student, Linda Brown, who was forced to attend an all-black school in Kansas even though an all-white elementary school was only a few blocks from her home. In 1954, the U.S. Supreme Court struck down the practice of racial segregation in public schools ("separate but equal"). The court ruled that the 14th Amendment of the U.S. Constitution prohibited states from denying equal protection of the laws to persons within their jurisdiction.[88] Following the success of *Brown*, many other liberal organizations turned to the courts in the 1950s and 1960s, as many judges were seen as more progressive on social issues than were many state and local governments. In addition to civil rights associations like the NAACP, consumer rights advocacy organizations, women's and pro-choice groups, and environmental organizations all used lawsuits—especially pursued in federal courts—to advance their causes.

Beginning in the 1970s, many conservative groups started pushing lawsuits to advance their agendas, in part because they had more sympathizers sitting on the federal and state benches. The increase in litigation by interest groups has been well documented: between 1953 and 1993, the number of U.S. Supreme Court cases drawing interest group attention

New York World-Telegram and the Sun Newspaper Photograph Collection, Library of Congress Prints and Photographs Division, Washington D.C. [LC-US262-123956]

Lawyers for the NAACP (Thurgood Marshall, center) confer at the U.S. Supreme Court prior to oral arguments for *Brown v. Board of Education* (1954).

[86] Robert Hogan, "State Campaign Finance Laws and Interest Group Electioneering Activities," *Journal of Politics* 67 (2005): 887–906.

[87] Nownes and Freeman, "Interest Group Activity in the States."

[88] *Brown v. Board of Education of Topeka*, 347 U.S. 483 (1954).

increased from just 13 percent to 92 percent of all cases.[89] When an interest group is not an immediate party in a lawsuit, its lawyers may choose to file an amicus curiae brief (amicus curiae is Latin for "friend of the court"). These written briefs, which are usually filed on appeal of a case in either state or federal court, offer supplemental legal arguments that attempt to influence the reasoning of the court. Although not always prevailing, lawsuits can deliver results for interest groups that are otherwise unattainable in other political arenas.[90]

The Dynamics of State Interest Group Systems

How do state interest group systems evolve over time, how are they comparatively different from one another, and which groups tend to hold the upper hand in a state's system? As studies on the dynamics of state interest group systems make evident, the concern voiced by critics of pluralist theory—that the system is biased in favor of economic interests—appears to be supported by empirical data.

The Advocacy Explosion

Paralleling the trend in Washington, D.C., the number and types of interest groups in the American states greatly expanded during the 1960s and 1970s.[91] The rise of public interest groups in the American states and communities was not limited to newfangled nonprofit public interest groups pushing postmaterialist values. The rise of liberal-leaning citizen groups in the 1960s and 1970s helped to fuel a conservative backlash.

During the 1970s and 1980s, conservative public interest groups, such as the Eagle Forum, with over 30 state chapters; National Right to Life; and the Christian Coalition established themselves as key political actors in many states. As countervailing forces, these groups continue to serve as foils to the liberal groups that emerged out of the social changes begotten from the 1960s.

There was a simultaneous backlash in the business community. In response to the strengthened public interest lobby as well as to the prowess of organized labor, which had reached its zenith of influence in the 1950s, businesses began forming their own peak associations.[92] Today, corporate interests dominate the universe of state interest group systems. According to the most recent survey of interest groups registered in the states, enterprises comprise nearly three-fifths of all registered groups, with associations accounting for an additional 22 percent. Membership-based groups only account for 19 percent of all registered interest groups, down from 31 percent of all groups in 1980.[93]

The number of professional associations registered in the states, particularly ones representing business and trade interests, also rose in the 1970s and 1980s. The sharp rise was fueled in part by the surge in the number of white-collar jobs and women entering the workforce. By one count, the number of professional associations nationally increased from just 6,500 national organizations in 1958 to more than 23,000 by 1990.[94] Whereas some of these professional associations are well-established and have active chapters in the states, others such as the Montana Bed and Breakfast Association, the Mid-Atlantic

[89] Andrew Koshner, *Solving the Puzzle of Interest Group Litigation* (Westport, Conn.: Greenwood Press, 1998).

[90] Donald R. Songer and Ashlyn Kuersten, "The Success of Amici in State Supreme Courts," *Political Research Quarterly* 48 (1995): 31–42; Melinda Gann Hall, "Constituent Influence in State Supreme Courts: Conceptual Notes and a Case Study," *Journal of Politics* 49 (1987): 1117–24; and Lee Epstein and C. K. Rowland, "Debunking the Myth of Interest Group Invincibility in the Courts," *American Political Science Review* 58 (1991): 206–17.

[91] Nownes, *Pressure and Power*.

[92] Jeffrey Berry, *The Interest Group Society*, 3rd ed. (New York: Longman, 1997).

[93] Anderson et al., "Mayflies and Old Bulls."

[94] Theda Skocpol, Marshall Ganz, and Ziad Munson, "A Nation of Organizers: The Institutional Origins of Civic Voluntarism in the United States," *American Political Science Review* 94 (2000): 527–46.

Alpaca Association, and the Oregon State Beekeeper's Association are relatively new.

Density and Diversity of State Interest Group Systems

The explosion of interest groups has not been consistent across all states, policy domains, or types of interests represented in a state's interest group system. The states have considerable variation in terms of the composition of interest groups. Interest group power, in turn, is not distributed evenly across the systems. So, why are state interest group systems different from one another?

Following the pluralist logic that groups emerge when a disturbance in the status quo occurs, the number and types of interest groups will grow as a society becomes more complex. There are considerable differences in the size, strength, and dynamics of state economies. As a state's economy grows, so does the number of interest groups operating in that state.[95] States with the largest economies invariably have the most interest groups. In 1997, for instance, Texas and California both had over 2,000 interest groups with registered lobbyists, Illinois had over 1,500, and Pennsylvania, Minnesota, New York, Ohio, Missouri, Florida, Michigan, and Massachusetts all had more than 1,000. At the other end of the spectrum, five states— Rhode Island, Wyoming, New Hampshire, Delaware, and Hawaii—all had less than 300 interest groups with registered lobbyists.

As competition for resources among registered organizations in the states increases, however, interest group systems gradually become denser and the expansion rate of

the system slows down.[96] A state's **interest group system density** refers to the number of functioning groups relative to the size of the state's economy. Wealthier states tend to have more interest groups, in part because governments are able to attract new businesses by increasing their expenditures. In states with fairly dense interest group systems, the relative power of each group is lessened. A state's **interest group system diversity**, in contrast, refers to the spread of groups across various social and economic realms. Interest group diversity is positively related to a state's economic diversity.[97]

There is a tremendous amount of diversity in terms of the kinds of interest groups that have representation in a given state. In some states, such as New Mexico, California, Montana, and Wyoming, nearly one out of every three interest groups with a registered lobbyist is a nonprofit organization. In New Jersey, by way of contrast, only 14 percent of all groups are in the nonprofit sector. The Dakotas, followed closely by Montana, lead the way with the highest percentage of membership organizations, with roughly 30 percent of their interest group systems composed of groups with individuals as members. Less than 14 percent of all groups are membership-based in Pennsylvania and New Jersey, with Texas having the fewest, at only 11.7 percent. Texas is the state with the highest percentage (71.5 percent) of interest groups that are enterprises; in Wisconsin, less than 40 percent of all groups with a registered lobbyist are enterprises. At 31.6 percent, North Carolina has the highest percentage of associations, with Idaho a close second; the percentage in Utah, by contrast, is roughly half that amount.

---

[95] David Lowery and Virginia Gray, "The Density of State Interest Group Systems," *Journal of Politics* 55 (1993): 191–206.

[96] Virginia Gray and David Lowery, *The Population Ecology of Interest Representation: Lobbying Communities in the American States* (Ann Arbor: University of Michigan Press, 1996).

[97] Virginia Gray and David Lowery, "The Expression of Density Dependence in State Communities of Organized Interests," *American Politics Research* 29 (2001): 374–91; and Virginia Gray and David Lowery, "The Institutionalization of State Communities of Organized Interests," *Political Research Quarterly* 54 (2001): 265–84.

Several factors seem to contribute to the density and diversity of a state's interest group system. States with more competition among the parties also tend to have denser interest group systems, as the lack of single-party rule perhaps exacerbates policy uncertainty and, thus, more intergroup competition. The legislatures of states with denser interest group systems tend to be less productive, as measured by the proportion of all bills introduced that are passed. Interestingly, states that have the initiative process also tend to have an increased number and a greater diversity of active interest groups. One study finds that states that allow the initiative process had on average 17 percent more interest groups between 1975 and 1990, after controlling for other factors that might lead to interest group growth, than states without the process.[98] A parallel study finds that actual initiative use by a state leads to a general increase in the number of membership groups, associations, and not-for-profit organizations that have registered lobbyists in the state, indicating that the institution of direct democracy can increase the aggregate size as well as the diversity of state-level interest groups.[99] Finally, states with more diverse interest group systems tend to adopt public policies that are more distributive and progressive.[100]

In states with dense and diverse interest group systems, it is difficult for a single interest to dictate the overall policy agenda of state government. But even in these states with more diversified economies, interest groups are often able to carve space for themselves within a policy domain that is central to their policy objectives, where they become a dominant force. The number of participants in these policy niches tends to be limited in scope, with the vested interests holding considerable influence. In ensuring its survival, a successful interest group is able to stake out its own niche within a given policy domain.

Interest Group Competition: Who's Got Clout?

Today, most states and many communities have much more diversified economies than they did a half century ago. This economic change has led to a robust competition among a variety of private and public sector interest groups that battle over the making of public policy. Yet, private economic interests tend to dominate interest group systems. For example, the oil industry remains king in Alaska and Louisiana, the agriculture lobby reins supreme in Iowa and South Dakota, ranching interests continue to be a strong force in Nebraska, and the tourism industry holds an upper hand in Florida, Nevada, and Hawaii. Although the company town, communities literally built by firms to house their employees, disappeared from the local landscape long ago,[101] some towns—Bentonville, Arkansas, the corporate headquarters of Wal-Mart, comes to mind—are still dominated by a single industry.

An interest group's clout, or relative influence, is largely determined by its own internal resources, but it is bounded by external conditions. Internal resources include a group's political, organizational, and managerial skills as well as its finances, the size and geographical distribution of its membership, its political cohesiveness, and its long-term relations with public officials. A group's policy goals are also conditioned by external factors, such as the political climate of the state or community, including partisan identification, political culture, issues and events, and public opinion. Although it is difficult, if not impossible, to precisely measure a group's "clout," these internal and external factors affect the ability of an interest organization to wield influence and power within a state or community.

[98] Frederick Boehmke, "The Effect of Direct Democracy on the Size and Diversity of State Interest Group Populations," *Journal of Politics* 64 (2002): 827–44.

[99] Daniel Smith and Caroline Tolbert, *Educated by Initiative: The Effects of Direct Democracy on Citizens and Political Organizations in the American States* (Ann Arbor: University of Michigan Press, 2004).

[100] Sarah Morehouse and Malcolm Jewell, *State Politics, Parties and Policy*, 2nd ed. (New York: Rowman & Littlefield, 2003).

[101] John Gaventa, *Power and Powerlessness: Quiescence and Rebellion in an Appalachian Valley* (Champaign-Urbana: University of Illinois Press, 1980).

When lacking in clout, some groups opt to team up with other organizations to build coalitions. Rather than acting independently and going it alone, it sometimes makes strategic sense for an organization to form alliances with other like-minded groups, especially if competition increases among groups in the system.[102]

Most Influential Interests in the 50 States

Is it possible to rank the most powerful interests in the 50 states? Drawing on data collected by researchers in all 50 states, Table 5.1 categorizes interest organizations by their effectiveness, listing the 20 most influential interests in the states in 2002 (with comparison rankings from 1985). The table reveals how some sectors of interest organizations are influential interests across many states, whereas others are only effective in a few states. General business organizations, most notably the Chamber of Commerce, and teachers' associations, such as the American Federation of Teachers and the National Education Association, are powerful interest groups in all 50 states today, just as they were in 1985. Interest groups representing energy utilities, insurance companies, hospitals, lawyers, and manufacturers are also forces to be reckoned with in most states. Although liquor, wine, and beer interests are not nearly as powerful, they have a presence in all 50 states. The brewer Anheuser-Busch, for instance, maintains active lobbies in all the states because alcohol policy is largely regulated by the states. On the other hand, groups representing senior citizens, forest products, mining companies, and tobacco companies have a strong presence in only a handful of states.

Overall, the relative power of interest groups across the 50 states has remained fairly constant over time. Column 1 of Table 5.1 reveals little change between 1985 and 2002 regarding their relative strengths and weaknesses. In addition to the aforementioned economic interests, groups representing physicians, general farm organizations, and realtors have retained their strength through the years. Although minimal, some change has occurred across some of the sectors: hospital and nursing home associations, the insurance industry, gaming, and hunting and fishing interests have all become relatively stronger (including the venerable NRA), whereas energy corporations and their associations, banks, and other financial enterprises have become weaker players.

Despite some flux in the relative strength of the different sectors represented in state interest group systems, economic groups remain powerful players in most states, just as they were back in the 1950s when the first survey of interest groups was conducted.[103] This has led some observers to ask whether a corporate bias in the interest group systems of the states exists. One recent study—which finds that 77 percent of the total universe of state interest groups is made up of for-profit organizations—seems to confirm Schattschneider's prediction that private interest organizations will dominate the interest group system.[104] Yet, the dominance of business interests is not hegemonic. Business interests do not control all policy niches. As state economies increase in size, business interests tend to fragment to some degree.[105] As interest group systems become more and more crowded and complex, it is possible that powerful groups—including business associations and firms—may lose their "clout."[106]

Relative Impact of Interest Groups

Interest group strength can also be measured with a

[102] Clive Thomas and Ron Hrebenar, "Who's Got Clout?" *State Legislatures*, April 1999, 30–34; Kevin Hula, *Lobbying Together: Interest Group Coalitions in Legislative Politics* (Washington, D.C.: Georgetown University Press, 1999); and Michael T. Heaney, "Outside the Issue Niche: The Multidimensionality of Interest Group Identity," *American Politics Research* 32 (2004): 1–41.

[103] Belle Zeller, *American State Legislatures*, 2nd ed. (New York: Thomas Y. Crowell, 1954).

[104] Anderson et al., "Mayflies and Old Bulls."

[105] Lowery and Gray, "Bias in the Heavenly Chorus."

[106] Schattschneider, *The Semisovereign People*; and Schlozman and Tierney, *Organized Interests and American Democracy*.

Table 5.1

The 20 Most Influential Interests in the 50 States (2002 and 1985)

2002 Ranking (1985 Ranking)	Interest Organization	Number of States in Which Interest Ranked Among		
		Most Effective	Some What Effective	Less or Not Effective
1 (2)	General business organizations (state chambers of commerce, etc.)	40	12	5
2 (1)	Schoolteachers' organizations (NEA and AFT)	37	12	2
3 (6)	Utility companies and associations (electric, gas, water, and telephone/telecommunications)	24	26	6
4 (13)	Insurance: general and medical (companies and associations)	21	19	15
5 (17)	Hospital and nursing homes associations	21	18	13
6 (8)	Lawyers (predominantly trial lawyers and state bar associations)	22	15	15
7 (4)	Manufacturers (companies and associations)	18	20	19
8 (9)	General local government organizations (municipal leagues, county organizations, and elected officials)	18	17	17
9 (11)	Physicians and state medical associations	17	16	19
10 (10)	General farm organizations (state farm bureaus, etc.)	16	16	18
11 (3)	Bankers' associations	15	15	22
12 (5)	Traditional labor associations (predominantly the AFL-CIO)	13	16	22
13 (19)	Universities and colleges (institutions and employees)	13	13	26
14 (12)	State and local government employees (other than teachers)	11	15	26
15 (22)	Contractors, builders, and developers	13	11	26
16 (14)	Realtors' associations	13	10	27
17 (16)	K–12 education interests (other than teachers)	9	12	29
18 (15)	Individual traditional labor unions (Teamsters, UAW, and other unions)	8	14	29
19 (27)	Truckers and private transport interests (excluding railroads)	9	11	31
20 (35)	Sportsmen and hunting and fishing groups (including anti–gun control groups)	9	10	32

Source: Clive Thomas and Ronald Hrebenar, "Interest Groups in the States," in *Politics in the American States*, 8th ed., ed. Virginia Gray and Russell Hanson (Washington, D.C.: CQ Press, 2004).

fivefold typology that assesses the overall impact of interest groups relative to other actors (most notably political parties) in a state's political system. Last updated in 2002, a survey of the 50 states reveals that the power of interest groups compared to that of other actors can be considered dominant in seven states, dominant-complementary in 21 states, complementary in 17 states, complementary-subordinate in five states, and subordinate in no states.[107] Table 5.2 provides the overall impact of interest

groups in the 50 states. Slightly less than half of the states today are categorized as dominant-complementary. Why are interest group systems in some states more dominant than in others? Although it's difficult to precisely answer this question, states with less robust economies tend to have political systems with more dominant interest groups. Conversely, states with larger economies tend to have interest groups that are weaker or more complementary relative to other actors, such as parties.[108]

Table 5.2

Classification of the Overall Impact of Interest Groups, 2002

Dominant	Dominant-Complementary	Complementary	Complementary-Subordinate
Alabama	Arkansas	Colorado	Delaware
Florida	Arizona	Connecticut	Minnesota
Louisiana	Alaska	Indiana	Rhode Island
New Mexico	California	Maine	South Dakota
Nevada	Georgia	Maryland	Vermont
South Carolina	Hawaii	Massachusetts	
West Virginia	Idaho	Michigan	
	Illinois	Missouri	
	Iowa	New Hampshire	
	Kansas	New Jersey	
	Kentucky	New York	
	Mississippi	North Carolina	
	Montana	North Dakota	
	Nebraska	Pennsylvania	
	Ohio	Utah	
	Oklahoma	Washington	
	Oregon	Wisconsin	
	Tennessee		
	Texas		
	Virginia		
	Wyoming		

Source: Clive Thomas and Ronald Hrebenar, "Interest Groups in the States," in *Politics in the American States*, 8th ed., ed. Virginia Gray and Russell Hanson (Washington, D.C.: CQ Press, 2004).

[107] John Heinz et al., *The Hollow Core* (Cambridge, Mass.: Harvard University Press, 1993); and Thomas and Hrebenar, "Interest Groups in the States."

[108] Heinz et al., *The Hollow Core*; and Mark Smith, *American Business and Political Power* (Chicago: University of Chicago Press, 2000).

Summary

Political parties and interest groups hold different levels of power in states and localities, and these levels can vary over time. Sometimes, interest groups are subservient to parties; at other times, the relationship appears to be reversed. Regardless of whether they are understood as responsible or functional organizations, the two major political parties are essential players in state and local politics. Parties help to structure the electoral and governing environments in states, which in turn affect the parties. The partisan identification and political ideology of a state's electorate, which are not always synonymous, help to shape the organization and the governance strategies of the parties. Furthermore, the strength of state parties is ever-shifting in terms of their electoral, organizational, and governance strength, with considerable differences across the states. Like parties, interest groups are political institutions that operate as rational actors. Some employ lobbyists to place pressure on public officials. Others use issue advocacy, electioneering, and litigation to advance their collective goals. Whatever their tactic, interest groups are constantly fighting to shape the political terrain, molding it to reflect their image. Because economic and political resources are not distributed evenly across society, some interests are more easily articulated and aggregated than others. As such, not all societal interests are equally represented in states and communities by organized interests, nor are they all heard by elected officials and policy makers.

Key Terms

Caucus

Closed primary

Contract lobbyist

Direct primary

Disturbance theory

Electioneering

Free-rider problem

Functional party model

In-house lobbyist

Interest group system density

Interest group system diversity

Issue advocacy

Lobbying

Mobilization of bias

Nonpartisan blanket primary

Office-block ballot

Open primary

Party boss

Party-column ballot

Party fusion

Party identification

Pluralism

Political action committee (PAC)

Potential interest

Public good

Responsible party model

Selective benefit

Semiclosed primary

Semiopen primary

Top-two blanket primary

Watchdog

6

State Legislatures

INTRODUCTION

State legislatures provide a vital link between a state's citizens and its government—they are the "guts of democracy," as a seasoned legislative scholar once wrote.[1] State legislators are closer to the people they represent than any other state or federal elected official. Their job is neither glamorous nor well paid, but it is essential in the process of translating the wishes and needs of a state's citizens into public policy.

Because the job of the state legislature is so difficult and so important, the states have constantly tinkered with their institutions to improve their performance. These bodies have undergone particularly radical change in the past generation. A prime motivator of this period of reform was the set of U.S. Supreme Court decisions in the 1960s mandating that states redraw their legislative districts every ten years. Regular redistricting has stirred the political pot, leading to significant political changes in every state. In addition, two major reform movements have recently swept the country: legislative professionalism in the 1970s and 1980s and term limits in the 1990s. Each wave of reform was motivated by the optimistic assumption that institutional change would improve legislative performance. But defining good legislative performance and deciding upon the best way to achieve it have been matters of continuing debate.[2]

Other changes in the state legislatures have not been matters of institutional reform. Dramatic social changes in the 1960s and 1970s allowed for greater diversity in participation in American politics, and these changes were reflected first and to the greatest extent in the state legislatures. It is now common for women and members of minority racial and ethnic groups not only to serve in state legislatures but also to hold the highest leadership positions there. It is not even surprising anymore to find legislators who are openly homosexual. And because state legislatures are a prime political training ground,[3] the demographic diversity of today's national leaders was foreshadowed in the states. Long before Nancy Pelosi was speaker of the U.S. House of Representatives, Vera Katz was speaker of the Oregon House; 33 other women have also led a state legislative chamber to date.[4] And before Barack Obama became president, Deval Patrick (Massachusetts) and David Paterson (New York) were African-American governors.

[1] Alan Rosenthal, "The Legislative Institution: In Transition and at Risk," in *The State of the States*, ed. Carl E. Van Horn, 2nd ed. (Washington, D.C.: CQ Press, 1993), 115.
[2] Alan Rosenthal, *Heavy Lifting: The Job of the American Legislature* (Washington, D.C.: CQ Press, 2004).
[3] Michael B. Berkman, "State Legislators in Congress: Strategic Politicians, Professional Legislatures, and the Party Nexus," *American Journal of Political Science* 38 (1994): 1025–55.
[4] Center for American Women and Politics, "Women State Legislators: Leadership Positions and Committee Chairs 2005," fact sheet (New Brunswick, N.J.: Rutgers University, 2005).

In this chapter, we consider state legislatures and their role in state government, reflecting on the dramatic changes in these bodies in recent decades. What does a legislature do, and how does it do it? Who are state legislators? How do they get into office, and how do they behave once they are there? We also discuss states' efforts to improve their legislatures through institutional reform. As clearly as anywhere in government, institutional reform in the state legislature has affected politics and policy—but not always in the ways that reformers intended.

State Legislatures: The Basics

As lawmaking institutions, state legislatures are quite similar to one another and to the U.S. Congress. Forty-nine state legislatures have **bicameral** structures, with two independent chambers (the **unicameral** Nebraska Legislature has only a chamber); a **bill** must pass through both chambers in exactly the same form to become law. One chamber is called the Senate, and the other chamber is usually called the House of Representatives, although some states use other names, such as the House of Delegates in Virginia and the Assembly in California. Houses have more members than do senates, typically about two or three times as many, and so they have smaller districts. Senators are most commonly elected to four-year terms from **single-member districts** (SMDs); that is, districts from which they are the only senator; house members are usually called representatives and elected to two-year terms from SMDs.[5] Some legislators (about 13 percent of them

nationwide) are elected from districts with more than one member serving in them, like members of the U.S. Senate (two of whom serve each state). These are called **multimember districts** (MMDs). Table 6.1 lists how the different state legislatures vary on these characteristics. MMDs used to be more common in state legislatures because they reduce the difficulty of drawing districts (since fewer districts need to be drawn). But MMDs are now used less often because they seem to diminish the representation of racial minorities.[6]

State Legislative Elections

There are 7,382 men and women serving in the 50 state legislatures, with from 20 in the Alaska State Senate to 400 in the New Hampshire House of Representatives. Each of these legislators was elected to his or her seat.[7] So, to understand state legislatures and state legislators, you must first understand state legislative elections.

---

[5] In 12 states, senators have two-year terms, and in five states, representatives have four-year terms.

[6] Bernard Grofman and Lisa Handley, "The Impact of the Voting Rights Act on Black Representation in Southern State Legislatures," *Legislative Studies Quarterly* 16 (1991): 111–28.

[7] All these legislators were elected to their seats except for those few at any given time who have been appointed to serve out the remainder of a term for an elected legislator who died or resigned.

Table 6.1

State Legislatures, Terms, Seats, and Multimember Districts (MMDs)

State	Name of Both Chambers Together	Senate			Name of Chamber	House		
		Length of Term	Number of Seats	% MMDs[a]		Length of Term	Number of Seats	% MMDs[a]
AL	Legislature	4	35	0	House*	4	105	0
AK	Legislature	4	20	0	House*	2	40	0
AZ	Legislature	2	30	0	House*	2	60	100%
AR	General Assembly	4	35	0	House*	2	100	0
CA	Legislature	4	40	0	Assembly	2	80	0
CO	General Assembly	4	35	0	House*	2	65	0
CT	General Assembly	2	36	0	House*	2	151	0
DE	General Assembly	4	21	0	House*	2	41	0
FL	Legislature	4	40	0	House*	2	120	0
GA	General Assembly	2	56	0	House*	2	180	0
HI	Legislature	4	25	0	House*	2	51	0
ID	Legislature	2	35	0	House*	2	70	0
IL	General Assembly	4	59	0	House*	2	118	0
IN	General Assembly	4	50	0	House*	2	100	0
IA	General Assembly	4	50	0	House*	2	100	0
KS	Legislature	4	40	0	House*	2	125	0
KY	General Assembly	4	38	0	House*	2	100	0
LA	Legislature	4	39	0	House*	4	105	0
ME	Legislature	2	35	0	House*	2	151	0
MD	General Assembly	4	47	0	House of Delegates	4	141	67%
MA	General Court	2	40	0	House*	2	160	0
MI	Legislature	4	38	0	House*	2	110	0
MN	Legislature	4	67	0	House*	2	134	0
MS	Legislature	4	52	0	House*	4	122	0
MO	General Assembly	4	34	0	House*	2	163	0
MT	Legislature	4	50	0	House*	2	100	0
NE	Legislature	4	49	0	**	**	**	**
NV	Legislature	4	21	11%	Assembly	2	42	0
NH	General Court	2	24	0	House*	2	400	88%
NJ	Legislature	4	40	0	General Assembly	2	80	100%
NM	Legislature	4	42	0	House*	2	70	0
NY	Legislature	2	62	0	Assembly	2	150	0
NC	General Assembly	2	50	0	House*	2	120	0
ND	Legislative Assembly	4	47	0	House*	4	94	100%

(Continues)

State Legislatures, Terms, Seats, and Multimember Districts (MMDs)—(continued)

State	Name of Both Chambers Together	Senate			Name of Chamber	House		
		Length of Term	Number of Seats	% MMDs[a]		Length of Term	Number of Seats	% MMDs[a]
OH	General Assembly	4	33	0	House*	2	99	0
OK	Legislature	4	48	0	House*	2	101	0
OR	Legislative Assembly	4	30	0	House*	2	60	0
PA	General Assembly	4	50	0	House*	2	203	0
RI	General Assembly	2	38	0	House*	2	75	0
SC	General Assembly	4	46	0	House*	2	124	0
SD	Legislature	2	35	0	House*	2	70	100%
TN	General Assembly	4	33	0	House*	2	99	0
TX	Legislature	4	31	0	House*	2	150	0
UT	Legislature	4	29	0	House*	2	75	0
VT	General Assembly	2	30	77%	House*	2	150	39%
VA	General Assembly	4	40	0	House of Delegates	2	100	0
WA	Legislature	4	49	0	House*	2	98	100%
WV	Legislature	4	34	100%	House of Delegates	2	100	40%
WI	Legislature	4	33	0	Assembly	2	99	0
WY	Legislature	4	30	0	House*	2	60	0

[a]This is the percentage of districts that have more than one member serving in them.
*House of Representatives.
**Nebraska's unicameral legislature has only a senate.

Source: Council of State Governments, *Book of the States 2006* (Lexington, Ky.: Council of State Governments, 2006); and the National Conference of State Legislatures' Web site, www.ncsl.org/programs/legismgt/about/legislator_overview.htm.

The Paradox of Competition in State Legislative Elections

Political competition is vital to a healthy representative democracy. When any candidate could win an election, each one works hard to appeal to voters. This energetic campaign activity raises voters' interest in, and understanding of, the race, the office being contested, and the candidates. Furthermore, elected officials who anticipate a close race in the next election pay close attention to what their constituents want them to do in office, and they make every effort to serve and represent them well. When a race is not competitive—that is, when only one candidate has a chance of

winning—neither the voters nor the candidates take much interest in it. Elected officials who feel safe in office have little electoral incentive to do anything special for their constituents. Of course, elected officials also serve their districts for other, less selfish reasons, but the fear of losing the next election is a strong institutional motivation for politicians.

Are state legislative elections competitive? Recent election results suggest a paradoxical answer to this question. As you saw in Chapter 5, recent elections have yielded remarkably similar numbers of Democratic and Republican state legislators overall nationwide. Before the Democrats picked up 322 seats in their big wins in the 2006 midterm elections, they had a mere one-seat advantage out of 7,382. This looks like very close competition. But in individual state legislative races, there is precious little political competition. Many state legislative races are routinely won by 10 or 20 percent.[8] In fact, 35 percent of the winners of state legislative general elections in 2004 and 2006 did not even have an opponent.[9]

If state legislative elections overall reflect the close competition between the political parties that we have seen in recent presidential elections and in Congress, why are the races for most individual state legislative seats so uncompetitive? The answer has to do with (1) how people vote in state legislative elections and (2) the way state legislative districts are drawn. That is, we can explain this paradox by understanding voting for state legislators and how our electoral institutions translate these votes into state legislative seats.

Party, Incumbency, and Voting Decisions in State Legislative Elections

Consider the nature of state legislative elections. First, the size of legislative districts varies dramatically from state to state based on the number of seats in a chamber and the number of people living in the state, from California's senate districts with 887,000 people in them to New Hampshire's house districts with only 3,220 people. But the average state house district has about 55,000 people in it, and the average senate district has about 150,000. Thus, even compared

to members of the U.S. House (with about 650,000 constituents), state legislators have small districts. And because Americans tend to live near those who are like themselves racially, socially, and economically, these small districts are also relatively homogeneous. That is, whereas a congressional district may stretch hundreds of miles and encompass farms, small towns, suburbs, and urban areas, a state legislative district may cover as little as a few square miles in a heavily populated city or a dozen sparsely populated counties peopled only with farmers and small-town folks.

The small size of these districts also works against voters getting information about state legislative races. These districts usually do not include an entire **media market**, so advertising on TV and radio is uneconomical, since many viewers will be outside of the district at which the ad is aimed.[10] Local TV news almost never covers state legislative elections, largely for the same reason—any given legislative race is not meaningful to very many viewers.[11] And since Americans tend to get their political information from mass media advertisements and news, these races are virtually invisible to most voters.

Finally, state legislative races are typically overshadowed by candidates "up the ticket" for Congress, governor, and president.[12] People have a limited attention span for politics, and state legislative races are not nearly as relevant to most people as are those other races. So, voters step into the booth with a pretty good idea about how they will vote in these more visible races, but they typically have given little thought at all to their state legislative vote.

---

[8] Richard G. Niemi, Lynda W. Powell, William D. Berry, Thomas M. Carsey, and James M. Snyder Jr., "Competition in State Legislative Elections, 1992–2002," in *The Marketplace of Democracy*, ed. Michael P. McDonald and John Samples (Washington, D.C.: Brookings Institution, 2006); and Robert E. Hogan, "Institutional and District-Level Sources of Competition in State Legislative Elections," *Social Science Quarterly* 84 (2003): 543–60.

[9] John McGlennon and Cory Kaufman, "Expanding the Playing Field: Competition Rises for State Legislative Seats in 2006," report from the Thomas Jefferson Program in Public Policy (Williamsburg, VA: College of William and Mary, 2006); and National Conference of State Legislatures, http://www.ncsl.org/programs/press/2004/unopposed_2004.htm.

[10] Gary F. Moncrief, Peverill Squire, and Malcolm E. Jewell, *Who Runs for the Legislature?* (Upper Saddle River, N.J.: Prentice Hall, 2001), ch. 4.

[11] Jeff Venezuela, "Midwest Local TV Newscasts Average 36 Seconds of Election Coverage in Typical 30-Minute Broadcast," press release (Madison: UW NewsLab, University of Wisconsin–Madison, 2006).

[12] Richard G. Niemi and Lynda W. Powell, "Limited Citizenship? Knowing and Contacting State Legislators after Term Limits," in *The Test of Time*, ed. Rick Farmer, John David Rausch Jr., and John C. Green (Lanham, MD: Lexington, 2003).

Regardless of the lack of information about the state legislative candidates that they bring into the voting booth, voters always[13] have one important piece of information on which to base their vote—the candidates' party affiliations, as written on the ballot. Thus, in conjunction with voters' own party leanings, the candidates' party likely determines most votes in state legislative races. When you know nothing else about a candidate, why not vote for the one from the party with which you typically agree? And because state legislative districts are relatively politically homogeneous, this voting based on party affiliation generates very little two-party competition in these elections.

Another effect of the low level of information that voters have about state legislative races is that if a voter simply recognizes one of the names on the ballot, he or she may be more likely to vote for that candidate. And why might a voter be more likely to have heard about one candidate than another? Incumbency is the biggest reason. The current state legislator— the **incumbent**—has campaigned before, has gotten his or her name in the newspapers for legislative accomplishments, has perhaps been seen by the voter in a parade or at a meeting of a group, or has sent newsletters about his or her service to the voter for the past two years or more. Furthermore, this information is likely to have been positive because it has largely been controlled by the incumbent himself or herself. Thus, all things being equal, this name recognition tends to work to the incumbent's advantage in the voting booth.

Campaigns can also increase name recognition; in fact, that is largely what they

are designed to do. State legislative campaigns have traditionally been pretty down-home affairs, being run from a kitchen table and a home computer, with a small group of the candidate's friends and neighbors going door to door, distributing campaign brochures, putting up yard signs, and so forth.[14] Candidates can also increase their name recognition among voters by winning the endorsements of newspapers and interest groups that are important to voters in their districts.[15] And, on average, the more money a candidate spends on the campaign, the more votes he or she will receive.[16] Of course, the effects of incumbency and campaign spending are intertwined; interest groups may try to gain access to legislators by making campaign contributions to them. Thus, incumbents' electoral chances are improved both by the name recognition they earn from serving in the legislature and by having more money to spend on their campaigns than their challengers.

The results of state legislative elections confirm this line of thinking—incumbent state legislators who run for reelection win overwhelmingly, especially where legislators are well-paid and have plenty of staff.[17] Incumbents are sometimes challenged successfully, even in their party's primary, but the defeat of a state legislative incumbent is so rare as to be newsworthy.

On the other hand, voters' lack of information about state legislative candidates— even incumbents—means that one bad piece of information may be enough to turn out of office even a long-term legislator. For example, after Pennsylvania lawmakers voted themselves a pay raise in 2005, the state's media wrote

---

[13] Except Nebraska, where state legislative elections are nonpartisan.

[14] Tom Loftus, *The Art of Legislative Politics* (Washington, D.C.: CQ Press, 1994); Moncrief, Squire, and Jewell, *Who Runs for the Legislature?*; and Ralph G. Wright, *Inside the Statehouse: Lessons from the Speaker* (Washington, D.C.: CQ Press, 2005).

[15] R. W. Lariscy, S. F. Tinkham, H. H. Edwards, and K. O. Jones, "The 'Ground War' of Political Campaigns: Nonpaid Activities in U.S. State Legislative Races," *Journalism and Mass Communication Quarterly* 81 (2004): 477–97.

[16] Anthony Gierzynski and David Breaux, "Legislative Elections and the Importance of Money," *Legislative Studies Quarterly* 21 (1996): 337–57.

[17] Robert E. Hogan, "Challenger Emergence, Incumbent Success, and Electoral Accountability in State Legislative Elections," *Journal of Politics* 66 (2004): 1283–303; David Breaux, "Specifying the Impact of Incumbency on State Legislative Elections," *American Politics Quarterly* 18 (1990): 270–86; and William D. Berry, Michael B. Berkman, and Stuart Schneiderman, "Explaining Incumbency Re-Election," *American Political Science Review* 94 (2000): 859–74.

stories about various perks of office that these legislators enjoyed, such as generous pension benefits, lobbyist wining and dining, tickets to Steelers and Eagles games, and so forth. So, in 2006, Pennsylvania voters finally noticed their state legislators—and threw them out in record numbers, including some key leaders.[18]

Thus, state legislative races are typically determined by incumbency and the partisan alignment of the district, and this helps explain the dearth of district-level competition in state legislative races. But this is not the whole story. Next, we consider an institutional factor that helps complete our explanation—the mechanisms by which state legislative districts are drawn.

State Legislative Redistricting

Each state legislator is elected from a specific, legally defined subsection of the state: his or her legislative district. A state's legislative map is defined by a law (or laws) specifying exactly down which streets the district boundaries run, placing every square foot of the state into one and only one senate and house district. Precisely where each of these lines runs is determined as a matter of public policy based on various criteria, some legally established and some established simply by custom and preference. Because of these criteria, districts are not just shaped by geographic features (like rivers or mountain ranges) nor can they neatly follow other political boundaries (like county or city lines). Furthermore, the U.S. Supreme Court requires that these districts be redrawn every ten years to reflect changes in a state's population. How these districts are drawn has a lot to do with explaining the lack of political competition in state legislative races.

"One Person, One Vote" Before the early 1960s, states rarely redrew their legislative district boundaries because **redistricting** causes political conflict. Changing district boundaries means moving some of a legislator's former constituents to a new district and bringing in new people to take their place. Although legislators might want to gain constituents who would vote for them and lose constituents who would vote against them, they can never be sure which are which. Furthermore, legislators invest considerable time and effort building favorable name recognition in their districts through campaigns, newsletters, personal favors, professional service, and the like.[19] As a result, legislators generally favor the status quo in anything relating to their elections— the current arrangements got them elected, so why change things? And before the 1960s, they didn't, sometimes for many decades.

The problem with this bias toward the status quo was that although the district boundaries remained the same, the states' populations were constantly shifting. In particular, people moved from the countryside, where most people lived in 1900, to the cities, where most people lived in 1960. Because of this migration, even districts that were equal in population in 1900 were very unequal by 1960, when some states suffered extreme legislative **malapportionment**; that is, the unequal representation of people living in different districts. For example, Connecticut's districts were so malapportioned that a party controlling districts containing as little as 12 percent of the state's population could have had a majority of seats in its state house.[20]

But in a series of decisions beginning in 1962, the Supreme Court ruled that districts of unequal population in the same legislative chamber[21] violated the Equal Protection

---

[18] Alan Greenblatt, "Perks That Kill," *Governing*, July 2006, 18.

[19] Robert G. Boatright, "Static Ambition in a Changing World: Legislators' Preparations for, and Responses to, Redistricting," *State Politics and Policy Quarterly* 4 (2004): 436–54.

[20] Richard K. Scher, Jon L. Mills, and John J. Hotaling, *Voting Rights and Democracy* (Chicago: Nelson-Hall, 1997).

[21] This principle of equal-population districts applies only within a given chamber. So, for example, Texas House districts may have more people in them than North Carolina House districts, but all Texas House districts must be equal in population.

Clause of the 14th Amendment and were, therefore, unconstitutional.[22] The Court established the principle of "one person, one vote,"[23] whereby all votes in a state must be of equal value. In malapportioned districts, the value of a person's vote in a smaller district is worth more than that of a person in a larger district. So, a person in a sparsely populated rural house district of 5,000 people would have three times the influence in an election as a person in a more densely populated urban house district of 15,000 people—1/5,000 versus 1/15,000. And influence in an election is influence in the legislature.

Responding to these Supreme Court decisions, the states spent the rest of the 1960s undertaking the politically wrenching task of completely redrawing their state legislative (and congressional) districts so that they would be equal in population based on the 1960 U.S. Census.[24] In most states, the legislatures passed legislation to redraw their own districts, but sometimes, the courts had to step in. For example, the failure of Illinois's legislature and governor to agree on a set of legislative districts led to that state's infamous "bed-sheet ballot" in the 1964 general election, a 33-inch ballot on which every voter in the state had to choose between 236 candidates for 177 state house seats.[25] But by the end of the 1960s, every state had redrawn its legislative districts equally. The result was a shift in power from the rural areas of the states to the urban and suburban areas, reflecting the end of the malapportionment bias under which many legislatures had long suffered.[26]

Drawing New Districts Of course, because Americans are highly mobile, those equal-population districts did not stay equal for long. To maintain the one person, one vote standard, states must go through the legislative redistricting process after the national census *each decade* to adjust to the population shifts that occurred since the previous census. But if redistricting in the 1960s was like a Category 4 hurricane, the regular decennial redistricting is only like a Category 1 in most states. Yes, it causes a significant political battle in every state every decade, but policy makers have developed the processes and skills required to fight those battles in a relatively orderly way. And the changes that are now made each decade are not nearly as large as those that were required in the 1960s, when policy makers had to make up for generations of malapportionment.

One exception to this was the Texas redistricting wars after the 2000 U.S. Census. Republican Congressman Tom DeLay, then majority leader in the U.S. House, did not like the congressional districts drawn by the Democrat-controlled Texas state legislature in 2002 (recall that a state's legislature draws its congressional districts too). After Texas Republicans took control of the state legislature later that year, DeLay had a novel idea—why not *re*-redistrict? That is, he convinced the legislature to draw a new set of congressional districts that would be more favorable to Republicans. After superheated political fighting—including the spectacle of Democratic state legislators twice fleeing the state to deprive the legislature of a quorum—the Republicans succeeded in passing a

---

[22] The key cases on state legislative redistricting in this period were *Baker v. Carr*, 369 U.S. 186 (1962); *Reynolds v. Sims*, 377 U.S. 533 (1964); and *Lucas v. 44th General Assembly of Colorado*, 377 U.S. 713 (1964).

[23] At the time, the principle was referred to as "one man, one vote," but we prefer the less sexist phrasing.

[24] Gordon E. Baker, *The Reapportionment Revolution* (New York: Random House, 1966).

[25] James L. McDowell, "The Orange-Ballot Election: The 1964 Illinois At-Large Vote and After," *Journal of Illinois History* 10 (2007): 289–314.

[26] Stephen Ansolabehere and James M. Snyder Jr., "Reapportionment and Party Realignment in the American States," *University of Pennsylvania Law Review* 153 (2004): 433–57.

districting plan that ended up increasing that party's numbers in the U.S. House.[27] Before DeLay's maneuver, no one had tried to redistrict more than once a decade, and opponents of the plan fought it unsuccessfully all the way to the U.S. Supreme Court.[28] It remains to be seen how many states will take advantage of this new opportunity, but the heavy political toll[29] of this extraordinary redistricting in Texas suggests that it will be uncommon.

Most states take one of two approaches to redistricting, adopting their new maps either through the regular legislative process or through a nonpartisan or bipartisan commission.[30] With either method, decisions must be made about exactly where to draw the district lines and what criteria should be used to do so. First, any redistricting plan must meet at least two criteria:

- Each district must be geographically **contiguous** (all its area must be connected by land—except for islands).
- Districts must be just about equal in population, as of the most recent census.[31]

No map that fails to meet these criteria will hold up to a federal court challenge.

But beyond these two legal absolutes, a variety of criteria may be used to draw a "good" legislative map. Some argue that legislative districts should be compact, follow local government boundaries, or reflect "communities of interest" (groups of people with common racial, ethnic, or economic interests).[32] Different types of people advocate different criteria. For example, legislators themselves prefer districts full of voters from their own party so that they can win reelection easily, while the parties would rather see their voters spread around more evenly so as to establish a modest majority in as many districts as possible, thereby winning more seats.[33]

Racial and ethnic representation has long been an important consideration in legislative redistricting. Multimember districts were once used to dilute minority voters' power, but this use of MMDs was banned by the federal **Voting Rights Act of 1965**.[34] In the 1980s, the Supreme Court seemed to encourage drawing "majority-minority" districts by packing enough of those of a given race or ethnicity—generally, African Americans or Latinos—into a district so as to elect one of their own.[35] But in the 1990s, the Court appeared to change its mind, holding that race could not be the primary consideration in drawing a district.[36]

[27] Layla Copelin, "DeLay and His Legacy Are Both on Trial," *Austin (Tex.) American-Statesman*, 18 December 2005, p. A1; David Espo, "Top Court Rules States Free to Redistrict," *Sacramento Bee*, online ed., 28 June 2006; and Tim Storey, "Supreme Court Tackles Texas," *State Legislatures*, April 2006, 22–24.

[28] *League of Latin American Citizens v. Perry*, 548 U.S. 399 (2006).

[29] For example, it was largely during this political battle that DeLay allegedly committed the acts for which he was later indicted and had to resign from Congress.

[30] Michael P. McDonald, "A Comparative Analysis of Redistricting Institutions in the United States, 2001–02," *State Politics and Politics Quarterly* 4 (2004): 371–95.

[31] The U.S. Supreme Court allows the largest and smallest districts in a state legislative chamber to vary by as much as 10 percent.

[32] Jason Barabas and Jennifer Jerit, "Redistricting Principles and Racial Representation," *State Politics and Policy Quarterly* 4 (2004): 415–36.

[33] Brian F. Schaffner, Michael W. Wagner, and Jonathon Winburn, "Incumbents Out, Party In? Term Limits and Partisan Redistricting in State Legislatures," *State Politics and Policy Quarterly* 4 (2004): 396–414; and David Butler and Bruce Cain, *Congressional Redistricting: Comparative and Theoretical Perspectives* (New York: Macmillan, 1992).

[34] Grofman and Handley, "The Impact of the Voting Rights Act."

[35] *Thornburg v. Gingles*, 478 U.S. 30 (1986).

[36] *Easley v. Cromartie*, 532 U.S. 234 (2001).

Race continues to be a consideration for redistricters because (1) it is illegal to draw maps deliberately to disenfranchise minority voters; (2) partisanship and race are closely intertwined in the United States, and it is legal to draw maps for partisan advantage;[37] and (3) all things being equal, many people believe that fairness in the representation of minorities is important. Add to this the potential for the Supreme Court to weigh in on the subject again, and you can see that race will factor into legislative redistricting for the foreseeable future.

Three general forces shape the final decisions on state legislative district boundaries:

- Conflicts of interest among those charged with drawing the maps (in most cases, state legislators and political parties),
- The general public's lack of concern with the redistricting process, and
- The lack of agreed-upon criteria for redistricting.

The state legislative districts that result from these forces have at least two characteristics.[38] First, they tend to be electorally safe for most of the current incumbents and their parties, especially when the maps have to be approved by the legislature. The price of a legislator's vote for a plan may be a favorable district. Such **incumbent-protection districts** have lopsided partisan balances and incorporate as much of an incumbent's previous district as possible. The effect of such districts is often to freeze the political status quo, with incumbent legislators being even more difficult to defeat than normal and the overall balance of the parties' seats in the legislature being reified. This status quo bias is strongest when both parties have a say in the process, whether due to **divided government** or by the use of a bipartisan redistricting commission.

The second effect of these redistricting forces is that when one party controls the redistricting process, whether by having unified government or controlling the redistricting commission, that party will try to draw districts that improve its chances of winning seats in the state legislature. This is done by spreading out some of its opponent's voters so that they are less than a majority in many districts—so-called **cracking**—and **packing** many of the others into a few seats so as to "waste" all their votes over 50 percent. Such machinations often require irregular, if not downright tortured, boundaries as districters search for just the right balance of partisan votes. This is called political **gerrymandering**, after the 19th-century Massachusetts political boss and U.S. vice president Elbridge Gerry. Because the districts Gerry drew to maximize his party's advantage were so weirdly shaped, a political cartoonist once drew it as a salamander, hence the name. But with today's detailed census and voting databases and Geographic Information System (GIS) software, redistricters now outdo even Gerry in their creativity in pursuing political advantage (e.g., see Figure 6.1).

Ohio's current state legislative map provides a good example of the effect of partisan gerrymandering.[39] As is well-known from presidential elections, Ohio's electorate is split virtually 50–50 between the parties. What's more, 2006 was a terrible year for the GOP in the Buckeye State. A major financial scandal and a retiring governor with the lowest poll ratings in the country led the party to landslide losses in the races for governor, U.S. senator, secretary of state, treasurer, and attorney general for the first time in over ten years.[40] But Republicans controlled redistricting in Ohio in 2001, and their effective cracking and packing of voters

[37] *Easley v. Cromartie.*

[38] McDonald, "A Comparative Analysis."

[39] Caroline J. Tolbert, Daniel A. Smith, and John C. Green, "Support for and the Mobilizing Effects of Election Reform Ballot Propositions" (paper presented at the annual meeting of the American Political Science Association, Philadelphia, September 2006).

[40] Alan Ehrenhalt, "Party Lines," *Governing*, January 2007, 11–12.

Figure 6.1

The Texas 17th State Senate District is a good example of partisan gerrymandering. This district consists of about one quarter of the city of Port Arthur, linked by marshland, Galveston Bay, and some lightly populated portions of Galveston Island and Bend and Bazoria counties to the west side of Houston. Analysts argued that drawing the district in this way caused a Democratic senator to be defeated—not surprisingly, Republicans controlled this redistricting.

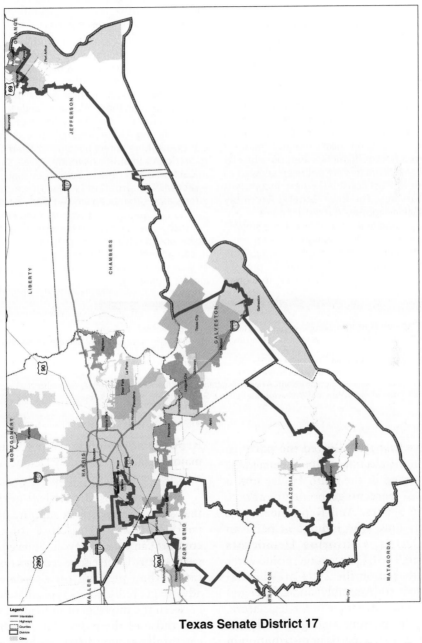

Texas Senate District 17

Source: Layla Copelin, "Redistricting Drama Heading to the Courtroom after State Board's Contentious Vote, Challenges to Maps Move Forward," Austin (Tex.) American-Statesman, 26 July 2001, p. A1.

INSTITUTIONS MATTER

IOWA'S NONPARTISAN REDISTRICTING INSTITUTION

Iowa has a unique redistricting system that seems to eliminate political gerrymandering and incumbent protection.[a] In the Hawkeye State, nonpartisan legislative staff are assigned to draw districts for their state house and senate and congressional districts based almost solely on simple population data (rather than the detailed demographic and political data used elsewhere), with an eye toward not splitting political units (like cities and counties) between different districts, when possible. By law, these redistricters are not even allowed to know (or at least consider) where incumbent legislators live. The Iowa General Assembly must officially approve the district maps drawn in this way, and legislators may ask the staffers to redraw the plan. But usually the staffers' first or second plan is passed into law, largely due to public and media pressure that the process be nonpartisan. The result is that Iowa has

legislative and congressional districts that are more competitive for both incumbents and parties than those in other states.

Many other states have nonpartisan or bipartisan redistricting commissions, but the maps they produce tend to be biased toward either partisan advantage or incumbent protection,[b] even if they are a bit more competitive than those adopted strictly through the legislative process.[c] There has been a flurry of redistricting reform proposals in recent years, but even where voters have been offered new redistricting institutions in initiatives, such as in California and Ohio in 2005, they have been rejected. The problem is that these reform efforts have often been viewed, fairly or not, as partisan power grabs.[d] Given that redistricting has such a direct impact on the interests of those politicians who have the responsibility for doing it, can an institution be adopted in the other 49 states that purges it of politics? The prospects are not promising.

[a] Alan Greenblatt, "Monster Maps: Has Devious District-Making Killed Electoral Competition?" *Governing* 19, no. 1 (2005): 46–50.
[b] Michael P. McDonald, "A Comparative Analysis of Redistricting Institutions in the United States, 2001–02," *State Politics and Politics Quarterly* 4 (2004): 371–95.
[c] Jamie L. Carson and Michael H. Crespin, "The Effect of State Redistricting Methods on Electoral Competition in United States House of Representatives Races," *State Politics and Policy Quarterly* 4 (2004): 455–69.
[d] Sam Hirsch and Thomas E. Mann, "For Election Reform, A Heartening Defeat," *New York Times*, online ed., 11 November 2005; and Jill Sanders, "Setting Political Boundaries Done in Variety of Ways across the Country," *Sacramento Bee*, online ed., 3 November 2005.

in legislative districts allowed the party to emerge from the election with a 7 percentage point advantage in the Ohio House and a whopping 27 percentage point advantage in the Ohio Senate. And Republicans are not the only ones who indulge in partisan gerrymandering. California Democrats gerrymandered a 10 percentage point voter advantage (based on the 2004 presidential election) into a 20 (Assembly) and 25 (Senate) percentage point advantage in the legislature. Political gerrymandering (among other things) also yielded a bizarre partisan distribution in the New York legislature, with the Senate

Republicans holding a 9 percentage point majority and the Assembly Democrats holding a 44 percentage point majority.

But a proposed political gerrymander that shaves the partisan support of majority party legislators too close for their own comfort can cause a revolt. So even when one party controls the entire redistricting process, rather than pushing for extreme partisan advantage, redistricters typically compromise between the interests of individual legislators and those of the party. This leads to many electorally secure districts along with some effort toward partisan advantage, especially in districts where no incumbent is seeking reelection.[41]

Furthermore, some states have constitutional provisions or statutes that limit gerrymandering in some way. For example, 21 states require that county or municipal boundaries be followed to the greatest extent possible while meeting the one person, one vote standard.[42] Nineteen states require that districts be compact, and ten require that old districts be preserved as much as possible. Because these provisions are vague (for example, "as much as possible" is certainly debatable), politically motivated redistricters are not completely thwarted. But these provisions give those arguing—whether in court or the legislature—against egregious political gerrymandering more ammunition for their cases.

The Paradox of Competition in State Legislative Elections Revisited

This sort of voting and redistricting results in the paradox we introduced above for state legislative elections—close competition between the parties in the aggregate (or at least a good reflection of the state or national electorate's partisan balance) but little competition in individual races. State legislative districts that tend to be homogeneous due to their relatively small size and Americans' increasingly segregated living patterns are further homogenized and manipulated during the redistricting process, resulting in near certainty about which party will win each seat in the general election.[43] Furthermore, incumbents' advantages in name recognition and campaign spending stifle competition even in party primaries. And although redistricters

cannot predict future population shifts, they now have greater skill, more sophisticated technology, and more detailed data to pursue their goals than ever before. For example, in California's 2004 general election, of the 153 congressional and state legislative seats up for election, none of them changed parties—and this is in a state with state legislative term limits that are supposed to decrease incumbents' dominance in elections.

State Legislators: Who Are They?

Soon after these 7,382 state legislators have won their individual elections, they meet in their respective state capitols to begin work. These people make big decisions about public policy and the allocation of state government resources that affect your life every day, so who they are makes a difference. Although any generalization about these thousands of unique individuals glosses over a lot of differences, it is useful to take a look at them in broad strokes to begin to understand how well the legislature represents the citizens of the states.

The average state legislator is a 53-year-old white man, in business or a lawyer, who is married and has lived in the same area most of his life.[44] Thus, like most political elites in this country, state legislators do not represent the diversity of the American population in many ways. Non-Latino whites make up only about 70 percent of our population, about half of us are women, most of us are not lawyers or businessmen, and most of us relocate at least a couple of times in our lives.[45] But if we look past the simple averages, and especially if we look at changes in state legislatures in recent years,

[41] Schaffner, Wagner, and Winburn, "Incumbents Out, Party In?"

[42] Barabas and Jerit, "Redistricting Principles and Racial Representation"; and Jonathon Winburn, "The Realities of Redistricting: Political Control and Partisan Consequences" (Ph.D. diss., Indiana University, Bloomington, 2005).

[43] Alan Greenblatt, "Monster Maps: Has Devious District-Making Killed Electoral Competition?" *Governing*, January 2006, 46–50.

[44] National Conference of State Legislatures, "Legislator Demographics," 2006, http://www.ncsl.org/programs/legman/about/demographic_overview.htm.

[45] U.S. Bureau of the Census, *The Statistical Abstract of the United States, 2005*, http://www.census.gov/statab/www/.

we see a much more varied demographic picture for state legislators than for any other set of state or federal elected officials.

Women in the State Legislature

First, consider the representation of women in state legislatures. No woman had served in a state legislature until 1894, when three women were elected in Colorado. In the following 80 years, women made some progress but not much. In 1971, at the beginning of the modern women's movement in this country, only 4.5 percent of state legislators were women. But since then, women have made steady gains so that after the 2006 election, they constituted 23.5 percent of state legislators. Indeed, the influx of women was one of the most dramatic changes in these bodies in the late 20th century. And just as important, more of them are assuming leadership positions in state legislatures.[46] Women continue to gravitate toward committees in the areas of health, education, and social welfare, but they also receive fair representation on the powerful fiscal committees in state legislatures.[47] And although it was not until the 1980s that the first women assumed the top leadership positions of house speaker and senate president, as of 2006, 33 women from 17 states had done so.[48]

However, women are not represented equally well in all states. As Figure 1.1 in Chapter 1 showed, the percentage of women in state legislatures varies dramatically, ranging from 43.3 percent in the Arizona Senate to only 2.2 percent in the South Carolina House. States in the West and the Northeast tend to have more women legislators, and those in the Southeast tend to have fewer (except for North Carolina and Florida).

Why has women's representation in state legislatures increased so dramatically since the 1970s, and why is there such variation in women's representation across the states? Recent scholarship can give us some insight into these questions. For example, state legislatures with lower pay and shorter sessions and those that use MMDs tend to have more women.[49] The standard explanation for this has to do with a bias against women serving in elective office, a carryover from the prefeminist period. Seats in full-time, high-pay legislatures and single-member districts may seem more valuable, generating more competition for them and the tendency to fill them with men. Supporting this explanation is the finding that when a state's electorate and party leaders hold more traditional attitudes toward religion and gender roles, women are less well represented in its legislature.[50] This explanation also accounts for the upward trend in women's overall representation since 1971, a time when women were moving in greater numbers into many nontraditional professions and attitudes toward their role in society were changing. There is evidence that women's continuing underrepresentation in state legislatures is also affected by their greater overall hesitancy to enter political races than men.[51]

---

[46] Susan J. Carroll, "Women in State Government: Historical Overview and Trends," in *The Book of the States 2004*, vol. 36 (Lexington, Ky.: Council of State Governments, 2004).

[47] Robert Darcy, "Women in the State Legislative Power Structure: Committee Chairs," *Social Science Quarterly* 77 (1996): 888–98.

[48] Center for American Women and Politics, "Women State Legislators"; and Robert Tanner, "Female State Leaders Double since 2000," *Chicago Sun-Times*, online ed., 3 April 2007.

[49] James D. King, "Single-Member Districts and the Representation of Women in American State Legislatures: The Effects of Electoral System Change," *State Politics and Policy Quarterly* 2 (2002): 161–75; and Peverill Squire, "Legislative Professionalization and Membership Diversity in State Legislatures," *Legislative Studies Quarterly* 17 (1992): 69–79.

[50] Kevin Arseneaux, "The 'Gender Gap' in State Legislative Representation: New Data to Tackle an Old Question," *Political Research Quarterly* 54 (2001): 143–60; John F. Camobreco and Michelle A. Barnello, "Postmaterialism and Post-Industrialism: Cultural Influences on Female Representation in State Legislatures," *State Politics and Policy Quarterly* 3 (2003): 117–38; and Kira Sanbonmatsu, *Where Women Run: Gender and Party in the American States* (Ann Arbor: University of Michigan Press, 2006).

[51] Richard L. Fox and Jennifer L. Lawless, "Entering the Arena? Gender and the Decision to Run for Office," *American Journal of Political Science* 48 (2004): 264–80.

Racial and Ethnic Minorities in the State Legislature

State legislative representation for members of racial and ethnic minorities has also improved in recent decades but for different reasons than those for the improvement in women's representation. In 1969, there were only 172 African-American state legislators (about 2 percent); this had increased to 438 by 1991 and 607 by 2003 (the last year data are available), or 8.2 percent of legislators.[52] Thus, the proportion of African Americans in state legislatures now better represents their proportion in the population (12.8 percent) than does the proportion of women in state legislatures. On the other hand, there were 140 Latino state legislators in 2003 (1.8 percent), far less than Latinos' 13.7 percent share of the population. In 2003, there were also 72 Asian-American legislators and 36 Native American legislators.

Why has the representation of racial and ethnic minorities in state legislatures improved? The **Voting Rights Act (VRA) of 1965** had a lot to do with it, especially in the South, which has the states with the largest proportions of blacks. By banning practices that discouraged blacks from voting, getting rid of the MMDs that diluted their votes, and encouraging districts with a majority of blacks to be drawn where possible, the VRA helped to increase the number of African-American state legislators in the states of the old Confederacy from three in 1965 to 176 as early as 1985.[53] Efforts to draw majority-minority districts in the 1980s and 1990s also helped increase black representation in legislatures outside the South. Latino representation has been helped by these events to some degree, but the biggest reason for their

greater numbers in state legislatures in recent years is simply immigration. But currently, they are probably the most underrepresented demographic group due to their historical lack of political participation.[54]

As with women, the percentage of racial and ethnic minorities in state legislative chambers varies dramatically across the states (see Table 6.2), but much of this cross-state variation is easy to explain. The percentage of blacks or Latinos in a state's legislature is largely a function of their percentage in the state's population.

There is considerable debate about the effect of drawing state legislative districts to be homogeneous on race or ethnicity. On one hand, if people vote along racial or ethnic lines, majority-minority districts should lead to proportional minority representation in the state legislature. But some argue that minority groups' political and policy interests are better served by having some level of influence in many districts, regardless of the race of the legislator. For example, by packing African-American voters (who predominantly vote Democratic) into fewer districts to ensure that some black legislators are elected, Republicans may be more likely to win in other districts that have been stripped of Democratic voters.[55] This raises a potential conflict between policy representation (based on voters' policy needs and desires) and descriptive representation (based on voters' demographic characteristics).[56]

The Impact of Broader Representation

What difference does the improvement in African-American, Latino, and women's state

---

[52] Samantha Sanchez, *Money and Diversity in State Legislatures, 2003* (Helena, Mont.: Institute on Money in State Politics, 2005).

[53] Grofman and Handley, "The Impact of the Voting Rights Act"; and Janine A. Parry and William H. Miller, "'The Great Negro State of the Country?' Black Legislators in Arkansas, 1973–2000," *Journal of Black Studies* 36 (2006): 833–72.

[54] Rodney Hero, F. C. Garcia, J. Garcia, and H. Pachon, "Latino Participation, Partisanship, and Office Holding," *PS: Politics and Political Science* 33 (2000): 529–34.

[55] David Lublin, *The Paradox of Representation* (Princeton, N.J.: Princeton University Press, 1999).

[56] Rodney E. Hero and Caroline J. Tolbert, "Latinos and Substantive Representation in the U.S. House of Representatives: Direct, Indirect, or Nonexistent?" *American Journal of Political Science* 39 (1995): 640–52.

Table 6.2

African-American and Latino State Legislators

State	African Americans as % of State Population (2005)	% African-American State Legislators (2006)		Latinos as % of State Population (2005)	% Latino State Legislators (2007)	
		Senate	House		Senate	House
AL	26	22.9	24.8	2	0.0	0.0
AK	4	5.0	0.0	5	0.0	0.0
AZ	4	0.0	1.7	29	20.0	18.3
AR	16	8.6	12.0	5	0.0	0.0
CA	7	5.0	5.0	35	45.0	12.5
CO	4	5.7	4.6	19	5.7	6.2
CT	10	8.3	6.6	11	0.0	4.0
DE	21	4.8	7.3	6	0.0	2.4
FL	16	17.5	14.2	19	7.5	11.7
GA	30	19.6	21.1	7	0.0	1.7
HI	2	0.0	2.0	8	4.0	0.0
ID	1	0.0	0.0	9	0.0	1.4
IL	15	15.3	16.9	14	5.1	6.8
IN	9	8.0	8.0	5	0.0	1.0
IA	2	0.0	3.0	4	0.0	0.0
KS	6	5.0	4.0	8	0.0	3.2
KY	8	2.6	5.0	2	0.0	0.0
LA	33	23.1	21.9	3	0.0	0.0
ME	1	0.0	0.0	1	0.0	0.0
MD	29	21.3	22.7	6	2.1	2.1
MA	7	2.5	3.8	8	2.5	1.9
MI	14	13.2	12.7	4	2.6	1.8
MN	4	0.0	1.5	4	1.5	1.5
MS	37	21.2	28.7	2	0.0	0.0
MO	12	8.8	10.4	3	0.0	0.6
MT	0	0.0	0.0	2	0.0	1.0
NE	4	2.0	N/A	7	2.0	N/A
NV	8	14.3	9.5	24	4.8	4.8
NH	1	0.0	1.0	2	0.0	0.5
NJ	14	12.5	13.8	15	0.0	5.0
NM	2	0.0	2.9	43	33.3	42.9
NY	17	12.9	14.7	16	6.5	8.7
NC	22	14.0	15.8	6	2.0	0.8
ND	1	0.0	0.0	2	0.0	0.0
OH	12	12.1	14.1	2	0.0	0.0
OK	8	4.2	3.0	7	0.0	0.0
OR	2	10.0	0.0	10	0.0	1.7
PA	11	8.0	7.4	4	0.0	0.5
RI	6	2.6	4.0	11	2.6	2.7
SC	29	17.4	20.2	3	0.0	0.8
SD	1	0.0	0.0	2	0.0	0.0

(Continues)

African-American and Latino State Legislators—(continued)

State	African Americans as % of State Population (2005)	% African-American State Legislators (2006)		Latinos as % of State Population (2005)	% Latino State Legislators (2007)	
		Senate	House		Senate	House
TN	17	9.1	16.2	3	0.0	1.0
TX	12	6.5	9.3	35	16.1	20.7
UT	1	0.0	1.3	11	3.4	1.3
VT	1	0.0	0.7	1	0.0	0.0
VA	20	12.5	11.0	6	0.0	1.0
WA	4	2.0	2.0	9	2.0	2.0
WV	3	0.0	2.0	1	0.0	0.0
WI	6	6.1	6.1	4	0.0	1.0
WY	1	0.0	0.0	7	0.0	3.3
US average	13	7.7	8.5	14	3.3	3.2

Note: The columns show the percentage of members in each chamber who are African American (2006) or Latino (2007) and the state population percentages for 2005. These are the most recent data available for each of these characteristics.

Source: Joint Center for Political and Economic Studies, "Black Elected Officials Roster-2006 Black State Legislators" (Washington, D.C.: Joint Center for Political and Economic Studies); Evan Bacalao, res. assoc., National Association of Latino Elected and Appointed Officials; and U.S. Bureau of the Census, *Statistical Abstract of the United States,* http://www.census.gov/statab/www/ranks.html.

legislative representation make in public policy or governance? Scholars have begun to explore this difficult question by assessing the degree to which these state legislators differ from white male legislators. For example, we know that African-American and women legislators tend to be more interested than their white male colleagues in education, social welfare, and (for women) health care policy.[57] These preferences are seen in differences in the committees they serve on, the bills they introduce, and the way they vote on legislation. And political scientists have recently found evidence that as these groups become better represented in state legislatures, their preferences are better reflected in public policy,[58] although not always.[59]

African-American state legislators are more likely to have started their political careers in social movement groups, churches, or unions, while white legislators are more likely to have started in local government positions.[60] Black legislators are also more likely to have a pessimistic view of race relations than whites, even feeling that black interests and they themselves are given short shrift in the state legislature. Indeed, they may have good reason to feel this way. One study of attitudes in and around the North Carolina statehouse[61] supports this belief, showing that, all things being equal, lobbyists and white legislators there have less respect for African-American legislators than their white colleagues. Interestingly, journalists' attitudes were not found to be racially biased in this way.

The differences between women and men state legislators were fairly stark in the 1970s

[57] Kathleen A. Bratton and Kerry L. Haynie, "Agenda Setting and Legislative Success in State Legislatures: The Effects of Gender and Race," *Journal of Politics* 61 (1999): 658–79.

[58] C. T. Owens, "Black Substantive Representation in State Legislatures from 1971–1994," *Social Science Quarterly* 86 (2005): 779–91; and Robert R. Preuhs, "The Conditional Effects of Minority Descriptive Representation: Black Legislators and Policy Influence in the American States," *Journal of Politics* 68 (2006): 585–99.

[59] Caroline J. Tolbert and Gertrude A. Steuernagel, "Women Lawmakers, State Mandate, and Women's Health," *Women and Politics* 22 (2001): 1–39.

[60] James Button and David Hedge, "Legislative Life in the 1900s: A Comparison of Black and White State Legislators," *Legislative Studies Quarterly* 21 (1996): 199–218.

[61] Kerry L. Haynie, *African American Legislators in the American States* (New York: Columbia University Press, 2001).

and 1980s, when women were first making inroads at the statehouse. Aside from their having a somewhat different policy agenda, female legislators tended to be older, have fewer children, be unmarried or divorced, be social workers or teachers rather than lawyers, and be less politically ambitious.[62] But as the novelty of women serving in elected office has worn off in recent years, these differences between the sexes in the statehouse have vanished, with female state legislators now being just as likely to be young, with children, and married as their male colleagues. On the other hand, the ideological gender gap among American voters is even more obvious in the statehouse, with the average female legislator being more liberal on social issues, the environment, gun control, and abortion regulation, regardless of her party or the characteristics of her district.[63] Women also engage in more constituent service and are more cooperative, consensus-building, and egalitarian in the legislative process.[64]

Of course, for any underrepresented group, achieving its political goals requires more than just gaining a few seats in the legislature. As we shall see, real policy making requires legislative majorities. But there are two important ways minorities can have influence. First, women and minorities can gain committee or chamber leadership positions.[65] These positions have been filled increasingly by women and minorities in recent years, largely in proportion to their numbers in their chambers.[66] On the other hand, women have been more successful in attaining the top jobs in their chambers than members of minority groups. For example, as

of 2008, 37 women had served as a senate president or house speaker, but only ten African Americans had done so. The second way that women and minorities have gained influence in state legislatures is by forming informal legislative groups, such as a Black Legislators' Caucus or a Conference of Women Legislators. Such groups provide training and mentoring for new legislators, a sense of group cohesion among its members, and a vehicle with which to mobilize blocs of votes that can be used to gain support from other legislators on issues important to the group.[67]

The Job of the State Legislature

The state legislature has three basic duties:

- To help establish and revise the state's laws and constitution
- To oversee the activities of the executive branch as it implements the state's laws
- To represent the interests of the state's citizens before the state government

Although there is some overlap in these duties, it is useful to discuss them separately, especially when considering the impacts of institutions on how well they are accomplished.

Lawmaking

The state legislature's primary duty is to consider the public problems of the state and

---

[62] Anne Marie Camissa and Beth Reingold, "Women in State Legislatures and State Legislative Research: Beyond Sameness and Difference," *State Politics and Policy Quarterly* 4 (2004): 181–210.

[63] Sarah Poggione, "Exploring Gender Differences in State Legislators' Policy Preferences," *Political Research Quarterly* 57 (2004): 305–14.

[64] Lyn Kathlene, "Power and Influence in State Legislative Policy-Making: The Interaction of Gender and Position in Committee Hearing Debates," *American Political Science Review* 88 (1994): 560–76.

[65] Robert R. Preuhs, "Descriptive Representation, Legislative Leadership, and Direct Democracy: Latino Influence on English Only Laws in the States, 1984–2002," *State Politics and Policy Quarterly* 5 (2005): 203–24; and Cindy S. Rosenthal, *When Women Lead: Integrative Leadership in State Legislatures* (New York: Oxford University Press, 1998).

[66] Darcy, "Women in the State Legislative Power Structure"; Byron D'Andra Orey, L. Marvin Overby, and Christopher W. Larimer, "African-American Committee Chairs in American State Legislatures" (University of Nebraska–Lincoln, 2006).

[67] Tracy Osborn, "Women Representing Women: Pursuing a Women's Agenda in the States" (Ph.D. diss., Indiana University, 2004).

make or modify state law to address them. This is a huge job; the state legal code consists of thousands of laws touching on every facet of life and business, and every one of these laws has been passed by the legislature over the years.[68] Everything that a state or local government official does must be authorized by the legislature. Gay rights, education from preschool to the Ph.D., prisons and homeland security, public health and driver's licenses, road building, and coal mine regulation—all these and much more are considered in depth in a state legislature each year. And the number of formal proposals, or **bills**, to change state law each year is immense. For example, in their 2005–2006 legislative session, members of the Michigan House and Senate considered 4,227 bills and passed 681 of these into law, with these new laws filling over 1,500 pages in the Michigan Compiled Laws.[69] By any standard, state legislators' lawmaking job is large and important, and they take it seriously.

The process by which a state legislature makes law is complex and difficult—and for a good reason. Mark Twain once said, "No man's life, liberty, or property is safe while the legislature is in session,"[70] and like all good jokes, this one has a large measure of truth in it. Americans tend to be suspicious of government, so we make the legislative process slow and difficult to reduce the risk of unwise or dangerous state government action. In fact, on average, only about 20 percent of the bills that a state legislature considers actually become law.[71] In the end, a bill must pass both chambers of the legislature by at least a majority vote and then be signed by the governor (or have the governor's veto overridden by the legislature) to become law.

The basic legislative process in the states is quite similar to that of Congress. First,

someone says, "There ought to be a law!" Legislators are in the business of making law, so they are always on the lookout for good ideas. They get ideas from their constituents, the news, and especially lobbyists and interest groups, which are the main source of bill ideas. Such groups have very specific interests that can be affected—positively or negatively—by state policy, so they have a strong incentive to get organized and present their ideas to legislators for consideration. Regardless of the source of the idea, when a legislator files a bill with the clerk of the chamber, he or she becomes its **bill sponsor** and formally begins the legislative process.

After a bill is introduced in one chamber in this way, it is assigned to a **standing committee** for consideration. This committee will specialize in the bill's policy area, so the legislators on it will likely have some expertise in the subject. The committee holds a public hearing to gather information about the bill's potential effects and its political support. Often, a bill that seems like a good idea to one group would have bad consequences for others. Sometimes the state agency that would be assigned to implement the bill sees problems with it that need to be considered.

After hearing these arguments, the committee deliberates. If the problems raised about the bill are sufficiently worrisome, the committee may simply not report it back to the full chamber (or report it unfavorably), and it will not become law in the current legislative session. Standing committees serve the important function of screening out bad, weak, or politically unpalatable bills. There is no reason to waste the full chamber's time considering bills that have obvious problems. But state legislative committees tend to be weaker than their congressional counterparts,

---

[68] This is true except for those relatively very few laws that are passed through the initiative process.

[69] See the Michigan Legislature's excellent website to examine their laws, bills, committee reports, and other legislative documents: http://www .legislature.mi.gov. Today, most state legislatures have websites like this that allow you to search for various legislative documents and laws.

[70] Tommy Neal, *Learning the Game: How the Legislative Process Works* (Denver, CO: National Conference of State Legislatures, 2005), 33.

[71] This varies quite a bit, with Colorado passing more than 50 percent of its bills and Massachusetts passing less than 5 percent in a typical year; see Council of State Governments, *The Book of the States 2006*.

so they are much less likely to screen out bills before they get to the floor.[72] In fact, in many states, if a sponsor really wants to get his or her bill passed in committee, he or she can do so. And about a quarter of state legislative chambers require that their committees report all bills assigned to them to the full chamber, whether favorably or not.[73]

Even if the committee agrees with the general idea behind a bill, its hearing often highlights weaknesses in it. In such cases, the committee will **amend** the bill, typically with the sponsor's permission. In the end, if the committee is convinced of the amended bill's merit, it will vote to report it to the full chamber for further consideration.

At this point in the process, in most chambers (especially in houses), the majority party leader (whether the speaker of the house, president of the senate, or person with some other title) has a critical opportunity to affect the bill's fate, particularly if he or she opposes the bill. Standing committees report far more bills than their full chambers can reasonably consider, and one of the majority party leader's important functions is to manage this bottleneck by selecting which bills will be considered on the **chamber floor**.[74] A number of factors go into a leader's decision about which bills the chamber will consider. First, these leaders typically prefer uncontroversial bills that will waste less of the chamber's precious floor time. Such bills are also less likely to be publicly controversial; controversy could threaten the party's majority in the next election. Less commonly, the majority leader will kill bills he or she does not want to see debated on the floor, whether for policy or political reasons. Perhaps the debate would expose rifts among legislators of his or her own

party or perhaps voting on the bill would be politically damaging for some majority party legislators facing tough reelection campaigns. Finally, and probably least frequently, the majority party or its leader may have a policy agenda that would be helped by killing or advancing a particular bill, and the leader uses his or her **gatekeeping** power to do so.

On the floor of the full chamber, legislators first consider amending the bill. Various legislators, especially the bill's sponsor and members of the committee that reviewed it, may speak to describe the bill's intent and its political support and opposition (if any). Sometimes, suggestions for modifications are offered, with the floor typically deferring to the wishes of the bill's sponsor and committee members about these proposed amendments. To reduce controversy and increase the chances of passing the bill, sponsors usually agree to most amendments, unless they think that they would undermine the original intent of the bill.

Finally, the chamber votes on the bill, and a majority vote passes it in that chamber.[75] Since the goal of the legislative process up to the floor vote is to screen out bills that are flawed or lack political support, most bills that survive to the chamber floor not only pass there but also pass by a wide margin. So, a legislator's default floor vote is "aye"; in other words, legislators need a reason to vote against a bill on the floor rather than for it. So, why might a legislator vote "nay" on a particular bill? Certainly, if he or she knows something special about that bill, perhaps by having followed its discussion in committee or having heard from a constituent about it, that information will factor into his or her vote. But since lawmakers vote every year on hundreds

---

[72] Wayne Francis, *The Legislative Committee Game: A Comparative Analysis of Fifty States* (Columbus: Ohio State University Press, 1989).

[73] Council of State Governments, *The Book of the States 2006*, 178–80.

[74] A few states, like Colorado, limit the ability of the majority leader to screen out bills from floor consideration, requiring a floor vote on every bill that is reported out of committee. This reduces both the power of the majority leader and the amount of deliberation any given bill can have on the floor.

[75] This is except for special types of bills that require a supermajority vote, such as bills for borrowing money or votes to override a governor's veto.

of often very technical and arcane bills on a wide range of topics, they usually know little about any given bill when they vote on it.

The most common reason why legislators vote against a bill is if it somehow hurts their district and, thereby, hurts their reelection chances. But typically, most bills either have no direct impact on a legislator's district or are too complex or unfamiliar for the legislator to know about any such impacts. In such cases, legislators usually take cues about voting from their colleagues.[76] Most legislative chambers have a large electronic "tote board" that tells everyone how each legislator has voted during a **roll call**. Legislators first look to the votes of members of their own party, especially those on the committee that considered the bill. If all their co-partisans are voting one way on a bill, they will likely vote that way too. Legislators also consider the votes of those from similar and neighboring districts. Lacking other information, voting with their colleagues who are similarly positioned helps legislators avoid casting a vote that may hurt their district or come back to haunt them in a reelection campaign. Legislative leaders usually advise their co-partisans about how to vote for their districts' interests, even if that sometimes means voting against the party's position. Rarely is a party leader so desperate for a vote that he or she will encourage—or even allow—a legislator to vote against his or her district. And a party leader who insists on many such votes will not likely be the leader for long.

If a bill manages to pass all these hurdles successfully in its chamber of origin, it is sent over to the other chamber, where the entire process is repeated—introduction, committee evaluation, and floor consideration and voting. As in its chamber of origin, if the bill fails to pass any of the hurdles in the second chamber, it dies for the session. Even if the bill passes the other chamber, it may be amended during the process. Since a bill must pass both chambers in identical form before it can become law, the different versions must be reconciled and then voted on again in each chamber. This may be done by one chamber simply accepting the other chamber's version, or if neither chamber acquiesces, a temporary **conference committee** may be convened to craft a bill that can pass both chambers.

Typically, conference committee members are appointed by the leaders of each party in each chamber and include the bill's primary sponsor in each chamber and the leaders of the standing committees that heard the bill. If the conference committee can reach a compromise, it reports it out to both chambers (if no agreement can be reached, the bill dies). On each chamber floor, legislators can vote only "aye" or "nay" on a conference committee bill, with no amendments being allowed. But even more than regular bills, conference committee bills usually pass on the floor. Too much effort has been put into them by this point in the process for them to fail.

Once both chambers pass the bill in identical form, it is sent to the governor. If the governor approves of the bill, he or she signs it, and the process is complete—the bill becomes state law on its effective date, as specified in the bill. Alternatively, the governor can veto the bill, sending it back to the legislature for further consideration. As you will read about in the next chapter, governors' veto powers vary significantly among the states, with many governors having a much more powerful veto than that of the president. But regardless of the type of veto used, the legislature always has the opportunity to **override** it, usually through a **supermajority** vote (i.e., a vote greater than a simple 50 percent majority, such as two-thirds or three-fifths) on the bill in each chamber. But a governor's veto is very hard to override. Governors do not veto bills lightly or often, so when they do, they take them seriously and often use considerable

[76] This process is best described in the context of congressional roll call voting in John W. Kingdon, *Congressmen's Voting Decisions*, 3rd ed. (Ann Arbor: University of Michigan Press, 1989).

political resources to make sure they are not overridden.[77]

Overseeing the Executive Branch

Although it is neither as formal, nor time-consuming, nor well publicized as lawmaking, another important duty of the state legislature is to oversee the executive branch's **implementation** of state law and programs. In effect, the legislature acts like the board of directors of a very large corporation (the state bureaucracy), setting general policy and then checking up now and then to make sure that the agencies are executing that policy as the legislature intended.

The most obvious way for the legislature to control policy implementation by an agency is to specify very clearly what that agency is supposed to do in its original legislation. The more detailed the legislation, the less discretion an agency has in implementing the policy and, therefore, the more likely it will follow **legislative intent**. For example, if the legislature passes a law that states simply, "The Department of Natural Resources (DNR) shall regulate deer hunting," the agency has enormous leeway to determine the regulations it deems necessary and desirable to regulate hunting. Such regulations may turn out to be completely at odds with what legislators actually had in mind when they passed the bill. Maybe the DNR decides to regulate deer hunting by banning it outright, whereas the rural legislators who championed the bill really wanted regulation that would promote hunting. Had these legislators been more specific in the legislation, the DNR probably would have given the lawmakers the regulations they wanted. Indeed, legislators write very specific legislative language when

they want to force a recalcitrant agency or governor into implementing legislation a certain way.[78]

But most of the time there are far too many details and uncertainties in running an agency or enforcing a law for legislators to anticipate when they pass legislation. So, they give agencies great flexibility to make the multitude of specific, but important, policy decisions needed to fill in these details. Arguably, these decisions are best made by those with specialized training and experience, such as those who run the executive agencies. For example, who would you rather see set the exact dates or kill limits for deer hunting: generalist state legislators or professional wildlife managers in the DNR? Furthermore, these detailed decisions can often be made only after seeing how a new law actually works in practice.

The legislature can also check up on an agency to make sure that it is implementing policy according to legislative intent. Such **ex post oversight** can be done through either fire alarm or police patrol activities.[79] Fire alarm oversight occurs in response to a problem that has been pointed out to a legislator. This commonly occurs as a result of legislators' **casework** for their constituents, helping them with problems they have with state government. Although most constituent concerns are not caused by an agency violating legislative intent, casework can sometimes call attention to systematic problems with an agency that need to be addressed by the legislature. But probably more effective control results from the fact that agency officials know that the citizens with whom they work *could* complain to their state legislators. This encourages these officials to implement policy conscientiously

---

[77] Vicky M. Wilkins and Garry Young, "The Influence of Governors on Veto Override Attempts: A Test of Pivotal Politics," *Legislative Studies Quarterly* 27 (2002): 557–76.

[78] John D. Huber, Charles R. Shipan, and Madelaine Pfahler, "Legislatures and Statutory Control of Bureaucracy," *American Journal of Political Science* 45 (2001): 330–45; and Craig Volden, "A Formal Model of the Politics of Delegation in a Separation of Powers System," *American Journal of Political Science* 46 (2002): 111–33.

[79] Mathew D. McCubbins and Thomas Schwartz, "Congressional Oversight Overlooked: Police Patrols versus Fire Alarms," *American Journal of Political Science* 28 (1984): 165–79.

and to provide good public service. The media provide another important source of fire alarm oversight. When reporters uncover problems in state government, lawmakers take notice, holding hearings to investigate problems and changing policy as required.

State legislatures also have more systematic, ongoing methods of overseeing their executive branches, more like police patrols than fire alarms. For example, legislators use their regular hearings on the agencies' budgets to hold their directors accountable. Experienced and influential budget committee members often specialize in specific agencies' budgets so that over time, they learn the ins and outs of those agencies and can question these officials based on their in-depth knowledge. Likewise, **administrative rules review committees**, bodies of the legislature that review the myriad rules that agencies issue each year in implementing policy, can conduct police patrol oversight. Such rules and budget reviews can be more or less rigorous, depending on a legislature's institutions.[80] Finally, most state auditors work for the legislature, conducting financial and program evaluations of state agencies, both routinely and in response to legislative requests. In some states, the auditor is a very powerful legislative oversight institution.[81]

But in general, state legislatures do not oversee the executive branch very well or very often, for a number of reasons. First, the state executive branch is large and complex; by comparison, the state legislature is very small. Even the best-staffed legislatures in the largest states do not have enough resources to examine closely what every state agency is doing all the time. But even if they had the resources, legislators simply have little incentive to invest their time in effective executive oversight. Legislators are far more interested in lawmaking. Regardless of the relative impact of the two activities on a state's government and citizens, most legislators probably get more electoral and professional payoff from introducing bills that their districts favor, even if those bills fail, than from spending countless hours trying to understand the intricacies of an executive agency and how well it is following legislative intent. On the other hand, lawmakers can gain some political points by helping constituents who have problems with executive agencies, which encourages at least some legislative oversight.[82]

Representation

The third major duty of the state legislature is to represent the interests of the state's citizens to state government.[83] Legislators are the closest state government policy-making officials to the people in the sense that their districts are relatively small and are distributed throughout the state in proportion to the population, they spend most of their time in these districts, and they must face reelection frequently. All this makes representing their districts as natural to legislators as breathing, and they do it in a variety of ways.

First, legislators sponsor bills and vote on legislation to benefit the people and businesses in their districts. Sometimes, a legislator's political ideology or party allegiances will affect how he or she votes on bills,[84] but it

[80] Brian J. Gerber, Cherie Maestas, and Nelson C. Dometrius, "State Legislative Influence over Agency Rulemaking: The Utility of ex Ante Review," *State Politics and Policy Quarterly* 5 (2005): 24–46.

[81] W. Daniel Ebersole, "Trends in State Government Accounting, Auditing and Treasury," in Council of State Governments, *The Book of the States 2005*, vol. 37 (Lexington, KY: Council of State Governments, 2005).

[82] Christopher Reenock and Sarah Poggione, "Agency Design as an Ongoing Tool of Bureaucratic Influence," *Legislative Studies Quarterly* 29 (2004): 383–406.

[83] Malcolm E. Jewell, *Representation in State Legislatures* (Lexington: University Press of Kentucky, 1982); Michael A. Smith, *Bringing Representation Home: State Legislators among Their Constituencies* (Columbia: University of Missouri Press, 2003); and Ronald E. Weber, "The Quality of State Legislative Representation: A Critical Assessment," *Journal of Politics* 61 (1999): 609–27.

[84] Shannon Jenkins, "The Impact of Party and Ideology on Roll-Call Voting in State Legislatures," *Legislative Studies Quarterly* 31 (2006): 235–57.

is the interests of the district—or at least the legislator's perceptions of those interests—that drive most legislative policy making. Even legislative party leaders help legislators represent their districts this way, even if it means voting against the party on a particular bill. These leaders know that voting against the district's interests imperils a member's reelection chances, which thereby threatens the party's legislative influence. For example, a Democratic state senator from a rural part of Georgia is certainly not going to vote in favor of a gun control bill that her party is supporting. Gun control may be seen as a law enforcement and public safety issue to Democrats from Atlanta, but it is seen as a threat to hunting and her rural constituents' traditional way of life. The result of legislators' close attention to their districts is that despite all the forces that influence state public policy—especially those of interest groups, which you read about in Chapter 5—a state's overall public policy follows its citizens' general ideology and values remarkably closely.[85]

State legislators also represent their constituents' interests in a variety of other ways. For example, in casework, legislators act as ombudsmen for those constituents struggling with the state bureaucracy. Legislators also represent their constituents by pursuing **pork barrel** projects—specific public construction and economic development projects for their districts.[86] Even conservative legislators who are ideologically opposed to government seek out pork for their districts. Legislators believe that bringing home the bacon helps their election chances, and legislative leaders shower the districts of their electorally threatened co-partisans with such "worthy projects."[87]

Finally, out of a broader sense of responsibility, some legislators also think of themselves as representing certain classes of people, whether they live in their districts or not. This may be because a legislator has an interest in a certain business or profession, such as when a legislator who is a farmer or a pharmacist watches out for these interests in the state legislature. But this type of representation is most consciously felt by legislators who are women or members of a racial or ethnic minority group. These legislators often assume the responsibility to watch out for other members of their group, regardless of where they live in the state.[88]

The Collective Action Problem

State legislatures' three basic jobs—lawmaking, oversight of the executive branch, and representation—are difficult under the best of circumstances, but our state constitutions make them even harder by establishing an unwieldy and complex institutional legislative structure. Think about it. A state legislature consists of dozens of people from all around the state, each with different interests, ambitions, and goals, converging on the statehouse for perhaps only a few months out of the year to deal with a wide range of very complex problems. Most maddeningly, every one of these people has an equal say in any final decision of the body, and none of them can be fired or expelled by anyone in the group.[89] Two parallel sets of people (senators and house members) are working at the same time on the same problems, and the

---

[85] Robert S. Erikson, Gerald C. Wright, and John P. McIver, *Statehouse Democracy: Public Opinion and Policy in the American States* (New York: Cambridge University Press, 1993).

[86] Joel A. Thompson and Gary F. Moncrief, "Pursuing the Pork in a State Legislature: A Research Note," *Legislative Studies Quarterly* 13 (1988): 393–401.

[87] Michael C. Herron and Brett A. Theodos, "Government Redistribution in the Shadow of Legislative Elections: A Study of the Illinois Member Initiative Grants Program," *Legislative Studies Quarterly* 39 (2004): 287–312.

[88] Anne Marie Camissa and Beth Reingold, "Women in State Legislatures and State Legislative Research"; and Haynie, *African American Legislators*.

[89] Most legislatures have methods by which under very unusual circumstances—usually involving legislators convicted of crime—they can expel members, but such actions are extremely rare.

groups must agree in the end. Plus, all their deliberation and decision making occur in public view (or at least with the media paying attention), and all the people making these decisions are on very short-term contracts—contracts that most of them would like to see renewed. The final kicker is that although they must work together to accomplish their job, they are held accountable in elections only as individuals. If you have ever worked on a group project for a class, you know just how tricky this last arrangement can be.

Political scientists and economists call this a **collective action problem**—how to get a group of people to work together to accomplish a common goal.[90] You see these difficulties everywhere, from a sorority trying to run a fundraiser to an international airline trying to move people around the world. Different organizations solve the problem in different ways. In a small group, like a sorority, it may be done by informal consensus-building. In a large business, like an airline, it is usually done by setting up institutions, such as a command-and-control organizational structure and a division of the work among different units, such as sales, accounting, and customer service. Because of its unique constitutional arrangements, a state legislature must use a variety of techniques—both institutions and informal norms—to overcome its collective action problem and get its job done. The process that results is complex and rarely pretty, but it can work. Of course, there is always room for improvement, and the states are continually tinkering with their legislative institutions to improve their performance.

The basic strategy that legislatures use to solve their collective action problem is to divide themselves on two dimensions along which state policy varies—policy type and

policy preference—and then assign leaders the responsibility of organizing individual members in these subgroups. Three important state legislative institutions are used to do this—committees, party caucuses, and leaders. By dividing up policy problems among their standing committees, making sure that both parties are represented at all stages of the legislative process, and assigning leadership responsibilities to some of its members, state legislatures go a long way toward dealing with their collective action problem and getting their job done for the state.

Committees

Legislatures must address a vast range of public issues, everything from preventing birth defects to cemetery regulation, and they must have information and expertise on all these issues so that nothing gets forgotten and good decisions can be made on any problem that arises. Like Congress, state legislatures divide themselves into various standing committees to do this.[91] Each committee specializes in one area of policy—say, agriculture or transportation—so its members gain special knowledge and experience on it. When voting on a bill on the chamber floor, legislators typically look to members of the bill's committee for guidance because these are the legislature's in-house experts on the subject. Each committee has members of both parties, so different policy perspectives are represented in the preliminary review of bills and a variety of members are available to help non–committee members make decisions later in the process.

But in comparison with those of the U.S. House of Representatives, state legislative standing committees typically have much less control over legislation, especially relative to

[90] Lawrence Becker, Doing the Right Thing: Collective Action and Procedural Choice in the New Legislative Process (Columbus: Ohio State University Press, 2005).

[91] James Coleman Battista, "Re-Examining Legislative Committee Representativeness in the States," *State Politics and Policy Quarterly* 4 (2004): 135–57; L. Marvin Overby and Thomas A. Kazee, "Outlying Committees in the Statehouse: An Examination of the Prevalence of Committee Outliers in State Legislatures," *Journal of Politics* 62 (2000): 701–28; and Nancy Martorano, "Balancing Power: Committee System Autonomy and Legislative Organization," *Legislative Studies Quarterly* 31 (2006): 205–34.

the chamber leaders.[92] Whereas committees in the U.S. House are the primary center of policy-making activity, in most state legislatures, more policy making gets done in party caucuses, in leaders' offices, and on the chamber floor. Most important, the seniority norm that determines the chairs and membership of congressional committees does not exist in most state legislatures, so state legislative committees are much less stable than those in Congress, forming and disbanding from session to session and with their members changing committee assignments frequently. Thus, committees in most state legislatures are weaker than those in Congress.

Party Caucuses

In addition to developing some expertise in all the policy areas that state government handles, legislatures also try to ensure that most major points of view are considered in the discussion of every policy. Without the representation of these views, the legislature loses legitimacy as a policy-making institution. State legislatures represent these policy positions by organizing themselves along the most obvious characteristic of American electoral politics—the two-party system. Because Democrats and Republicans have basic differences in their inclinations toward most of the areas of state policy, organizing the legislature by party also organizes it by policy preference, even if in an imperfect way.

The importance of party as an organizing principle in state legislatures cannot be overstated. Besides those in Nebraska's nonpartisan unicameral body, over 99 percent of state legislators are elected as either a Democrat or Republican.[93] The two **party caucuses** in each chamber meet frequently to discuss strategy and policy; in some chambers, the most crucial policy decisions are made in the majority party caucus rather than in committee or on the floor. Members of each party usually sit together on the chamber floor, with members of the other party on "the other side of the aisle," literally. Although members of the same party do not always agree on policy—far from it, in some chambers—a legislator's party affiliation is the single most important predictor of how he or she will vote on bills, even more important than his or her general political ideology.[94] This similarity in roll call voting is the result of shared policy preferences, a sense of common cause against the other party in the chamber, and legislators' use of their co-partisans as **voting cues**.

To understand why any state legislature acts as it does, you have to know the party distribution in its chambers. The party that has a majority of members in a chamber is said to "control" that chamber—and for good reason. Because a majority must vote in favor of a bill in committee and on the floor for it to pass, the party with the majority—if its members vote together—can pretty much do anything it wishes. As a longtime West Virginia Legislature staffer once told one of us, "If the majority wants to paint its chamber polky dot, you'd better buy the paint because we're going to paint it polky dot." In fact, the majority party can have influence far out of proportion to its representation in the chamber. For example, if it sticks together, a party with 51 percent of the seats can win 100 percent of the decisions even though it has only one or two more members than the minority party. Because of this inordinate power, gaining a majority in a chamber is the holy grail of state legislative parties.

---

[92] Richard Clucas, "Improving the Harvest of State Legislative Research," *State Politics and Policy Quarterly* 3 (2003): 387–419.

[93] Twelve state legislators in 2007 had not been elected as either a Democrat or Republican: six Progressives and one independent in Vermont, two independents in Maine, one independent in Kentucky, one Constitution Party member in Montana, and one write-in candidate in Massachusetts who was a Democrat but not the nominee of that party in the 2006 election. See Council of State Governments, *The Book of the States 2007*.

[94] Jenkins, "The Impact of Party and Ideology"; and Gerald C. Wright and Brian F. Schaffner, "The Influence of Party: Evidence from the State Legislatures," *American Political Science Review* 96 (2002): 367–80.

On the other hand, sometimes a legislative majority party is not cohesive. In fact, perhaps surprisingly, the larger the majority, the less party members tend to stick together and the less overt power the party can exert over legislative decision making.[95] When the parties' percentages in a chamber are close—say, the 51 percent to 49 percent Democratic majority in the Indiana House following the 2008 election—the majority party must work extremely hard to maintain control over legislation and, indeed, to maintain their majority in the next election. The minority party smells success just a few votes away, so it scrambles to gain whatever advantage it can, whether to win passage of legislation or to position bills and votes to use as campaign issues in the next election. But a minority party facing a lopsided partisan split—say, the Hawaii Senate Republican's minority of only 8 percent—knows that the only way it will ever manage to pass a bill is with the help of many majority party members, so it tries hard to avoid partisan conflict. And because majority party members are not threatened by the minority in such chambers, they don't mind working with them from time to time. In fact, when a majority party is not threatened by a large minority, it often crumbles into factions, making legislative conflict less along partisan lines than along regional, ethnic, or economic lines.[96] In such legislatures, parties are not a relevant organizing principle, making the collective action problem more difficult to overcome.

In 2008, State Representative Karen Bass (D-Los Angeles) became the speaker of the California State Assembly, making her the first African-American woman to be the majority party leader in a state legislative chamber.

Brian Baer/Landov Media

[95] Nancy Martorano, "Cohesion or Reciprocity? Majority Party Strength and Minority Party Procedural Rights in the Legislative Process," *State Politics and Policy Quarterly* 4 (2004): 55–73.

[96] V. O. Key Jr., *Southern Politics* (New York: Vintage, 1949).

Legislative Leadership

Once they have organized themselves along party and policy lines, legislators select from among themselves various leaders, for both their parties and committees, whose responsibility it is to move the group along toward making collective decisions. The fundamental problems of collective action in the state legislature—as opposed to in a corporation or the executive branch—are that all the members of the legislature are constitutionally equal and no one is responsible for achieving its common goal. To address these problems, legislators give various leaders special powers and the responsibility to see that the group's tasks are accomplished.

The two basic types of leaders reflect the organizing principles of a state legislative chamber: committee chairs and party leaders. Committee chairs call committee meetings, schedule which legislation is to be heard and voted upon, and have what can often be significant procedural powers to organize and structure committee hearings and votes. Committee chairs are typically members of the majority party; a corresponding minority party leadership position is usually established for each committee, but the minority party committee leader has far less power than the chair. Of course, since committees are less powerful in most state legislatures than in Congress, committee chairs are less powerful in the states as well.

On the other hand, party leaders are usually much more important in state legislatures than in Congress. State legislative party leadership is focused on a single office for each party in each chamber. The leader of the majority party is the most powerful person in a chamber,

serving as the presiding officer in all 49[97] of the state houses of representatives (usually called the "speaker") and in 24 state senates (usually called the "senate president").[98] The lieutenant governor presides over the senate floor proceedings in 26 states, but in most of these, the real power still rests in the hands of the majority party's leader (usually called the "president pro tempore" in these cases). Minority party leaders are important players in the legislative process, but most have far fewer powers and responsibilities than the majority leaders. There are also several lower leadership positions in each party in each chamber that as a group make up the party leader's team.

The power and importance of state legislative party caucus leaders are suggested by the informal names they sometimes acquire, like the "Four Tops" in Illinois and the "Big Five" in California (which includes the governor).[99] Most important, state legislative majority party leaders have an especially strong hand in the legislative process.[100] For example, these leaders usually appoint committee chairs and members, so they have leverage over the output and proceedings of those bodies. Being a committee chair or on the party leadership team usually boosts a legislator's pay, power, and prestige, so these positions are coveted and those holding them are beholden to the party leader who appointed them. Party leaders also often negotiate among themselves and with the governor, representing their caucuses on important bills, especially the budget. Party leaders may also control much of the legislature's staff, and its offices and parking spaces. In short, party leaders, especially majority party leaders, can dominate state legislatures.

On the other hand, these leaders cannot just do whatever they wish. They are elected

---

[97] There are only 49 state houses of representatives, since the unicameral Nebraska legislature only has a senate.

[98] Keith E. Hamm and Gary F. Moncrief, "Legislative Politics in the States," in *Politics in the American State*, ed. Virginia Gray and Russell L. Hanson, 8th ed. (Washington, D.C.: CQ Press, 2004). Note that in certain very rare political circumstances, a minority party member may become a chamber's presiding officer, as is currently the case in the Pennsylvania House. See Eric Kelderman, "Battles for Gavels Kick off 2007 Sessions," *Statelines.org*, online ed., 11 January 2007.

[99] Kent D. Redfield, "What Keeps the 4 Tops on Top? Leadership Power in the Illinois General Assembly," in *Almanac of Illinois Politics: 1998*, ed. David A. Joens and Paul Kleppner (Springfield, IL: Institute of Public Affairs, 1998); and Andy Furillo, "'Big 5' Put a Range of Issues on the Table," *Sacramento Bee*, online ed., 25 August 2005.

[100] Richard A. Clucas, "Principal-Agent Theory and the Power of State House Speakers," *Legislative Studies Quarterly* 26 (2001): 319–38.

by their caucuses, and if they fail to help their co-partisans meet their goals, they will not be reelected to their position in the next legislative session.[101] But the overthrow of a party leader is rare because most leaders work hard to help the members of their caucuses meet their goals. First and foremost, this means helping legislators overcome the collective action problem to achieve their policy-making goals. That is, these leaders are accountable to their caucuses for the policy output of the legislature. They are the ones who make sure the system runs smoothly so that members can pass legislation that is important to them and their constituents. Without strong leadership taking collective responsibility for the output of the chamber, very little would ever get done.

Legislative party leaders also work hard to help their caucus members get reelected. Traditionally, they have done this in a variety of ways, from making sure they do not cast votes on legislation that will be used against them by election opponents to helping them pass bills and get projects that they can tout in their own election campaigns. Leaders help train new members about constituent service and media relations, and they even work to draw legislative districts in ways that advantage members of their caucuses (see "State Legislative Redistricting," above).

In recent years, many legislative leaders have gone beyond these traditional approaches and begun to take an active role in their caucus members' actual campaigns.[102] Given the importance of a majority in the legislative process, these leaders focus especially on gaining or maintaining a chamber majority. The basic electoral strategy for state legislative party leaders to gain or maintain a chamber majority is as follows:

1. Use their powerful positions in the legislature to attract lots of campaign contributions.

2. Hire and train top-flight campaign personnel.

3. Identify those districts in their chamber that are likely to have close races in the general election, perhaps due to the lack of an incumbent or changing demographics.

4. Inundate these few targeted competitive races with massive campaign resources in an effort to swing them to their party.

Legislative party leaders are in a unique position to pursue this **targeting electoral strategy**. Their extra influence over the legislative process can attract plenty of campaign contributions from groups anxious to influence policy. They can take a statewide perspective, learning where the competitive seats are and making the hard decisions about which candidates would and would not benefit from extra campaign help. By concentrating money and campaign expertise in a few targeted districts, these leaders use their party's resources efficiently.

Because the leaders of both parties are more or less equally adept at this targeting strategy, legislative campaign activity is very uneven in a state. As we have seen, most general election state legislative races are blowouts, with a minimal amount of campaign activity and spending. But a handful of races scattered around the state see intense campaign battles, with perhaps ten times the amount of campaign funds being spent as in nontargeted races, lots of TV and radio ads, out-of-town campaign managers and workers, and so forth. Targeted state legislative races can become proxy battlegrounds for the parties statewide, being run by the legislative leaders' campaign experts, with the candidates themselves being almost irrelevant. But few of these candidates complain (at least very loudly) because the leaders are helping them win their races.

---

[101] Clucas, "Principal-Agent Theory."

[102] Richard A. Clucas, *The Speaker's Electoral Connection: Willie Brown and the California Assembly* (Berkeley, CA: IGS Press, 1995); Anthony Gierzynski, *Legislative Party Campaign Committees in the American States* (Lexington: University Press of Kentucky, 1992); Loftus, *The Art of Legislative Politics*; and Wright, *Inside the Statehouse.*

In summary, state legislators solve the collective action problem posed by their states' constitutions by establishing institutions: standing committees, party caucuses, and committee and party leaders. Without such institutions, state legislatures would not be able to accomplish any of their three jobs. This is an example of how institutional arrangements can cause a problem and how the establishment of additional institutions can help overcome those problems.

State Legislative Reform

The states frequently try to improve their legislatures by tinkering with their institutions, rules, and processes. Sometimes, these reforms are dramatic, affecting the very foundations of these bodies. Not surprisingly, major institutional reforms are usually controversial, generating deep debate over just what a state legislature should be. Interestingly, the two most influential waves of state legislative reform in the past 40 years were driven by apparently contradictory ideas about just this question.[103] Some argued that a legislature should have sufficient resources to be a strong force in state government. These people advocated legislative professionalism, and the major institutional changes in state legislatures in the 1970s and 1980s reflected this value. Other reformers focused more on who state legislators were than on the institution, arguing that legislators ought to be as much like the average citizen as possible. Such "citizen-legislators" would provide a counterweight to those in the state capital whose pro-government biases could distort public policy. The most significant reform that these people advocated was state legislative **term limits,** a reform adopted by many states in the 1990s.

What were the goals of the advocates of these reforms? What impacts, intended and unintended, have they actually had on state politics and policy? The answers to these questions are not straightforward, but we begin to explore them in this chapter's final section.

Legislative Professionalism

In the 1950s and 1960s, a consensus developed among scholars, journalists, and good government advocates that state legislatures were simply not up to the task of governing modern state governments.[104] After World War II, state governments took great strides in their program responsibilities and administrative capacity. But state legislatures' capacity for sound planning, decision making, and analysis had not kept pace with the rest of state government. Indeed, state legislatures in 1965 looked much more like those in 1865 than of those in 2009. Legislative sessions typically lasted only a month or two, with many legislatures meeting only biannually. Most legislators had no office, with only a desk on the chamber floor to call their own. Staff was minimal; a legislator might share a secretary with ten colleagues, and that secretary would be employed only during the short legislative session. In 1971, a think tank, the Citizens Conference on State Legislatures (CCSL), published a detailed and influential study derisively titled "The Sometime Governments."[105] This book graded each state legislature on a range of criteria, primarily having to do with institutional effectiveness and efficiency. The CCSL found just about every state legislature sorely lacking on most of its criteria.

With Congress as a model, these reformers and researchers argued that state legislatures

---

[103] Thad Kousser, *Term Limits and the Dismantling of State Legislative Professionalism* (New York: Cambridge University Press, 2005).

[104] Peverill Squire, "Historical Evolution of Legislatures in the United States," *Annual Review of Political Science* 9 (2006): 19–44; Alexander Heard, ed., *State Legislatures in American Politics* (Englewood Cliffs, N.J.: Prentice Hall, 1966); and James Nathan Miller, "Hamstrung Legislatures," *National Civic Review* 54 (1965): 178–87.

[105] Citizens Conference on State Legislatures, *The Sometime Governments* (New York: Bantam, 1971).

lacked three things to deal effectively with all the policy problems facing the states: time, staff, and pay. Legislatures needed longer, annual sessions. They needed more staff to provide information and expertise for their policy deliberations and to give them independence from their traditional sources of policy information—interest groups and executive agencies. And legislators needed to be paid more so that lawmaking could be less of a hobby and more of a profession. Without a salary that allowed them to support their families, legislators needed another full-time job—or to be independently wealthy, supported by someone else, or retired, each of which has its biases. Such moonlighting could distract legislators from their duties at the statehouse and cause conflicts of interest in working on legislation.[106]

Given the very unusual combination of a consensus about what needed to be done, media pressure to do it, and expanding state budgets that allowed them to be able to afford it, the states adopted a wide variety of **legislative professionalism** reforms in the 1970s and 1980s. Not every state professionalized its legislature completely—far from it. But all states progressed along the professionalism continuum to some degree. States with larger, more urban, growing, and diverse populations, like Illinois, Massachusetts, and especially California, professionalized their legislatures sooner and more thoroughly than those smaller, more rural, and more homogeneous states, like New Hampshire, Wyoming, and Arkansas, who retain their **citizen-legislatures** even today.[107] In other words, the states that needed the extra help in dealing with their public problems tended

to beef up the capacity of their legislatures. Figure 6.2 breaks down today's state legislatures into three categories according to their level of professionalism, based on session length, members' salaries, and number of staff.[108]

The Impact of State Legislative Professionalism Have these professionalized legislatures lived up to the reformers' expectations? Although they have been better able to "perform [their] role in the policymaking process with an expertise, seriousness, and effort comparable to that of other actors in the process,"[109] these reforms have had some unexpected—and not universally praised—side effects. Political scientist Alan Rosenthal, a leader in the professionalism movement in the 1960s, has more recently criticized the reforms for promoting careerism among legislators, weakening legislative leadership, politicizing staff and the legislative process generally, polarizing the parties in the legislature, and reducing civility in these bodies.[110] That is quite an indictment for reforms that were once so universally advocated.

Other scholars have identified a variety of other effects of state legislative professionalism, many of whose value is open to debate. Political scientist Morris Fiorina argues that professionalism increased the number of Democrats in state legislatures because they are more likely than Republicans to be attracted by the relatively modest salaries even the professionalized bodies offer and the activist approach to government they encourage.[111] From this line of argument, some drew the hypothesis that professionalized

[106] H. W. Jerome Maddox, "Opportunity Costs and Outside Careers in U.S. State Legislatures," *Legislative Studies Quarterly* 20 (2004): 517–44.

[107] Neil Malhotra, "Government Growth and Professionalism in U.S. State Legislatures," *Legislative Studies Quarterly* 31 (2006): 563–84; James D. King, "Changes in Professionalism in U.S. State Legislatures," *Legislative Studies Quarterly* 25 (2000): 327–44; Christopher Z. Mooney, "Citizens, Structures, and Sister States: Influences on State Legislative Reform," *Legislative Studies Quarterly* 20 (1995): 47–68; and Bill Boyarsky, *Big Daddy: Jesse Unruh and Art of Power Politics* (Berkeley: University of California Press, 2008).

[108] Peverill Squire, "Measuring Legislative Professionalism," *State Politics and Policy Quarterly* 7 (2007): 211–27.

[109] Christopher Z. Mooney, "Measuring U.S. State Legislative Professionalism: An Evaluation of Five Indices," *State and Local Government Review* 26 (1994): 70–78, 74; see also Ann O'M. Bowman and Richard C. Kearney, *The Resurgence of the States* (Englewood Cliffs, N.J.: Prentice Hall, 1986).

[110] Rosenthal "The Legislative Institution."

[111] Morris P. Fiorina, *Divided Government*, 2nd ed. (New York: Longman, 2002).

Figure 6.2

State Legislative Professionalism

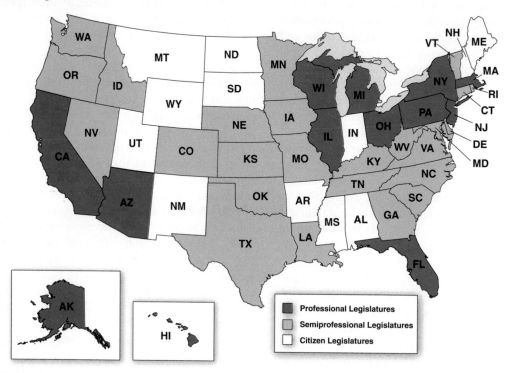

Note: Legislative professionalism is measured based on legislative salary, session length, and staffing, all compared to the U.S. Congress, using 2003 data.

Source: Peverill Squire, "Measuring Legislative Professionalism," *State Politics and Policy Quarterly* 7 (2007): 211–27.

legislatures spent more than nonprofessional legislatures, and one early study appeared to support this proposition.[112] But a more recent study by Neil Malhotra has shown that, when controlling for the public problems in each state, professional legislatures spend no more than do citizen-legislatures.[113] On the electoral side, whereas Berry, Berkman, and Schneiderman demonstrate that incumbents in professional legislatures are especially safe

in their reelection bids,[114] Squire finds that these legislatures have fewer uncontested races, suggesting increased competition.[115] Regarding constituency service and representation, Cherie Maestas finds that professional legislatures attract lawmakers who are especially attentive to the needs of their constituents—because they are more ambitious.[116] Interestingly, Squire shows that although citizens in states with professional legislatures have more contact

[112] S. Owings and R. Borck, "Legislative Professionalism and Government Spending: Do Citizen Legislators Really Spend Less?" *Public Finance Review* 28 (2000): 210–25.

[113] Neil Malhotra, "Selection Effects and the Impact of Legislative Professionalism on Government Spending" (Stanford University, Department of Political Science, 2007).

[114] Berry, Berkman, and Schneiderman, "Explaining Incumbency Re-Election."

[115] Peverill Squire, "Uncontested Seats in State Legislative Elections," *Legislative Studies Quarterly* 25 (2000): 131–46.

[116] Cherie Maestas, "The Incentive to Listen: Progressive Ambition, Resources and Opinion Monitoring among State Legislators," *Journal of Politics* 65 (2003): 439–56.

with their legislators, they are less satisfied with their legislature.[117] So, although legislative professionalism has largely fulfilled reformers' hopes of a more active, influential, and coequal legislative branch of state government, it has also had some peripheral effects that need to be considered when judging the reform.

Term Limits

In the late 1980s and early 1990s, some reformers began arguing that ordinary Americans, not professional politicians, ought to serve in state legislatures and Congress, contending that such citizen-legislators would bring some common sense to government.[118] Libertarian and Republican activists tapped into Americans' mistrust of government, a deep-rooted political value stretching back to Thomas Jefferson and other thinkers of the American Revolution. In particular, these reformers focused on the lack of competition in legislative elections and the high rate of incumbent reelection. Their remedy? Specific and reasonably short restrictions on the number of times a legislator could be reelected: legislative term limits.

Term limits was a very popular reform among voters. From 1990 to 2000, 21 states enacted the reform for their state legislators.[119] This is an extraordinarily swift reform adoption, especially for such a significant change. The way this reform was adopted in these states is quite telling of its politics. Nineteen of these 21 states adopted their limits through an initiative, usually with the help of a national advocacy group called U.S. Term Limits.[120] Of the states that allow initiatives, only two (North Dakota and Mississippi) voted against having

term limits.[121] Furthermore, only two state legislatures (Utah and Louisiana) limited their own terms through regular legislation—and Utah lawmakers did so under the imminent threat of an initiative with even more severe limits than they themselves passed.

We see a similar pattern at the national level. Term limits were part of the Republican Party's 1994 Contract with America, the set of campaign promises that helped them break the Democrats' 40-year grip on the U.S. House of Representatives. But during the 12-year period of mainly Republican control after 1994, Congress never limited its own members' terms. In fact, many of those who favored term limits as insurgent candidates in 1994 became much less enamored of them as their congressional careers lengthened, continuing to run even after their own self-imposed limits. Clearly, it is far easier to convince voters than legislators of the wisdom of term limits. But this is not only because legislators just want to keep their jobs, although that is surely part of it. As we shall see, there are also legitimate policy reasons for opposing term limits, just as there are legitimate reasons for supporting them.

Legislative term limits are not uniform among the states that have them, varying in two important ways (see Table 6.3). First, states limit their legislators to different numbers of terms. Members of the lower chambers in Arkansas, California, and Michigan can have the fewest terms, being allowed to serve only three two-year terms. At the other extreme, Louisiana, Nevada, and Oklahoma allow their legislators to serve for 12 consecutive years. The second way term limits vary is whether the limit represents a lifetime ban or just a restriction on consecutive terms. Taking these

---

[117] Peverill Squire, "Professionalization and Public Opinion of State Legislatures," *Journal of Politics* 55 (1993): 479–91.

[118] For example, see George F. Will, *Restoration: Congress, Term Limits, and the Recovery of Deliberative Democracy* (New York: Free Press, 1993).

[119] In 1995, the U.S. Supreme Court held that a state cannot limit the terms of its members of Congress (*U.S. Term Limits, Inc. v. Thornton*, 514 U.S. 779).

[120] Kousser, *Term Limits*.

[121] Alaska and Illinois also have a form of the initiative, but these states have not voted on term limits.

Table 6.3

State Legislative Term Limits

State	Year Enacted	House Limit (years)	House Year of First Impact	Senate Limit (years)	Senate Year of First Impact	Lifetime or Consecutive Term Ban?
Maine	1993	8	1996	8	1996	Consecutive
California	1990	6	1996	8	1998	Lifetime
Colorado	1990	8	1998	8	1998	Consecutive
Arkansas	1992	6	1998	8	2000	Lifetime
Michigan	1992	6	1998	8	2002	Lifetime
Florida	1992	8	2000	8	2000	Consecutive
Ohio	1992	8	2000	8	2000	Consecutive
South Dakota	1992	8	2000	8	2000	Consecutive
Montana	1992	8	2000	8	2000	Consecutive
Arizona	1992	8	2000	8	2000	Consecutive
Missouri	1992	8	2002	8	2002	Lifetime
Oklahoma	1990	12	2004	12	2004	Lifetime
Nebraska	2000	n/a	n/a	8	2006	Consecutive
Louisiana	1995	12	2007	12	2007	Consecutive
Nevada	1996	12	2010	12	2010	Lifetime

Source: National Conference of State Legislatures, http://www.ncsl.org/programs/legman/about/states.htm.

two factors together, Arkansas, California, and Michigan have the most restrictive term limits, with short limits and a lifetime ban. On the other hand, Louisiana's 12-year limit on only consecutive terms probably does not impede the ambitions of Bayou State politicians very much. Perhaps not coincidentally, Louisiana is one of the two states where term limits were adopted not by initiative but by the legislators themselves. Also, term limits were struck down by four state supreme courts (those of Massachusetts, Oregon, Washington, and Wyoming), typically because they restrict a person's right to vote for whom he or she wishes. In contentious moves, the Utah and Idaho state legislatures actually repealed their own term limits.[122]

The Impact of State Legislative Term Limits Term limits go straight to the heart of the most basic forces that political scientists believe shape legislative behavior: incumbent security, the influence of seniority and apprenticeship, and, most importantly, legislators' drive to be reelected. Therefore, scholars have spent considerable effort both assessing the reform's effects on state policy and politics and using the reform as a way of testing legislative theory.[123] Indeed, some of the most extensive collaborative research efforts ever undertaken by state politics scholars have been marshaled recently to evaluate the impacts of term limits.[124]

The predictions that term limits' advocates and detractors made about the reform's

[122] Daniel A. Smith, "Overturning Term Limits: The Legislature's Own Private Idaho?" *PS: Political Science and Politics* 36 (2003): 215–20.

[123] Christopher Z. Mooney, "Thank You, Paul Jacob: Term Limits as a Boon to Legislative Scholarship," (paper presented at the Midwest Political Science Association conference, Chicago, IL, 2008).

[124] Karl T. Kurtz, Bruce Cain, and Richard G. Niemi, eds., *Institutional Change in American Politics: The Case of Term Limits* (Ann Arbor: University of Michigan Press, 2007); John M. Carey, Richard G. Niemi, and Lynda W. Powell, *Term Limits in the State Legislatures* (Ann Arbor: University of Michigan Press, 2000); and Marjorie Sarbaugh-Thompson, Lyke Thompson, Charles D. Elder, John Strate, and Richard C. Elling, *The Political and Institutional Effects of Term Limits* (New York: Palgrave-Macmillan, 2004).

effects during the battles over its adoption in the 1990s were usually vague and often contradictory. Proponents argued that term limits would purge state legislatures of career politicians, providing more opportunity for average citizens to serve.[125] Since these citizen-legislators wouldn't worry about reelection, they could vote their own consciences on legislation and avoid a narrow focus on their districts' interests and pork barrel politics. Furthermore, the leverage of lobbyists and interest groups over lawmakers would be decreased, since that leverage is largely derived from campaign contributions, which would be less important to citizen-legislators. On the other hand, term limits' critics argued that the reelection motive encourages legislators to represent their constituents well; under term limits, representation would suffer.[126] But most worrisome, term limits would strip legislatures of their institutional knowledge. By purging the legislature of its "old heads,"[127] those senior members who knew how state government worked and had a deep, long-term understanding of a state's policy problems, term limits would reduce the quality of legislation and subvert the legislature's influence relative to that of other actors in the process, such as interest groups, the governor, executive agencies, and even their own staff.

Unfortunately, since it has not been long since any state legislators actually reached their maximum number of terms and were forced from office, it's too early to make authoritative judgments about term limits' effects. But even so, we are already beginning to see some important changes in the politics of the 15 states where term limits are still in effect—but not all these changes were the ones predicted by either their opponents or proponents.

First, consider how term limits have influenced elections. Advocates thought that they would increase competition in state legislative elections by eliminating many incumbents, and one early study suggested that this might be true.[128] But several later studies have shown that competition and campaign spending are probably no different under term limits.[129] In fact, competition may even decrease; more incumbents seem to be running unopposed, with potential candidates simply waiting for their legislator's limit to be reached, at which time they all join in the fray for the open seat. We also see a steady stream of state house members running for state senate seats whenever they come open, so that term-limited senates may soon be made up almost entirely of former house members.[130] This may increase the legislative expertise and experience of state senators relative to state

[125] John H. Fund, "Term Limitation: An Idea Whose Time Has Come," in *Limiting Legislative Terms*, ed. Gerald Benjamin and Michael J. Malbin (Washington, D.C.: Congressional Quarterly Press, 1992); Mark P. Petracca, "The Poison of Professional Politics," *Policy Analysis*, online ed., 151 (1991); and Will, *Restoration*.

[126] Amihai Glazer and Martin P. Wattenberg, "How Will Term Limits Affect Legislative Work?" in *Legislative Term Limits: Public Choice Perspectives*, ed. Bernard Grofman (Boston: Kluwer, 1996); and Nelson Polsby, "Limiting Terms Won't Curb Special Interests, Improve the Legislature, or Enhance Democracy," *Public Affairs Report* 31 (Spring 1990): 9. Note that these same arguments arose again in the short-lived attempt by Pennsylvania governor Ed Rendell to adopt term limits in the Keystone State in 2007; see Daylin Leach, "Don't Dumb Down the Legislature," *Philadelphia Daily News*, online ed., 27 April 2007.

[127] Christopher Z. Mooney, Jason Wood, and Gerald C. Wright, "Out with the Old-Heads and in with the Young Turks: The Effects of Term Limits in Semi-Professional State Legislatures," in *Legislating without Experience: Case Studies in State Legislative Term Limits*, ed. Rick Farmer, Christopher Z. Mooney, Richard Powell, and John Green (Lanham, MD: Lexington Books, 2008).

[128] Kermit Daniel and John R. Lott Jr., "Term Limits and Electoral Competition: Evidence from California's State Legislative Races," *Public Choice* 90 (1997): 165–84.

[129] Sarbaugh-Thompson et al., *The Political and Institutional Effects of Term Limits*; Scot Schraufnagel and Karen Halperin, "Term Limits, Electoral Competition, and Representational Diversity: The Case of Florida," *State Politics and Policy Quarterly* 6 (2006): 448–62; and Seth Masket and Jeffrey B. Lewis, "A Return to Normalcy? Revisiting the Effects of Term Limits on Competitiveness and Spending in California Assembly Elections," *State Politics and Policy Quarterly* 7 (2007): 20–38.

[130] Kousser, *Term Limits*.

representatives, leading senates to dominate houses.[131] Term limits also seem to stir the political pot generally, with termed-out legislators running more frequently for local offices and Congress and local officials seeking slots opened up by term limits.[132]

Also contrary to reformers' hopes, term limits have made few changes in the demographics of state legislatures, although they may have accelerated ongoing trends toward more representation for women and minorities by forcing some long-serving white male incumbents from their seats.[133] On the other hand, term limits have increased **legislative turnover** in most states, bringing in the new blood that reformers predicted.[134] But perhaps more significantly, the first wave of limits purged states' cadres of senior legislators.[135] Especially in citizen-legislatures that were term limited, like in Arkansas, where staff and legislative sessions are very restricted, these old heads' deep and extensive knowledge of state politics and policy counterbalanced the power and resources of interest groups and executive agencies.[136] So, as term limits got rid of these "entrenched incumbents," as reformers had hoped, they also deprived the legislature

of an important resource, as opponents feared. Furthermore, term-limited legislators appear to be more partisan and less knowledgeable than non-term-limited legislators.[137]

Term-limited legislators tend to be less focused on their districts, more concerned with statewide issues, and more willing to vote their own minds on legislation.[138] They also spend less time campaigning and raising money. These are all results that reformers would applaud. On the other hand, term-limited legislators do not appear to spend any more time studying and developing legislation than their non-term-limited counterparts. So, what are they doing with their time? Term-limited legislators put in extra effort during the beginning and end of their legislative careers on activities with which non-term-limited legislators are less concerned. Political scientist Renee Van Vechten explains this with her "2-2-2 Rule" in California: "The first two years they're learning. The next two years they're legislating. The final two years they're looking for a job."[139] That is, the shorter the term limits, the greater the proportion of a legislator's career is spent gearing up and winding down.

---

[131] Kathryn A. DePalo, "Truly the 'Upper' Chamber? Relations between the House and Senate after Term Limits," (paper presented at the annual State Politics and Policy Conference, Temple University, Philadelphia, PA, 2008).

[132] Christopher Z. Mooney, "The Effects of Term Limits in Professionalized State Legislatures," in Farmer et al., *Legislating without Experience*; Richard J. Powell, "The Impact of Term Limits on the Candidacy Decisions of State Legislators in U.S. House Elections," *Legislative Studies Quarterly* 25 (2000): 645–61; Rebecca A. Tothero, "The Impact of Term Limits on State Legislators' Ambition for Local Office: The Case of Michigan's House," *Publius* 33 (2003): 111–22; Jeffrey Lazarus, "Term Limits' Multiple Effects on State Legislators' Career Decisions," *State Politics and Policy Quarterly* 6 (2006): 357–83; and Jennifer A. Steen, "The Impact of State Legislative Term Limits on the Supply of Congressional Candidates," *State Politics and Policy Quarterly* 6 (2006): 430–47.

[133] Gary Moncrief, Lynda Powell, and Tim Storey, "Composition of Legislatures," in Kurtz, Niemi, and Cain, *Institutional Change in American Politics*; Schraufnagel and Halperin, "Term Limits."

[134] Gary F. Moncrief, Richard G. Niemi, and Lynda W. Powell, "Time, Term Limits, and Trends in Membership Stability in U.S. State Legislatures," *Legislative Studies Quarterly* 29 (2004): 357–81.

[135] Mooney, Wood, and Wright, "Out with the Old-Heads and in with the Young Turks."

[136] Art English and Brian Weberg, "Term Limits in the Arkansas General Assembly: A Citizen Legislature Responds," Joint Project on Term Limits case study report (Denver, CO: National Conference of State Legislatures, 2004), http://www.ncsl.org/jptl/casestudies/Arkansasv2.pdf.

[137] Thad Kousser and John Straayer, "Budgets and the Policy Process," in Kurtz, Niemi, and Cain, *Institutional Change in American Politics*; Schaffner, Wagner, and Winburn, "Incumbents Out, Party In?"; and Marjorie Sarbaugh-Thompson, Lyke Thompson, Charles D. Elder, Meg Comins, Richard C. Elling, and John Strate, "Democracy among Strangers: Term Limits' Effects on Relationships between State Legislators in Michigan," *State Politics and Policy Quarterly* 6 (2006): 384–409.

[138] John M. Carey, Richard Niemi, Lynda W. Powell, and Gary F. Moncrief, "The Effects of Term Limits on State Legislatures: A New Survey of the 50 States," *Legislative Studies Quarterly* 31 (2006): 105–34; and Lynda W. Powell, Richard G. Niemi, and Michael Smith, "Constituent Attention and Interest Representation," in Kurtz, Niemi, and Cain, *Institutional Change in American Politics*.

[139] Steve Law, "Lawmaking Talent Lost through Revolving Door," *Statesman Journal Online*, 13 February 2000, 9.

Because term limits disrupt relationships among legislators, reduce their understanding of the rules of the legislature and their appreciation for its institutions, and make them in a hurry to make their mark, they have caused the legislative process itself to be messier, more chaotic, more partisan, more rancorous, more confrontational, and less predictable than without term limits.[140] Although you might think that this sounds bad, some term limits supporters are so suspicious of government that they welcome such legislative gridlock as a way of keeping the state from making new inroads into people's lives.[141]

Term limits have also reduced the influence of the legislature on state policy relative to the governor, executive agencies, and legislative staff, just as its critics predicted.[142] This shift in power is especially noticeable in technical and ongoing areas of policy, like the state budget, where a deep understanding of policy history and state government is vital.[143] Term limits may also weaken legislative leaders, something both hoped for by term limits' proponents and feared by their opponents.[144] Throwing out strong leaders opens up the legislature to more people, but it restricts its ability to speak with a powerful voice when negotiating with the governor and other outsiders. On the other hand, a major study in Michigan has suggested that term limits may actually increase legislative party leaders' control of the chamber simply because no one else knows what is going on.[145] It isn't yet clear what impact the reform will have on interest groups' overall influence in the legislative process, but it appears that lobbyists are working harder in term-limited legislatures and that their influence is more evenly distributed than previously.[146]

Thus, term limits have had a variety of impacts on those state legislatures subject to them. Are they good or bad? The jury is still out, and more time must pass before we can fully understand their effects. But beyond simply needing better information about term limits' effects, different people will make different value judgments about these effects. For example, is it good or bad that state legislatures have less influence on public policy, as compared to governors and executive agencies? Should we be concerned or pleased that legislators are more partisan and less attentive to their districts in term-limited legislatures? Will less experienced legislators make better or worse public policy? These are values questions that need to be discussed by citizens and policy makers as term limits become part of the political landscape of many states.

[140] Kousser and Straayer, "Budgets and the Policy Process"; Sarbaugh-Thompson et al., "Democracy among Strangers"; and Alan Greenblatt, "The Truth about Term Limits," *Governing*, January 2006, 24–28.

[141] Law, "Lawmaking Talent Lost," 15.

[142] Carey et al., "The Effects of Term Limits"; and Carey, Niemi, and Powell, *Term Limits in the State Legislatures*.

[143] Kousser and Straayer, "Budgets and the Policy Process."

[144] Eric Kelderman, "Term Limits Take out Legislative Leaders," Stateline.org, online ed., 25 April 2006.

[145] Sarbaugh-Thompson et al., "Democracy among Strangers."

[146] Christopher Z. Mooney, "Lobbyists and Interest Groups," in Kurtz, Cain, and Niemi.

Summary

State constitutions charge their legislatures with difficult responsibilities—to set the state's public policy, oversee its executive branch, and represent its citizens' values and interests before the government. But these constitutions also make it very difficult for legislatures to do these jobs well by setting up a bicameral process, having lawmakers equal in power and elected frequently, and making it difficult to pass laws. Over the years, state legislatures have developed a variety of processes and institutions that help them overcome these obstacles and do their jobs. Standing committees, political parties, and legislative leaders all help legislatures solve their collective action problem. Never content with these arrangements, reformers continually advocate and make institutional changes in state legislatures to improve their performance.

But what constitutes good legislative performance, and what is the best way to achieve it? As you have seen, these questions cannot be answered easily. At its root, the answer to the first question must be based on our political values. Should legislatures engage in the technical evaluation of policy problems and quiet, fact-based debate and compromise or should they be a forum for the clear exchange of divergent views, ending with a majority vote to decide any conflicts? Do we value efficiency or deliberation, effectiveness or fairness? Do we value all of them? Is there an inherent conflict between any of these values?

Should we encourage public participation in the legislative process even if it slows down decision making? Is the efficiency that strong leadership gives us beneficial even if it means that some views are ignored in the process? Should the opinion of the majority always decide policy no matter how badly it hurts the minority? These are questions for citizens and politicians to decide in the public arena. In some respects, the two major legislative reform movements of recent years reflect the tension between these values. The professionalism movement was an attempt to bring more efficiency and rational decision making into lawmaking, whereas the term limits movement was an attempt to link the legislature more closely to the people of the state.

Once these values are decided, political scientists can assess whether they are being reflected in a specific set of state government institutions and policies. We have done some of this in this chapter. But given the differences among the states, the ongoing tinkering with their legislative institutions, and especially the conflicting values that may be used to evaluate a legislature, no institutional design is going to be ideal. However, we should be encouraged by the fact that state policy makers care enough about our legislatures to continue working to improve them. As citizens, we must be vigilant to see that our values are indeed reflected in this, our closest political institution—the state legislature.

Key Terms

Administrative rules review committee

Amend

Bicameral

Bill

Bill sponsor

Casework

Chamber floor

Citizen-legislature

Collective action problem

Conference committee

Contiguous

Cracking

Divided government

Ex post oversight

Gatekeeping

Gerrymander

Implementation

Incumbent

Incumbent-protection district

Legislative intent

Legislative professionalism

Legislative turnover

Malapportionment

Media market

Multimember district

Override

Packing

Party caucus

Pork barrel

Redistricting

Roll call

Single-member district

Standing committee

Supermajority

Targeting electoral strategy

Term limits

Unicameral

Voting cue

Voting Rights Act of 1965

7

Governors

INTRODUCTION

The governor is the single-most visible and powerful person in state government. As the official head of state (like the president of the United States or the queen of England), the governor symbolizes the state to people, organizations, and other governments, in and out of the state. So, when Governor Tim Kaine visited the campus of Virginia Tech just after the April 2007 shooting rampage, he demonstrated the sympathy of all Virginians for the plight of those affected, just as Governor Kathleen Sebelius's visit to Greensburg the following month showed the compassion of Kansans for that tornado-ravaged town (see the chapter-opening photo).[1] And on a more positive note, when Delaware governor Ruth Ann Minner flew to Europe to promote economic development in her state with the German minister of economics and the Italian Chamber of Commerce, she was singing the praises of the workers and business opportunities in her home state.[2] Governors also meet with schoolchildren and sports champions, business and community leaders, delegations of foreign dignitaries, and many others, showing these people their states' concern for them and those people they represent.

Like the president, a governor is also the state's chief executive officer and policy maker, taking a major role in formulating, enacting, and implementing a wide range of public policy. Given the size and complexity of modern state governments, few administrative jobs in the world compare to being the governor of even the smallest state. Only a few countries are as big and complex as California or New York, and even medium-sized states, like Louisiana and South Carolina, are about the size of smaller, but important, countries, such as Ireland and Israel. And certainly few corporations match any of the states in terms of their annual budget, number of employees, and scope of activities.

Thus, being governor is a big job with big responsibilities, and we recognize successful governors accordingly. Indeed, more presidents have been governor than any other type of office or position. In 49 of the 56 presidential elections in U.S. history, at least one of the major party candidates for president or vice president had been a governor; often, more than one governor was on the ticket.[3] Other important positions are regularly filled by former governors, too, including key federal-level cabinet positions, seats in the U.S. Senate, and top executive positions in business, education, and the arts.

[1] Roxana Hegeman, "Rescuers Comb through Rubble," *(Springfield, Ill.) State Journal-Register,* 7 May 2007, p. 2.

[2] "Gov. Minner to Meet with DaimlerChrysler, AstraZeneca in Germany and Italy Next Week," press release, Office of the Governor, State of Delaware, 31 March 2005.

[3] Thad Beyle, "Governors," in *Politics in the American States,* 8th ed., ed. Virginia Gray and Russell L. Hanson (Washington, D.C.: CQ Press, 2004).

But American governors have not always been as powerful as they are today. In fact, out of fear of tyranny and the memory of severe royal governors, when the original 13 colonies set up their state governments, they made their governors very weak indeed. An important scholar of early state governors argued that one such governor "had just enough power to sign the receipt for his salary."[4]

But as the states grew in population and their governments expanded and became more complex, Americans soon realized that their governors needed to be more than just symbolic leaders or simple bureaucrats. Because of the office's pivotal role in state government, the institution of the governorship has been the focus of large and small reforms since the beginning of our nation. These reforms have reflected the political values held most deeply by Americans at different points in history and in different parts of the country.[5] As a result, the 50 governors' offices are diverse in their duties and powers, and these differences have important impacts on policy and governance. We focus on the governor's office as an institution rather than the personality of the person temporarily in the position.

In this chapter, we look at how today's governors are elected, what kinds of people win those races, and the institutional and informal powers of the office. Then, we bring all this together by discussing how three governors use their powers to accomplish three of a governor's main jobs—chief policy maker, chief administrator, and intergovernmental relations manager.

[4] Leslie Lipson, *The American Governor: From Figurehead to Leader* (Chicago, Il.: University of Chciago Press, 1939).
[5] Coleman B. Ransone Jr., *The American Governorship* (Westport, Conn.: Greenwood, 1982); and Nelson C. Dometrius, "Governors: Their Heritage and Future," in *American State and Local Politics: Directions for the 21st Century*, ed. Ronald E. Weber and Paul Brace (New York: Chatham House, 1999).

Gubernatorial Elections

In general, gubernatorial races are the most important elections on a state's political calendar, often drawing even more interest in a state than presidential elections. All but two states now hold gubernatorial elections every four years (New Hampshire's and Vermont's governors still serve two-year terms), with 34 of these being held in the even-numbered year in which no presidential election is held (for example, 2006, 2010, and 2014).[6] Nine states elect their governors to four-year terms during presidential election years, and five states hold their gubernatorial elections in odd-numbered years (see Figure 7.1). Thirty-five states limit their governors to two consecutive terms; Virginia is the last state to limit its governors to one term.

Voting for Governor

When a citizen enters the booth, how does he or she decide which gubernatorial candidate to choose? Recall our discussion of voting in state legislative races (Chapter 6), and think how that might apply to voting for governor. We know that voters have much more specific information about gubernatorial candidates

[6] Council of State Governments, *The Book of the States: 2006*, vol. 38 (Lexington, Ky.: Council of State Governments, 2006), table 4.1.

Gubernatorial Election Cycles[a]

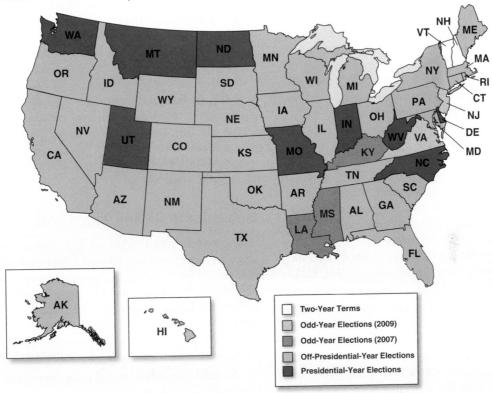

Legend:
- Two-Year Terms
- Odd-Year Elections (2009)
- Odd-Year Elections (2007)
- Off-Presidential-Year Elections
- Presidential-Year Elections

[a]Election cycle coding as follows:

Two-year: Every even-numbered year (for example, 2008, 2010, and 2012).
Odd-year elections 2009: Every fourth odd-numbered year, with the next election being held in 2009 (for example, 2009, 2013, and 2017).
Odd-year elections 2007: Every fourth odd-numbered year, with the last election being held in 2007 (for example, 2007, 2011, and 2015).
Off-presidential-year elections: Even-numbered years when no presidential election is held (for example, 2006, 2010, and 2014).
Presidential-year elections: Years when presidential elections are held (for example, 2008, 2012, and 2016).

than they do about state legislative candidates.[7] Because the race is run statewide, gubernatorial candidates can advertise on television and radio more cost-effectively than those running for the legislature. Campaigning also has economies of scale, so a gubernatorial candidate can transmit more sophisticated messages across the state more frequently. But more importantly, political parties, interest groups, and the general public all recognize the governor's office as a uniquely important position in the state. As a result, gubernatorial candidates can raise more money to get their messages out to the public, groups will make their preferences in the race widely known, and voters will simply spend more time and energy paying attention to the race than they do for lower-level offices.

But what kind of information actually influences how people vote in gubernatorial elections? First, not surprisingly, voters are

[7] Randall W. Partin, "Campaign Intensity and Voter Information: A Look at Gubernatorial Contests," *American Politics Research* 29 (2001): 115–40; and E. Freedman and F. Fico, "Whither the Experts? Newspaper Use of Horse Race and Issue Experts in Coverage of Open Governors' Races in 2002," *Journalism and Mass Communication Quarterly* 81 (2004): 498–510.

most likely to vote to reelect popular incumbent governors. For example, Pennsylvania governor Ed Rendell was so popular in 2006 that he was able to raise taxes significantly and still handily beat a popular Pittsburgh Steelers Hall of Famer (Lynn Swann) for reelection. Interestingly, an incumbent governor's popularity can rub off on the candidate of his or her party even if the incumbent is not running for reelection.[8] Second, voters hold incumbent governors accountable for the state's economy, especially its unemployment rate.[9] Furthermore, the effect of a state's economy on gubernatorial voting appears to be highly nuanced, suggesting that voters are quite sophisticated in making their decisions. For example, voters seem to hold a governor accountable for the state's economy only when his or her party controls both the legislature and the governor's office[10] and only in election years, when campaigning makes getting this information relatively easy.[11]

But not surprisingly, most Americans don't vote only on their understanding of the candidates and issues, even in gubernatorial elections.[12] Like for other offices, voters use some shortcuts that allow them to make a reasoned vote for governor with a minimum amount of effort. The most important of these shortcuts is political party; people tend to vote for the gubernatorial candidate to whose party they feel closest. And unlike his or her public record and policy positions, in practice, a candidate has little control over his or her party affiliation. Other factors affect gubernatorial voting that candidates have even less control over. In particular, national-level forces, such as the country's economy and the popularity of the president, can influence people's votes for governor.[13] But as gubernatorial campaigns have become more costly, sophisticated, and personality-based, the link between gubernatorial voting and presidential approval has weakened, with people voting more on party, the issues, and the candidates in the race.[14]

Gubernatorial Campaign Costs

The growing importance of governors and state governments has caused gubernatorial campaigns to become increasingly costly and competitive over the past 25 years. A serious gubernatorial campaign even in a small state now costs millions of dollars. The average cost has more than doubled between 1980 and 2000, even when controlling for inflation.[15]

Spending on gubernatorial campaigns varies dramatically from race to race and from state to state. Not surprisingly, this variation is not random.[16] For one thing, gubernatorial races are more expensive in larger states because more voters need to be persuaded there. For example,

[8] James D. King, "Incumbent Popularity and Vote Choice in Gubernatorial Elections," *Journal of Politics* 63 (2001): 585–97.

[9] John E. Chubb, "Institutions, the Economy, and the Dynamics of State Elections," *American Political Science Review* 82 (1988): 133–54; and Lonna Rae Atkeson and Randall W. Partin, "Economic and Referendum Voting: A Comparison of Gubernatorial and Senatorial Elections," *American Political Science Review* 89 (1995): 99–107.

[10] Kevin M. Leyden and Stephen A. Borrelli, "The Effect of State Economic Conditions on Gubernatorial Elections: Does a Unified Government Make a Difference?" *Western Political Quarterly* 48 (1995): 275–90.

[11] Jason A. MacDonald and Lee Sigelman, "Public Assessments of Gubernatorial Performance," *American Politics Quarterly* 27 (1999): 201–15.

[12] Eric R. A. N. Smith, *The Unchanging American Voter* (Berkeley: University of California Press, 1989).

[13] Chubb, "Institutions, the Economy, and the Dynamics of State Elections."

[14] Stephen A. Salamore and Barbara G. Salamore, "The Transformation of State Electoral Politics," in *The State of the States*, 2nd ed., ed. Carl E. Van Horn (Washington, D.C.: CQ Press, 1993).

[15] Thad Beyle, "Gubernatorial Elections, Campaign Costs and Powers," in *The Book of the States: 2007*, vol. 39 (Lexington, Ky.: Council of State Governments, 2007).

[16] Malcolm E. Jewell and Sarah M. Morehouse, *Political Parties and Elections in American States*, 4th ed. (Washington, D.C.: CQ Press, 2001), 163–66; and Thad Beyle, "Governors: The Middlemen and Women in Our Political System," in *Politics in the American States*, 6th ed., ed. Virginia Gray and Herbert Jacob (Washington, D.C.: CQ Press, 1996).

in 2002, a total of $155.8 million was spent by gubernatorial candidates in New York, while those in Nebraska only spent $1.7 million. But other factors can also cause gubernatorial campaign costs to increase. In general, the more uncertain the outcome of an election, the more likely candidates will spend freely to win it. So, costs are low when a popular governor is running for reelection, since his or her opponents (and interest groups and other contributors) will be less inclined to "invest" in their lost cause, while a sure winner has little incentive to spend exorbitantly. So, when competition is closest, no incumbent is running, and the partisan balance is even, gubernatorial campaign spending is the highest.

But why have gubernatorial campaigns overall become so much more expensive in recent years? It is an issue of both supply and demand. On the supply side, the importance of the governor's office and state government in general has made a wide range of interest groups and businesses more than willing to contribute money to candidates who they think will pursue their interests once in office. Gubernatorial candidates even tap groups, businesses, and individuals outside of their state for contributions. For example, California governor Arnold Schwarzenegger raised millions in out-of-state campaign fundraisers in 2005.[17] Ironically, Illinois governor Rod Blagojevich raised millions at fundraisers in California that same year.

There have also been more **self-financing candidates** in governor races recently, just as there have been in congressional races.[18] A multimillionaire may worry little about spending $5–10 million or more in pursuit of a challenging opportunity for public service. Two such men spent a total of over $70 million in the New Jersey governor's race in 2005.[19] In California, it costs so much to run for governor that one political scientist quipped, "[T]he rich and famous only need apply."[20] Yet, even the super-rich Schwarzenegger had to solicit contributions; he could not afford the $75 million it cost to reelect him in 2006.[21]

So, the money is available to gubernatorial candidates—at least to those who look viable— but why do they need so much of it? First, the importance of the governor's office attracts many highly qualified and well-financed candidates. Gubernatorial races routinely attract popular U.S. senators, congresspersons, big-city mayors, and other elected statewide officials as well as successful and well-heeled businesspeople and even celebrities, like NBA Hall of Famer Charles Barkley and actor–movie producer Rob Reiner. Such candidates have the knowledge, desire, and money to employ the most up-to-date tools of modern campaigning, including hiring campaign professionals, doing extensive polling, and— most important and expensive—producing slick television ads and running them heavily on stations throughout the state.[22]

Another factor contributing to gubernatorial candidates' insatiable need for campaign funds is the demise of the state political party as a vehicle for campaigning in the general election.[23] Parties almost never get involved in gubernatorial primary elections, which means that candidates have to develop and fund their own campaigns from the start. So, once they win the primary, they are understandably reluctant to hand over control of their successful

---

[17] Gary Delsohn, "3-State Swing to Raise Funds," *Sacramento Bee*, online ed., 20 May 2005.

[18] Jennifer A. Steen, *Self-Financed Candidates in Congressional Elections* (Ann Arbor: University of Michigan Press, 2006).

[19] Robert Tanner, "Democrats Win 2 Governorships," *(Springfield, Ill.) State Journal-Register*, 9 November 2005, p. 8.

[20] Bruce Cain, quoted in Aaron C. Davis, "Only Rich Need Apply," *San Jose (Calif.) Mercury News*, online ed., 5 April 2006.

[21] Dan Walters, "This Is the Week the Race for Governor Shifted into High Gear," *Sacramento Bee*, online ed., 24 March 2006.

[22] Salamore and Salamore, "The Transformation of State Electoral Politics."

[23] Sarah McCally Morehouse, *The Governor as Party Leader: Campaigning and Governing* (Ann Arbor: University of Michigan Press, 1998).

campaigns to others. This personalized approach to running a campaign costs more because the campaign organizations have to be reinvented each election, and the professional campaign consultants who travel from state to state and campaign to campaign to run them are more expensive than simply tapping into the expertise of homegrown party officials.

Finally, the demand for gubernatorial campaign spending has grown so dramatically simply because campaigns are longer and more competitive these days. As soon as the votes are counted in one election, potential candidates for the next contest begin jockeying for favor with the media, interest groups, and potential donors. This is especially the case in those 36 states with gubernatorial term limits, where open races occur at least every two cycles, but it is true even when an incumbent is likely to run again.

Election Outcomes

So, once the smoke clears and the votes have been counted, what can we say about the outcomes of gubernatorial elections? To begin to answer this, remember what we know about voting and campaigns. Because party matters a great deal in voters' decision making, it should not be surprising that the candidate from the dominant party in a state usually wins. But given the high profile of gubernatorial elections and their candidates and the millions of dollars that are spent on their campaigns, the competition between major party gubernatorial candidates in general elections has become closer than ever in most states.[24] Recently, personality-driven campaigns have led to gubernatorial wins for Republicans in such strongly Democratic states

as Massachusetts, California, and New York and for Democrats in the Republican-dominated states of Virginia, Kansas, and Wyoming. Thus, almost no state's governorship is safe for one party or the other anymore, and competition for these offices is intense.[25]

This intense competition can also be seen in the rate of incumbent governor reelection. From 1970 to 2005, of the 286 incumbent governors seeking reelection, 74 percent were successful.[26] That may sound like a high reelection rate, but compared to the much higher rates for state legislators, members of the U.S House, and even U.S. senators (whose prestige of office and constituency parallel those of governors), we see that incumbent governors are relatively vulnerable. Much of this vulnerability is due to the fact that as chief executives, governors are held accountable for a state's problems to a much greater degree than are legislators.[27] In fact, the only major office with a worse reelection rate in recent years is that other chief executive of a large and complex government—the president of the United States.

Today's Governors: Who Are They?

Who are today's governors? Although each one has his or her own personal history, experiences, and background, we can make some generalizations about them. First, as a group, they are a long way from the political hacks who often occupied governors' mansions before the 1960s.[28] Today's governors are younger and better educated

---

[24] Kenneth Dautrich and David A. Yalof, "The State of State Elections," in *The State of the States*, 4th ed., ed. Carl E. Van Horn (Washington, D.C.: CQ Press, 2006).

[25] Dan Seligson, "Home State Blues: Republicans Face Tough Foes in Red State Democratic Governors," *Campaigns & Elections*, online ed., August 2005.

[26] Beyle, "Governors."

[27] David R. Mayhew, *Congress: The Electoral Connection* (New Haven, Conn.: Yale University Press, 1974).

[28] Larry Sabato, *Good-Bye to Good-Time Charlie: The American Governorship Transformed*, 2nd ed. (Washington, D.C.: CQ Press, 1983).

than those in years gone by, they have been highly successful in their chosen fields before becoming governor, and they often move on to important and powerful careers after being governor. Governors fight hard to win their jobs, and while in office, they energetically pursue their vision of the state and its government. To better understand who today's governors are, let's consider both their career paths and what is perhaps the most striking trend in American governors today: the rise of the woman governor.

Career Path

The Rise to Governor What does the résumé of today's typical governor look like? Because the governorship is the top political job in a state, governors often have considerable and progressive experience in state and local government. Governors typically start out their careers in the local or state legislature or in law enforcement, often as a local prosecutor. They have almost always been to college, and they frequently have a postgraduate education, especially in law. Governors were interested in politics, policy, and government from an early age, and their careers reflect this.

We can get a feel for the progressive nature of the state political career ladder by considering the last job of some recent governors.[29] The most common job these people last had before becoming governor was as a statewide elected official, like lieutenant governor or secretary of state. Statewide officials face the same voters they do in a gubernatorial race, and they have already served and are known among that constituency. Charlie Crist (Florida) and Jay Nixon (Missouri) were attorneys general before becoming governor, while Beverly Perdue (North Carolina) was lieutenant governor and Jack Markell (Delaware) was state treasurer. The next most common former

job among governors is member of Congress. This indicates that being governor is typically seen as a step up from Congress in today's political career ladder. In 2006, Nevada's Jim Gibbons and Ohio's Ted Strickland took this route to the governor's mansion.

Some governors move straight up from the state legislature, such as Minnesota's Tim Pawlenty and Oklahoma's Brad Henry, but fewer make this jump now, as the governor's office has become more attractive and more fought over than in years gone by. A few governors come straight from positions in the criminal justice system, such as Oregon's Ted Kulongoski, who was a state supreme court justice, while a few others step up from big-city mayors' offices, like Pennsylvania's Rendell.

The power and prestige of the governor's office also hold considerable cachet for those who have been successful outside of government. Such outsiders have occasionally gained governorships throughout our history. For example, on his way to the White House, Woodrow Wilson moved from the presidency of Princeton University to New Jersey's governor's mansion in 1911. But in recent years, successful businesspeople are more frequently taking their first step into politics by running for the governor's office, which appears to many to be quite like that of a manager in private business. Governors George W. (Texas) and Jeb (Florida) Bush each went straight from private business into the governor's mansion. California's Schwarzenegger and Minnesota's Jesse Ventura were in the entertainment industry before becoming governor (although Ventura had also served a stint as the mayor of a small Minneapolis suburb). Besides these well-known examples, others with a lower profile have moved straight from the private sector to the governor's office, including Rhode Island's Don Carcieri, North Dakota's John Hoeven, and New Jersey's Jon Corzine.

---

[29] Beyle, "Gubernatorial Elections, Campaign Costs and Powers."

Beyond the Governor's Mansion If the governor's office is the pinnacle of a state's political ladder, what can a governor do for an encore? This is an especially important question for those many governors in recent years who have been elected to office in their 30s and 40s, with the prospect of a long postgubernatorial life. Most former governors today continue to do what former governors have always done—put together a lucrative portfolio of business activities that can include legal work, lobbying, public speaking, university teaching, corporate board service, and public relations work. And who can blame them for cashing in a little on their years of experience and many contacts made in state government? Being governor is an extremely demanding job, and governors earn nowhere near the salary of a Fortune 100 company CEO, a comparable position in the private sector.

But many of today's former governors continue to work in the public realm, sometimes in addition to their private ventures. Former governors serve on various top-level public commissions and boards at both the state and national levels, such as the national commission investigating the 9/11 terrorist attacks, 30 percent of whom were former governors. Former governors often serve on presidents' cabinets and as ambassadors; President Bush, a former governor himself, used them extensively in these ways. Several former governors have served on the U.S. Supreme Court, although none has done so since California governor Earl Warren became chief justice in 1953. Two former governors, Virginia's L. Douglas Wilder and California's Jerry Brown, took unusual postgubernatorial jobs—as mayors of troubled cities in their states. California's Brown has more recently been elected the state's attorney general, another seeming backward step in the political ladder. Recently, former governor Roy Romer of Colorado may have taken on one of the most difficult jobs of all—superintendent of the distressed Los Angeles School District.

Of course, the fact that the job of a governor is more like that of the president of the United States than any other job in the country makes the nation's governors a natural talent pool for future presidents. This has been true throughout U.S. history, as 17 of our 44 presidents (39 percent) were former governors (the 2008 presidential election notwithstanding). Indeed, as of 2008, former governors had served as president for 108 years of the nation's 220-year history under the U.S. Constitution—almost 50 percent of the time. From 1977 to 2009, a former governor occupied the Oval Office in all but four years. Only President George H. W. Bush had not been a governor—but two of his sons were. While we often think of the U.S. Senate as a natural training ground for presidents, the 2008 election of Barack Obama was the first time a sitting member of Congress was elected to the presidency since John F. Kennedy in 1960; the last one before Kennedy was Warren G. Harding in 1920!

Of course, only a small percentage of former governors actually become president, but just as important is the idea that a governor could become president. Thus, governors are thought of as being "presidential timber" by the media, the political parties, and, just as importantly, the governors themselves. This burnishes the image of both governors and their offices, attracting higher-quality candidates to run for the office and giving sitting governors more influence, both within and outside of their states. And a governor's presidential aspirations may even be good for a state, as he or she strives to perform well to gain favorable publicity. For example, the performance of Massachusetts governor Mitt Romney in managing Boston's "Big Dig" highway reconstruction was seen by many as having implications for his (ultimately unsuccessful) 2008 presidential bid, giving him an incentive to do the job well.[30]

---

[30] Glen Johnson, "Gov. Romney's Future May Hinge on Big Dig," *Sacramento Bee*, online ed., 18 July 2006.

Women and Minorities as Governor

Until quite recently, governors were almost exclusively white men. But in the past two decades, progress has been made in electing governors who are more representative of the sex and race of all Americans,[31] just as progress has been made in electing more representative state legislatures, as we discussed in Chapter 6.

The most sweeping change to the demographics of American governors has been with the election of many women to the post in recent decades. Prior to 1974, only three women had ever served as governor, and these were spouses of former governors who were term limited, were banned from office for official malfeasance, or had died. These governors were clearly elected as surrogates for their husbands; one even ran under the slogan "Two governors for the price of one," and another used the slogan "Let George [her husband] do it."[32]

In 1974, Connecticut's Ella Grasso, a former state legislator, Connecticut secretary of state, and U.S. congressperson, became the first woman elected governor on her own merits;[33] she was soon followed by Washington State's Dixy Lee Ray in 1977. Three more women were elected to governorships in the 1980s, and six more in the 1990s. This pace has continued to accelerate in the 2000s, with 11 women being elected governor in the first eight years of the 21st century. Indeed, six women were elected or reelected in 2006—fully 17 percent of those winning gubernatorial elections that year. In addition to those women who have been elected governor since 1982, seven women have succeeded to the governorship when the elected governor died, resigned, or was impeached, serving anywhere from several days to three years. Jane Dee Hull of Arizona and Jodi Rell of Connecticut succeeded to their governorships and were later elected in their own right.

Thirty women have served as governor (see Table 7.1). Most of these women have been Democrats, but the balance is not too lopsided (19 Democrats and 11 Republicans). Perhaps more important, the states that have elected these women represent the country very broadly, with 23 states having had a woman governor. Clearly, the rise of the woman governor is not a regional, partisan, or ideological phenomenon. And as women continue to serve as governors, Americans will become accustomed to seeing women in powerful executive positions in government, allowing candidates to be judged more on their qualifications than their sex. This levels the playing field for female candidates and can improve sexual representation in all public offices. Hillary Clinton's run for president in 2008 was probably helped significantly by the rise of woman governors in the 1990s and 2000s—or, more accurately, the old bias against electing women to executive office was reduced by these governors' success.

Better racial and ethnic gubernatorial representation has been harder for the states to achieve than better sexual representation. But some nonwhites have been elected in recent years, especially in those states with smaller proportions of whites than the nation as a whole. Hawaii, with its polyethnic population where whites are in the minority, has elected three Asian American governors. New Mexico has the country's highest proportion of Latinos, and it has elected three Latino governors recently, including its current governor, former Clinton cabinet secretary Bill Richardson. New Mexico's neighbor, Arizona, also elected a Latino governor, as has Florida.

---

[31] As to sexual orientation, no openly gay person has ever been elected governor of a U.S. state. New Jersey's former governor Jim McGreevy announced that he was gay when he resigned in 2004. His resignation was prompted by ethical and legal questions regarding having sexual relations with an aide and engaging in improprieties in the awarding of contracts, not his sexual orientation.

[32] Quoted in Susan J. Carroll, "Women in State Government: Historical Overview and Current Trends," in *The State of the States*, vol. 36 (Lexington, Ky.: Council of State Governments, 2004).

[33] Grasso was reelected in 1978 but resigned in 1980 for health reasons, dying soon after.

Table 7.1

Woman Governors

Name	State	Party	Dates of Service
Wives of Former Governors			
Nellie Taylor Ross	Wyoming	D	1925–1927
Miriam "Ma" Ferguson	Texas	D	1925–1927, 1933–1935
Lurleen Wallace	Alabama	D	1967–1968[a]
Elected in Their Own Right			
Ella Grasso	Connecticut	D	1975–1980[b]
Dixy Lee Ray	Washington	D	1977–1981
Martha Layne Collins	Kentucky	D	1983–1987
Madeleine M. Kunin	Vermont	D	1985–1991
Kay A. Orr	Nebraska	R	1987–1991
Joan Finney	Kansas	D	1991–1995
Barbara Roberts	Oregon	D	1991–1995
Ann Richards	Texas	D	1991–1995
Christine Todd Whitman	New Jersey	R	1994–2001
Jeanne Shaheen	New Hampshire	D	1997–2003
Jane Dee Hull[c]	Arizona	R	1997–2003
Judy Martz	Montana	R	2001–2005
Ruth Ann Minner	Delaware	D	2001–2009
Linda Lingle	Hawaii	R	2002–
Janet Napolitano	Arizona	D	2003–2009
Kathleen Sebelius	Kansas	D	2003–
Jennifer Granholm	Michigan	D	2003–
Kathleen Blanco	Louisiana	D	2004–2008
M. Jodi Rell[d]	Connecticut	R	2004–
Christine Gregoire	Washington	D	2005–
Sarah Palin	Alaska	R	2007–
Beverly Perdue	North Carolina	D	2009–
Successors			
Vesta M. Roy	New Hampshire	R	1982–1983
Rose Mofford	Arizona	D	1988–1991
Jane Dee Hull[c]	Arizona	R	1997–2003
Nancy P. Hollister	Ohio	R	1998–1999
Jane Swift	Massachusetts	R	2001–2003
Olene Walker	Utah	R	2003–2005
M. Jodi Rell	Connecticut	R	2004–
Jan Brewer	Arizona	R	2009–

[a] Died in office.
[b] Resigned for health reasons.
[c] Jane Dee Hull succeeded to office upon the resignation of Fife Symington in 1997 and then was elected to a full term in her own right in 1998.
[d] M. Jodi Rell succeeded to office upon the resignation of John Rowland in 2004 and then was elected to a full term in her own right in 2006.

Source: Adapted from Thad Beyle, "Gubernatorial Elections, Campaign Costs and Powers," in *The Book of the States: 2007*, vol. 39 (Lexington, Ky.: Council of State Governments, 2007), table D.

Latinos make up a large percentage of voters in both these states. In 1990, Virginia's Wilder became the first African American to be elected a state governor.[34] Although 20 percent of Virginia's population is African American, the seven other states with higher proportions of black residents have never elected an African American governor.

Recently, three nonwhite men were elected governor in states where members of their racial groups make up only a small proportion of voters, and another nonwhite man—who is also disabled—became governor through succession. In 1996, Washington State's Gary Locke was the first Asian American to be elected governor of a mainland state; only about 6 percent of Washingtonians are Asian Americans. In 2006, Deval Patrick was elected governor of Massachusetts, a state whose population is only about 7 percent African American. In 2007, Louisiana elected second-generation Indian American Bobby Jindal governor. In addition, in March 2008, New York lieutenant governor David Paterson became governor when Governor Eliot Spitzer resigned after a prostitution scandal. Paterson is not only African American but also legally blind. Thus, while racial and ethnic minorities are much underrepresented in the ranks of the nation's governors, the recent elections of Locke, Patrick, and Jindal—and the elections of Paterson and several other nonwhites to statewide offices—in states where people of their own race are in the distinct minority suggest that more governors of color may be elected in the coming years.

The Powers of the Governor

Once in office, what does a governor do, and how does he or she do it? The answer to these questions is not as clear-cut as it may be for officials of the other two branches of state government. Legislators pass laws, and judges interpret and enforce laws by deciding on cases, but what exactly do governors do? We see them in the media giving speeches, meeting with various officials and schoolchildren from around the state, visiting disaster areas, and so forth, and we are vaguely aware that they somehow run state government—but what does that mean?

Governors have three basic jobs—helping set public policy for the state, directing the state government **bureaucracy**, and acting as the point person for relations with people and governments outside of state government, including the state's local governments, other state governments, the national government, businesses, and even foreign countries. How do governors accomplish these three jobs? In order to understand this fully, we must first look at the powers available to a governor.

As with presidential power, gubernatorial power is largely the power to persuade.[35] One way or the other, most of the people who governors need to help them govern the state can choose to ignore or even work against the governor's goals if they want to do so. But governors have a variety of tools—both institutional and informal—that, when used skillfully, can make them a more "persuasive." In this section, we describe these tools, or **gubernatorial powers**, and how they can be useful to a governor. We also describe how some of these powers vary among the states and over time and how this translates into important variations in gubernatorial control of state government. Once we have an understanding of these individual powers, in the following section, we provide examples of how three current governors have put them together to accomplish each of a governor's three main jobs.

---

[34] The first African American to serve as governor took office over 100 years before Wilder. In 1872, during the Reconstruction era after the Civil War, as the president pro tem of the Louisiana state senate, P. B. S. Pinchback became governor upon the death of the sitting governor, Oscar Dunn.

[35] Richard E. Neustadt, *Presidential Power and the Modern Presidents* (New York: Free Press, 1990).

Institutional Powers

First, consider the institutional powers that states give their governors, largely through their constitutions and statutes. These are powers that a state's policy makers have consciously decided to give to their governors. In recent decades, the states have increased their governors' powers in each of these areas, but significant variation remains in the institutional powers states grant to their governors.

Budget-Making Authority As you will see in Chapter 10, the budget is one of the most concrete expressions of a state's public policy. Almost everything a state does, from providing needy children with health care to housing prisoners to building and maintaining roads, requires spending money, and the budget plans and authorizes all the state's spending. Although the budget must pass the state legislature each year[36] through the regular legislative process, all but a few states give the governor special powers to influence the budget process that they do not have in regular lawmaking.

In the early years of the republic, state government was small and simple and so was its budget. Then, state budgets tended to be written piecemeal in various legislative committees based on each agency's spending needs. But as state government grew in complexity and size, it became evident that such a haphazard budgeting process allowed for overlap, mismanagement, and fraud. One of the most enduring reforms of the **Progressive era** was the unified **executive budget**, a system of state budget-making where the governor is given the responsibility to assess the state's spending needs and develop a single budget proposal for the legislature to consider. Developing a unified executive budget may

seem more like an administrative pain in the neck than an important political power, especially because the legislature can make virtually any modifications in the proposal that it wants to, but this authority to propose the budget is widely seen by administrators, legislators, interest groups, and political scientists as probably the governor's most important institutional power.[37]

Why is developing the budget such an important gubernatorial tool? It comes down to logistics. Consisting of hundreds of pages of very small type outlining exactly how the state will spend its money for the entire year, the budget is extremely large, complex, and technical. The governor has a large budget office staff and perhaps hundreds of other people in the offices throughout the executive branch helping him or her put this document together for the better part of a year. The legislature has only two or three months and very limited staff to review the proposal, and at the same time, they are also taking care of thousands of other pieces of legislation. The result of this imbalance is that the legislature only can review the budget around the edges, with most of the governor's proposal usually being adopted. Beyond the power to propose a state's budget, most governors also have special veto powers for spending bills (see below) and the ability to estimate revenue for the coming year (which can sometimes allow the governor to justify cuts or expansions in spending, as desired). All this adds up to real power for the governor over anyone or any group that wants to determine state government spending—which is just about everyone involved in state policy making.

On the other hand, special fees and taxes that are **earmarked** in statutes for particular purposes can limit governors' budget-making power by reducing the discretion with which

---

[36] For those few states that still do biennial budgeting, it must pass through the legislature every two years.

[37] Dall W. Forsythe, *Memos to the Governor: An Introduction to State Budgeting*, 2nd ed. (Washington, D.C.: Georgetown University Press, 2004); Charles Barrilleaux and Michael Berkman, "Do Governors Matter? Budgeting and the Politics of State Policymaking," *Political Research Quarterly* 56 (2003): 409–17; Thad L. Beyle, "The Governor's Formal Powers: A View from the Governor's Chair," *Public Administration Review* 28 (1968): 540–45; and E. Lee. Bernick, "Gubernatorial Tools: Formal and Informal," *Journal of Politics* 41 (1979): 656–65.

they can target spending. For example, gasoline taxes that are earmarked for building new roads cannot be used to buy textbooks or even fund mass transit. A governor's control over the budget is reduced in proportion to the amount of the state's revenue that is designated for some predetermined purpose.

Veto As discussed in Chapter 6, a governor's only institutional role in the state legislative process is at the end, when, after both chambers have passed a bill in identical form, the governor chooses whether to sign it into law or to veto it in some fashion, sending it back to the legislature for further consideration. Legislatures have the opportunity to **override** a veto by voting again in favor of the bill in both chambers but usually by a **supermajority** vote. Given the difficulty of mustering a supermajority on a controversial measure (and a bill is controversial by definition if it has been vetoed by the governor), and given the other powers and respect typically accorded a governor, vetoes are very difficult to override.[38] For example, during his 14-year tenure in Wisconsin in the 1980s and 1990s, Republican governor Tommy Thompson made 1,937 legislative vetoes, and the Democrat-controlled Wisconsin Legislature failed to override any of them.[39]

Governors in different states have different levels of veto power. All governors can execute a full, or "package," veto on bills—the same veto power that the president has. But in most states, the governor's veto power is even stronger than that of the president. First, 43 governors have **line-item veto** power on **appropriations bills**; that is, the ability to veto a single expenditure item (literally, a line in a budget bill) while letting the rest of the bill pass into law.[40] This way, the legislature cannot hold the entire budget hostage for a single spending item that the governor thinks is unnecessary (say, a bridge or a new fire truck for a town). The line-item veto allows the governor to remove such items surgically from the budget. Presidents have long coveted this power,[41] but the U.S. Constitution grants them only the **full veto**.[42]

Twelve states also grant their governors a second kind of enhanced veto for appropriations bills: a **reduction veto**. A reduction veto allows the governor to reduce the amount that is authorized to be spent on a budget item. This way, governors avoid the all-or-nothing choice of the line-item veto on each project, allowing them simply to scale back what they see as excessive spending on a useful project. Six states give their governors even greater power with the **amendatory veto**, which allows them to send a budget item or a bill back to the legislature with a message asking for a specific change.[43] Then, the legislature can either override the veto by passing the original bill or item with a supermajority vote or pass the governor's suggested language with a simple majority vote. Because it is often much easier to generate a simple majority to agree with the governor than to generate a supermajority to oppose him or her, this is a powerful tool. Finally, Wisconsin gives its governor the ability to veto individual words, letters, and digits within single sentences in appropriations

---

[38] Vicky M. Wilkins and Garry Young, "The Influence of Governors on Veto Override Attempts: A Test of Pivotal Politics," *Legislative Studies Quarterly* 27 (2002): 557–76.

[39] Steven Walters, "Thompson's Legacy," *Milwaukee (Wisc.) Journal-Sentinel*, 24 December 2000, pp. 1A and 10A.

[40] Daniel C. Vock, "Govs Enjoy Quirky Veto Power," *Stateline.org*, online ed., 24 April 2007.

[41] Deb Reichman, "Bush Urges Senate to Pass Line-Item Veto," *Sacramento Bee*, online ed., 27 June 2006.

[42] In 1996, Congress tried to give the president an item veto through legislation, but the Supreme Court held that this was unconstitutional. See *Clinton v. City of New York*, 524 U.S. 417 (1998).

[43] In addition to Alabama, Illinois, Massachusetts, Montana, New Jersey, and Virginia, South Dakota gives its governor the amendatory veto when the legislature is in session, and Wisconsin does so on budget bills; Vock, "Govs Enjoy Quirky Veto Power."

bills, making this the most powerful veto of all (see Institutions Matter).

These states give governors special veto powers on appropriations bills to help reduce state spending. In particular, reformers hoped these special vetoes would allow the governor to cut out unnecessary pork barrel projects. The idea was that while legislators have an incentive to pass such district-specific largesse and inflate the state budget, governors, with their statewide perspective, may be less prone to do so. But while this institutional tool may make sense in theory, there is little evidence that these special vetoes do in fact reduce state spending.[44]

On the other hand, the veto is a very powerful political weapon for the governor, and these special vetoes certainly enhance this power. And the veto is useful to a governor in more ways than one. Of course, the full veto helps governors stop legislation that they do not wish to become law, and the special vetoes allow them to reduce or eliminate specific spending. But these blunt effects of the veto are really only the last resort of governors who cannot get their way in a more subtle fashion. Because the process of passing a bill is complex and difficult, as you saw in Chapter 6, legislators do not want their bills vetoed. Therefore, vetoes may have their greatest effect through their threat rather than their actual use. If a legislator knows that the governor disapproves of a piece of legislation, the existence of a strong veto power gives that lawmaker great incentive to work with the governor prior to its passage and modify it as necessary to win a gubernatorial signature. Even more subtly, a governor can threaten to veto a legislator's pet bill as leverage to get help on a totally unrelated piece of legislation. Indeed, when a governor actually has to use the veto, it is usually an indication of weakness. In practice, governors typically use the veto quite sparingly, unless they are faced

with a legislature with a majority of the other party—which is why governors Thompson and Jim Doyle used it so often in Wisconsin.

Appointment Power The states vary in the power they give their governors to make appointments to positions in government. These include appointments to judgeships and various boards and commissions, but the most important powers of appointment tend to be those to top posts in the executive branch. Governors who can appoint their people to many or most of the policy-making and upper-management positions in the executive branch can control better the bureaucracy and policy implementation.[45] This helps a governor get policies administered as he or she wants them to be, and it forces those who want something from a particular agency to come to the governor (or the governor's appointee) to get it. Broad appointment powers also allow governors to reward their supporters by giving them positions of prestige and power. Such appointments can also be bargaining chips for a governor in dealing with state legislators or others in the policy-making process. In short, a governor who controls many jobs in state government is more powerful than one whose appointment power is more limited.

Governors' appointment powers vary in two important ways. First, some states allow for the direct and independent election of various top-level executive branch officials, including the lieutenant governor, attorney general, secretary of state, and treasurer, among others. When these officials are elected independently, not only can governors not order them around, but they may also actually be rivals for power. Sometimes, these executives are from the other party and are bent on working against the governor as a precursor to their own gubernatorial runs.[46] Remember that many governors held one of these independently

---

[44] J. A. Dearden and T. A. Husted, "Do Governors Get What They Want? An Alternative Examination of the Line-Item Veto," *Public Choice* 77 (1993): 707–23.

[45] Thad Beyle, "Being Governor," in Van Horn, *The State of the States*, 4th ed.

[46] Beyle, "Being Governor."

INSTITUTIONS MATTER

VANNA WHITE MEETS FRANKENSTEIN: WISCONSIN'S POWERFUL VETO

Wisconsin has long given its governors a uniquely powerful veto, but it has been whittling away at this power in recent years. Until a constitutional amendment banned the practice in 1990, governors could veto individual words, letters, digits, and even punctuation marks within appropriations bills to create whole new words, numbers, and sentences that sometimes had an entirely different meaning from the original bill. They called this variant of the line-item veto the "Vanna White veto," after the game show personality who constructs words one letter at a time.[a] Former Governor Tommy Thompson, a Republican, used this power extensively when facing a state legislature with a Democratic majority in the 1980s. The 1990 amendment was a reaction to what some saw as an abuse of this power. But after this limitation, the Wisconsin Constitution still allowed governors to delete whole words and individual digits from different sentences. They called this the "Frankenstein veto," since it allowed the construction of new sentences out of multiple sentences through this partial veto process. The excerpt from the vetoed 2005 budget bill below demonstrates how effective this power could be. With these vetoes, Democratic Governor Jim Doyle angered the Republican-majority legislature by giving the secretary of administration the power to shift money around in the state's funds, something that greatly enhanced the governor's control of the state budget. As Thompson's and Doyle's actions show, a governor whose party is in the minority in the legislature can use a strong veto as leverage over the outcome of legislation. The legislature had often challenged these powerful vetoes in court, but the state's supreme court regularly upheld their constitutionality.[b] Following what some saw as another abuse of this veto, this time by Doyle in 2005, its opponents again worked to change the state's constitution. As a result of these efforts, in April 2008, the state's voters approved an amendment that banned the Frankenstein veto. However, the amendment still allowed vetoing of individual words or digits within a single sentence.[c] As such, Wisconsin's governor continues to have what is probably the strongest veto power in the country.

Cited segments of 2005 Assembly Bill 100:

SECTION 9255. Appropriation changes; other.
(1) STATE AGENCY APPROPRIATION LAPSES TO THE GENERAL FUND.

	(b) *Prohibited appropriation lapses and transfers.*
Vetoed In Part	The secretary of administration may not lapse or transfer
Vetoed In Part	moneys to the general fund from any appropriation account specified in paragraph if the lapse or transfer would violate a condition imposed by the federal

government on the expenditure of the moneys or if the **Vetoed** lapse or transfer would violate the federal or state **In Part** constitution.

(2) TRANSFER FROM GENERAL FUND TO TAXPAYER **Vetoed** PROTECTION FUND. There is transferred $36,000,000 from **In Part** the general fund to the taxpayer protection fund . **Vetoed In Part**

Note: Wisconsin's "Frankenstein veto." Governor Jim Doyle completely changed the meaning of these paragraphs of Wisconsin's 2005 budget bill with the Frankenstein veto (the grayed-out words have been vetoed). As passed by the legislature, the bill said that the secretary of administration could *not* transfer these funds to the general fund; with the veto, the secretary is explicitly authorized to make such transfers. Through a constitutional amendment in 2008, Wisconsin's voters restricted the Frankenstein veto to words and digits within individual sentences in a bill.

[a] Steven Walters, "Vetoes Strike at Spending Power," *Milwaukee (Wisc.) Journal-Sentinel*, 30 July 2005, p. A1.
[b] Mike Nichols, "See, It's Easy to Abuse This Veto," *Milwaukee (Wisc.) Journal-Sentinel*, 30 July 2005, p. B1.
[c] Ryan J. Foley, "'Frankenstein' Veto Slain by Voters," *Madison (Wisc.) Capital Times*, online ed., 1 April 2008.

elected executive positions themselves before moving up to the governorship.

A second way that gubernatorial appointment powers vary among the states is how far up into the managerial positions of the bureaucracy a state's **civil service system** reaches. At one time, governors gained political power from handing out as many as 20,000 **patronage jobs** to political supporters and their families. Although no one begrudges a governor the power to appoint the top managers of state government so that he or she can hold the bureaucracy accountable and set public policy, many of these positions—such as workers on road construction crews and driver's license examiners—clearly had no policy-making power. Although a state legislator might not be persuaded to vote for a governor's bill by the offer of a road crew job, he or she might be happy to get one of these jobs for a constituent or supporter. States with extensive civil service systems hire more workers through merit testing, giving governors less power over the bureaucracy and fewer political bargaining chips. But the lack of independently elected statewide executives and the ability to hire and fire top agency managers without the approval of the state legislature are the most important facets of this gubernatorial power.

Tenure Potential A governor is more powerful if those with whom he or she deals in the political process believe that he or she may be around for a long time. Governors who will soon be leaving office have less to threaten or offer those with whom they negotiate. State bureaucrats, interest groups, and legislators (at least where no legislative term limits are in place) may be able to simply wait out a governor who will soon be replaced, giving them little incentive to compromise.

Governors' institutional tenure potential varies in two ways: term length and term limits.[47] One of the major institutional reforms of the 1960s and 1970s for governors was the lengthening of their terms. In 1960, many states elected their governors to two-year terms; today, only Vermont and New Hampshire do. Governors elsewhere serve four-year terms. Gubernatorial term limits make a governor a **lame duck** as soon as he or she has won the last election allowed. Although term limits have been a feature of some governorships for many years, the legislative term limits movement also affected some governorships. Fourteen of the 21 states that passed legislative term limits in the 1990s enacted gubernatorial term limits at the same time. Currently, 34 states limit their governors to two four-year terms, whereas 14 states have no limits.[48] Governors of Utah can serve up to three four-year terms, and those of Virginia can serve only a single four-year term.[49]

Gubernatorial Staff A governor's personal staff can be considered an institutional power.[50] Although staffing varies more from governor to governor in a given state than do other institutional powers, it still must be approved in a state's budget, and as such, it is statutory. These staff can include press spokespeople, legislative liaisons, and deputy governors to coordinate policy areas that spread out over a variety of agencies, such as education or drug enforcement. Unlike cabinet secretaries and other managerial appointees, these staff are solely responsible to the governor and should have no mixed loyalties. They have no agencies or interest groups to appease, and their appointments are not typically subject to legislative approval. Staff serve as additional eyes, ears, feet, and hands for the governor, greatly extending his or her

---

[47] The length of time a governor may actually serve also depends on voters (and, in some cases, federal prosecutors), but term limits and term length are the institutional aspects of tenure potential.

[48] See Council of State Governments, *The Book of the States 2006*, vol. 38 (Lexington, Ky.: Council of State Governments, 2006), table 4.1.

[49] Rob Gurwitt, "The Last One-Term Statehouse," *Governing*, October 2005, 36–42.

[50] Robert J. Dilger, "A Comparative Analysis of Gubernatorial Enabling Resources," *State and Local Government Review* 26 (1995): 118–26.

reach and information-gathering ability. And because staff serve solely at the governor's discretion, and because their fate is inextricably linked to that of the governor, a good staff acts simply as a proxy for the governor. The flipside of this is that when these staff generate controversy, whether because of ethical issues or due to concern over how high their salaries are (reaching upward from $100,000 annually for top gubernatorial staff), this controversy reflects directly on the governor.

The number of staff that a governor has varies dramatically across states, from a dozen close aides and secretaries to an extended office of well over 100 staffers in a variety of roles. In general, governors' staffs are much larger today than they were even 20 years ago, and they are the largest in more populous states.[51] In some states, the budget office is housed in the governor's office and considered part of the governor's staff. This unit has the primary responsibility for developing the governor's budget proposal and monitoring the budget's execution throughout the fiscal year. As governors have gained more control over the budget, these offices have been increasingly shifted to the governors' direct control rather than being an independent unit. Indeed, for many governors, the state budget office now acts as one of the main tools for controlling the bureaucracy and guiding policy, much the same way that presidents now use the federal Office of Management and Budget.[52]

Instruments to Set the Legislative Agenda

Most governors have two institutional powers that give them some influence over the legislature's **policy agenda**. First, at the beginning of each legislative session, most governors give a **State of the State address** to the legislature, much like the president's annual State of the Union address. This major address is an opportunity for governors to identify what they think are the most important problems for their legislatures to tackle that session and to offer a list of proposals for the legislature to consider.[53] Of course, the legislature is not bound to follow the agenda the governor lays out in his or her speech, but traditionally, the governor's proposals receive serious consideration. Indeed, legislators will complain of a lack of leadership if the governor's proposals are not clear in the State of the State speech.

The other institution that lets governors set the legislative agenda is their power to call the state legislature into **special session** after it has adjourned its regular session. Just the threat of a special session can be a potent weapon in part-time legislatures because it would require these members to sacrifice extra time from their regular jobs. Such legislators may quickly give in to the governor's legislative demands to avoid this overtime work, for which they do not receive extra pay.[54]

More importantly than simply assembling legislators in a special session, most governors are empowered to set a limited agenda for that session, in effect forcing legislators to consider a specific issue. For example, in 2006, Governor Rick Perry ordered the Texas Legislature into special session to deal with public school financing issues, and California's Schwarzenegger called a special session to deal with prison overcrowding.[55] Calling a special session not only shows the legislature that the governor really cares about an issue but also puts the media spotlight on the legislature's deliberations, increasing pressure on it to act.

---

[51] Margaret R. Ferguson, *The Executive Branch of State Government* (Santa Barbara, Calif.: ABC-CLIO, 2006), 176–79.

[52] Forsythe, *Memos to the Governor.*

[53] Margaret R. Ferguson, "Gubernatorial Policy Leadership in the Fifty States" (Ph.D. diss., University of North Carolina at Chapel Hill, 1996).

[54] Legislators usually receive expense money for these special sessions to cover their meals, hotels, and so on, but they do not receive extra salary for them.

[55] "Perry Expands Call," *Austin (Tex.) American-Statesman,* online ed., 11 May 2006; and Andy Furillo, "Governor Wants Special Session on Prisons," *Sacramento Bee,* online ed., 26 June 2006.

Although the governor may force the legislature into special session on a particular issue, the governor cannot force the legislature to pass anything. A recalcitrant legislature can simply adjourn a special session without taking any action. Occasionally, a battle royal ensues as the governor keeps calling the legislature into special session and the legislature keeps adjourning without acting; in 1999, this happened in Illinois over the budget.[56] But this sort of brouhaha is rare because the media, the public, and rank-and-file legislators quickly get fed up with the spectacle and the expense, giving both legislators and the governor the incentive to settle their differences.

Executive Orders Governors, like presidents, can make executive orders, which are official pronouncements mandating certain government actions.[57] Such orders are public written documents, typically filed with the secretary of state or some other official for public access. Executive orders have the force of law, but their scope is usually limited. The power of governors to make executive orders varies on whether they are authorized by statute, constitution, or simply tradition; by the areas of policy in which a governor is authorized to make such orders; and whether these orders can be reviewed by the legislature or are subject to any other restrictions.[58] Governors are typically authorized to make executive orders in four policy areas: to reorganize or control the bureaucracy; to call out the National Guard to respond to emergencies or crises; to set up commissions to study particularly vexing policy problems; or to respond to federal rules, regulations, and initiatives. The stronger the legal basis for these executive orders, the

broader the scope of their power, and the fewer restrictions or less oversight of them, the more potent a tool they become for a governor.

In 2006, New Jersey's Corzine used an executive order as a powerful and effective weapon in his fight with his state legislature over a tax increase.[59] Faced with a budget deficit, the speaker of the assembly wanted to cut expenses, whereas the governor wanted to raise the sales tax one cent. In a game of political chicken, the start of the fiscal year arrived on July 1 with no agreement, no budget, and, therefore, no money to pay state workers. Corzine upped the ante by issuing an executive order that closed down all nonessential[60] state government services— parks, beaches, driver's license testing stations, bureaucratic agencies, and so forth. Even Atlantic City's casinos were closed down because the required state inspectors were laid off. For ten days, the shutdown went on—even over the important Fourth of July holiday. Finally, the governor got his way (with perhaps at least a little compromising), and he rescinded the order. States where governors have a weaker executive order power might have seen a different outcome.

Formal Powers: Comparing the States
Figure 7.2 shows how today's governorships differ in their institutional powers.[61] Even though all state governors are stronger today than in the past, this map demonstrates that the institutional powers of different states' governors vary a great deal. Although most governorships fall into the middle range, 12 of them are either quite strong or quite weak compared to these institutions in the other states. This map also gives some

[56] Doug Finke. "Under Pressure: Groups Push Jones on Budget Cuts Vote," *(Springfield, Ill.) State Journal-Register*, 4 October 2007, p. 1.

[57] Cynthia J. Bowling, Margaret R. Ferguson, and Colleen Clemons, "Executive Orders in the American States" (paper presented at the 6th Annual State Politics and Policy Conference, Lubbock, Tex., 2006).

[58] Council of State Governments, *The Book of the States: 2005*, vol. 37 (Lexington, Ky.: Council of State Governments, 2005), 222–24.

[59] Tom Hester Jr., "Gov. Jon Corzine Shuts Down New Jersey Government," *(Springfield, Ill.) State Journal-Register*, 2 July 2006, p. 7; and "Corzine's Cuts: Hard to Some, Soft to GOP," *Philadelphia Inquirer*, online ed., 11 July 2006.

[60] Prisons, hospitals, and other services deemed essential continued to operate.

[61] Thad Beyle and Margaret Ferguson, "Governors and the Executive Branch," in *Politics in the American States*, 9th ed., ed. Virginia Gray and Russell L. Hanson (Washington, D.C.: CQ Press, 2008).

Figure 7.2

Governor's Institutional Powers

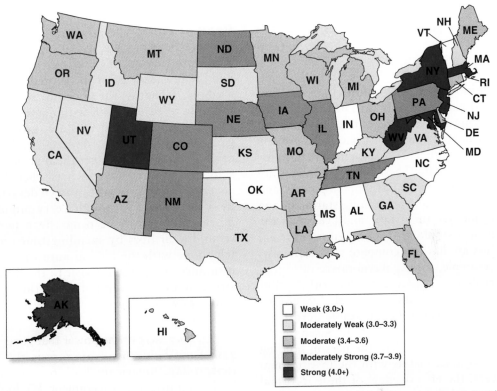

Weak (3.0>)

Moderately Weak (3.0–3.3)

Moderate (3.4–3.6)

Moderately Strong (3.7–3.9)

Strong (4.0+)

Note: This figure compares governorships' institutional power based on appointments, independently elected executives, tenure potential, the state budget, party control of the legislature, and the veto.

Source: A modification of an index developed in Thad Beyle and Margaret Ferguson, "Governors and the Executive Branch," in *Politics in the American States*, 9th ed., ed. Virginia Gray and Russell L. Hanson (Washington, D.C.: CQ Press, 2008).

hints about what types of states tend to develop weaker or stronger gubernatorial institutions.

First, the states of the South tend to have weaker governorships, probably a legacy of the reaction to the strong **Reconstruction** governors in the post–Civil War era. Second, more populous and more urban states tend to have more powerful governorships, whereas smaller, rural states tend to have weaker ones. This might be a case of states arming their governors with just the level of power they need to deal with the forces at work in their states. Governors in large or urban states must contend with both more diverse public

problems and a broader range of actors in the policy-making arena, such as big-city mayors, strong unions, major industries and corporations, and so forth. Perhaps these governors need greater institutional power just to do their jobs as well as those governors with less institutional power do in the small, rural states where they are big fish in a small pond. Finally, and although it is not obvious in this map, those states with more liberal citizens tend to have stronger governorships. Perhaps liberals appreciate strong, active government, whereas conservatives prefer weaker, limited government. On the other hand, the causal effect may also run the other way. One study has found that regardless of the ideology of a state's citizens, its political party tendencies, or its economic and demographic characteristics, states with stronger governors tend to have more liberal policies.[62]

Informal Powers

In addition to the institutional powers that states give their governors as a matter of policy, the circumstances of the office, the state, and the incumbent himself or herself also provide a governor with more or less effective tools for running the state. These informal powers are not as obvious as the institutional powers, and their potency can vary among states, among governors within a state, and even over the term of a single governor. Some informal powers are hard to compare systematically. For example, some governors are just more charismatic or intelligent than others. But several important dimensions of a governor's informal power are comparable across the states and across time and are based on the office itself rather than the person holding it. Of course, just as with the institutional powers, the effectiveness of these informal powers in helping governors manage a state and achieve their policy agendas depends in large part on the skills of the governor in using them. But unlike the institutional powers, informal powers can often be a double-edged sword, either helping or hurting a governor, depending on circumstances and the governor's skill.

The first three of these informal powers we discuss are largely things that affect governors' **political capital**; that is, their perceived political power in the eyes of state legislators, interest groups, or whomever else the governor wants to influence. The last two informal powers we discuss involve a governor's political power relative to other actors in the state's political process.

Head of State The governor is a state's symbolic **head of state**, just as (as mentioned above) the queen of England is for her country and the president is for the United States as a whole.[63] That is, the governor represents the state to people both within and outside of the state. As head of state, governors gain political capital by undertaking largely ceremonial duties that get them around the state in a positive way, such as when Texas governor Rick Perry visits a town devastated by a hurricane. Although Perry might be more effective in helping these people rebuild their lives by spending time on the telephone with the federal authorities and insurance companies, a visit to the disaster site conveys the sympathy of the entire state—as well as earning the governor some political capital.

Another facet of the power that governors gain from being head of state is the fact that, today, Americans look for executive leadership from our government. We look to the governor, the president, and the mayor when we want government to act rather than the state legislature, the Congress, or the city council. Governors can benefit from this attitude by stepping into the role forthrightly, pursuing an active policy agenda in the legislature and taking a strong hand with the executive agencies. Although other state government officials may chafe under such an "imperial" governor, like the general public, they too expect the governor to lead and will complain if such leadership does not materialize. Indeed, one study found that even in a highly partisan legislature, bills the

---

[62] Charles Barrilleaux, "Governors, Bureaus, and Policymaking," *State and Local Government Review* 31 (1999): 53–59.

[63] The role of head of state is actually a formal gubernatorial duty in the sense that it derives from state statutes and constitutional provisions. But the political and policy importance of the role is derived from a governor's choices about the use of this duty. In this sense, the head of state role is an informal power.

governor advocated were regularly supported even by members of the opposite party—except during election years.[64]

Certainly, the expectation of gubernatorial leadership can backfire on the governor if things do not go well. A governor who is not a strong and visible leader may lose influence with the people and state officials. Some argued that this was in part what led to California governor Gray Davis's recall in 2003.[65] Furthermore, governors are often blamed for state actions, even if they had little to do with them. A clear example of this goes back to the 1950s and 1960s, when many states implemented their first sales tax. Shopkeepers upset with the tax would often ring up the price of an item at the cash register, adding, "And a penny for the governor." This practice went on for many years after the sales tax was introduced and the governor responsible for it was out of office.[66] Thus, symbolizing state government is most beneficial for a governor when things are going well in the state.

Public Opinion Closely associated with the power of being head of state is the effect of public opinion on a governor's informal power. Governors have long used the argument that their statewide electoral mandate gives them the backing of the state's people for whatever they wanted to do. But since the recent advent of state-level public opinion polling, a governor's support among the people can be assessed more finely and followed as it changes throughout the term.[67] A governor riding high in the polls will be quick to point out this fact to obstinate legislators or bureaucrats. Legislators, in particular, are much more susceptible to a popular governor's request because they have to face the voters themselves. And although the chance to have a well-liked governor appear with a legislator in his or her district may entice that lawmaker to be more compliant with that governor's wishes, no legislator wants to be associated with an unpopular governor.

Governors understand the importance of public opinion, and they do what they can to keep their ratings high. They monitor the ratings closely through their own internal office polls (sometimes run through their campaign offices to avoid any suggestion of impropriety), and they appear at popular, nonpolitical functions, like the state fair and ribbon-cutting ceremonies for new highways, among other events. Some governors go even further, such as when California's Schwarzenegger bought television ads and executed a public image "makeover" after his poll numbers began to drop in his first term.[68] On the other hand, if a governor's efforts to improve his or her public approval ratings are too obvious, they can backfire, such as when Illinois's Blagojevich ordered some state workers to write letters to the editors of various newspapers supporting one of his programs.[69] When this was made public, it probably hurt Blagojevich's image more than it helped it.

Some of a governor's popularity is beyond his or her control. Governors of large states tend to have lower ratings, whereas governors of less populated states tend to be more popular. Larger states tend to have more, larger, and more complex public problems than other states, and that makes the job of governor more difficult. Furthermore, as in elections, the

---

[64] Thad E. Hall, "Changes in Legislative Support for the Governor's Program over Time," *Legislative Studies Quarterly* 27 (2002): 107–22.

[65] Michael Lewis, "The Personal Is the Antipolitical," *New York Times Magazine* 153 (2003): 40–130.

[66] Philip J. Roberts, *A Penny for the Governor, a Dollar for Uncle Sam: Income Taxation in Washington* (Seattle: University of Washington Press, 2002).

[67] Richard G. Niemi, Thad Beyle, and Lee Sigelman, "Gubernatorial, Senatorial, and State-Level Presidential Job Approval: The U.S. Officials Job Approval Ratings (JAR) Collection," *State Politics and Policy Quarterly* 2 (2002): 215–29.

[68] Gary Delsohn, "Governor Embarks on Image Change," *Sacramento Bee*, online ed., 26 July 2005.

[69] Bernard Schoenburg, "Senior CMS Workers Urged to Push Education Plan," *(Springfield, Ill.) State Journal-Register*, 15 April 2005, p. 11.

national economy is an important influence on gubernatorial popularity.[70] On the other hand, the state economy is also a factor here, especially the state's economy relative to that of other states,[71] and governors probably have at least some control over this. A governor's perceived success—or lack thereof—in handling a major state crisis can affect his or her popularity. West Virginia's Joe Manchin saw his popularity rise dramatically when he was seen as effectively handling a coal-mining disaster in 2006, whereas Louisiana's Kathleen Blanco's approval went down fast after the Hurricane Katrina debacle. Governors' own actions—or those of their appointees—can also affect their popularity if they result in scandals, as was the case recently for Ohio's Bob Taft and Kentucky's Ernie Fletcher—both now *former* governors.

Mass Media Attention Governors can also work to affect their popularity through the skillful use of the mass media. In fact, the governor's office is especially well positioned to gain political capital from the effective use of print, broadcast, and even online media, and the special attention they get from the mass media relative to other state policy makers is one of their primary informal powers.

Governors attract media attention for a variety of reasons but mainly because it is just easier to report and understand state government by focusing on the governor. First, the governor is a single, authoritative news source. Who speaks authoritatively for the legislature, the courts, or the bureaucracy? No one. Who appears more reliable and unbiased to talk about a given issue: the governor or an interest group spokesperson?

Certainly, important, thoughtful, and honest people work in all those other institutions, but in none is there a single, recognizable news source that a reporter can go to time and again for the final word on that institution's position on an issue. And the governor is clearly an important and well-known person whose actions are significant to a lot of people. As we noted at the start of the chapter, more people know who the governor is than any other public official in every state.[72]

Keep in mind that news organizations are in business to attract readers, viewers, or listeners. It is easier to do this when discussing a familiar person than a more obscure official—like the state speaker of the house—who, although important, would need to be introduced to the media consumer before getting to the heart of the story. Americans' attention span for political news is short, especially for news about state politics.[73] As a chief executive, the governor is easier to understand than the legislature—both for media consumers and for reporters. The governor is like the boss of the state or the parent of the family; this is a role with which people are familiar, even if it does distort reality. Legislatures are complex, mysterious, and unfamiliar, so it is harder to write a relatively short, understandable news story about them. Legislators, especially legislative leaders, also try to work with the media, but they are generally less successful because they have a less media-friendly institution to explain.

It is also no accident that governors' power and prestige rose in the 1960s and 1970s just as television became the main source of political news for Americans.[74] Governors are particularly attractive for television

[70] James D. King and Jeffrey E. Cohen, "What Determines a Governor's Popularity?" *State Politics and Policy Quarterly* 5 (2005): 225–47.

[71] Jeffrey E. Cohen and James D. King, "Relative Unemployment and Gubernatorial Popularity," *Journal of Politics* 66 (2004): 1267–82.

[72] Peverill Squire and Christina Fastnow, "Comparing Gubernatorial and Senatorial Elections," *Political Research Quarterly* 47(1994): 705–20.

[73] G. Patrick Lynch, "The Media in State and Local Politics," in *Media Power, Media Politics*, ed. Mark J. Rozell (Lanham, Md.: Rowman & Littlefield, 2003).

[74] Dometrius, "Governors."

news, where stories are much shorter than in newspapers and rely more on pictures. A governor speaking at a press conference or giving a speech makes pretty good television; a governor touring a disaster site or visiting a state facility or cutting a ribbon on a new highway is even better. The state legislature in session makes bad television (except as a background shot while the reporter speaks); legislative negotiations and discussions are even worse.

Governors work hard to make the reporters' job easy for them. They hire professional media relations staff (many of whom are former statehouse reporters themselves) to develop effective press releases and manufacture television-friendly media events at times convenient for news deadlines. Some governors even send out prepackaged video clips of themselves making brief comments on current issues. This allows those television stations without the resources to have their own statehouse reporter—which comprise most stations these days—to air footage that looks like their own reporter actually interviewed the governor. Of course, governors are not likely to send out footage that makes them look bad, so although they are helping the station get good video for the nightly news, the governors also present themselves in a very good light without fear of any tough questions from reporters. This can only help a governor's popularity. On the other hand, it raises serious questions about the quality and ethics of journalism about state government.

Partisan Balance in the State Legislature

A governor's informal power also depends on the partisan balance in the state legislature. Legislators who are in the governor's party are thought of, and often think of themselves, as loyal lieutenants of the governor. In particular, an important job of the legislative leaders of the governor's party is to marshal the party's members behind the governor's bills.[75] Therefore, governors who have a majority in both legislative chambers—a situation known as **unified government**—can get their bills passed if the party sticks together. But ironically, governors with the most lopsided legislative majorities often have the hardest time leading their legislative co-partisans, as that venerable scholar of state politics, V. O. Key Jr., documented in the Democrat-dominated state legislatures in the South in the 1940s.[76] Sometimes, a governor of the other party can work with a legislative majority better because the expectations of their cooperation are more realistic. For example, Democratic governor Mark Warner surprised observers by being able to work with the Republican majority in the Virginia General Assembly to solve their recent fiscal problems.[77]

But **divided government** typically makes it more difficult for a governor to pass his or her legislative agenda. In such cases, not only does the legislative majority have basic ideological differences with the governor, but the party also has an electoral incentive at least to offer alternative positions on key issues, if not to sabotage the governor's efforts actively. Of course, when the legislature and the governor are at loggerheads publicly, the governor's advantage with the media really helps in the battle over public opinion, but only if the governor uses the media cleverly. Furthermore, sometimes the legislature can work against the governor so subtly that the public does not recognize its obstructionism. Divided government has become much more common in recent decades, encouraged by legislative professionalism and the personalization of gubernatorial campaigns.[78]

[75] Malcolm E. Jewell and Marcia Lynn Wicker, *Legislative Leadership in the American States* (Ann Arbor: University of Michigan Press, 1994).

[76] V. O. Key Jr., *Southern Politics in the State and Nation* (New York: Knopf, 1949).

[77] Gurwitt, "The Last One-Term Statehouse."

[78] Morris P. Fiorina, *Divided Government*, 2nd ed. (Boston: Allyn & Bacon, 1996).

Big Government and Rivals for Power

Finally, governors gain informal power to the extent that they (1) preside over a large and powerful state government and (2) have few other heavyweight political actors in the state. If state government is powerful and important, the person who runs it—the governor—must be dealt with in any policy discussion. Similarly, governors from large states are seen as somehow more important, newsworthy, or powerful than those in smaller states. For example, governors of New York, California, and Ohio are far more likely to be mentioned in the press as potential presidential contenders than governors of North Dakota, Hawaii, and Utah—although the candidacies of Arkansas's Bill Clinton, Vermont's Howard Dean, and New Mexico's Bill Richardson may belie this generalization. Also, governors who have less competition for political attention and power in their state, such as from large urban centers, major corporations, or a large federal government presence, are the biggest fish in the pond and, therefore, are more powerful. For example, the governor of Maryland must contend with a major city dominating its state and with the federal government, for which many of its residents work. As such, the mayor of Baltimore and even the president are rivals for the governor's power and prestige. The governor of Maine, on the other hand, lacking such competition, can dominate state politics more easily.

Unfortunately for governors, these two factors are usually inversely related with one another—large states have both big state governments and many competing power centers, balancing off these forces of gubernatorial influence in most states. For example, New York governors run a massive and diverse operation, but they must also contend with the political power and influence of the mayor of New York City, the many Fortune 500 corporations headquartered there,

and so forth. On the other hand, governors of Wyoming have a relatively small government to run, but because it is the biggest operation in the state, they gain significant informal clout by doing so.

The Three Jobs of the Governor

Today's governor has three basic jobs: chief policy maker, chief administrator, and intergovernmental relations manager. Each of these is a demanding and complicated task that requires all of a governor's institutional and informal powers as well as his or her personal knowledge, skills, and abilities. In this section, we bring together what you have learned about gubernatorial powers to demonstrate how three current governors have tackled these jobs.

Chief Policy Maker: Charting the Course

The first American states wanted their governors to be mere administrators, simply following the orders of the all-important state legislatures. But over time, fear of a strong governor declined and Americans grew disenchanted with legislature-driven government. As a result, governors gained considerable power and responsibility. Today's governors are expected to set the course of state government by taking the lead in policy making. This is not to say that governors are dictators; they certainly are not. But the governor sets the tone in state policy making, and all other people involved in the process look to him or her for guidance.

Political scientist Nelson Dometrius describes gubernatorial policy making as having four stages: agenda setting, policy development, enactment, and implementation.[79] We'll discuss

---

[79] Dometrius, "Governors."

policy implementation in the next section, but we take up the first three here. These three stages take place primarily, but not exclusively, in and around the legislative process. Although, in theory, the legislature is the main policy-making branch of the government, in practice, today's legislature takes its lead on most big issues from the governor.[80]

Setting the policy agenda means defining for the legislature, other relevant policy makers, and the general public which public problems are most important. The state could address countless problems at any given time, but because its resources are limited, policy makers must choose carefully which problems are most pressing and where the state can do the most good. Every state capital is swarming with people and organizations trying to get policy makers to address their pet problem, everything from regulating or subsidizing new birth technologies to banning or instituting the death penalty. The person who can define the most important issues has tremendous power.[81] Wise governors use their powers judiciously to do just that.

Once the most important public problems have been identified, the potential solutions to these problems also need to be prioritized. Every public problem has many potential solutions. These are not all likely to work equally well, and neither are they equally feasible, either economically or politically. The governor has a large staff of analysts, in addition to the entire state executive branch, to develop, weigh, and modify the various alternatives.

Finally, decisions ultimately must be made about which solution the state will try for a given problem on the agenda. As you saw in Chapter 6, the state legislative process is complex and requires strong leadership to pass the laws that determine state policy. Even though the governor has only a small formal role in the legislative process (in signing or vetoing a bill), and legislators are very concerned about broaching the constitutional boundaries between the branches,[82] all those in and around the process expect the governor to engage informally in the process at all stages. And because governors care about which policies are enacted, they routinely get actively involved in the legislative process. California governor Arnold Schwarzenegger was deeply involved in the legislative process when he tried to influence changes in the state's legislative redistricting policy.

Governor Arnold Schwarzenegger and Legislative Redistricting Reform
Republican movie star–businessman Arnold Schwarzenegger became governor of California in 2003 after winning the extraordinary recall election that ousted Gray Davis. During the campaign, Schwarzenegger ran as a reform candidate—a breath of fresh air who would solve all of California's very serious problems (including the biggest state budget deficit in national history and electricity blackouts around the state).[83] As an outsider candidate with no political baggage and lots of money and popular appeal, Schwarzenegger won over an electorate fed up with the status

---

[80] Alan Rosenthal, *Heavy Lifting: The Job of the American Legislature* (Washington, D.C.: CQ Press, 2004), ch. 9.

[81] John W. Kingdon, *Agendas, Alternatives, and Public Policies* (Glenview, Ill.: Scott, Foresman, 1984).

[82] Rosenthal, *Heavy Lifting*.

[83] The discussion in this section is based on a variety of newspaper articles published in the *Sacramento Bee*, including Daniel Weintraub, "Pushing Broad Agenda, Governor Will Go Both Ways," 22 March 2005; Tom Chorneau, "Governor Says Special Election Would Return Power' to the People,'" 19 May 2005; Dan Walters, "Jackson Upstages Schwarzenegger—Portent for Governor's Crusade?" 14 June 2005; Gary Delsohn, "Governor Cites Prop 13 to Open Election Drive," 15 June 2005; Gary Delsohn, "Field Poll: Special Election Turns off Voters," 21 June 2005; Jim Sanders, "Flawed Measure Ignites New Flap," 15 July 2005; Gary Delsohn, "Governor, Allies Spent $23 Million," 2 August 2005; Beth Fouhy, "So Close, yet So Far: How Election Compromise Talks Fell Through," 29 August 2005; Gary Delsohn and Laura Mecoy, "Governor's' Reforms' Get Cold Shoulder," 9 November 2005; and Steve Lawrence, "Senate Likely to Revisit Redistricting Issue This Week," 18 June 2006.

California's governor Arnold Schwarzenegger takes his 2005 "Year of Reform" proposals straight to the citizens of his state.

quo, sweeping to victory in one of the most raucous and unusual gubernatorial elections in the nation's history.

Arriving in Sacramento with very high approval ratings, Schwarzenegger dove right into policy making. After some initial legislative successes, he ended his first full year in office (2004) frustrated by the Democrat-controlled state legislature and his lack of experience in working with such an institution. So, he decided to make 2005 his "Year of Reform" for California, setting his agenda explicitly in his State of the State speech kicking off the legislative session in January, proposing a wide range of institutional and legal changes. He followed this speech with a series of personal appearances around the state to gather support. Using his advantages with the media and his position as head of state to the utmost, he pressured the legislature by appealing directly to their constituents. Although his popularity had ebbed somewhat from its lofty postelection heights, it was still

in the 60 percent approval range, and he used this to try to steamroll the legislature into passing his proposals.

At the top of Schwarzenegger's reform agenda was a plan to change legislative redistricting procedures; that is, the way congressional and state legislative maps were drawn in the state. California used the regular legislative process to redistrict, but Schwarzenegger argued that this caused a **conflict of interest** for legislators, eliminating political competition as they drew districts to protect themselves and their parties. Schwarzenegger proposed that a panel of three retired judges draw the maps instead. Along with legislative redistricting reform, Schwarzenegger's agenda included calling for limits on state government spending, tenure restrictions and performance pay for public school teachers, cutbacks in the state workers' pension plan, and a variety of other reforms, large and small.

Unfortunately for Schwarzenegger, he made a fundamental mistake in setting his Year of

Reform agenda—he simply asked for too much. The speaker of the California Assembly likened Schwarzenegger's agenda to "dropping a hand grenade on the Legislature."[84] Governors have more success in the legislature when they restrict the size of their agendas, focusing only on a few top priorities.[85] And not only did Schwarzenegger set a large agenda, but he also set a controversial one. Each of these reforms was opposed by powerful interest groups, and because Schwarzenegger linked his ideas into a reform package, their opponents joined forces to fight them all together. So, for example, although teachers' and other public employees' unions had no direct interest in legislative redistricting, they made common cause with legislators who opposed it in exchange for their opposition to other reforms the unions opposed. Schwarzenegger himself helped solidify this coalition with unfortunate off-the-cuff comments to the news media, such as when he outraged a nurses' union by suggesting that he was "kicking their butts" in the legislature.[86]

Schwarzenegger's personal popularity, use of the media, and head-of-state role were not enough to overcome his problems with a divided government and a too-large, too-controversial agenda, and his redistricting plan, the centerpiece of his reform agenda, bogged down in the legislature. In 2004, the popular, newly elected governor had played roughly with the legislature, vetoing hundreds of bills and using all of his budget powers to get what he wanted. Legislators remembered this, making them even less willing to work with him in his Year of Reform. So, in March 2005, Schwarzenegger again pulled off the gloves, this time threatening to go directly to the people with an initiative if the legislature refused to adopt his redistricting plan. This was an especially potent threat, given that the governor himself had recently gained office through his predecessor's recall,

another direct democracy mechanism. Over the next three months, as he continued to work with legislative leaders on a compromise redistricting plan, the threat of the initiative hung in the air.

Schwarzenegger wanted his plan in place quickly so that new districts could be drawn for the 2006 legislative election. This was the businessman talking—let's just get it done. But even though they were sympathetic to the political need for change in the redistricting process, legislative leaders held out for a compromise that would reform redistricting in the next scheduled round after the 2010 U.S. Census. Finally, after a failure to agree on a plan with legislators, on June 13, Schwarzenegger issued an executive order calling for a special election in November to vote on, among other things, his Proposition 77 redistricting initiative.

The development of Schwarzenegger's redistricting plan was relatively simple, given the nature of the issue. But during the campaign, the exact content of Proposition 77 became an issue. Although Schwarzenegger's staff spent months tinkering with the proposal, the final version that was certified by the California secretary of state's office had what was referred to as a "clerical error," making it different from the version that was on the petitions circulated for the measure. This discrepancy caused a minor uproar during the campaign, including a lawsuit brought by the proposal's opponents to get it tossed from the ballot. Although the Schwarzenegger team won the case in the California Supreme Court, it distracted them from their main job at that time—working on the initiative campaign. Schwarzenegger himself also spent most of the summer of 2005 negotiating with legislative leaders in hopes of arriving at a compromise before the last day the secretary of state would allow the proposition to be pulled from the ballot (August 18).

---

[84] Quoted in Delsohn and Mecoy, "Governor's' Reforms' Get Cold Shoulder."

[85] Margaret Robertson Ferguson, "Chief Executive Success in the Legislative Arena," *State Politics and Policy Quarterly* 3 (2003): 158–82.

[86] Quoted in Delsohn and Mecoy, "Governor's' Reforms' Get Cold Shoulder."

While Schwarzenegger and his staff were distracted, Proposition 77's opponents were focused on campaigning. The coalition against this and his three other reform propositions spent tens of millions of dollars on TV ads during the summer of 2005, while Schwarzenegger failed to get his campaign off the ground. The governor had pegged these propositions' success to his personal prestige, and as his opponents' TV ads attacked him directly, his popularity ratings plummeted into the 30–40 percent range. By the time Schwarzenegger's campaign got under way in the fall, it was too late. Proposition 77 was defeated at the ballot box by a 3 to 2 margin.

Even though Schwarzenegger failed to reform the way California draws its legislative districts—and even though Schwarzenegger is not exactly a typical governor—his story illustrates many of the ways that governors can use their powers in their role as chief policy maker. He used his popularity, his staff, his position as head of state, an executive order, and his State of the State speech to force the legislature at least to consider his reform. But his problems with divided government, missteps with the media, declining popularity, and lack of governmental experience were just insurmountable. But as is so often the case in policy making, his reform may only have been temporarily defeated. Only a few months after Proposition 77's ignominious defeat, the California Senate again worked on a legislative redistricting bill in the spring 2006 legislative session. And Schwarzenegger seemed to learn from his political mistakes. By the end of 2006, he had changed his image, moved toward the center of the political spectrum, and won reelection handily.[87] Whether he tries again to reform the state's redistricting process depends on whether he and his advisors decide that his first pass at the reform was defeated due to bad political decisions and low political capital or simply due to the time not being right for the reform in California.

Chief Administrator: Managing the Bureaucracy

The original job of the governor was strictly to implement the laws passed by the state legislature by supervising various agencies staffed by nonpolitical workers. In the beginning of the republic, these duties and workers were few. But as the nation and its needs for public services grew, so did the responsibilities of the executive branch of state government. Today, state and local governments comprise the largest employer in each state. Almost 16 million people work for state and local governments nationwide, including over a million each in California, New York, and Texas.[88] Even the states with the fewest state and local employees—Vermont, Wyoming, and the Dakotas—each have over 40,000 of them. All but a small percentage of these workers serve in the executive branches. As these executive agencies have grown, so has the importance of the governor's job of managing them.

The bureaucracy of the executive branch is the quiet giant of government. Although the media often report about the courts, the legislature, and the governor, it is the bureaucracy that carries out the important day-to-day jobs of government, from teaching our children and college students, to testing new drivers for their licenses, to guarding prisoners, to caring for patients in public hospitals, and so much more. And in the process of doing this work, bureaucrats—those who work in the executive branch, including your professors, if you are attending a state university—control a lot of public policy, both formally and informally.

Formally, high-level administrators write **administrative rules** to implement state law. By necessity, legislation is written in general language. Legislators have neither the time nor the expertise to go into detail about, say, how a school curriculum ought to be written

[87] Peter Hecht, "Governor's Decisive U-Turn," *Sacramento Bee*, online ed., 10 November 2006.

[88] Kendra A. Hovey and Harold A. Hovey, *CQ's State Fact Finder* (Washington, D.C.: CQ Press, 2007), 114.

or how deer hunting ought to be regulated. The agencies charged by the legislature with carrying out these general policies use their staff and expertise to write these detailed rules and regulations.

Informally, bureaucrats, even **street-level bureaucrats**, make decisions every day that have the power of the state behind them.[89] When a police officer chooses between giving you a warning or writing you a ticket when he catches you driving five miles per hour over the speed limit, that matters a lot to you personally. When police officers as a group make similar decisions, they are setting public policy for the state at the street level.

The speed limit serves as a good example of how the bureaucracy helps set policy, both formally and informally. First, the legislature charges the Department of Transportation (DOT) with setting speed limits on public roads throughout the state. Next, the DOT sets the limit at 65 miles per hour on a specific stretch of highway by writing an administrative rule. Finally, the police implement a speed limit in practice of, perhaps, 72 miles per hour on that stretch of highway; that is, they do not charge anyone with speeding until they go faster than 72. Of course, if you do not want a ticket, you should not go faster than the posted speed limit because you never know for sure what the informal limit is on a particular stretch of road.

Given the importance of the bureaucracy in setting and implementing policy and the governor's historic role as chief executive, it should not be surprising that most governors spend a good deal of time trying to impose their will on their executive branch. This is no small task; the state bureaucracy is a mammoth operation, and the governor is but one person, perhaps with several dozen staff. Most state workers are far removed from the governor, doing their jobs as they have always done them and watching governors come and go. Furthermore, government workers hold a strong ethic that they are experts in their fields and that they should be allowed to do their jobs without undue political influence from above. This value of **neutral competence** is strong in government service, with roots in the Progressive era civil service reforms. On the other hand, elected officials appreciate **political accountability** in the bureaucracy so that the "will of the people"—or, more accurately, the will of the elected official in question— is reflected in policy implementation. Although recent research suggests that a mix of gubernatorial appointees and merit-based employees in a state agency workforce enhances its efficiency,[90] the tension between these two values pervades the relationship between governors and the bureaucracy.[91]

Not surprisingly, governors appreciate political accountability in the bureaucracy, but bureaucratic neutral competence helps governors tremendously by making the huge ship of state run smoothly on a daily basis. Judicious management of the state bureaucracy can give governors enormous impact on public policy, and many of their powers are useful in doing so. Sometimes, governors just need to communicate their preferences clearly; often, bureaucrats are happy to do what the governor wants, as long as they know what that is and if it fits with their professional norms. Such communication can occur through the governor's staff interacting with agency officials, gubernatorial appointments to policy-making and management positions in the agency, and executive orders, among

[89] Norma M. Riccucci, *How Management Works: Street-Level Bureaucrats and Welfare Reform* (Washington, D.C.: Georgetown University Press, 2005).

[90] George A. Krause, David E. Lewis, and James W. Douglas, "Political Appointments, Civil Service Systems, and Bureaucratic Competence: Organizational Balancing and Executive Branch Revenue Forecasts in the American States," *American Journal of Political Science* 50 (2006): 770–87.

[91] Charles Barrilleaux, "Statehouse Bureaucracy: Institutional Consistency in a Changing Environment," in Weber and Brace, *American State and Local Politics*.

other gubernatorial powers. But sometimes, a governor has strong policy preferences that are at odds with the norms and preferences of bureaucrats. In such circumstances, a governor must work harder to manage the bureaucracy. Such was the case with Governor Rod Blagojevich and the Illinois State Board of Education in 2004.

Governor Rod Blagojevich and the Illinois State Board of Education

At the beginning of 2004, a year after becoming the first Democratic governor in Illinois since 1976, Rod Blagojevich was flying high.[92] He had strong poll numbers and a solid Democratic majority in both chambers of the General Assembly. These allowed him to pass most of his legislative agenda the previous year. But his top priorities were in education policy, and in this area, the state Board of Education (BOE) stood in his way.

The 1970 Illinois Constitution established the BOE as an independent agency, overseen by nine board members appointed by the governor on a staggered basis so that no governor could appoint a majority in a single term. The director of the agency, the state superintendent of education, was also appointed for a long term, yielding some degree of independence from the current governor. This arrangement reflected the belief of members of the 1970 constitutional convention that education policy should be above politics and that neutral competence, rather than political accountability, should be the dominant value in implementing it.

In 2003, the BOE and superintendent had frustrated and embarrassed Blagojevich by, among other things, refusing to cancel

a contract for its Washington lobbyist, criticizing the governor's education proposals and budget, and submitting its own budget request to the legislature that far exceeded what the governor wanted to spend. So, in 2004, Blagojevich decided to make every effort to get control of the BOE and the implementation of state education policy. To do this, he tried an approach that many governors have tried lately—bureaucratic reorganization.[93] Bureaucratic reorganization involves rearranging the lines of authority and duties of various offices and departments. Governors often justify such changes as an effort to increase an agency's efficiency, but usually, at least part of the goal is to change power relationships to allow the governor more control over it. This is what Blagojevich was up to in 2004. But unlike many reorganizations that can proceed simply by executive order, the arrangements that Blagojevich wanted to change were written into the state's constitution, so he had to go through the legislature to get the job done.

Blagojevich began his campaign to get control of the BOE with his State of the State speech, just as Schwarzenegger began his redistricting reform campaign in California. But Blagojevich's 2004 speech was unprecedented in its focus and intensity. Blagojevich devoted virtually his entire 90-minute speech to lambasting the BOE. He dubbed it a "Soviet-style bureaucracy" that stymied education in the state with red tape and top-heavy spending on administration rather than on teachers and schoolbooks. He slammed several large books onto the podium, saying that they were the "2,800 pages [of] rules and regulations" under which the BOE

---

[92] The discussion in this section is based on a variety of newspaper articles, including Diane Rado and Ray Long, "Blagojevich Sets School Power Grab," *Chicago Tribune*, 14 January 2004, p. 1; Stephanie Banchero and Tracy Dell'Angela, "Educators Jabbing at Governor's School Fix," *Chicago Tribune*, 18 January 2004, p. 1; Diane Rado and Ray Long, "Schools Could Get $2.2 Billion but Blagojevich Doesn't Want State Education Panel Handling It," *Chicago Tribune*, 23 March 2004, p. 1; Ray Long and Christi Parsons, "Madigan Condemns Governor's School Plan," *Chicago Tribune*, 6 May 2004, p. 1; Adriana Colindres, "Lawmakers Give Governor Power to Remake Education Board," *(Springfield, Ill.) State Journal-Register*, 23 July 2004, p. 1; Adriana Colindres, "Governor Shakes up State Education Board with New Appointees," *(Springfield, Ill.) State Journal-Register*, 14 September 2004, p. 1; and Diane Rado, "Junk-Food Ban Faces School Board Critics: State Panel Questions Governor's Proposal," *Chicago Tribune*, 16 March 2006, p. 3.

[93] Alan Greenblatt, "A Rage to Reorganize," *Governing*, March 2005, 30–35.

forced schools to work. He proposed a plan to shift almost all the BOE's functions to an agency directly under the governor's control (which is how the state education authority is organized in many states), with the governor appointing the top administrators of that department. The board would be left as a small education policy "think tank" with little policy-making power.

Throughout the spring legislative session, the governor fought to pass his BOE reorganization bill. He and his staff spent a good deal of time working with the media, making his case to the public, and he tried to leverage the fact that he had unified party government by counting on the votes of Democrats in the legislature. He used his budgetary powers to entice the BOE to drop its opposition to the plan by linking a $2.2 billion school construction program to it. And he had tenure potential in his favor; as a popular governor early in his first term, all those involved knew that they may well have to work with him for a long time.

But critics argued that this reorganization was simply an unconstitutional power grab. The BOE itself worked with the media and the legislature to fight Blagojevich's plan, and various influential education interest groups mobilized to support the BOE. The board had allies in the legislature, as such independent boards often do. For years, the legislature's education committees had worked closely with the BOE and the teachers' and school administrators' organizations that opposed the reorganization. But most important, the speaker of the Illinois House of Representatives, Michael Madigan, opposed the plan on constitutional grounds. Madigan had special moral authority here—as a young man, he had been a delegate at the 1970 constitutional convention that established the BOE.

Near the end of the legislative session, the governor and the speaker worked out a compromise that both gave Blagojevich the power over education policy that he wanted and passed constitutional muster with Madigan. The new arrangement kept the BOE intact, but it let new governors choose five of the nine board members and the superintendent upon taking office and the other four board members two years later. And it also allowed Blagojevich to appoint an entirely new board and superintendent immediately, which he did. So, although Blagojevich did not get the exact organizational arrangement that he wanted, he did get what he ultimately desired—control over state education policy.

For example, after these institutional changes, the BOE always followed the governor's lead in its budget requests. And at the other end of the spectrum, when he was unable to pass a highly visible junk food ban for schools in the legislature, he simply had his newly compliant board order such a ban. The downside of all this for the governor was that with full responsibility for education policy, only he was left to blame for problems in the area. For example, in 2006, when major foul-ups with contracts caused standardized testing for schoolchildren across the state to be delayed, the governor had to take the heat himself.

Intergovernmental Relations Manager: Working Well with Others

Since the modern age of state governors began in the 1960s, an increasingly important job for these chief executives has been acting as the point person for relationships between their states and other governments, including local governments, other state governments, the national government, and even foreign governments and Indian tribal governments.[94] Today's global economy and fast communication and transportation mean that people, businesses, and governments interact with one another constantly and repeatedly, as

---

[94] Todd Milburn, "Governor Agrees to New Casino Deal with Tribe," *Sacramento Bee*, online ed., 8 August 2006; and Kevin Yamamura, "Schwarzenegger Slams House Republicans for Immigration Reform Plan Delays," *Sacramento Bee*, online ed., 21 June 2006.

we discussed in Chapter 2. Commerce, social problems, and crime move freely across state borders, as they do, perhaps a little less freely, across international borders. Four states border Mexico, ten border Canada, 16 others have ocean coastlines, and every state has at least one international airport. As the central coordinating figure in state government, governors have by necessity taken on the role of intergovernmental relations (IGR) manager.[95]

Many of these IGR interactions are financial, especially with so many federal grants coming to the states and state and federal grants going to local governments. This net of financial transactions has drawn the three levels of American government so close that it is often hard to tell where one leaves off and another begins. For example, a state government employee might award a contract to a construction company to spend federal money to build a city street. As this example suggests, private firms are also a very important part of this mix of relationships.

Governors play an important role in coordinating these financial relationships, but their IGR duties go far beyond this. As head of state, a governor works with representatives of other governments in negotiations over mutual and competing interests in much the same way that the president does this in international relations.[96] But given the complexity of the relationships and the number of other governments with which governors must deal,

their job may be even more difficult in this respect than that of the president (although the stakes are undoubtedly not as high). The gubernatorial job of IGR manager is made more difficult by the fact that it is both newer and less well defined than the job of either chief policy maker or chief administrator. Therefore, governors must use their powers creatively to be successful IGR managers. Arizona governor Janet Napolitano certainly found this to be true when she wrestled with international border security in her role as IGR manager.

Governor Janet Napolitano and International Border Security

International borders appear to have a clarity and precision that belie the fact that much is vague and subjective in borderland regions, where societies, norms, and rules intermingle.[97] In such areas, governors' institutional powers are less important in IGR management than their informal powers and relationship-building skills. Arizona governor Janet Napolitano has found this to be the case in her management of one of the most complex and important policy issues facing her state—international border security.[98]

The U.S.-Mexico border is the epicenter of some of the knottiest social, political, and policy problems in the United States today—illegal immigration, drug trafficking, and homeland security. And because they all arise from people

---

[95] Beyle, "Governors: The Middlemen and Women."

[96] Peter Hecht, "Blair, Schwarzenegger Make Global Warming Deal," *Sacramento Bee*, online ed., 31 July 2006.

[97] Joachim Blatter, "Beyond Hierarchies and Networks: Institutional Logics and Change in Transboundary Spaces," *Governance* 16 (2003): 503–26.

[98] The discussion in this section is based on a variety of newspaper articles, including Ralph Blumenthal, "Citing Border Violence, 2 States Declare a Crisis," *New York Times*, 17 August 2005, p. 14; Arthur H. Rotstein, "Napolitano Checks out Border Safety in Statewide Tour," *Associated Press State and Local Wire*, online ed., 2 November 2005; Jacques Billeaud, "Arizona Governor Four Months ahead of Bush on Border Troops," *Associated Press State and Local Wire*, online ed., 16 May 2006; Lara Jakes Jordan, "Homeland Security to Probe Border Strategy," *Associated Press Online*, 23 August 2005; John Pomfret, "At Front Line of Immigration Debate; Ariz. Governor Favors Tough Enforcement but Humane Treatment," *Washington Post*, 31 May 2006, p. A03; Blake Schmidt, "Utah Governor Visits Guardsmen," *Yuma (Ariz.) Sun*, online ed., 13 June 2006; Paul Davenport, "Napolitano Signs Pact for National Guard Border Duty," *Associated Press State and Local Wire*, online ed., 2 June 2006; Jacques Billeaud, "Governor Vetoes Bill to Pay for Sending Troops to the Border," *Associated Press State and Local Wire*, online ed., 10 March 2006; Robert Tanner, "Swamped with Illegal Immigrants at Home, Governors Pushing for Action in Washington," *Associated Press*, online ed., 27 February 2006; Arthur H. Rotstein, "Illegal Immigration Top Story of 2005 in Arizona," *Associated Press State and Local Wire*, online ed., 31 December 2005; Lisa Riley Roche, "Huntsman Hopes to Rally Western Governors," *Deseret (Utah) Morning News*, online ed., 8 November 2005; "Governors Announce Steps on Cross-Border Safety," *Associated Press State and Local Wire*, online ed., 21 June 2005; Scott Baldauf, "Border States Forge Their Own Foreign Policy," *Christian Science Monitor*, 10 July 2000, p. 2; and Jacques Billeaud, "Ariz. Gov. Vetoes Criminal Immigrant Bill," *Sacramento Bee*, online ed., 18 April 2006.

and goods crossing governmental borders, they are also IGR problems. Furthermore, no state can deal with these problems by itself; the problem in any given state is affected by the actions of the federal government, the Mexican government, the state's local governments, and other state governments. Within each state, local governments and their schools, law enforcement agencies, public hospitals, and the like bear the brunt of many of these problems. The federal government runs the Border Patrol and has official responsibility for international border checkpoints and security. Governors have little official authority over any of these political actors, so they must use informal methods to deal with public problems regarding border security.

With her state's 350 miles of highly porous international border, these problems are high on Napolitano's policy agenda, and almost all her work on them has involved IGR. Divided government has hampered her ability to pass legislation to facilitate her efforts. But because the issue of border security splits opinion in the Republican Party so badly,[99] the legislature has not been able to pass legislation that causes too much trouble for Democrat Napolitano, who has successfully vetoed several high-profile border security bills that she did not like.

Napolitano has worked with the federal government on border issues in a variety of ways, although sometimes not very cooperatively. A former U.S. attorney, Napolitano is a tough negotiator and familiar with Washington. After unsuccessfully negotiating with the U.S. Department of Homeland Security for various resources for Arizona during her first two years in office, in February 2005, she used her budget powers to send the federal government a bill for $118 million for the costs of imprisoning illegal immigrants who had been convicted of crimes in Arizona. She argued that these people were the federal government's responsibility because it had a duty to secure the international borders. Even though this move was largely symbolic—the bill was never paid—she showed skill in using the media and her position as head of state to draw national attention to the issue. Another such move was her executive order later in 2005 declaring a state of emergency on the border following a series of violent incidents there. This declaration not only again drew national media attention but also made millions of state and federal dollars available to her to pay for more security. Napolitano also sent National Guard troops to the border four months before President Bush ordered them there in 2006. The National Guard serves both the state and federal governments as well as often helping local governments, so its use always involves the governor's IGR role.

Napolitano has also worked closely with other governors in her efforts to solve Arizona's border security problems. Her 2005 state emergency declaration was done in coordination with New Mexico governor Bill Richardson making the same declaration in his state, giving the announcement more publicity value—two governors are better than one. We do not know whether Napolitano and Richardson tried to get Texas governor Rick Perry and California's Schwarzenegger (the other two U.S. governors of states on the U.S.-Mexico border) to join them in the declaration, but partisan politics may have been at play. Republicans Perry and Schwarzenegger likely are not as inclined to embarrass President Bush as are Democrats Napolitano and Richardson. Also in 2005, Napolitano served as the vice chair of the Western Governors Association (WGA). At the WGA's annual conference, after a closed-door, governors-only discussion of the issue—out of earshot of the media—she and Utah governor Jon Huntsman pushed through a resolution calling on the federal government to be tougher on border security. In 2006–2007, Napolitano served as president of the **National Governors Conference**, where she worked to get that organization to lobby for more federal border help.

---

[99] James A. Barnes, "Wedge Issue Could Splinter GOP Base," *National Journal* 37 (2005): 3006–8.

Napolitano also worked on the issue with her counterparts in the six Mexican states that border the United States. These Mexican governors are just as concerned with the public problems at the border as officials in the United States because they must deal with the effects of organized crime, violence, and drug and immigrant trafficking on their side of the border too. The governors of Arizona, New Mexico, Texas, and California, along with these Mexican governors, belong to the Border Governors Association, an organization that deals with issues these states have in common. In 2005, Napolitano and Governor Eduardo Bours of Sonora (the Mexican state bordering Arizona) made an official agreement to coordinate their border security strategies, especially in sharing information and conducting joint law enforcement exercises and operations. Such cross-border intergovernmental cooperation has become increasingly frequent and effective in recent years.[100]

Finally, Napolitano has also worked closely with local government officials in Arizona on border security issues, mostly in informal ways. For example, her office staff has been working with the counties on the border to apply for federal aid to help cover the school, social services, and law enforcement costs caused by illegal immigration and drug smuggling. And as part of her efforts to assess the impact of illegal immigration on Arizona, school districts were ordered to reveal how many children of illegal immigrants they enrolled.

Summary

Today's American governors are among the most powerful and important public officials in the country. The 50 governors are an impressive bunch, with future cabinet secretaries, ambassadors, and perhaps even presidents among them. They are also a diverse bunch, with many more women and nonwhite men among them than ever before. The states provide their governors with more powerful offices than at any other time in history, and their informal powers can be tremendous if used skillfully. And to get their jobs done, governors need all these powers. Next to the president, the job of state governor is probably the most difficult in the country. Governors are responsible for leading the reform of policy and its implementation within their states, and they must interact with other governments— from the smallest town in their state to the governments of other nations—to serve their states' needs. We have seen three examples of how governors have faced important problems in their states, and we have seen that even with all their power and prestige, they do not always succeed. But as the 21st century begins, it is clear that there is not a more challenging place for an ambitious and talented person wishing to serve the public than the office of state governor.

---

[100] Edgar Ruiz, "Regional Cooperation: The Border Legislative Conference," *Spectrum* (Fall 2004): 20–21.

Key Terms

Administrative rules
Amendatory veto
Appropriations bill
Bureaucracy
Civil service system
Conflict of interest
Divided government
Earmark
Executive budget
Full veto
Gubernatorial powers

Head of state
Lame duck
Line-item veto
National Governors
    Conference
Neutral competence
Override
Patronage job
Policy agenda
Political accountability
Political capital

Progressive era
Reconstruction
Reduction veto
Self-financing candidates
Special session
State of the State address
Street-level bureaucrats
Supermajority
Unified government

8

The Court System

INTRODUCTION

I n this chapter, we describe the wide variety of courts and judicial activity in the states and consider the effects of these differences. State court systems are very complex, and most people don't understand even their own state's system well. But understanding state courts and how they work can have a significant impact on your life—especially when it's your day in court.

Ironically, some people think they know a good deal about the legal system, when, in fact, their beliefs are often mistaken. Courtroom and law enforcement dramas have long been among the most-watched shows on TV, and now we can even see the "real" criminal justice system in action on *Cops*, *Judge Brown*, and the like. In fact, the cable network truTV is entirely devoted to criminal justice reality shows and dramas. But perceptions of the judicial system formed by watching TV often do more to distort our view of this important branch of government than to enlighten us. For example, dramatic courtroom battles are far less common than tedious negotiations; rather than sensational murder trials, the vast majority of criminal cases are for minor offenses, such as drug possession, simple assault, or drunk and disorderly conduct. And despite the extensive media coverage of the U.S. Supreme Court, state courts handle far more cases than federal courts. In reality, the state supreme courts together handle 100 times more cases than the U.S. Supreme Court does. And notwithstanding urban legends and the occasional news story of multimillion-dollar jury awards for scalding hot coffee or whiplash, most lawsuits result in either no or a modest amount of money being awarded to the injured party.

The application of law through the judicial system has been an aspect of government that has concerned people deeply since time immemorial because those who interpret and enforce the law—judges and the police—literally have life and death power over us. Not surprisingly, then, the American states have spent considerable energy over the years trying to figure out how to get their judicial systems right. Because of this, the three themes of this book—institutions, reform, and comparison—become thoroughly intermingled when discussing the courts. The states have continually tinkered with their judicial institutions, and the history of these reforms reflects the history of Americans' values. And because it seems to be so much harder to get our judicial institutions right—or because the social conditions surrounding the courts change more often—and because the courts must do so many different jobs, the institutions of the states' judicial branches vary far more than those of either their executive or legislative branches. In this chapter, we explore both the causes and effects of this institutional variation in an attempt to understand the *real* reality of our state court systems.

Two Essential Distinctions in the American Legal System

We begin our discussion of the state courts by presenting two sets of basic distinctions in American law: state versus federal courts and criminal versus civil law. Much of the complexity of the state court systems can be clarified by understanding these distinctions.

State Courts in the Federal System

As with everything else in American government and politics, the administration of justice is complicated by federalism. But while most people can easily distinguish between their state legislature and Congress and between their governor and the president, the distinction between federal and state courts is less well-understood.

In every state, a parallel set of federal and state court systems exists. Each state is served by state and federal trial and appellate courts. The court system that a case goes into depends primarily on the nature of the crime or conflict involved. Basically, if the crime or conflict is about a federal law, the case goes into the federal court system; if it is about a state law, it goes into the state court system. Whether a law is a state law or a federal law is somewhat idiosyncratic, depending on the actions of Congress and the state legislatures over the years, but some generalities can be made.

First, understand that by far, most legal cases are handled in state courts under state or local law. For example, in a typical recent year, whereas 80,424 criminal cases went through federal courts, fully 5,287,438—98.5 percent of all cases—went through the state courts.[1] Most of the crimes you have heard of—like assault, murder, and robbery—as well as almost all traffic infractions are violations of state laws or local ordinances. Federal crimes typically involve federal officials (like assassinating the president), interstate activity (like taking a stolen car across a state border), or activities that were outlawed by Congress for some historical reason (like bank robbery and kidnapping). The proportion of state versus federal cases is even more lopsided for civil cases (which we discuss in the next section) like lawsuits for injuries and for family law cases (like divorce and child custody).

Sometimes, it is not obvious whether state or federal law is at issue in a case. For example, when a person is arrested for the possession or sale of illicit drugs, he or she may be charged with the violation of either federal or state law. In such cases, the state and federal prosecuting authorities typically negotiate which system to pursue the charges in, with the decision often being based on the resources and interests of the arresting authorities. It can even happen that if a case is lost in one system, it can be brought again in the other system. In this way, federalism can add both flexibility and complication to lawsuits and criminal cases.

Criminal versus Civil Law

The second legal distinction that you need to understand when thinking about state court systems is the difference between criminal and civil law.[2] State courts deal with cases involving both of these types of law. Criminal cases involve the government prosecuting a person for violating a specific criminal statute, whether this involves doing something that is prohibited (e.g., stealing a car) or failing to do something that is required (e.g., having car insurance). Criminal cases are initiated by government prosecutors. In state court systems, head prosecutors are typically elected at the county level,[3] and they have different titles

---

[1] These figures are for cases that were concluded in 2002, the most recent year for which complete data are available; see the National Center for State Courts, http://www.ncsconline.org; and the Bureau of Justice Statistics, http://www.bjs.gov.

[2] Lawrence Baum, *American Courts: Process and Policy*, 5th ed. (Boston: Houghton Mifflin, 2001), ch. 7.

[3] In a few states, these head prosecutors are appointed by the governor or an other executive official.

in different states, like the district attorney or the state's attorney. These top prosecutors supervise an office of perhaps dozens of assistant prosecutors, depending on the size of the **jurisdiction**. Their job is to follow up on the criminal investigations of the police, decide whether cases are worth bringing to trial, negotiate with defense attorneys, and act as the people's lawyer in cases that go to trial.

On the other hand, civil cases involve noncriminal legal conflicts between people, corporations, or even the government. A civil case may arise out of a dispute over a contract, where one party to the contract feels that another party has not lived up to his or her obligations under it, or a dispute where one party claims to have been injured (whether bodily, psychically, or monetarily) by another party, such as in an automobile accident. Civil cases are brought by the party that feels he or she (or it, in the case of a corporation or governmental unit) has been injured, the **plaintiff**, against the party that allegedly has done the injury, the **defendant**. The case is all about the plaintiff trying to get the defendant to make the injury right, usually by giving the plaintiff a certain amount of money. Lawyers in civil cases make arguments based on case law, or **common law**, a traditional system of law about disputes over contracts and injuries that has evolved case by case over the last 500 years or so, first in England and then in the United States.

The Organization of State Court Systems

The states organize their courts in a variety of ways, and these institutional differences can affect the efficiency, and perhaps even the fairness, of the administration of justice. But generally, state court systems have the same basic hierarchical structure, with each level having its unique role in the process. Figure 8.1 shows this generic state court system structure. To oversimplify, **trial courts** establish the facts of a case and apply the law, **intermediate courts of appeal** judge any questions of fairness about the trial, and the **supreme court** decides whether a law or legal procedure is allowable under the state's constitution. The pyramidal structure of Figure 8.1 reflects not only the fact that these courts' authority flows hierarchically from the top to the bottom but also the fact that the number of cases handled by these courts drops dramatically as you move up the pyramid.

Trial Courts

If you have ever seen *Law & Order*, *Judge Judy*, or almost any other courtroom drama or reality show, you have been watching a trial court. TV shows focus on trial courts because this is really the only level of court that could make for watchable drama. The proceedings of intermediate courts of appeal and supreme courts are exciting only to those involved in the cases themselves and to legal scholars. But it is also appropriate that trial courts get the most public attention because the vast majority of cases begin and end there. Indeed, virtually every case starts in a trial court, and only about 1 percent[4] of them get any farther.

Whether a case is civil or criminal, trial courts have two basic functions: (1) to establish the facts of the case and (2) to apply the relevant law to these facts, whether case law or criminal statute. As straightforward as this may sound, this process contains considerable room for judgment—and for error.

Procedures and Decision Making The fundamental job of any court system is to resolve disputes between parties and to back these resolutions with the authority of the state. Trial courts are the first step toward such a resolution. To this end, the first thing a trial court must do is determine the disputed facts of the case. For example, a prosecutor alleges

---

[4]Shauna M. Strickland, *State Court Caseload Statistics, 2003* (Williamsburg, Va.: National Center for State Courts, 2004).

Figure 8.1

A Generic State Court System Structure

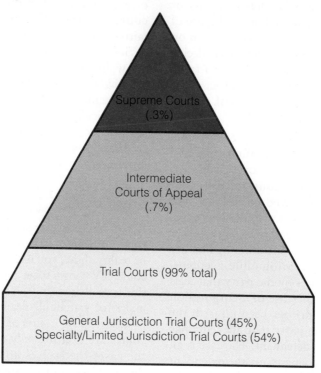

Supreme Courts
(.3%)

Intermediate
Courts of Appeal
(.7%)

Trial Courts (99% total)

General Jurisdiction Trial Courts (45%)
Specialty/Limited Jurisdiction Trial Courts (54%)

Note: The figures given are the percentage of cases in all state court systems that are disposed of in each type of court. These caseload data are for 2002, the most recent year for which these data are available.

Source: Shauna M. Strickland, *State Court Caseload Statistics, 2003* (Williamsburg, Va.: National Center for State Courts, 2004).

that Bryan Kaneski stole a certain Nikon camera from the 2003 Toyota Camry with Kentucky license plate number 715-H93 on May 16. By pleading not guilty, Bryan disputes this claim of fact—he did not take that camera from that car on that day. Did DeQuardo's Restaurant serve Maria Butsch tainted pizza that made her sick on June 2, as she alleges? If the owner of DeQuardo's disputes this claim of fact, they may go to court to get a definitive resolution of this civil dispute. In addition to such factual disputes, the parties may also disagree about which specific statute or case law applies to these facts.

Trial courts resolve legal disputes between two parties through a process of **adversarial argument** and **adjudication** by a neutral third party. Both sides make their best argument in

court, usually with the help of a trial lawyer who understands the legal system. Each side makes its case through legal and logical analysis, by questioning witnesses who may have relevant information, and by presenting any documents and physical evidence that might support their story. This process will sound familiar to viewers of courtroom dramas. But unlike on TV, real trials have almost no surprises because both sides not only should know in advance what their witnesses will say but also usually know who the opposition's witnesses are and what they will say.

This adversarial approach to judicial decision making requires that both sides do their best to sharpen their arguments and counter those of the opposition. The idea is that through this competitive process, both sides have an incentive to make their best case before the neutral third party who resolves the conflict by deciding which version of the facts and the law to accept. So, who is this neutral third party? A trial court has two possibilities. First, a **jury** may make the decision. Trial juries consist of about a dozen citizens, selected randomly, often from voter registration lists. Their job is to listen to both sides' arguments and the presiding judge's instructions and then to render a verdict—an authoritative decision—about the dispute.

Thus, in a jury trial, the judge is just there to make sure that the trial is conducted fairly, in accordance with the relevant rules and laws. Of course, a judge can have considerable impact on the jury's verdict by how he or she runs the trial, decides on procedural questions, and instructs the jury before its deliberations. But the final decision making on the dispute, in terms of both the facts and the application of the law, is done by the jury.

Juries can be unpredictable. Unlike judges, who have extensive legal training and experience, juries represent a cross-section of the community. For good or ill, they may be swayed by factors other than a strict interpretation of the law. Trial lawyers may even purposely appeal to jury members' emotions, in addition to the law or facts, in arguing that, for example, a doctor's neglect led to a child's death or disability. We have all seen media reports of runaway juries awarding seemingly outrageous sums in lawsuits or freeing "obviously guilty" defendants.[5]

Despite the potential for an appeal to a higher court in some circumstances, the fact that a successful trial ends in an authoritative decision on the dispute makes the parties in the case very nervous. Think about it. Suppose a person ran their car into yours, causing $2,000 worth of damage, and you took him to court

to get this money. The trial might result in you getting all that $2,000 or getting nothing. And criminal defendants walk into the courtroom to hear a decision that could send them to prison for years or release them immediately. The magnitude of these consequences and the uncertainty of the outcomes encourage most defendants, plaintiffs, and prosecutors to minimize the unpredictability of a trial as much as possible. This dynamic leads to two common characteristics of state court trials.

First, despite what you see on TV, by far most trials do not use juries but rather are **bench trials**, at which a single judge not only runs the trial but also makes the final decision on the facts and the law. Judges are far more predictable than juries because they usually follow standard legal practice and interpretation closely. Also, where discretion is possible, experienced trial court judges have long records that help the parties in the case evaluate how they are likely to rule. Although the assignment of judges to cases is typically done by a neutral court administrator, lawyers may have some influence in getting a sympathetic judge.

The second result of trial uncertainty is that the vast majority of legal disputes are settled between the parties before they even get to trial. By one estimate, only 1 percent of civil disputes filed in trial courts are decided at trial,[6] and a vast and unknown number get settled before they even get formally filed. In criminal cases, the uncertainty of conviction and sentencing frequently encourages the defense and prosecution to agree on a **plea bargain**, a reduction in charges or sentence in exchange for a guilty plea from the defendant. For example, a prosecutor with shaky evidence of drunk driving might allow the defendant to plead guilty to reckless driving, a crime that carries far less penalty and social stigma. Plea bargaining assures the prosecutor of a

---

[5] Eric Helland and Alexander Tabarrok, "Runaway Judges? Selection Effects and the Jury," *Journal of Law, Economics, and Organization* 16 (2000): 306–33.

[6] Henry R. Glick, "Courts: Politics and the Judicial Process," in *Politics in the American States*, 8th ed., ed. Virginia Gray and Russell L. Hanson (Washington, D.C.: CQ Press, 2004).

conviction, while it allows the defendant to avoid the possibility of a more severe sentence.

Plea bargaining has pros and cons.[7] On one hand, it is an efficient way to administer justice. If all the cases filed in state trial courts had to be settled with a full trial (especially a jury trial), the cost to the state would be astronomical and the already-slow progress of cases through the system would grind to a halt. On the other hand, people charged with a crime may be intimidated into pleading guilty even if they are innocent. This pressure may be especially difficult to withstand for defendants who are poor and poorly educated. In addition, plea bargaining may leave victims of crime feeling that they have not received justice. Thus, the efficiency of plea bargaining may come at the expense of fairness in the trial courts.

Uncertainty in trial courts also influences how civil cases are handled. Not every disagreement needs to be settled in court. Going to court is expensive, time-consuming, and uncertain, so often just the threat of a lawsuit gives the parties enough incentive to work out a deal. In difficult disputes, this can turn into a game of chicken, with both sides putting off a settlement until the very last minute. In fact, many civil suits are settled "on the courthouse steps," with the parties resolving the dispute privately as their court date looms.

Like with plea bargaining, these **out-of-court settlements** increase the efficiency of the civil justice system, but they also have their downside. Most obviously, this process benefits those with more experience in the judicial system and more resources—especially

money.[8] But beyond this, some argue that the prevalence of out-of-court settlements has encouraged unscrupulous people to abuse the civil law system by suing big companies and wealthy individuals for damages that never occurred.[9] A company may settle such a baseless case simply because of trial uncertainty, the cost of defending itself in court, and the potential for the bad publicity that the suit might bring. On the other hand, trial lawyers, victims' rights groups, and consumer groups argue that civil lawsuits are an important check on the rich and powerful, keeping them accountable for damages their actions may cause to even the poorest person. In this sense, this system offers an avenue for average citizens to fight big companies and institutions—and even the government.[10]

Although juries add considerable uncertainty to judicial decision making, trial court judges are certainly not just legal robots who make decisions mechanically. A case probably wouldn't even get to court if there was no uncertainty about the facts or the law, since a plea agreement or out-of-court settlement would be in the best interests of the negligent or guilty party. Strong professional norms restrain judges from letting their personal preferences color their decisions, but political scientists have found evidence that judges' backgrounds and values can sometimes influence them. For example, one study found that trial court judges hand out somewhat longer prison sentences as they get closer to their reelection dates.[11] Judges appear to be concerned with appearing

[7] George Fisher, *Plea Bargaining's Triumph: A History of Plea Bargaining in America* (Stanford, Calif.: Stanford University Press, 2003).

[8] James G. Lakely, "Bush Hits' Frivolous Lawsuits,'" *Washington Times*, online ed., 16 December 2004; Joel B. Grossman, Herbert M. Kritzer, and S. Macauley, "Do the' Haves' Still Come out Ahead?" *Law and Society Review* 33 (1999): 803–10; W. F. Samuelson, "Settlements out of Court: Efficiency and Equity," *Group Decision and Negotiation* 7 (1998): 157–77; and Herbert M. Kritzer, "Contingent-Fee Lawyers and Their Clients: Settlement Expectations, Settlement Realities, and Issues of Control in the Lawyer-Client Relationship," *Law and Social Inquiry* 23 (1998): 795–821.

[9] Even an interest group is organized to fight this problem, as they see it. They have a telling name: the Lawsuit Abuse Reform Coalition. See Lawsuit Abuse Reform Coalition, http://www.lawsuitabusereform.org.

[10] Jeff Yates, Belinda Creel Davis, and Henry R. Glick, "The Politics of Torts: Explaining Litigation Rates in the American States," *State Politics and Policy Quarterly* 1 (2001): 127–43.

[11] Gregory A. Huber and Sanford C. Gordon, "Accountability and Coercion: Is Justice Blind When It Runs for Office?" *American Journal of Political Science* 48 (2004): 247–63.

"soft on crime" just before they face the voters. Other studies have found that female judges give longer sentences to rapists and that judges who are evangelical Protestants are more conservative in death penalty, obscenity, and gender discrimination cases.[12] Although judges probably don't consciously let these factors bias their decisions, unconscious bias may creep in when ambiguity about the facts and law in a case gives a judge discretion.

It should be clear by now that trial courts have a very different approach to decision making than the legislative or executive branches. First, while governors and legislators can consider a variety of points of view, the only information a trial court judge or jury can consider comes through the formal, adversarial process. In fact, any communication by either party in the case with the judge or jury outside of the formal trial procedures is not only inappropriate but also illegal. Second, like all courts, trial courts are passive decision makers. Whereas a governor or legislator can identify a public problem and propose a solution for it, judges can make decisions only about questions that are brought to them. Finally, judges decide on specific disputes about specific facts and law in specific cases. Legislatures (and, to a large degree, governors) make policy decisions that apply equally to everyone. Although state courts—especially supreme courts—sometimes make broader policy informally (as we will see later), the main focus of judicial decision making is always on the individual case at hand.

Courts of Limited Jurisdiction All states have trial courts of **general jurisdiction;** that is, courts where virtually any type of legal case can be tried, criminal or civil. But 40 states also have various trial courts of **limited jurisdiction** specializing in a particular type of case. Such courts are an institutional way to increase the efficiency of the court system.

Some courts of limited jurisdiction simply handle minor matters. For example, traffic court personnel spend most of their time processing violations and assessing fines, with only the occasional dispute over a ticket. On the civil side, **small claims courts** handle suits claiming damages of up to, say, $5,000 or $10,000, depending on the state. For example, landlord–tenant disputes typically go to small claims courts. Small claims court proceedings can be pretty informal, often with the parties presenting their own arguments—without lawyers—to an **adjudicator**. The filing fee for bringing such a suit is kept low (perhaps $20), making these courts very accessible. But the relatively small amounts of money involved and the informality of the proceedings do not mean that traffic and small claims courts can be treated lightly. Their decisions have the force of law, the same as in any other trial court.

Some states also have **problem-solving courts**—courts of limited jurisdiction that focus on certain technical areas of the law, allowing judges to become experts in and help solve disputes on these subjects fairly and expeditiously. Common problem-solving courts include family courts (divorce and child custody issues), probate courts (wills and estates), **drug courts, mental health courts,** and tax courts. Colorado even has water courts to settle disputes over that precious commodity in that arid state.

Courts of limited jurisdiction are used heavily in the states that have them, where fully two-thirds of trial court cases are filed in them. In fact, there are over 13,000 of these courts, as compared to just over 2,000 trial courts of general jurisdiction.[13] If a party in a case is not satisfied with the decision of a court of limited jurisdiction, he or she can often appeal to a trial court of general jurisdiction for a new trial. But relative to the number of cases that these courts handle, this is done infrequently, indicating that these institutions are indeed

[12] Donald R. Songer and Kelly A. Crews-Meyer, "Does Gender Matter?" *Social Science Quarterly* 81 (2000): 750–62; and Donald R. Songer and Susan J. Tabrizi, "The Religious Right on the Court," *Journal of Politics* 61 (1999): 506–26.

[13] National Center for State Courts, *Examining the Work of State Courts, 2003* (Williamsburg, Va.: National Center for State Courts, 2004).

INSTITUTIONS MATTER

TEEN COURTS

Juvenile offenders are difficult for the state court systems to handle. In particular, first-time offenses for younger teens are typically minor and impulsive, like smashing a store window on a dare or shoplifting a six-pack of beer. Ending up in the regular (adult) criminal justice system for such offenses can often do more harm than good for both the teenaged offender and society, traumatizing the teen or indoctrinating him or her into the culture of crime. Traditional juvenile courts are problem-solving courts that have tried to address the special needs of these young people, but they often fail.

In the 1990s, many states and local governments around the country established a new set of institutions to help these offenders—teen courts.[a] Teen courts allow first-time offenders the chance to keep their criminal records clear by pleading guilty and submitting themselves to the judgment of a panel of trained teen volunteers. Typically, the members of this teen jury are not from the same town or neighborhood as the offender, allowing for anonymity for both the offender and the jurors. The jury listens to the story of the offense and the offender's explanation of the crime and its circumstances and then suggests a "sentence." This sentence may consist of community service—like working with younger kids, helping the aged with chores, fines or restitution, or tasks like writing an essay about the crime or an apology letter to the victim.[b] Studies of teen courts suggest that this innovative institution may not only reduce **recidivism** among youthful offenders but also encourage civic engagement by both offenders and jurors.

[a] Madelyn M. Herman, "Teen Courts: A Juvenile Diversion Program," Knowledge and Information Services, National Center for State Courts, 2002, http://www.ncsconline.org/WC/Publications/KIS_JuvJus_Trends02_TeenPub.pdf.
[b] Amanda Reavy, "Teen Jury Focuses on Peer Influence," *(Springfield, Ill.) State Journal-Register*, 19 May 2008, p. 1.

useful in expediting the fair administration of justice in the states.

Intermediate Courts of Appeal

Trial courts establish the facts of a case and apply the law to those facts. But we have all heard about those who have lost in court "appealing" their decision. What does that mean?

First, it is important to understand that a person cannot appeal a trial court decision simply because he or she doesn't like the verdict. Perhaps surprisingly, the legitimate grounds for an appeal in civil or criminal law have nothing to do with the facts of the case. An appeals court never deals with questions of facts; these are determined by the trial court.

A case can be appealed based only on questions about either the fairness of the trial or the constitutionality of the law involved.

Most state court systems have two levels of appellate courts: intermediate courts of appeal and the supreme court. In general, intermediate courts of appeal decide questions about the trial's fairness, while supreme courts consider questions of constitutionality.

The Role of the Intermediate Courts of Appeal
Intermediate courts of appeal (ICAs) have jurisdiction over those cases that are appealed from trial courts with general jurisdiction. In essence, ICAs act as a check to ensure that trials are carried out fairly. Without such oversight, trial judges could act arbitrarily and tyrannically, something that the nation's founders feared. The Fifth Amendment to the U.S. Constitution gives Americans the right to a fair trial, and the ability to appeal a trial court's decision plays a large part in maintaining that right.

Originally, the oversight of trial courts was one of the main jobs of state supreme courts. But by the mid-20th century, as states' populations and economies grew, many of their supreme courts became overloaded with relatively routine appeals, denying them the time they needed to consider the deeper issues of law raised only occasionally by certain important cases.

ICAs are an institutional reform designed to relieve this burden on state supreme courts. ICAs decide on appeals that do not raise general points of law, allowing the supreme courts to consider only the most significant cases, as we will discuss later. Fifty years ago, only 13 states had ICAs; today, 40 states do. Those ten states without ICAs tend to be small or lightly populated states with less complex economies, such as Delaware, Maine, and Montana.

By relieving the supreme courts of the burden of routine appeals, ICAs help ensure that the state court system makes fair, timely, and consistent decisions.[14] They promote fairness by reviewing trials where proper procedures may not have been followed. They promote timeliness by eliminating the backlog that an overworked supreme court can generate. They promote consistency by ensuring that trial judges and juries around the state apply legal procedures and law the same way.

Procedures and Decision Making The procedures and decision making of ICAs differ markedly from those of trial courts. First, all appeals are heard only by judges, never by a jury, and they are usually heard by more than one judge, perhaps three to five of them. No witnesses testify, and no physical evidence is presented. Witnesses and evidence are used in trials to determine the facts of the case, but these case facts are not relevant in an appeal. Instead, the defense and plaintiff or prosecution simply offer arguments about the trial's fairness. These arguments are made in **legal briefs**, documents in which the parties point out what they see as the problems

with the trial and respond to the arguments made in the other party's brief. The primary evidence at an appeal is the **trial transcript**, the official record of events in the trial. Typically, the parties to the case don't even attend ICA hearings, whereas they almost always attend the trial. Only their lawyers appear before the ICA to represent their interests, and these are usually specialists in legal appeals, not the same lawyers who argued the trial. Indeed, for some appeals, legal arguments are made completely through their legal briefs, with no public hearing whatsoever.

ICAs also differ from trial courts in their decision making. After hearing or reading both sides' arguments, the panel of judges votes on the appeal, with the majority determining the verdict. Typically, the panel hearing the appeal does not consist of all the state's ICA judges. The judges are divided, usually geographically, into panels of three or five judges to cover their large caseloads more efficiently. Only for certain especially important or controversial cases will a state's ICA sit en banc; that is, as a whole.

In the end, the decisions of trial courts and ICAs have a fundamental, important difference. In trial court, case facts are determined and decisions involve the application of law. That is, in criminal cases, people can be found guilty and sentenced to jail, and in civil cases, fault can be assigned and judgments awarded. But in ICAs, the judges' decision is about the original trial itself—was it fair or not? If the ICA holds that the trial was fair or, more specifically, if it fails to accept the exact arguments of unfairness brought in the appeal, the decision of the trial court stands. On the other hand, if the ICA accepts the argument that the trial was flawed, either it can order the lower court to correct the sentence or judgment or it can overturn the entire decision, necessitating a completely new trial. Sometimes, after a trial's verdict has been overturned on appeal, the prosecutor or the party to the lawsuit that won the original trial decides not to pursue a new trial. For example, the appeals court may decide that the camera

---

[14] Roger A. Hanson, *Appellate Court Performance Standards and Measures* (Williamsburg, Va.: National Center for State Courts, 1999).

in the defendant's possession on the night of the robbery cannot be used as evidence because the police discovered it in an illegal search. Without that piece of evidence, the prosecutor may decide that she cannot win a second trial and so she drops the case. But that is a decision made by the prosecutor; ICAs only make decisions about the procedures of the trial, not the facts of a case or its verdict.

Supreme Courts

Shirley Abrahamson, the chief justice of the Wisconsin Supreme Court, once quoted a 19th-century journalist who wrote that "things were so quiet on the Wisconsin State Supreme Court that you could hear the justices' arteries clog."[15] Abrahamson was making the point that while state supreme courts were once quiet legal backwaters, that is certainly not true today. In the 21st century, state supreme courts regularly make decisions that have momentous impacts on their states' residents, businesses, and local governments. On all matters of a state's law, its supreme court is the final arbiter.[16] This is why these courts are also called **courts of last resort**. Furthermore, in most states, the supreme court also runs the state's entire court system and regulates its legal profession. Thus, a state's supreme court dominates its entire legal system.

Jurisdiction Trial courts have **original jurisdiction** over the vast majority of cases in a state's legal system, and ICAs handle the trial court appeals on issues of procedural fairness. So, what cases do supreme courts handle? In part, this depends on whether a state has ICAs. In the ten states that don't have them, the supreme courts' **dockets** are largely made up of the same sort of routine fairness appeals that occupy the time of ICAs. But in states with the three-tiered system shown in Figure 8.1, supreme courts have significant discretion over which cases they hear, making them very important actors in state government and policy.

In the 40 states with ICAs, the state supreme courts handle three types of cases. First, they hear cases about the balance of power in state government at the highest levels. In particular, when the state legislature and the governor have a conflict over their constitutional powers, they can bring suit directly in the supreme court.[17] These interbranch conflicts usually don't involve disputes of fact, so no trial is needed. Rather, the conflicts are over the interpretation of a state's constitution, so the supreme court can be asked directly to decide the question.

Second, in some states, the supreme court is required to hear appeals of certain criminal convictions. Most commonly, trials resulting in a death sentence must be reviewed by the supreme court regardless of the facts of the case, what happened in the trial, or even the defendant's wishes. The states vary on which other cases their supreme courts are required to hear on appeal and the percentage of the supreme court's docket made up of such cases. For example, one study found that as much as 17 percent of Georgia's state supreme court docket consists of these mandatory appeals, whereas south of its border, in Florida, mandatory appeals account for only about 2 percent of the docket.[18]

Finally, and perhaps most significantly, a state supreme court also hears those appeals of trial court and ICA decisions that it chooses

---

[15] Shirley S. Abrahamson, "Homegrown Justice: The State Constitutions," in *Developments in State Constitutional Law*, ed. Bradley D. McGraw (St. Paul, Minn.: West, 1985): 315.

[16] The U.S. Supreme Court may overturn a state supreme court's decision but only based on some aspect of the U.S. Constitution, not state law. Texas and Oklahoma each have two supreme courts, one for civil cases and one for criminal cases, but each of these has the last word for the cases it hears.

[17] "Iowa Court Decision a Victory for State Legislatures," *NCSL News*, online ed., 17 June 2004, http://www.ncsl.org/programs/press/2004/pr040617.htm.

[18] Fred Cheesman, Roger A. Hanson, and Brian J. Ostrom, "Caseload and Timeliness in State Supreme Courts," *Caseload Highlights: Examining the Work of State Courts* 7, no. 2 (2001): 1–6.

to hear because of these cases' potential implications for public policy and state law. In this respect, state supreme courts are much like the U.S. Supreme Court. If a party in a case does not feel that the trial was fair, and if the ICA decision went against him or her or if the case involves a dispute over the constitutionality of a state law, that party may **petition** the supreme court to hear the case. But most of these petitions are denied; nationwide, supreme courts grant only about 7 percent of these requests.[19]

State supreme courts grant these requests for discretionary hearings very carefully, with the aim of clarifying the interpretation of their states' law. Trial courts and ICAs follow the lead of their supreme court closely in applying state statutes and case law both because of judicial norms and because a supreme court can overturn lower court decisions. So, supreme courts choose to hear cases on which their decisions can be used as examples for lower courts facing similar cases.

In particular, supreme courts agree to hear cases that raise ambiguous legal questions that are common to a class of cases. This ambiguity often leads to inconsistency in trial court and ICA decisions. Without clear guidance on a point of law raised in cases facing them, lower court judges will simply use their own best legal judgment when making decisions. But if judges' judgments vary, decisions on similar cases will vary from judge to judge. Because the consistent administration of justice is one of the hallmarks of a fair legal system and because the state supreme court has the responsibility to maintain a fair legal system in the state, it agrees to hear cases that allow it to clear up these ambiguities.

At any given time, a state law may be ambiguous for at least two reasons. First, a new statute may need to be interpreted by the supreme court to help judges, the police, lawyers, and the public understand it exactly in practice. For example, in the past few years, several states have banned "aggressive driving" in response to the deaths, injuries, and property damage caused by road rage.[20] Since these statutes are the result of the legislative process, they typically don't define "aggressive driving" clearly. This leaves it up to police officers and trial court judges to decide whether a person's specific behavior in a case violates the law. If conflict over or inconsistency in how these officials interpret these laws arises, a representative aggressive-driving case will make its way to the state's supreme court for clarification.

Legal ambiguity can also be caused by changes in society, the economy, or even technology. For example, suppose that state statutory and case law have traditionally given visitation rights to noncustodial parents in divorce cases.[21] But what if a nonmarried, live-in couple has a child and one of the partners moves out? Should that person be given visitation rights? Maybe this is so similar to the traditional divorce situation that trial judges consistently rule that traditional divorce case law applies. But what if a couple had a child but never lived together and simply stopped being romantically involved? Can the divorce analogy be applied here for child custody? What about a couple (married or not) who had a child using a sperm donor? Is the man entitled to visitation rights after a breakup? What if a lesbian couple has a child through sperm donation? What about a couple who used both sperm and egg donation to produce a child?

As the facts in these cases move farther from those in established case law, the legal questions become more ambiguous and court decisions become less consistent. By hearing a representative case of this type, a supreme

---

[19] National Center for State Courts, *Examining the Work of State Courts*.

[20] Victor E. Flango and Ann L. Keith, "How Useful Is the New Aggressive Driving Legislation?" *Court Review* 40, nos. 3–4 (2004): 34–43.

[21] Related to this example, consider the way the legal definition of "parent" evolved in the following cases before the California Supreme Court: *In re Nicholas H.* (6 June 2002) 28 Cal. 4th 56; *In re Jesusa V.* (16 April 2004) 97 Cal.App. 4th 878; and *Elisa B. v. Superior Court* (22 August 2005) 118 Cal.App. 4th 966.

court can make a definitive legal interpretation and bring consistency and fairness to such cases.

Procedures and Decision Making

State supreme court decision making is similar to that of ICAs, with no juries, witnesses, or physical evidence and with only lawyers making oral arguments and filing elaborate legal briefs that detail the parties' arguments. Supreme courts are made up of multiple judges (typically called "justices"), but unlike ICAs, supreme courts decide almost all cases en banc. Decisions are made with a majority vote; supreme courts have an odd number of justices (usually five to nine) to avoid ties.

Because a supreme court's decisions serve as precedents for its lower courts, they are usually supported by elaborate written opinions explaining their legal reasoning, especially for their discretionary cases. But because supreme court justices have sharp legal minds and strong opinions and because their discretionary cases are typically on debatable points of law, disagreement among them can arise. When one or more justices dissent from a case's majority opinion, he or she can write a dissenting opinion. A dissenting opinion can establish the arguments for future legal debate on a point of law, perhaps even signaling that the court might change its mind in the future if it has a personnel change.

The Administrative Duties of the State Supreme Court

In addition to making authoritative decisions on state law, most state supreme courts also administer the entire court system and regulate the legal professions in their state. These duties make supreme courts much more influential in state government and policy than they would be if they had only judicial powers. The chief justice is especially involved in these administrative activities, but the entire court has a responsibility and an important role to play here.

The supreme court is responsible for the smooth operation of the entire state court system as an organization. This involves hiring and supervising clerks, court bailiffs, court reporters, and others, buying supplies and dealing with the budget, among other duties. Each supreme court employs a **director of state courts** to do most of this day-to-day administrative work. A court director is a major state administrator, on the same level as a secretary of a cabinet-level state executive agency.

The state supreme court also regulates the legal and judicial professions in most states. In harmony with state statutes and often in collaboration with the state bar association, the court establishes professional and ethical standards for a state's lawyers and judges, runs training courses for new judges, and regulates the bar examinations that prospective lawyers must pass before being allowed to practice law in the state. The supreme court also establishes procedures for investigating and sanctioning judges and lawyers accused of unethical conduct. Charges of impropriety or incompetence against lawyers are common, largely because so many lawyers are in practice and they often deal with expensive and sensitive disputes. In most states, the supreme court, often with the state bar association, sets up a board to investigate and prosecute such charges in a quasi-judicial process. Supreme courts establish similar boards for judges. But because there are far fewer judges than lawyers and because judges, presumably, hold themselves to a higher ethical standard than lawyers, **judicial review** and sanction are relatively rare.

Of course, lawyers and judges are subject to criminal and civil law like everyone else. But these review boards are designed to evaluate and sanction behavior that, although maybe not illegal, might violate professional standards and ethics. For example, although it may not be illegal for a judge to direct profanity at a defendant, it is not the sort of behavior that is conducive to the proper administration of justice and thus a judicial review board could punish a judge for it.

Policy Making in the Courts

In your high school government class, you learned that the legislative branch makes law, the executive branch implements it, and the judicial branch interprets it. But as we have already seen, whereas the legislative branch certainly does make policy, the executive branch (especially the governor) does, too. What about the state judicial branch? Does it make policy too? In the narrowest sense that legislatures and governors establish statutes and official rules and regulations, no, judges do not make policy. But if we think of policy making a little more broadly, the state judicial branch—especially the supreme court—is very much involved in policy making.

Although the advisability and propriety of judicial policy making are debated,[22] the nature of law and the role the supreme court plays in the state legal system make it almost inevitable. In writing law, legislators cannot consider every eventuality, so statutes often have gray areas. In fact, legislators sometimes intentionally write bills ambiguously to help get them through the legislative process— ambiguous wording allows different legislators to believe different things about a bill and thus support it for different reasons. But the courts must enforce laws in specific cases based on specific factual circumstances. To do so, judges must decide on the exact meaning of a law. And because they have the power to make the definitive interpretation of state law, supreme courts have the clearest judicial policy-making power. Of course, this power is limited to ambiguously worded statutes and rules, the decisions can be overturned if the legislature clarifies the law, and the decisions can be made only on points of law that are brought before them in specific cases. But in practice, the interpretation of state law by the supreme court frequently has a significant impact on public policy.

One way to look for judicial policy making is by identifying those factors that affect supreme court justices' votes on cases. Certainly, the facts of a case and legal precedent ought to have a tremendous impact on judicial decision making; if not, our entire system of justice would be illegitimate. Fortunately, many studies have shown that case facts and existing legal decisions play dominant roles in the decisions of state supreme court justices. But dominant is not exclusive. These same studies show that several other factors can also affect supreme court justices' voting on cases.[23] First, the ideology of both a justice and the state's population can affect judicial decision making on issues where an ideological divergence of opinion is clear. For example, conservative justices as well as justices in conservative states are more likely to vote to uphold death penalty sentences than liberal justices or justices in liberal states, especially where these justices are elected.[24] Other studies have shown that a justice's political party,[25] gender,[26] and even religion[27] may sometimes influence his or her voting. Because these factors influence judicial decision making

---

[22] For example, consider the different opinions of two groups over the Massachusetts Supreme Judicial Court's decision that the state cannot ban same-sex marriage: Andrea Lafferty, "Massachusetts Supreme Judicial Court Legalizes Same-Sex Marriage!" Traditional Values Coalition, 2004, http://www.traditionalvalues.org/modules.php?sid=1323; and National Organization for Women (NOW), "NOW Leaders Applaud Massachusetts Supreme Court Ruling Favoring Same-Sex Marriage Rights," 2004, http://www.now.org/issues/lgbi/020604marriage.html.

[23] Paul Brace and Melinda Gann Hall, "The Interplay of Preferences, Case Facts, Context, and Structure in the Politics of Judicial Choice," *Journal of Politics* 59 (1997): 1206–31.

[24] Craig A. Traut and Carol F. Emmert, "Expanding the Integrated Model of Judicial Decision Making: The California Justices and Capital Punishment," *Journal of Politics* 60 (1998): 1166–80.

[25] Philip Dubois, *From Ballot to Bench* (Austin: University of Texas Press, 1980).

[26] Maldavi McCall, "Gender, Judicial Dissent, and Issue Salience: The Voting Behavior of State Supreme Court Justices in Sexual Harassment Cases, 1980–1998," *Social Science Journal* 40 (2003): 79–97; and Songer and Crews-Meyers, "Does Gender Matter?"

[27] Songer and Tabrizi, "The Religious Right on the Court."

systematically, over and above the effects of case facts and law, it is reasonable to say that the state supreme court is in the business of policy making.

But if justices' votes are affected by things that are irrelevant to the case before them— like their party or gender—is this not the very definition of biased judicial decision making? Perhaps. But judges are human, not legal machinery. They bring a lifetime of personal and professional experience to the bench, and perhaps it should not be surprising that this colors their thinking once they put on their robes. These biases may be small, and justices may do their best to eliminate them, but they do exist. In particular, these influences come into play when state supreme court justices interpret statutes and case law in ambiguous areas of law; that is, when they are effectively helping make public policy.

State supreme courts can also affect public policy through judicial review. Like the U.S. Supreme Court, the state supreme courts have the power to judge whether a statute violates the state's constitution and, if so, to nullify that law.[28] Especially since the 1970s, state supreme courts have been active in using judicial review, although their propensity to do so varies over time and among the states. One study examined over 3,000 judicial review cases heard by the 50 state supreme courts and found that almost 20 percent of the laws involved were overturned.[29] Another study found that the Washington State Supreme Court invalidated one out of every four laws it reviewed.[30] The influence of these decisions goes well beyond those directly involved in the case being reviewed, applying to everyone potentially affected by that law. The state legislature can initiate a change in the state constitution to reverse such nullification, but

this process is much more difficult than simply amending a statute. This gives considerable staying power to this sort of court-made constitutional law.

On the other hand, several factors work against the courts having a strong policy-making role in state government. Perhaps most important, the judicial branch has little policy-making legitimacy in popular American political culture. Judges' values are not supposed to enter into their decisions; they are just supposed to apply the law to the facts of the case. Judges are also supposed to evaluate each case individually, while policy making is about setting general rules. So, by admitting to making policy, a judge would be violating professional and cultural norms. Furthermore, unlike legislatures and governors, courts are passive decision makers, simply deciding on those cases brought before them. So, even if judges wanted to make policy, their agenda would be set to a much greater degree by events and outsiders than are the policy agendas of legislatures or governors.

Thus, although the nature of the job obliges state judges—especially those on the supreme courts—to influence public policy, norms and customs make the acknowledgment of that influence difficult. Indeed, if you ask a judge, even a state supreme court justice, if the courts make policy, he or she will likely deny it vehemently. In fact, it wasn't until recent decades that political scientists started studying whether even U.S. Supreme Court justices made decisions based on criteria other than case facts and the law.[31] But the evidence that the courts have substantial influence on policy makes it important even for those of us who never become directly involved in the court system to care about its institutions and performance.

[28] Laura Langer, *Judicial Review in State Supreme Courts: A Comparative Study* (Albany: State University of New York Press, 1999).

[29] Craig F. Emmert, "An Integrated Case-Related Model of Judicial Decisionmaking: Explaining State Supreme Court Decisions in Judicial Review Cases," *Journal of Politics* 54 (1992): 543–52.

[30] Charles H. Sheldon, "Judicial Review and the Supreme Court of Washington, 1890–1986," *Publius* 17 (1987): 69–89.

[31] Glendon A. Schubert, *The Judicial Mind: The Attitudes and Ideologies of Supreme Court Justices, 1946–1963* (Evanston, Ill.: Northwestern University Press, 1965).

Judicial Selection

Unlike almost any other type of American public official, state judges are selected in a variety of ways. Whereas all governors and state legislators are elected and all federal judges are appointed by the president, depending on the state and the level of the court, state judges may gain their judicial robes in any of five very different ways: appointment by the governor or state legislature, partisan or nonpartisan election, or a hybrid of election and appointment known as the **Merit Plan**. This variety of judicial selection methods demonstrates Americans' evolving attitudes and ambivalence about the role of judges in the political process.

It also offers political scientists a unique opportunity to examine how the institutions by which officials gain office affect their behavior in office.

Judicial Selection Methods

Figure 8.2 shows the ways the states select their supreme court justices. Some states use different selection methods for different courts; Indiana has the most diverse system, using three of the five selection methods for its trial courts alone. Some states' judicial selection systems also vary idiosyncratically. For example, in Illinois, Pennsylvania, and New Mexico (supreme court only), judges are initially elected in partisan elections,

Figure 8.2

Method of Selection of the State Supreme Court Justices

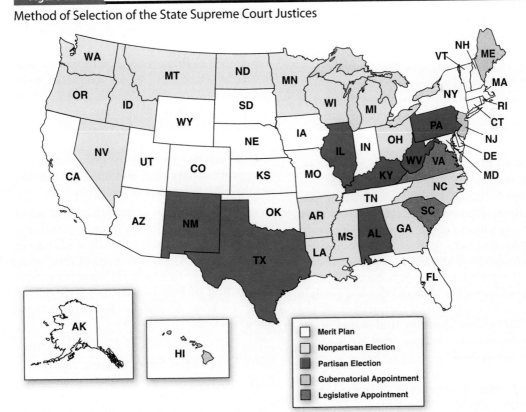

Source: Council of State Governments, *The Book of the States 2006* (Lexington, Ky.: Council of State Governments, 2006), 251–54.

but if they wish to serve a second term, they face only a **retention election**. But although classifying judicial selection methods can be a little tricky, important distinctions can be drawn. We describe the five methods as they are most commonly used.

Legislative Appointment Under the earliest state constitutions just after independence, most states' judges were appointed by their legislatures, reflecting the faith that the founders had in those representative assemblies. Today, only South Carolina and Virginia continue to select their judges this way. In these states, a legislative committee or commission screens candidates and reports its findings to the full legislature for a vote. These judges are appointed for a fixed term and subject to reappointment by the legislature.

Gubernatorial Appointment Three states—Hawaii, Maine, and New Jersey—continue to use the second-oldest method of selecting judges: gubernatorial appointment. In these states, the governor has almost unfettered discretion in appointing judges to a fixed term (with the caveats that judges can serve only until age 70 in New Jersey and legislative approval is needed for appointees in Maine and New Jersey).

Partisan Elections In 12 states, judges for at least some state courts are elected on partisan ballots. Just like governors and state legislators, those wishing to become a judge in these states must run for a party's nomination in a primary election (or gain the nomination in a convention) and then face an opponent from the other party (or parties) in a general election. Among the six states that use partisan elections for only some of their judges, all but New Mexico use them for trial courts, using other methods for judges on their supreme courts and ICAs.

Nonpartisan Elections The second-most common method of state judicial selection is nonpartisan election, with 21 states using this method for at least some of their courts. These elections are usually not held during the November general election but rather are held in the spring, often coinciding with nonpartisan municipal elections.

The Merit Plan The Merit Plan (also called the Missouri Plan, after the first state to adopt it) is the most widely used judicial selection method, with 24 states using some variant of it for at least some of their courts. The Merit Plan has three steps. First, a nominating commission is formed to recruit and evaluate potential judges. The composition of this commission varies from state to state, but it generally includes representatives of key government institutions (such as the state legislature, governor, and state supreme court) and the legal establishment (perhaps through the state bar association). For a specific judicial vacancy, the commission identifies a small number of qualified candidates (usually three) and sends their names to the governor. Next, the governor appoints one of the nominees to the vacancy for a short term, usually one to three years. Finally, once a new judge has served this probationary term, he or she faces the voters in a retention election. In a retention election, the question on the ballot is not which candidate the voter prefers but, rather, whether this judge should be allowed to have another (usually much longer) term. This probationary term and retention election are the unique features of the Merit Plan.

All this variation in how the states select their judges raises two obvious questions: (1) why don't all states select their judges the same way, as they do with most of their other government officials; and (2) what effect does the method of judicial selection have on the administration of justice? We turn to these questions next.

Why Do States Select Their Judges Differently?

Since the founding of the republic, Americans have debated how to select their state judges.

The explanation for the current variation in judicial selection methods lies in the evolution of Americans' values about our courts.[32] We establish institutions for selecting a class of public officials based on the functions that we believe these officials should perform and the values that we hold about these functions. The current variation in state judicial selection roughly follows the historic and geographic variation in Americans' beliefs about the proper role of the courts.

Our expectations for judges have never been as clear or as universally accepted as our expectations for most other officials. Some have debated the proper role of legislators and governors, but when push comes to shove, we want our legislators and governors to reflect our preferences, and we elect them directly to ensure that they do.

We are less certain about the proper role of judges in our representative democracy. For example, consider how you think judges should make decisions. Legal culture and norms hold that their decisions should be based only on the law and the facts of the case—this is the fair administration of justice that we prize. But what about when the fair administration of justice conflicts with public opinion? Such conflicts are more common than you might think. For example, an angry mob might want to lynch a person who they think got a too-lenient sentence for a particularly heinous crime. Most Americans would agree that the judge was right to ignore the wishes of this community and apply the law as passed by the state legislature. But what about when a law is passed by a state legislature or through a voter initiative that conflicts with the fundamental rules of governance or human rights set out in the state's constitution? Should a state supreme court override the current will of the people (the statute) in favor of the constitution, which

represents the will of the people at a previous time? In the federal court system, judges are appointed for life so that they can protect constitutional rights and values against the heat of current popular opinion. They have done this to protect the rights of minorities of all types, from African Americans trying to vote in the South to the Ku Klux Klan and neo-Nazi groups trying to hold rallies.[33] Is this the proper role of the courts?

Even if you agree that the judiciary should protect certain basic rights against popular opinion, consider other legal situations where the law and the facts are not clear-cut, giving a judge room for interpretation. To what extent should judges decide such cases using their professional judgment based on their years of legal training and experience, and to what extent should they reflect the values and preferences of the communities they serve? Furthermore, is there a difference between the ability of voters to understand the job of a judge, on one hand, versus that of a governor or legislator, on the other, such that we can trust the average person to know who would make a good governor or legislator but not who would make a good judge?

Different answers to these questions can be backed by good arguments, and this debate is reflected in the institutions the states use to select their judges.[34] As we have seen, the earliest state legislatures embodied what was seen as the only legitimate source of political power—the people. The British had used the colonial courts as instruments of royal oppression and thus the founders were suspicious of them, just as they were of governors. Thus, the first state governments subordinated the courts to the legislature by giving the latter the power to appoint judges. As state legislatures fell out of favor in the early 19th century, states embraced executive

---

[32] Charles H. Sheldon and Linda S. Maule, *Choosing Justice: The Recruitment of State and Federal Judges* (Pullman: Washington State University Press, 1997).

[33] Donald A. Downs, *Nazis in Skokie: Freedom, Community and the First Amendment* (South Bend, Ind.: University of Notre Dame Press, 1985).

[34] F. Andrew Hanssen, "Learning about Judicial Independence: Institutional Change in the State Courts," *Journal of Legal Studies* 33 (2004): 431–73.

leadership, including giving governors the power to appoint judges. Thus, in keeping with the strongly elitist tone of early American democracy, state judges were almost all appointed for the country's first half-century.

With the rise of Jacksonian democracy in pre–Civil War America, the states began electing many more of their officials directly, including judges. In 1832, Mississippi became the first to elect its judges, and by 1900, about 80 percent of the states did likewise. Like all officials in this era, judges were elected on partisan ballots, with the idea being that the party label would give voters an indication of the candidates' values and preferences. Thus, judges would reflect voters' values in the same way that legislators or governors would.

By the early 20th century, the good-government reformers of the Progressive Era advocated nonpartisan judicial elections. The Progressives valued judges who would decide cases fairly and impartially based on the law and the facts of the case. They felt that partisanship and political ideology should have nothing to do with the administration of justice, so it made no sense to select judges using those criteria. Nonpartisan elections would force voters to select judges on more job-related criteria, like their training and experience. North Dakota established the first nonpartisan judicial elections in 1910, and by 1952, 15 other states had done so.

Finally, in 1940, Missouri adopted the first Merit Plan, that hybrid of appointment and election. The values reflected by this institution were also a hybrid. The first part is the notion that judicial selection is best made by experts (the selection committee and the governor) because the job is highly technical and voters know little about it. But the retention election reflects the democratic impulse to give voters a way to evaluate their judges once the latter are in office. In this way, the Merit Plan is a scientific management approach to good government, an effort to appoint a qualified person to the post based on technical merit and then letting voters evaluate that person based on his or her subsequent performance on the job.

Thus, the diversity among the states in judicial selection reflects the diversity of our values about the role of judges over time and around the country. New states adopted the institution that reflected the values in vogue at the time of their statehood. For example, from 1846 to 1900, every state admitted to the union initially elected its judges on a partisan ballot.[35] Likewise, when states made major changes to their constitutions, they tended to adopt the method that better reflected the contemporary values about the judiciary. For example, in recent decades, Rhode Island, Delaware, New Hampshire, New York, Tennessee, and South Dakota all changed to the Merit Plan; since 1992, Mississippi, Arkansas, and North Carolina all moved in this direction by changing from partisan to nonpartisan elections.

Why have some states retained their older systems of judicial selection? This can often be explained simply by inertia and the difficulty of changing a state's constitution. For example, Article VI, Section 7, of the Virginia state constitution requires judges to be selected by the legislature, and this has not been changed since the constitution was adopted in 1776. In other states, even when the opportunity to change their selection method arose, it was not taken because the existing system reflected the values of the state well. For example, even though Illinois adopted a completely new constitution in 1970, it continued to elect its judges on a partisan basis due to the highly partisan and individualistic political culture of the state.

What Difference Does a Judicial Selection Method Make?

The variation in how states select their judges has given political scientists a unique

---

[35] Kermit L. Hall, "Progressive Reform and the Decline of Democratic Accountability: The Popular Election of State Supreme Court Judges, 1850–1920," *American Bar Foundation Research Journal* 2 (1984): 345–63.

opportunity to assess the impact of these selection methods and the impact of political institutions more generally. Before reviewing the results of recent research on this question, let's consider what effects reformers and their critics expected.

The original approach of appointing judges was criticized for reducing the independence of the courts and shifting political power to the appointing institution, whether it is the governor or legislature. One of the central principles of American government is the separation of powers among the three branches, and elite appointment may upset that balance.[36] Appointments might also affect the type of person who rises to the bench. For example, in South Carolina, one of only two states still using legislative appointment, almost all judges are former state lawmakers.

Judicial elections also have critics, with the American Bar Association being perhaps the most prominent among them.[37] Given the widespread use of judicial elections and the extensive debate about them over the past 100 years, these arguments are more extensive and multifaceted than those regarding judicial appointment.

First, judicial elections are criticized for being low-turnout, low-information events.[38] Few voters seem to know anything about candidates for state judgeships, especially below the supreme court level. Without such information, voters can't very well form and express a coherent preference about who should be a judge. As a result, people tend either to vote less or to fall back on voting cues that may be weakly related to their preferences, completely irrelevant, or even

misleading. In partisan elections, the party label may provide some information about a candidate's political values and policy preferences, but it says nothing about his or her fairness and judicial competence. And in nonpartisan elections and primaries, voters don't even have this limited information. This can sometimes cause problems. For example, because he had the same name as a popular state senator, an inexperienced lawyer on the verge of disbarment for a string of bad debts was once elected to the Texas Supreme Court. Luckily, the mistake was short-lived—eight months after his election, the judge quit and fled the country to escape federal charges related to hiring a hit man![39]

One of the reasons that voters know so little about judicial candidates is their professional norm against campaigning using anything other than basic résumé data. In essence, judicial candidates have traditionally been able to tell voters only where they went to law school and what jobs they have held. This information may be useful to voters who are very familiar with the legal profession, but it doesn't help most of us. For example, few voters would be able to rank the qualifications of two judicial candidates knowing only that one attended the College of William and Mary School of Law and served as a clerk in the U.S. Circuit Court of Appeals and that the other attended the John Marshall School of Law and was a partner in Fouts, Hicks, and Taylor, LLC.

The legal profession frowns on judicial candidates offering the sort of information that we expect from candidates for other offices—their opinions on the important issues on which they might be called to decide.

---

[36] Of course, because all federal judges are appointed by the president, the same argument could be made about the federal judiciary.

[37] For example, see American Bar Association, "Independence of the Judiciary: Judicial Elections Are Becoming More Politicized," 2006, http://www.abanet.org/publiced/lawday/talking/judicialelections.html.

[38] David Klein and Lawrence Baum, "Ballot Information and Voting Decisions in Judicial Elections," *Political Research Quarterly* 54 (2001): 709–28. On the other hand, recent research has shown that American voters may actually cast a more informed vote in judicial elections than had previously been thought; see Melinda Gann Hall and Chris W. Bonneau, "Predicting Challengers in State Supreme Court Elections: Context and the Politics of Institutional Design," *Political Research Quarterly* 56 (2003): 337–49; and Melinda Gann Hall and Chris W. Bonneau, "Does Quality Matter? Challengers in State Supreme Court Elections," *American Journal of Political Science* 50 (2006): 20–33.

[39] "The Sins of Justice Yarbrough," *Time*, online ed., 18 July 1977.

For example, no self-respecting judicial candidate would run a TV ad that said, "Mike Pyle for Judge—No More Coddling Criminals," even though we would not be surprised to see a state legislative candidate run such an ad—in fact, we would expect it.

The reason for this professional norm against policy-oriented information in judicial campaigns is the strong norm that judges should administer the law based only on the specific facts and the established law involved in each case. How would you like to be on trial on a charge of drunk and disorderly conduct—guilty or not—before the newly elected Judge Pyle fresh off his "law-and-order" election campaign? Or suppose you were suing a negligent doctor for botching a surgical procedure. Would you want to face a judge who gave campaign speeches against "excessive lawsuit settlements"? Governors and legislators are expected to have opinions on public policy and discuss them in their election campaigns; judges are expected to be unbiased.

Another important criticism of judicial elections arises from recent dramatic increases in campaign spending, especially in supreme court races.[40] Reformers are mostly troubled about how and why judicial candidates receive their campaign contributions. Lawyers and law firms have long been the major donors in these races, raising concerns about judicial fairness when these donors subsequently appear in court. And recently, interest groups have begun actively financing state supreme court races because of the broad judicial issues that are decided there.[41] Some groups have even been airing independent TV ads for the judicial candidates they favor, and these groups may not feel constrained by judicial norms about the content of these ads. Some interest groups have even begun targeting sitting judges they don't like, especially those who rule as unconstitutional those initiatives the groups just worked so hard to pass.[42]

But what really disturbs observers of state judicial elections about skyrocketing campaign finance is the potential for **conflict of interest**, especially when one side in a case is represented by a contributor and the other side is not.[43] For example, recently, just after a West Virginia Supreme Court justice was elected with the help of millions of dollars in campaign ads from a group associated with Massey Energy, he sat in judgment on that coal company's appeal of a $50 million settlement; a similar case also recently happened in Illinois with State Farm Insurance.[44] Like legislators who claim that campaign contributions do not affect their roll call votes, judges protest that this money causes "no bias or prejudice,"[45] but recent research suggests otherwise.[46] One way to avoid even the appearance of such bias is for a judge who has received contributions from a party to a case to **recuse** him or herself from deciding on it. These West Virginia and Illinois justices eventually recused themselves in Massey Energy and State Farm cases, respectively—but not before casting the

[40] Chris W. Bonneau, "What Price Justice(s)? Understanding Campaign Spending in State Supreme Court Elections," *State Politics and Policy Quarterly* 5 (2005): 107–25; and Eric Velasco, "Bids for State Court Carry High Price Tags," *Birmingham (Ala.) News*, online ed., 12 June 2006.

[41] Robert Lenzner and Matthew Miller, "Buying Justice," *Forbes*, 21 July 2003, 64; Zach Patton, "Robe Warriors," in *State and Local Government, 2007 Edition*, ed. Kevin B. Smith (Washington, D.C.: CQ Press, 2006); and Illinois Campaign for Political Reform, "Downstate Judicial Races Leave Records in the Dust," press release, 2006, http://www.ilcampaign.org/blog/2006/11/downstate-judicial-races-leave-records.html.

[42] Matthew Manweller, "The' Angriest Crocodile': Information Costs, Direct Democracy Activists, and the Politicization of State Judicial Elections," *State and Local Government Review* 37 (2005): 86–102.

[43] James Eisenstein, "Financing Pennsylvania's Supreme Court Candidates," *Judicature* 84 (2000): 10–19; and Michael J. Goodman and William C. Rempel, "In Las Vegas, They're Playing with a Stacked Judicial Deck," *Los Angeles Times*, online ed., 8 June 2006.

[44] Adam Liptak, "Justice Bemoans' Seat-Buying,'" *(Springfield, Ill.) State Journal-Register*, 1 October 2006, p. 4.

[45] Nevada Judge Gene T. Porter, quoted in Goodman and Rempel, "In Las Vegas, They're Playing with a Stacked Judicial Deck."

[46] Damon M. Cann, "Justice for Sale? Campaign Contributions and Judicial Decisionmaking," *State Politics and Policy Quarterly* 7 (2007): 281–97.

deciding votes in favor of the companies on earlier decisions.[47]

But even if there is no explicit quid pro quo on a case—which would be bribery and patently illegal—might a judge develop an unconscious bias on certain cases based on his or her campaign support? Furthermore, wouldn't we expect interest groups to support candidates who have a particular point of view, thereby trying to stack the judiciary in their favor? This happens all the time in legislative and gubernatorial races, so why is it problematic in judicial elections? And even if judicial decisions are never affected by campaign contributions, might just the appearance of such bias damage the public's opinion about the courts?[48] These questions raise important concerns about the wisdom of electing judges.

To address these fears, states have regulated judicial elections much more heavily than they have legislative and gubernatorial races. For example, some states enacted those judicial norms into law, restricting the policy statements that judicial candidates can make. But since 2002, federal courts have struck down many of these regulations, ruling that they violate the candidates' First Amendment right to free speech.[49] One case in Minnesota even struck down restrictions in nonpartisan elections on soliciting campaign funds from political parties, perhaps calling into question the future of nonpartisan elections.[50] In the coming years, it will be interesting to see whether professional norms alone will prevail or if judicial campaigns will simply become just like those for other offices.

After considering the arguments against judicial election and elite appointment, the Merit Plan may sound like a great idea. After all, who could argue against picking judges based on merit? And this hybrid of expert evaluation and voter double-checking through a retention election has been the most frequently selected format among the states that changed their judicial selection method since World War II. Most would agree that judges need certain technical expertise and training; not just anyone can be a judge. On the other hand, going back to Thomas Jefferson, Americans have strongly believed that the average citizen could serve well as a legislator; even the executive skills needed of a governor are probably more evenly distributed in the population than those skills needed to be a judge. Furthermore, the average person probably can't even determine who has the specialized skills a judge needs. Would you want your doctor or car mechanic to be selected by a popular vote or would you rather have them picked (or at least certified) by experts in their fields? The Merit Plan also reduces the temptation in appointment systems for judicial selection to be made on criteria other than pure technical merit, such as political party or returning a political favor.

On the other hand, we have to be careful not to take labels like "Merit Plan" at face value. What exactly does "merit" mean in this context? In practice, the answer is that merit is defined for this reform based on the values of a state's legal establishment. Old, established law firms, the state bar association, and their political allies tend to dominate Merit Plan nomination committees. These people know—and really care about—the difference between the John Marshall School of Law and the College of William and Mary School of Law. So they may well be the best people to evaluate judicial merit. But the social hierarchy of the legal profession suggests that there may be some differences in the types of lawyers selected to be judges through the Merit Plan and through

---

[47] Adam Liptak, "West Virginia Judge Steps out of Case Involving Travel Companion," *The New York Times*, online ed, 19 January 2008; Adam Liptak, "Case Studies: West Virginia and Illinois," *The New York Times*, online ed., 1 October 2006.

[48] James L. Gibson, "Challenges to the Impartiality of State Supreme Courts: Legitimacy Theory and' New-Style' Judicial Campaigns," *American Political Science Review* 102 (2008): 59–75.

[49] *Republican Party of Minnesota v. White*, 536 US 765 (2002).

[50] U.S. Eighth Circuit Court, *Dimick v. Republican Party of Minnesota* (No. 05–566).

Scott Olson/Getty Images

While this ad for attorneys Fetman and Garland may generate significant name recognition-and business-that could help them should they someday decide to run for an elective judgeship, it will not likely impress the legal establishment who control nominations in the Merit Plan judicial selection process.

elections or appointment. Consider the "See a Lawyer for 10 Bucks" guy who advertises on afternoon TV and city buses. He is not likely to attain a judgeship through the Merit Plan because he likely does not impress the legal establishment. But he might have a pretty good chance of winning a judicial election because of the name recognition that his TV and bus ads have generated, his money, and his self-promotional talent. The background, values, and clients of establishment lawyers can be quite different than those of lawyers who advertise on buses. Think about who gains and loses when these values are reflected in judicial decision making.

So far, we have considered reformers' arguments about the effects of these different judicial selection methods, but what has objective research told us about them? Recently, many scholars have studied the effects of these reforms, especially in state supreme courts. Some of these studies have even evaluated potential effects that reformers hadn't considered. For example, one study found that the judicial selection method doesn't affect how long justices serve,[51] while other studies have found conflicting evidence about the impact of selection method on the public's approval of their courts.[52] But a series of studies has allowed us to draw some general conclusions about two important hypothesized impacts of judicial selection method—the type of person who becomes a judge and the decisions made by judges once they are on the bench.

In considering the effect of the selection method on who becomes a judge, to date, scholars have

[51] R. L. Dudley, "Turnover and Tenure on State High Courts: Does Method of Selection Make a Difference?" *Justice System Journal* 19 (1997): 1–16.

[52] James P. Wenzel, Shaun Bowler, and David J. Lanoue, "The Sources of Public Confidence in State Courts: Experience and Institutions," *American Politics Research* 31 (2003): 191–211; Sara C. Benesh, "Understanding Public Confidence in America Courts," *Journal of Politics* 68 (2006): 697–707; and Gibson, "Challenges to the Impartiality of State Supreme Courts."

studied only judges' most obvious demographic characteristics. They have found that to a far greater degree than even other public officials, state judges are overwhelmingly middle-aged, middle class, white, and male. Again compared to other types of officials, their educational and professional experiences are pretty homogeneous; this is perhaps not surprising, since they are all in the same profession. But despite this pattern of homogeneity, political scientists have found that elections tend to reduce racial and ethnic diversity among judges and Merit Plans and appointment systems tend to increase it.[53] Why might this be so? First, because elections are decided on a majority-rule principle, if people tend to vote for those of their own racial or ethnic group (of course, an arguable assumption), only candidates from majority groups will win. On the other hand, with an appointment system or Merit Plan, the appointing officials may look at the totality of the bench and purposefully seek diversity, whether because they think that it is the right thing to do or as a way of rewarding certain constituencies. But if this is so, why do we find that women judicial candidates do worse in election systems, even though they constitute a slight majority in most states?[54] This may be attributed to a lingering gender bias in the electorate, something that affects elections for almost all offices.

Most political scientists studying judicial selection's effects have focused on judicial decision making because of its potential to affect the administration of justice and public policy. The general conclusion of these studies is that judicial selection does not affect judges' decisions much, if at all.[55] This is good—we hope that judges' decisions are driven by the law and the facts of the cases before them. The norm that judges should be impartial arbiters of justice appears largely to override any institutional differences among selection methods. But political scientists have found some minor impacts of the selection method on judicial decision making, primarily differences between elected judges on one hand and appointed and Merit Plan judges on the other, especially at the supreme court level.

First, as democratic theory suggests, elected judges' decisions tend to reflect the ideology and values of their state's citizens, especially on issues that are in the public eye, such as the death penalty.[56] This effect is stronger for competitive elections than for retention elections.[57] Moreover, elected judges tend to adjust their decisions as elections approach, both reflecting their state's ideology more closely[58] and issuing harsher criminal sentences.[59] Elections also lead to more plea bargaining, fewer trials,[60] and fewer dissenting opinions on controversial issues decided by supreme courts.[61] These suggest an effort by incumbent judges to reflect their constituents' values and reduce conflict, both of which might help their reelection chances.

[53] Barbara L. Graham, "Do Judicial Selection Systems Matter? A Study of Black Representation on State Courts," *American Politics Quarterly* 18 (1990): 316–36; and Mark S. Hurwitz and Drew Noble Lanier, "Explaining Judicial Diversity: The Differential Ability of Women and Minorities to Attain Seats on State Supreme and Appellate Courts," *State Politics and Policy Quarterly* 3 (2003): 329–52.

[54] Nicholas O. Alozie, "Selection Methods and the Recruitment of Women to State Courts of Last Resort," *Social Science Quarterly* 77 (1996): 110–26; Kathleen A. Bratton and Rorie L. Spill, "Existing Diversity and Judicial Selection: The Role of the Appointment Method in Establishing Gender Diversity in State Supreme Courts," *Social Science Quarterly* 83 (2002): 504–18; and Hurwitz and Lanier, "Explaining Judicial Diversity."

[55] Henry R. Glick and Craig F. Emmert, "Selection Systems and Judicial Characteristics: The Recruitment of State Supreme Court Justices," *Judicature* 70 (1987): 228–35.

[56] Brace and Hall, "The Interplay of Preferences, Case Facts, Context, and Structure."

[57] Traut and Emmert, "Expanding the Integrated Model of Judicial Decision Making."

[58] Melinda Gann Hall, "Constituent Influence in State Supreme Courts: Conceptual Notes and a Case Study," *Journal of Politics* 49 (1987): 1117–24; and Melinda Gann Hall, "Electoral Politics and Strategic Voting in State Supreme Courts," *Journal of Politics* 54 (1992): 427–46.

[59] Huber and Gordon, "Accountability and Coercion."

[60] Harold W. Elder, "Property Rights Structures and Criminal Courts: An Analysis of State Criminal Courts," *International Review of Law and Economics* 7 (1987): 21–32.

[61] Melinda Gann Hall, "State Supreme Courts in American Democracy: Probing the Myths of Judicial Reform," *American Political Science Review* 95 (2001): 315–30.

Judges elected on partisan ballots tend to vote in ways that reflect their partisanship,[62] and in civil cases, they all tend to grant higher awards to injured parties than judges selected through other systems.[63] Furthermore, partisan election results are influenced more by the judicial behavior of the incumbent judge running for reelection than are the results of nonpartisan and retention elections, which are more influenced by social and political events. This is the opposite of what Progressive era and Merit Plan reformers argued would be the case.[64]

Thus, although a state's judicial selection method can have a bit of an effect on who becomes a judge and how he or she decides, we can't say definitively which method is the best. Not only don't we understand completely the effects of these different methods but also, just as important, Americans hold ambiguous values about the role of the courts in government and about judges' behavior. Until we can agree on these values, the debate over judicial selection and the successive waves of reform that this debate spawns will likely continue.

Reform and the State Courts

The history of American state courts has been a history of institutional experimentation and reform. From partisan and nonpartisan elections to the Merit Plan, from intermediate courts of appeal to family and drug courts, from directors of state courts to boards to review attorney and judicial misconduct, the states have been trying to get the administration of justice right since the beginning of the republic. This is an especially difficult task because of the lack of a clear vision about what we want from our courts. Certainly, we

want fair and impartial adjudication of cases based on the facts and law, but we also value democracy, and as such, we want our courts to reflect the basic principles that our citizens hold dear. We also want the courts to guard the basic rights of minorities because besides being the right thing to do, we know that each of us will be in the minority sometimes, and we want our rights protected then.

Fulfilling all these needs is a tall order for the courts, so it should be no surprise that we never get them exactly right. Consider a few new reforms that have been touted recently and how they speak to the values we want our courts to reflect:

- CourTools—CourTools are a set of ten performance measures developed by the National Center for State Courts in an effort to make courts more user-friendly and efficient.[65] Aimed at evaluating court systems rather than specific judges, CourTools use both objective court data and surveys of those who have participated in the judicial system as parties to a case, jurors, witnesses, and family members.

- Court-stripping—"Court-stripping" refers to laws designed to change the jurisdiction of a type of case so as to improve the chances of court decisions that are preferred by those making the laws.[66] For example, before Republicans lost control of Congress in 2006, much court-stripping involved shifting the jurisdiction of cases like **class action lawsuits**, right-to-life decisions, and same-sex marriage questions from state courts to the federal courts.

- Judicial Accountability Initiative Laws (JAIL)—Advocated by the group Jail4Judges, JAIL would abolish the immunity against civil lawsuits held by

[62] Paul Brace and Melinda Gann Hall, "Justices' Response to Case Facts," *American Politics Quarterly* 24 (1996): 237–61; and Stuart S. Nagel, *Comparing Elected and Appointed Judicial Systems* (Beverly Hills, Calif.: Sage, 1973).

[63] Alexander Tabarrok and Eric Helland, "Court Politics: The Political Economy of Tort Awards," *Journal of Law and Economics* 42 (1999): 157–88.

[64] Hall, "State Supreme Courts in American Democracy."

[65] Zach Patton, "Judging the Judges," *Governing*, October 2006, 41–43

[66] "Congress and Court-Stripping: Just Keep Your Shirts On," *Church and State*, online ed., May 2004.

judges, juries, and others working in the court systems, establishing special boards to review court actions thought to be too lenient, too harsh, or just plain wrong—what JAIL advocates call "black-collar crime."[67] But in its first initiative vote, in South Dakota's 2006 general election, JAIL won only a 10.8 percent "yes" vote, indicating that this is a reform whose time has not yet come.

Summary

State court systems are both complex and diverse, and the central themes of this book—the importance of institutions, reform, and comparisons—become thoroughly intermingled when discussing them. Because the courts can have such an important and direct impact on a person's life, and because we have such mixed expectations for them, Americans have continuously reformed their judicial institutions, leading to the substantial state-to-state variation we see among them today. But through this complexity, we can both discern clear patterns and use this variation to understand how the states' institutions of justice work.

State courts settle civil and criminal disputes among people, corporations, and government entities. These courts work as a self-contained system within each state, working parallel to, rather than in competition with or as inferior to, the federal court system. State trial courts, intermediate courts of appeal (ICAs), and supreme courts each have an important and unique role in administering justice, with the supreme court being the final arbiter of the constitutionality and meaning of state law. Although their explicit job is just to interpret and apply the law in specific disputes, by doing so, the courts influence state public policy greatly. Unlike most other American public officials, state judges gain their positions through a variety of methods, including appointment by the governor or legislature, partisan and nonpartisan election, and the Merit Plan. Although scholars have found some significant impacts of the ways in which judges are selected, little evidence exists that judges selected in different ways behave radically differently from one another on the bench.

Key Terms

Adjudication	General jurisdiction	Plaintiff
Adjudicator	Intermediate courts of appeal	Plea bargain
Adversarial argument	Judicial review	Problem-solving courts
Bench trial	Jurisdiction	Recidivism
Class action lawsuit	Jury	Recuse
Common law	Legal brief	Retention election
Conflict of interest	Limited jurisdiction	Small claims courts
Courts of last resort	Mental health courts	Supreme court
Defendant	Merit Plan	Trial court
Director of state courts	Original jurisdiction	Trial transcript
Docket	Out-of-court settlement	
Drug courts	Petition	

---

[67] Nancy McCarthy, "South Dakota Measures Puts Judges on Edge," *California Law Journal*, online ed., November 2006.

9

The Structure of Local Governments

INTRODUCTION

The structure of American local governments today is the product of reforms that redesigned political institutions at the beginning of the 20th century. Some of these reforms have been discussed briefly in other parts of this book: nonpartisan local elections and direct democracy, for example. These are part of a larger package of institutional changes that fundamentally redefined how state and local politics work in much of the United States. Local political party organizations, or **party machines** that controlled public offices in many American cities in the 19th century, were the primary target of these reforms. We begin with a brief description of the major forms of local governments in the United States today and then examine the "machine" origins of American cities in order to understand how these local institutions have evolved into what they are today.

Many Americans might take for granted—or resent—the vast array of local governments in the United States. Local governments, including municipalities, counties, school districts, and numerous special service districts, provide a wide array of public services. Many Americans today reside in a town or city that is part of a larger county. Scattered across those two levels of government are school districts and various special districts that provide services to your place of residence. Given all these different types of local governments, your place of residence is likely located in several local governments simultaneously.

Forms of Local Government

Municipalities

Each state has its own unique rules about how municipal governments (cities, towns, and villages) are structured and how new municipalities are incorporated. Municipalities, like all local governments, are limited to doing only what their state says they may do. This concept, commonly known as **Dillon's rule**, means that a state legislature can make different rules about how various municipalities in a state might function. Many states have one set of rules for large cities (or special rules that affect only one city) and other rules for smaller municipalities. As we see below, these rules define what these places do and how they may do it. Larger, older cities often provide a wide range of general services—including police, fire protection, building inspections, water service, and many others. New cities may provide fewer services.

Counties

States are divided into geographic areas that perform some of the same functions as municipalities. Most states refer to these as counties, although they are known as boroughs in Alaska and parishes in Louisiana. Municipalities exist within counties,[1] and counties provide general services to portions of the county that are unincorporated (that is, outside city or town boundaries). Some counties contract with smaller cities and towns to provide a service the municipality does not offer. The range of public services provided varies substantially across the 3,000 counties in the United States. Counties are, traditionally, administrative and record-keeping jurisdictions for their states. County governments are thus often responsible for recording property records, conducting property tax assessments, administering elections, providing law enforcement, running jails, running courts, maintaining roads, and processing birth and death records.

Modern county governments have assumed many of the same responsibilities as large municipalities. In some ways, counties do even more than many large cities. Much of the federal and state money for health programs is spent in county hospitals and through county-administered health programs. Some states rely heavily on counties to regulate land use and development.

Special Districts

Special districts, or single-purpose governments, typically provide one particular service for an area. School districts may be the best-known single-purpose governments, but special districts supply dozens of different services (e.g., flood control, soil conservation, fire protection, and libraries). As of 2002, there were over 35,000 special districts in the United States. The geographic footprint of a special district may cut across city or county lines. A high density of special districts in an area can reduce the number of functions that a municipality might be engaged in.

The Rise of the Urban United States

Despite the huge number of cities, counties, and special districts that exist today, the United States began as a largely rural nation with little need for the public services that local governments provide today. In 1787, just 5 percent of its population resided in cities. As Figure 9.1 illustrates, few people lived in large, densely populated cities. As late as 1890, barely one-third of Americans lived in places

---

[1] In Virginia, municipalities are jurisdictions independent from the counties they are located in. In Connecticut and Rhode Island, county governments play no functional role.

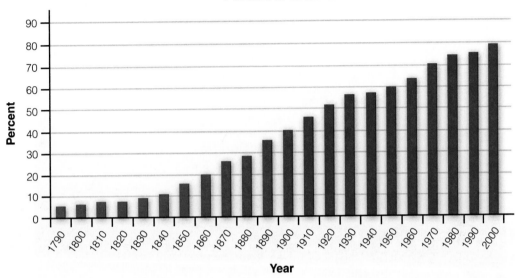

Figure 9.1

Percentage of Americans Living in Urban Places, 1790–2000

Source: U.S. Census Bureau data. Urban areas are defined as places with a population of over 2,500.

with a population greater than 2,500. Cities continued to be viewed by many as a threat to democracy, whereas agrarian communities were seen as the soul of pure democracy.

In 1850, there was only one U.S. city with a population over 500,000 (New York) and just five others with more than 100,000 residents: Baltimore, Boston, Philadelphia, New Orleans, and Cincinnati. By 1870—just 20 years later—there were 14 U.S. cities with over 100,000 people. By 1890, America had 28 cities with a population of 100,000 or more, with New York, Chicago, and Philadelphia each having over 1,000,000 people. By 1910, cities like Louisville, Minneapolis, Denver, Seattle, and Portland were all much larger than the second-largest American city was in 1850.[2]

Immigration

Although the United States largely remained a nation of small communities throughout the 19th century, its large cities were magnets for European immigrants. Immigrants were pushed from Europe by social transformations that moved peasants from their traditional lands by poverty and, for the Irish, by famine. They were pulled to the United States by the prospect of jobs associated with booming industrialization, by opportunities to farm, and by the prospect of political and religious liberties.

Millions of Irish and Germans emigrated from their native counties to the United States from 1850 to 1910. In 1890, there were nearly 2 million foreign-born Irish living in the United States, primarily in cities (this was equal to more than half the population of Ireland at the time). The social transformation produced by this immigration was profound. Prior to the 1840s, there was a limited measure of ethnic and religious heterogeneity in the United States. There were few Catholics or Jews and a limited range of

[2] Data from Campbell Gibson, "Population of the 100 Largest Cities and Other Urban Places in the United States: 1790–1990," U.S. Census Bureau. Population Division Working Paper no. 27, June (Washington, D.C.: U.S. Census Bureau, Population Division, 1998).

Hulton-Deutsch Collection/CORBIS

Dens of death. New York City's crowded shanties and tenements, circa 1880s; photo by Jacob Riis. Riis's muckraking photography turned public attention toward the problems of crowded, unsanitary housing and urban poverty and helped drive support for reforming city governments.

Protestant denominations, for example. In 1850, Catholics made up just 5 percent of the U.S. population. With mass emigration from Ireland, Germany, central Europe, Scandinavia, Russia, Italy, and elsewhere, ethnic and religious diversity increased dramatically. Millions of Catholics emigrated from Germany and Ireland from 1850 to 1910. Millions more emigrated from Italy, Poland, Austria, Czechoslovakia, Croatia, Hungary, Ukraine, and other nations in the first decade of the 20th century. By 1906, 17 percent of Americans were Catholic, making Catholics the single-largest religious group in the nation.[3] Millions of Jews also immigrated to American cities between 1880 and 1915— primarily from Eastern Europe (Poland, Latvia, Lithuania, the Ukraine, and Russia).

In 1910, there were 13.5 million people who were foreign-born living in the United States, mostly in cities.

The Need for Municipal Government

Multiple governments providing many public services are a relatively modern phenomenon. Governments played little role in providing social services or public services for much of the 19th century. No Social Security, no Food Stamps, no Medicaid, and no Environmental Protection Agency of the federal government existed at that time. The rapid **urbanization** of the United States largely outpaced the bare minimal levels of basic public services, such as sewerage, street lighting, and garbage

[3] Julie Byrne, *Roman Catholics and Immigration in Nineteenth Century America* (Research Triangle Park, N.C.: National Humanities Center, 2000).

Figure 9.2

Percentage Foreign-Born: Large Cities and Rural Areas, 1870–2000

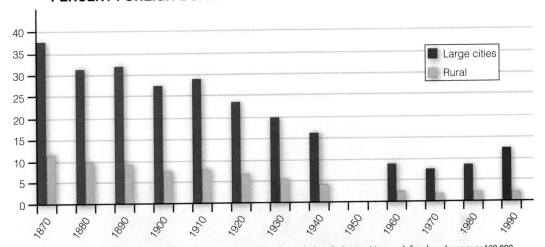

PERCENT FOREIGN-BORN: LARGE CITIES AND RURAL AREAS: 1870–2000

Note: Bars represent the percentage of residents who are foreign-born, for each decade. Large cities are defined as places over 100,000.

Source: Campbell Gibson and Emily Lennon, "Historical Census on the Foreign Born Population of the United States: 1850–1990," U.S. Census Bureau, Population Division Working Paper no. 29, February (Washington, D.C.: U.S. Census Bureau. Population Division, 1999).

collection as well as any publicly provided social welfare. As cities grew, the need for basic services also grew. Urbanization meant increased fire risks. Cities required sanitation (for humans and horses alike). The growth of manufacturing industries meant more people were crowded into polluted cities.

The provision of public services in this context was minimal and haphazard. Public and private police forces patrolled cities simultaneously. Fire departments were largely organized by volunteer groups, which often operated as private entities. Although Boston employed paid firefighters as early as 1678, few other U.S. cities followed Boston's lead over the next 200 years. New York City did not have paid firefighters until 1865.[4] Nineteenth-century local governments had developed with only minimal powers to regulate building standards, business practices, or public health. As there had never been

much need for a public sector prior to the 1870s or for public employees, there were few regulations regarding who city officials could hire or fire. In short, the need for effective local government outpaced the urbanization and development of U.S. cities.

Origins of Urban Party Machines

Urbanization created new demands for public services and also created new forms of politics. As Figure 9.2 illustrates, immigration built U.S. cities. Many of the new immigrants settled in cities and raised their families in cities. By 1870, 44 percent New York City's residents were born outside the United States; 48 percent in Chicago were foreign-born, as were 49 percent in San Francisco. The population of the 25 largest U.S. cities outside the South was at least one-quarter to one-third foreign-born in 1890.[5]

[4] Terry Golway, "Firefighters," *American Heritage Magazine* 56, no. 6 (November–December 2005).

[5] Campbell Gibson and Emily Lennon, "Historical Census on the Foreign Born Population of the United States: 1850–1990," U.S. Census Bureau, Population Division Working Paper no. 29, February (Washington, D.C.: U.S. Census Bureau, Population Division, 1999).

Growth of the Voting Population At the same time, the use of elections was expanding, although to a much more limited extent than what exists today. The number of voters in the United States increased dramatically after 1824. The size of the voting population continued to grow after the 1820s. Massachusetts and New York eliminated property requirements for voting in 1821, followed by Tennessee (in 1834), New Jersey (in 1844), and Virginia (in 1850). Connecticut removed the taxpaying requirement in 1845; Ohio did so in 1851.[6]

Thomas Nast cartoon of Boss Tweed and Tammany Hall politicians. The upper panel refers to a *New York Times* story uncovering $5.6 million paid to a Tammany-controlled firm (Ingersoll's Co.) that supposedly supplied carpets for the County Court House. The *Times* reported on numerous contracts that showed the city paid tens of millions of dollars to contractors selected by Tammany and to a firm owned by Tweed himself, with no evidence of any benefits for the city.

Source: *Harper's Weekly*, 19 August 1871, p. 764.

[6] Alexander Keysar, *The Right to Vote: The Contested History of Democracy in the United States* (New York: Basic Books, 2000), table A.2.

In the spirit of **Jacksonian democracy**, states were also expanding the range of offices subject to popular election. The first mayor of Chicago was elected in 1837 (he served one year). The first popular election of a Philadelphia mayor was held in 1840. With mass participation in federal, state, and local elections just emerging in the 1830s, there was a need for new methods to recruit candidates, communicate with voters, and earn voter loyalties. Out of this context, modern political parties were born—as institutions designed to meet the challenges of mobilizing regular people who had never before been allowed to play a role in elections.[7]

Early Political Parties A political group (in some cities, they were known as "clubs" before being called parties) seeking to control a city would need to organize the support of enough people in enough neighborhoods so they could win elections. Volunteer firehouses provided one base for organizing, as they were distributed in various neighborhoods across a city. Firehouses served as a sort of social center, as did local pubs. By the 1850s, volunteer fire departments were becoming more Irish and more Catholic.[8] Political clubs found the firehouse and pubs places to organize and recruit loyalists, and volunteer fire departments became political forces in large cities like New York, Baltimore, and St. Louis. Firehouses weren't simply a means that parties used to organize support but also provided "an arena in which those who wished to exercise political leadership could win men's loyalty by demonstrating their ability."[9] Machine politicians in several large cities came up through the ranks of firefighters, as did one of the nation's greatest political operatives, William "Boss" Tweed of New York City's **Tammany Hall** machine.[10]

Urban Party Machines

Urban political party organizations—known as machines—were born out of this 19th-century environment of industrialization, urbanization, rapid immigration, expanding democracy, and the absence of basic public services. These local party organizations gained and maintained control of cities by organizing neighborhoods to deliver votes for machine candidates on Election Day. One observer described machines as "quasi-feudal" because they were very hierarchical. At the top of the hierarchy sat the boss or the core group of leaders. The local boss and local party leaders might control the machine from the position of an elected office, but not every boss held local office. Below the boss and other organization leaders, a city was divided into districts (or **wards**), and each of these was divided into smaller units. Local neighborhoods, divided into **precincts**, were at the bottom of the hierarchy. Voters in neighborhoods remained loyal to the machine leaders when leaders provided them with favors or services. In immigrant neighborhoods where few residents had any political power or English language skills, relatively small favors might be mutually beneficial to party leaders and machine supporters alike. Irish Catholics were the backbone of machines in several, but not all, cities.

Favors that a machine organization provided to supporters could include help with finding a place to live, assistance with food (a turkey on Christmas), or help with home-heating fuel in winter. Services could include help with the police, help with finding a job, or help with making contacts in business.[11] Machines may have also helped immigrants obtain citizenship (so they could vote). Some machine organizations offered illicit businesses

---

[7] Richard Gunther and Larry Diamond, "Species of Political Parties," *Party Politics* 9 (2003): 167–99.

[8] Golway, "Firefighters."

[9] Amy Bridges, *A City in the Republic: Antebellum New York and the Origins of Machine Politics* (Ithaca, N.Y.: Cornell University Press, 1984).

[10] Amy Greenberg, *Cause for Alarm: The Volunteer Fire Department in the Nineteenth Century City* (Cambridge, Mass.: Harvard University Press, 1998).

[11] Steven P. Erie, *Rainbow's End: Irish Americans and the Dilemmas of Urban Machine Politics, 1840–1985* (Berkeley: University of California Press, 1988).

protection from law enforcement, thus earning the support of tavern owners, prostitution businesses, and gambling operations. A few city machines did have reformist intentions, establishing municipally owned utilities to improve water, sewer, and street-lighting services.

These 19th-century urban party machines operated as clientele parties; that is, the party machine (acting as a sort of patron) served working-class and immigrant voters (the clients) by providing personal favors in exchange for votes. Machine politics was most notable in large cities, but this style of local politics also operated in small towns and rural areas.[12] Support for a party machine organization was not based on ideology but on the leaders' personalities, ethnic solidarity, and/or neighborhood loyalties.[13] This being the case, a machine could operate with a Democratic Party label or a Republican Party label. Most were Democrat, yet the Philadelphia machine of 1867–1933 was Republican.[14]

Patronage

Clientele politics involves providing something of value in exchange for political support. Prior to the late 19th century, appointment to most government jobs was controlled by elected officials. Winning politicians had the power to fire government employees and replace them with their supporters. For urban party machines, public sector jobs were one of the more lucrative perks that they could use to reward the people who helped keep the machine running. This **patronage** system occasionally had a high cost for politicians. Carter Harrison Sr., the mayor of Chicago, was assassinated in his home in 1893 by a "disappointed office seeker."

Precinct-Based Politics

A political machine's ability to organize a city politically depended on its ability to maintain support at the neighborhood level. Many precincts had workers loyal to the party— perhaps led by a **precinct captain**—who provided information about residents' needs and their voting habits to people higher up the party machine hierarchy. Voters might support the machine in response to the patronage and favors it provided or as the result of friendship with party loyalists in neighborhoods or some common social bond with a precinct worker. Party organizations maintained contacts in neighborhoods by sponsoring picnics, sporting events, dances, and other social events "to keep people in the orbit of the machine."[15] Service as a precinct captain was a potential means for career advancement within the party organization.

District Elections, Large Councils

Given the concentration of different ethnic groups in distinct parts of a city and given neighborhood-based political loyalties that flowed from this, it was easier for a machine to organize a city on ethnic loyalties when representation on the city council was based on small geographic units. Local councils where each member was elected from a small geographic district helped to transfer ethnic-based neighborhood loyalties into political representation. City councils (or boards of aldermen) with a large number of districts allowed distinct, homogeneous neighborhoods to form the basis of an individual district. A smaller district would be more likely to be ethnically homogeneous and thus be easier to organize on the basis of common social bonds or patronage. This helped machine organizations

---

[12] Erie, *Rainbow's End.*

[13] Gunther and Diamond, "Species of Political Parties."

[14] Peter McCaffery, *When Bosses Ruled Philadelphia* (University Park: Pennsylvania State University Press, 1993).

[15] Clarence Stone, "Urban Political Machines: Taking Stock," *PS: Political Science and Politics* 29, no. 3 (1996): 446–50.

reach out to various ethnic groups concentrated in different parts of a city. As an example, in 1900, the Chicago City Council had 70 members, with two aldermen from each district, elected to two-year terms in partisan elections.

Partisan Elections, Party Ballot Machine control of a city required electing as many machine loyalists as possible to local councils and local offices. The "Democrat" or "Republican" name attached to a party organization provided a banner, or easily communicated brand label, under which the organization's local candidates sought office. Some parties also controlled a newspaper in a city to promote the organization and its candidates.[16] Early American elections were largely unregulated affairs, and secrecy was not always expected in voting. In some places, party organizations printed their own ballots to distribute to voters. Parties gave voters preprinted ballots listing the party's local candidates, with ballots listing only candidates preferred by the local party organization leaders. This helped the machine control who sought office, and it allowed party poll watchers to observe who voters were supporting. Party ballots printed in party newspapers could be clipped by voters to be cast when they arrived at the polling place. Party-printed ballots meant that there was little secrecy in voting, but it also provided a means of voting for new immigrants and others who were not literate enough to read a ballot and fill in without assistance the names of candidates they preferred. With much of the electorate having limited literacy, party-printed ballots made it possible for parties to communicate easily with voters and made it easier for many voters to participate in elections.

Timing of Elections Local party machines could have substantial influence on state and federal races if local elections were held at the same time as state or national contests. Local party organizations had incentives to bring their supporters to the polls in order to maintain control of the city. When local elections were contested in conjunction with state and federal races using **straight-ticket ballots**, machine organizations could deliver votes for the party's candidates seeking state and congressional offices, and they could have influence over presidential elections. High-profile state and national races, combined on the ballot with local contests, made it easier for machine organizations to mobilize a larger number of voters. Voter turnout in local elections is higher when local elections are held at the same time as national elections.[17] A local party machine's influence in the state or national party organizations as well as in state capitols and Washington, D.C., was enhanced by the local organization's ability to demonstrate that it could deliver votes for the party's candidates for higher office.

Corruption

Machines maintained voter support with patronage and favors and by building social bonds with their supporters. But some machine organizations also paid their supporters to show up to vote, and in parts of a city where support was weak, they could boost their vote share through electoral fraud—hence, the classic machine-inspired slogan "Vote early, and vote often." Stuffing ballot boxes and bribing people for votes were not uncommon, and they were not something limited to big cities.[18] Support at elections—whether earned or bought—was not always enough for a party machine to maintain control of a city. Kickback schemes required people who were given public jobs or awarded lucrative city contracts to pay back part of their salary or revenues to the machine organization. Bribes were offered

---

[16] Robert McChesney, *Corporate Media as a Threat to Democracy* (New York: Seven Stories Press, 1997).

[17] Zoltan Hajnal and Paul Lewis, "Municipal Institutions and Voter Turnout in Local Elections," *Urban Affairs Quarterly* 5 (2003): 645–68.

[18] Loomis Mayfield, "Voting Fraud in Early Twentieth-Century Pittsburgh," *Journal of Interdisciplinary History* 24, no. 1 (1993): 59–84; and Genevieve Gist, "Progressive Reform in a Rural Community: The Adams County Vote Fraud Case," *Mississippi Valley Historical Review* 48 (1961): 60–78.

to judges and other officials who needed to be brought on board. Bribes could also be used to control who won contracts to build city facilities. Alliances with business leaders were important to machine politicians, as business provided resources (money and jobs) for the machine, but machine politicians and machine loyalists also had personal financial interests in private real estate and development businesses and benefited from inside information about where their cities would need to buy land or build bridges and roads.

Who Benefited from the Machines?

It is clear that machines often aided illicit businesses and that many machine leaders enriched themselves personally through their corrupt political activities. Machines also operated cities inefficiently, as they needed an inflated number of public employees to boost their opportunities for handing out jobs as patronage. This inflated public sector came at a cost that was borne by taxpayers. When factors like these are considered, it might seem hard to conclude that urban machines provided benefits to anyone but the machine leaders. Machine bosses, like Tammany Hall's George Washington Plunkitt and Richard Croker, made it no secret that they got rich off of politics. As Plunkitt famously stated, "I seen my opportunities, and I took 'em."[19] Likewise, Croker claimed, "I work for my own pocket all of the time."[20]

Despite overt corruption and inefficiencies, however, some argue that machines acted as a humanizing force, making life better for masses of immigrants arriving to the United States.[21] For one thing, the level of corruption, although shocking by contemporary American standards, was not debilitating to local economies. As Chicago Mayor Carter Harrison Sr. noted in the late 1890s, the two major desires of machine politicians and regular Chicagoans were to make money and spend it. Machine corruption and graft—skimming from local contracts and insider trading in real estate markets—probably encouraged machine politicians to boost local economic development and pursue pro-growth strategies. More growth meant more graft, but it also meant more jobs. And because some key businesses could leave a city and move elsewhere if graft and corruption got too bad, there were limits to what machines could extract from businesses.[22]

Whatever their corrupt practices were, machines needed to win elections, and the greater the level of legitimate voter support they had, the better were their chances of winning. This meant they had to deliver something to voters—although contemporary studies suggest that machines had few decent-paying jobs to offer supporters.[23] Machines needed far more votes than they had city jobs to be filled. Machines were able to transfer real political power in many cities away from a minority of relatively affluent Protestants to the new Catholic majority. Others credit machines with contributing to the peaceful development of the United States by promoting personality-based and patronage-based politics rather than divisive ideological or radical class-based political divisions.[24] Although urban party machines championed

[19] William L. Riordan, *Plunkitt of Tammany Hall: A Series of Very Plain Talks on Very Practical Politics* (1905; reprint, New York: Bedford St. Martin's, 1993).

[20] Lincoln Steffens, *The Autobiography of Lincoln Steffens* (New York: Harcourt, 1968).

[21] Clarence Stone, "Urban Machines: Taking Stock," *PS: Political Science and Politics* 29 (1996): 450; and Steffens, *The Autobiography of Lincoln Steffens.*

[22] Rebecca Menes, "Corruption in Cities: Graft and Politics in American Cities at the Turn of the Twentieth Century," NBER Working Paper no. 9990, September (New York: National Bureau of Economic Research, 2003).

[23] Erie, *Rainbow's End.*

[24] Edward Banfield and James Q. Wilson, *City Politics* (New York: Vintage, 1963).

"the little guy," workers, and the immigrant, they rarely flirted with socialist ideology. They also frequently opposed union efforts to organize workers.[25]

But these latter points open urban party machines to further criticism. By emphasizing personal loyalties and patronage, and by opposing the emergence of organized labor (unions) in the late 19th century and early 20th century, machines may have hampered the upward mobility of the United States' less affluent urban immigrants.[26]

Demise of the Machines

Regardless of whether urban machines served their supporters well, the era of machines came to an end in the 20th century. As immigrants became more educated and affluent over time, the political base of urban machines weakened. Changes in federal laws produced a dramatic decline in immigration after 1910, further eroding the machine's base of support. Organized labor also became more influential in the early decades of the 20th century and competed directly with machines for the loyalty (and votes) of working-class people. After the Great Depression of the 1930s, the federal government became more active in providing for the basic needs of the poor. All these forces worked to dilute the influence of urban party machines.

Some big-city machines—but not all— can also be faulted for failing to respond adequately to the problems facing cities at the end of the 19th century. Many did a poor job of providing public services. Basic functions, such as streetcar service, street lighting, and sewers, were contracted to underfinanced private operators. Public health was also severely neglected. Basic services, such as municipal garbage removal, were sporadic.

The Urban Reform Movement

One reason for the demise of the urban party machines, then, is functional. Machines functioned poorly on several levels. Some functions that they had performed well, such as maintaining personal, ethnic-based loyalties and providing token material rewards for their supporters, also became less important as society gradually changed. The shortcomings of urban life grew more apparent. Sporadic epidemics made thousands ill, and by the late 1880s, people had knowledge that germs were spread more rapidly in crowded places. **Muckraking journalists** rallied the public against the dangers of crowded, inadequate urban housing and the exploitation of child labor in urban factories and publicized the dangers of slaughterhouses and mass-produced food sources.

But a major reason for the demise of the machines is that rules defining how cities were governed were changed to make it far more difficult for popular political organizations to control city affairs. Industrialization and urbanization happened quite rapidly in the later part of the 19th century. By the early 1900s, several social movements were forming in both the United States and Canada to combat the ill effects of industrialization and urban life. In this environment, reformers of various stripes battled party machines to restructure the organization of city governments.

Many reform proposals were attempts to systematically change the rules about how cities could function—to replace the 19th-century personal-based style of clientelism with a more impersonal bureaucracy. Urban reformers believed that raw politics as a method for governing cities could be improved with efficient public administration.[27]

[25] Dennis R. Judd and Todd Swanstrom, *City Politics: Private Power and Public Policy* (New York: Pearson Longman, 2004).

[26] Martin Sheffter, "The Emergence of the Political Machine," in *Theoretical Perspectives on Urban Politics*, ed. W. Hawley and M. Lipsky (Englewood Cliffs, N.J.: Prentice Hall, 1976); Bridges, *A City in the Republic*; and McCaffery, *When Bosses Ruled Philadelphia*.

[27] Kenneth Feingold, *Experts and Politicians: Reform Challenges to Machine Politics in New York, Cleveland and Chicago* (Princeton, N.J.: Princeton University Press, 1995).

Efficient administration included depersonalizing politics and replacing party loyalists in city departments with people who served because they had merit and specific job qualifications. Reformers wanted to insulate the functions of local governments from the influence of politicians who ruled because they could win elections.

Who Were the Reformers?

The various groups that worked to redefine local political institutions in the first two decades of the 20th century are loosely known as the **Progressive era** reformers. They should not be confused with the reform movement of the **Populist era**, discussed in previous chapters, although the goals of these groups often overlapped. The Populist movement of the late 19th century was largely centered in rural and agricultural areas and in western mining regions. Populists believed that government and business were dominated by elites conspiring against common people—particularly against farmers. Populists emphasized reforms that broke up concentrations of political and economic power and favored new rules that nationalized ownership of key industries and empowered common citizens (see Chapter 4). Populists are characterized as having disdain for experts and elites[28] and believed in strengthening the power of popular majorities (voters).

Progressives, in contrast, recognized that the concentration of political and economic power could be dangerous. Their targets of concentrated economic and political power included monopolistic trusts that controlled major industries, including beef, sugar, and oil. Party machines were targeted as concentrations of political power that dominated politics in many cities. Progressives also had a different vision for reform than Populists. Many Progressives believed that society could be improved through scientific study and better administrative practices and by limiting the power that wealthy corporations had in politics. As Wisconsin governor Robert M. Lafollette Sr. said, "My goal is not to smash corporations, but to drive them out of politics."

Progressives, as their name suggests, embraced what they viewed as the positive aspects of progress associated with the modern era: science, technology, and efficiency. Progressives believed that efficiency in business and government could be improved if the proper information was available and the best people were charged with implementing policy.[29] For example, Progressives believed that federal government agencies were needed to regulate private business practices and that local public health agencies were needed to collect data, such as vital statistics, that could be used to improve living conditions. Many Progressives embraced the idea that scientific management practices and practical expertise could replace politics in the administration of local government. They were not antidemocratic, but some Progressives found that popular partisan control of local governments could be a barrier to efficient administration.

Many Different Reform Groups

Many different reform groups emerged in the early 20th century, with very distinct agendas. Although they are now lumped together under the Progressive label, there was no single Progressive organization or overarching Progressive movement. There were Progressive, reformist wings in both the Republican and Democratic parties. While serving as the Democratic governor of New Jersey from 1911 to 1913, Woodrow Wilson fought local Democratic Party machines in his state by promoting direct primaries

---

[28] Richard Hofstadter, *The Age of Reform* (New York: Knopf, 1955).

[29] Samuel Haber, *Efficiency and Uplift: Scientific Management in the Progressive Era: 1885–1930* (Chicago: University of Chicago Press, 1964).

(see Chapter 3 and Chapter 5) and campaign finance regulations. At the same time, Teddy Roosevelt's wing of the Republican Party was promoting antitrust reforms to rein in the power of huge corporations. The Progressive era also corresponded with the rise of the modern conservation movement, which was dedicated to preserving natural resources and establishing national forests and parks. During this time, numerous other reform groups advocated for expanding the scope of public education, regulating investments in stocks and bonds, passing food safety laws, eliminating the exploitation of child labor, and improving working conditions. Religious groups and others also promoted the prohibition of alcohol as a remedy to many of the era's social ills.

Women as a Force for Social Reform

Women's groups were active in promoting Progressive reforms early in the 20th century. Lacking the power to vote, many politically engaged women sought to improve society and change policy by organizing groups that promoted reform goals.[30] In Chicago, the City Club and Women's City Club of Chicago conducted investigations of urban ills and published recommendations for reforms.[31] The Boston Women's Municipal League performed a similar role in that city. Influential women's clubs organized in most major cities. One study estimates that over 1,000,000 women participated directly in the reform movement under the banner of "municipal housekeeping"—championing reforms that improved sanitation, education, and public health.[32] Women's clubs united under the General Federation of Women's Clubs. Ellen Swallow Richards, an MIT-educated scientist, demonstrated the need for food safety laws. Jane Addams worked with the City of Chicago to improve garbage cleanup, sewers, drinking water, medical care, and street lighting.[33] In the early years of the 20th century, women also organized the backbone of the women's suffrage movement, and women played a major role in promoting reforms to legalize birth control.

Changing the Design of Local Institutions

The urban reform movement was born in this environment as a reaction against party machine dominance of local government. Groups advocating for new political arrangements formed in many American cities in the early years of the 20th century, and national organizations, including the U.S. Chamber of Commerce and the National Municipal League, provided urban reformers with ideas for reshaping local politics and the administration of local government. Many of these reforms, detailed below, linked improvements in administration with weakening the power of local party machines and made it more difficult for elected officials to affect how cities work.

How Did Local Institutions Change?

One prominent national advocacy group, the National Municipal League, offered reformers a blueprint for how to rebuild local political institutions so that the influence of mass-based political parties would be weakened and the influence of unelected experts would be increased. The National Municipal League publicized its ideas for reform in a **model city charter**. The first model charter was drafted after several years of conferencing among urban reform groups, including the City Club of New York and the Municipal

---

[30] Daphne Spain, *How Women Saved the City* (Minneapolis: University of Minnesota Press, 2000).

[31] Maureen A. Flanagan, "Gender and Urban Political Reform: The City Club and the Woman's City Club of Chicago in the Progressive Era," *American Historical Review* 95 (1990): 1032–50.

[32] Flanagan, "Gender and Urban Political Reform."

[33] Jane Addams, *Twenty Years at Hull House* (Chicago, 1910).

League of Philadelphia.[34] The model charter was an attempt to bring national attention to how various local experiments with new political arrangements "worked" (or "failed") in various cities. Elements of the model city charter were (and continue to be) updated periodically, and the earliest model charters embodied the Progressive reformers' ideal of how local government should function.

Because state laws define how charters for local governments are to be drawn, reform advocates had to lobby state legislatures to change state rules about local government arrangements. Progressive reformers were also able to define (or redefine) rules shaping local charters by electing sympathetic candidates as state legislators and governors. Some states had Progressive wings in both the Democratic or Republican parties, but Progressives were more often associated with the liberal wing of the Republican Party.

Although all these governors are often classified as Progressives, some emphasized social reforms (e.g., public health and improved public education) and economic reforms (e.g., regulating monopolies) when in office more than changes to political institutions. Reformers committed to changing the nature of local political institutions also lobbied state governments to grant cities **home rule** charters.

A Menu of Reforms

Prior to the Reform era (another name for the Progressive era), mayors in most large cities had few formal powers, with major decisions controlled by large city councils. Machine organizations exercised their influence over a city by controlling council elections. Some of these institutional arrangements were characterized as **weak mayor–council systems.** Voters elected the mayor and council separately, but weak mayors often had little formal influence over city budgets, city departments, or what the city council did. By the middle of the 1800s, most U.S. cities had a city council and mayor who shared legislative and administrative powers.[35]

This does not mean that American mayors had little influence over city affairs prior to the adoption of the reforms discussed below. Table 9.1 lists the results of a survey of historians that ranks the best and worst mayors in the United States from 1820 to 1990. The rankings here are probably biased toward overrepresenting better-known mayors, particularly from large eastern cities. There may have been several lesser-known mayors (terrible or excellent) from the South or West that these historians ignored. Nonetheless, most of the worst-rated mayors were machine operatives whose political influence stemmed not as much from the formal powers granted them in a city's charter but from their links with the party machine and their skill with clientele politics. At the top of the list of "worst" mayors is "Kaiser Bill" Thompson, who served three terms as mayor of Chicago. Thompson, a pro-German during World War I, fought against anticorruption reforms and allowed Chicago's gangsters to run unchecked (organized crime supplied the city with beer, wine, and liquor during the Prohibition era). After being defeated and investigated for fraud, he beat a reformist Prohibitionist incumbent to win a third term by promising to reopen the city's taverns.[36] Thompson died a rich man.

Other notorious pre–Reform era mayors include Frank Hague of Jersey City, whose influence in the national Democratic Party

[34] National Municipal League, *Municipal Program* (New York: Macmillan, 1900).

[35] Charles Adrian, "Forms of City Government in American History," in *Municipal Yearbook* (Washington, D.C.: International City Manager's Association, 1988).

[36] Melvin G. Holli, *The American Mayor: The Best and Worst Big City Leaders* (University Park: Pennsylvania State University Press, 1999).

Table 9.1

Scholars' Rankings of the Best and Worst Mayors in American History

Worst	
1. William H. "Kaiser Bill" Thompson	Chicago, 1915–1923, 1927–1931
2. Frank Hague	Jersey City, 1917–1947
3. James "Jimmy" Walker	New York, 1926–1932
4. James Michael Curly	Boston, 1914–1917, 1922–1925, 1930–1933, 1946–1949
5. Frank Rizzo	Philadelphia, 1972–1980
6. A. Oakley Hall	New York, 1868–1972
7. Dennis Kucinich	Cleveland, 1977–1979
8. Fernando Wood	New York, 1855–1958, 1860–1962
9. Sam Yorty	Los Angeles, 1961–1973
10. Jane Byrne	Chicago, 1979–1983
Best	
1. Fiorello La Guardia	New York, 1934–1945
2. Tom L. Johnson	Cleveland, 1901–1909
3. David Lawrence	Pittsburgh, 1946–1959
4. Hazen Pingree	Detroit, 1890–1897
5. Samuel "Golden Rule" Jones	Toledo, 1897–1904
6. Richard J. Daley	Chicago, 1955–1976
7. Frank Murphy	Detroit, 1930–1933
8. Daniel W. Hoan	Milwaukee, 1916–1940
9. Tom Bradley	Los Angeles, 1973–1993
10. Josiah "Great Mayor" Quincy	Boston, 1823–1828

Source: Melvin G. Holli, *The American Mayor: The Best and the Worst Big City Leaders* (University Park: Pennsylvania State University Press, 1999); from surveys of 120 experts about mayors of the largest U.S. cities between 1820 and 1990.

helped Franklin D. Roosevelt win the Democratic Party's nomination for president in 1932. Hague started as a precinct captain, earned a job as a city janitor, and ten years later was mayor. The Hague machine's skill at stuffing ballot boxes and other modes of voter fraud allowed Hague to dominate politics in his state for years. Hague also became a millionaire, despite a salary of $8,000 per year.[37] Conversely, the best-rated mayors are those who worked to reform city institutions.

It is important to consider that in the early decades of the 20th century, there were many ideas for changing how local political institutions operated, and these ideas have had a tremendous effect on defining how local governments work today.

Mayor–Council Government Progressives had conflicting views about how powerful a city's mayor should be and what the relationship between the mayor and council

[37] John Fund, "How to Steal an Election," *City Journal*, 2004, http://www.city-journal.org/printable.php?id=1701.

should be. Some early reformers believed that strong mayors were needed so that a reformist leader could take firm control of government and check the actions of the city council.[38] And by concentrating the control of city administration in one institution (the mayor's office) and legislative and policy-making power in another institution (the city council), reformers hoped that the separation of powers would produce better governance. A mayor with strong powers who was directly elected by the voters could also be held accountable at the ballot box. This idea of a strong, accountable mayor also reflected a business model of government. In a business corporation, for example, shareholders and a board of directors give a chief executive strong authority over the day-to-day operations of a business, and shareholders or the board can remove an executive if they are dissatisfied with the performance of the corporation. At the end of the 1890s, a strong mayor was seen as a cure to municipal corruption.[39]

The National Municipal League's first Model City Charter (of 1900) recommended that mayors be given strong executive powers. Under a **strong mayor–council system**, mayors are directly elected by the voters at the same time that the city council is. Depending on how many powers a city grants its mayor, a strong mayor may interact with a city council in a manner similar to how a governor interacts with a state legislature. A strong mayor can be given executive powers that include hiring and firing heads of city departments (and other staff), drafting budgets, and vetoing acts of the city council. Mayors may have even stronger powers if they are elected to long terms (four years rather than two), if they are not limited in how often they can seek reelection, if they don't have to share budget powers with the council, and if they have control over city schools. Figures 9.3 and 9.4 illustrate two versions of mayor–council government.

The second edition of the Model City Charter, published in 1915, gave up on the

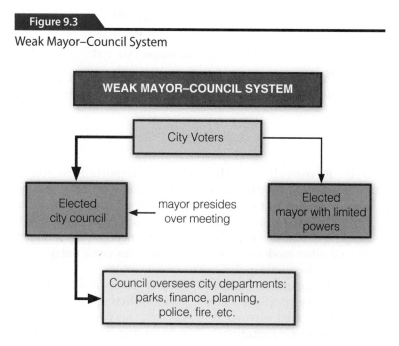

Figure 9.3

Weak Mayor–Council System

[38] Charles Adrian and Charles Press, *Governing Urban America* (New York: McGraw-Hill, 1977), 160.

[39] Victor S. Desantis and Tari Renner, "City Government Structures: An Attempt at Clarification," *State and Local Government Review* 324 (2002): 95–104.

Figure 9.4

Strong Mayor–Council System

STRONG MAYOR–COUNCIL SYSTEM

City Voters

Elected city council

mayor prepares budgets, can veto council, etc.

Elected mayor with strong powers

Mayor has substantial influence over city departments: parks, finance, planning, police, fire, etc.

strong mayor plan. Since then, subsequent Model City Charters in 1928, 1933, 1941, 1964, and 1989 advocated a **council–manager system** with an appointed city executive (see below). About one-third of U.S. cities had mayor–council forms of government as of 2002, but many have mayors who have limits on their formal executive powers. About 40 percent of mayor–council cities have mayors with strong powers to affect budgets and appointments of city staff.[40] Most American cities that have a mayor today, particularly in smaller cities, have mayors with weak executive powers. Just 12 percent of U.S. mayors have the responsibility for developing budgets, and just 17 percent of mayors have the power to appoint department heads. Less than 30 percent of U.S. mayors have the power to veto acts of their city's council. Eighty-five percent of American mayors' jobs are considered part-time positions.[41]

As Table 9.2 illustrates, many of the United States' largest cities have mayor–council systems of government today. These cities vary in how the mayor shares power with the city council.

Council–Manager Government After 1915, the National Municipal League began advocating for a council–manager form of government.[42] The council–manager system is the epitome of the business model of local government. Under this system, a small (five- to seven-member) council hires a professional administrator to implement its policies. The appointed executive is responsible for preparing the budget, directing the day-to-day operations of city departments, overseeing personnel management, and serving as the council's chief policy advisor.[43] City managers supervise city staff, and they recruit, hire,

[40] International City Managers Association, *2001–2002 Survey* (Washington, D.C.: International City Managers Association, 2002).

[41] http://www.ncl.org/publications/index.html.

[42] International City Managers Association, *The Council-Manager Form of Government* (Washington, D.C.: International City Managers Association, 2006).

[43] International City Managers Association, *Form of Government Survey* (Washington, D.C.: International City Managers Association, 2001).

Table 9.2			

Largest U.S. Cities with Mayor–Council Systems of Government

City	Population	Population Rank Grade		Council Elections
New York, NY	8,214,000	1st	B	51 districts
Los Angeles, CA	3,849,000	2nd	C	15 districts
Chicago, IL	2,833,000	3rd	B–	50 districts (wards)
Houston, TX	2,144,000	4th	C+	9 districts, and 4 at large
Philadelphia, PA	1,448,000	6th	B	10 districts, and 7 at large
Detroit, MI	871,000	11th	B–	9 at large
Jacksonville, FL	794,000	12th	B–	14 districts , and 5 at large
Indianapolis, IN	785,000	13th	B+	25 districts, and 4 at large
San Francisco, CA	739,000	14th	C	11 at large
Columbus, OH	733,000	15th	C	7 at large
Memphis, TN	670,000	17th	C+	13 districts
Baltimore, MD	631,000	19th	B–	18 districts
Boston, MA	591,000	22nd	B–	9 districts, and 4 at large
Seattle, WA	582,000	23rd	B	9 at large
Milwaukee, WI	573,000	25th	B	17 districts
Denver, CO	566,000	26th	B–	11 districts, and 2 at large
Louisville, KY	554,000	27th	n/a	26 districts
Nashville, TN	552,000	29th	C+	35 districts, and 5 at large
Albuquerque, NM	504,000	33rd	n/a	9 districts
Atlanta, GA	486,000	34th	C+	12 districts, and 3 at large
Fresno, CA	466,000	36th	n/a	7 districts
Cleveland, OH	444,000	40th	C	21 districts (wards)
Omaha, NE	390,000	42nd	n/a	7 districts
Oakland, CA	397,300	44th	n/a	7 districts, and 1 at large
Tulsa, OK	382,000	45th	n/a	9 districts
Honolulu, HI	377,000	46th	B	9 districts
Minneapolis, MN	372,000	47th	B+	13 districts (wards)

Source: Grade is the overall performance rating for the cities rated by the Government Performance Project, *Governing Magazine*, February, 2000.

and fire city employees within the boundaries of **civil service** rules. Cities with a pure form of the council–manager system either have no mayor or have a very weak mayor who serves on the council. Most U.S. cities have council–manager governments.[44]

Under the council–manager arrangement illustrated in Figure 9.5, the city council may appoint one of its own members to serve as a part-time mayor, but the mayor's role is largely ceremonial (e.g., attending functions and presiding over meetings). About 37 percent

[44] David Morgan, Robert England, and John Pellissero, *Managing Urban America* (Washington, D.C.: CQ Press, 2006).

Figure 9.5

Council–Manager System

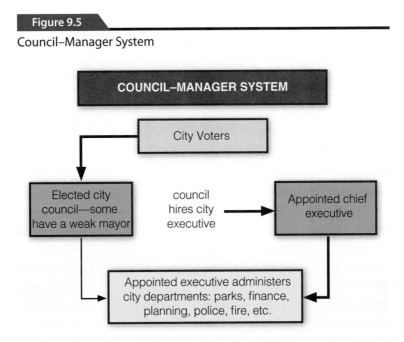

of council–manager cities have no elected mayor. Another 47 percent have a mayor elected by voters, but the mayor has no veto power and little executive power. Mayors in council–manager systems may nonetheless act as spokespersons for their community and, despite their limited executive power, may be the most visible representative of the community.

A council–manager system gives executive powers and administrative control to the council-appointed administrator, known as a city manager (in some places, the position is called the city administrator, chief executive officer, or chief administrative officer). Executive powers, such as the authority to prepare a budget or hire department heads, are granted to the unelected, professional executive who serves at the pleasure of the city council. A majority vote is required to fire a manager. Managers are expected to

stay clear of political disputes and should not engage in local political activity. Most city managers now have professional academic training (a master's degree), and most serve in their position for about five years and have about 17 years of job experience in public administration.[45] Many managers move from city to city during their careers, and city managers' salaries average over $160,000 in cities that have between 120,000 and 220,000 residents.[46]

Adoption of the council–manager reform was rapid and widespread. In 1908, Staunton, Virginia, became the first city to pass an ordinance that defined the authority of an appointed executive. In 1912, Sumter, South Carolina, was the first city to define a council–manager system in its charter, and Dayton, Ohio, became the first large city to adopt the council–manager system in 1913.[47] By 1915, 82 cities had adopted the system, and twice

[45] Worcester Regional Research Board, *Oh Manager, Where Art Thou? Best Practices for Selecting a City Manager*, ICMA salary survey (Worcester, Mass.: Worcester Regional Research Board, 2004).

[46] International City Managers Association, *The Council-Manager Form of Government*.

[47] http://www.ncl.org/npp/charter/process.html.

Table 9.3

Largest U.S. Cities with Council–Manager Systems of Government

City	Population	Population Rank Grade		Council Elections
Phoenix, AZ	1,512,000	5th	A	8 districts
San Antonio, TX	1,296,000	7th	B	10 districts
San Diego, CA	1,256,000	8th	B	8 districts
Dallas, TX	1,232,000	9th	C+	14 districts
San Jose, CA	929,000	10th	B–	10 districts
Austin, TX	709,000	16th	A–	6 at large
Fort Worth, TX	653,000	18th	n/a	9 districts
Charlotte, NC	630,000	20th	n/a	7 districts and 4 at large
El Paso, TX	609,000	21st	n/a	8 districts
Las Vegas, NV	552,147	28th	n/a	6 districts (wards)
Oklahoma City, OK	537,000	30th	n/a	8 districts (wards)
Tucson, AZ	518,000	32nd	n/a	7 at large
Long Beach, CA	472,000	35th	B	9 districts
Sacramento, CA	453,000	37th	n/a	8 districts
Kansas City, MO	447,000	39th	B–	6 districts and 6 at large
Mesa, AZ	447,000	38th	n/a	6 districts
Virginia Beach, VA	435,000	41st	B+	7 districts and 4 at large
Miami, FL*	404,000	43rd	n/a	5 districts
Colorado Springs, CO	369,000	49th	n/a	4 districts and 5 at large
Arlington, TX	362,000	50th	n/a	5 districts and 4 at large

*Miami is a hybrid mayor–commission system with an appointed city manager.
Source: Grade is the overall performance rating for the cities rated by the Government Performance Project, *Governing Magazine*, February, 2000.

as many more had by 1920.[48] The council–manager plan was subsequently adopted throughout the United States and is also used in Australia, Canada, the Netherlands, and New Zealand. Most U.S. cities and towns—particularly smaller places—now operate with some version of a council–manager system, often with the councils elected in nonpartisan elections. Of the 247 American cities with a population over 100,000, 144 (58 percent) use a council–manager system. Some of the largest cities using this system include Cincinnati, Dallas, Kansas City, Phoenix, and Las Vegas. Over 92 million Americans live in cities governed with a council–manager system.[49]

Table 9.3 lists the largest American cities that use the council–manager system of government today.

Council–Manager and Mayor–Council Blends

Cities continue to alter their charters to redefine the separation of powers between councils, mayors, and appointed city executives.

[48] International City Managers Association, *The Council-Manager Form of Government.*

[49] Adrian, "Forms of City Government in American History."

Some mayor–councils adopted rules that borrowed features of the council–manager system in order to increase the autonomy of professional administrators. As an example, San Francisco became the first mayor–council city to hire a professional administrator in 1931, yet it remained a relatively strong mayor–council system.[50]

More recently, some council–manager systems have adopted features from mayor–council systems to increase direct political control by voters.[51] Surveys of cities suggest that over the last 25 years, a large number of cities have been switching from mayor–council systems.[52] In larger cities, however, there may be greater public pressure to have political institutions that make it easier for citizens to hold elected officials directly accountable for how a city operates. This has led some council–manager cities to adopt some of the features of mayor–council systems, such as directly elected mayors as well as mayors with veto powers over councils.

Other council–manager cities have abandoned their council–manager systems. As examples, in 1999, Cincinnati voters approved a charter amendment that added a directly elected mayor to their council–manager system. The Cincinnati mayor has some elements of "strong mayor" powers, can veto the council, and has a role in selecting the city manager, but a city manager remains in charge of administering Cincinnati's city departments and implementing policies approved by the council. Voters in San Diego, a council–manager city, approved a referendum in 2004 to have a four-year experiment with a strong mayor–council system. The experiment began in 2006. Oakland, California, voters approved a similar experiment in 1998 at the request of then-mayor Jerry Brown. Four years later, they voted to make the strong-mayor system permanent. In contrast, Dallas voters rejected referendums in 2005 that would have replaced their council–manager system with a stronger mayor.

Commission System The National Municipal League was initially enthusiastic about a third form of local government: the commission system. The commission system was another attempt to isolate the administration of government from politics. Under this system, voters would select people, rather than a city council, to run city departments. A commission of these elected administrators shared executive and legislative powers.

In some early versions of the commission system, voters elected commissioners who would head specific city departments—for example, a finance commissioner, a public works commissioner, and a public safety (police and fire) commissioner. These commissioners would meet together as a council to pass city budgets (a legislative function), but each individual would be in charge of administering his or her own city department (an executive function). Most of these commission systems soon proved unworkable, as commissioners would promote the interests of their own departments over the general needs of the city, and it was difficult for anyone to coordinate city policy across rival city departments. Portland, Oregon, the 32nd largest U.S. city, is the only remaining large city to use the commission form of government. In Portland, voters elect a nonpartisan mayor and four nonpartisan commissioners, who serve together as a council. The mayor is in charge of assigning the administration of various departments to the four commissioners. Tulsa, Oklahoma, was one of the last remaining commission systems in a large city. Tulsa abandoned its commission form of government in 1989, switching to a mayor–council system.

[50] H. George Frederickson, G. A. Johnson, and C. Wood, "The Changing Structure of American Cities," *Public Administration Review* 64 (May 2004).

[51] Desantis and Renner, "City Government Structures."

[52] Frederickson, Johnson, and Wood, "The Changing Structure of American Cities."

At-Large Elections　In addition to altering the powers of mayors and city councils, many of the Progressive reforms from the early 1900s were aimed at changing how councils represented a city and how local elections were conducted.

Councils elected by individual districts increase opportunities for a political group or candidate to win support based on the social or ethnic bonds of specific neighborhoods. In district elections, only voters in the district vote for their representative. This meant that various ethnic minority groups concentrated in distinct neighborhoods could win council seats. Racial and ethnic minorities are more likely to win seats via districts than under citywide elections (known as at-large elections).[53]

In the early 1900s, Progressive reformers argued that at-large elections would make it more difficult for machines to organize cities from the precinct level up based on ethnic loyalties. In at-large elections, everyone in the city votes for each "position" on the city council. This allows a cohesive majority to sweep every council seat. At-large elections may also produce council representation with more of a citywide focus, whereas representatives elected by districts may have more parochial concerns. Most American cities now have at-large elections, although classic strong-mayor cities, and the 50 largest U.S. cities, are more likely to use district elections (see Tables 9.2 and 9.3). Some cities have representatives on their council elected partly by districts and partly citywide.

Since the 1970s, the U.S. Supreme Court has ruled that at-large elections may illegally dilute the influence of minority groups, and as a result, many larger cities (which have more minorities) have switched from at-large to district elections and other alternative election systems in recent decades (see Chapter 3).

Smaller Councils　Large councils elected by district made it easier to organize a city on ethnic and neighborhood lines, as more seats on the council allowed the city to be divided into many distinctive council districts. Reformers promoted smaller councils elected at large as a means to create governments that had a more "citywide" focus.

Nonpartisan Elections　Party labels allowed the machines an easy way to inform their supporters whom they should vote for. All they needed to do was select the candidates nominated by the machine organization listed as a Democrat (or Republican) candidate (depending on the city). Progressives and the National Municipal League promoted the idea that elections for local offices did not require partisan labels. This made it more difficult for low-literacy voters to support a party organization's candidate. Most U.S. cities now have nonpartisan elections, especially cities with council–manager forms of government.[54]

Australian Ballot　The urban party machine's ability to communicate with its supporters was also eroded with the introduction of the Australian ballot (also known as the secret ballot). Unofficial, party-printed ballots were favored by machines because they listed only one party's candidates (that of the machine organization). The government-printed Australian ballot, in contrast, listed candidates from all parties and required voters to pick and choose among them in a private voting booth without assistance. Australian ballots also allowed voters to "split their ticket" and vote for candidates from different political parties, thus weakening the influence of local precinct captains who had printed and distributed ballots.[55] New York adopted the Australian ballot throughout the state in 1890.[56]

---

[53] Richard Engstrom and Michael D. McDonald, "The Election of Blacks to City Councils," *American Political Science Review* 72 (1981): 344–54.

[54] Ninety percent of council manager cities have nonpartisan elections; Desantis and Renner, "City Government Structures."

[55] Some elite party officials may have allied with reformers in support of the Australian ballot to limit the influence of local precinct captains. John Reynolds and Richard McCormick, "Outlawing 'Treachery': Split Tickets and Ballot Laws in New York and New Jersey, 1880–1910," *Journal of American History* 72 (1986): 835–58.

[56] Gary Cox and Morgan Kousser, "Turnout and Rural Corruption: New York as a Test Case," *American Journal of Political Science* 25 (1981): 646.

In the southern and western regions of the United States, Australian ballots were adopted for different reasons. They made it difficult for third parties, such as the Populists, to win support from illiterate working-class voters who required party-printed, straight-ticket ballots.[57] Nonpartisan elections, contested with Australian ballots, likely made it much more difficult for party organizations to get their supporters to vote for machine candidates.

Off-Year Elections Elections happen in cycles. When local elections are held on separate dates than other elections (presidential, congressional, or gubernatorial), fewer people are likely to take notice. A study of cities in California found that when local elections were held jointly with presidential elections, turnout was 36 percent higher than when elections were held at times when there were not any higher-level offices up for election. Local elections held in sync with a gubernatorial race had a 21 percent higher turnout than a "local-only" election, and similar increases in turnout occur when local races are on the same ballot as a presidential primary.[58]

Voter Registration Prior to the late 1890s, there was little regulation of who could vote. Before then, a voter who arrived at the polls was automatically registered for the next election,[59] and party machines are reported to have created ways to offer immigrants "instant citizenship" to make them eligible for voting.[60] Repeat voting also inflated vote totals. One New York City election produced a reported turnout of 8 percent more than the total city voting population.[61]

By the early 1900s, many states attempted to combat electoral fraud by requiring that voters personally apply for registration before each election. Many early registration statutes applied only to the state's largest cities.[62] In 1908, the New York State Legislature passed regulations on voting, requiring that all voters in cities of over 1,000,000 people produce personal identification when voting and sign in when voting. Signatures could be matched to registration applications, and poll workers could query voters. Districts in New York City suspected of fraud-inflated vote totals in 1906 had substantially less voting in 1908.[63] As voter registration spread to other states, voter turnout in American elections fell sharply.[64]

Civil Service–Merit System Many federal government jobs became protected by civil service rules only after President James A. Garfield was assassinated in 1881 by a party activist who did not receive the patronage appointment he expected. The **Pendleton Act of 1883** established a Civil Service Commission that began to depoliticize (or bureaucratize) the hiring and firing of many federal employees. The modern civil service system requires that public employees should be hired only on the basis of merit (that is, based on job-specific qualifications) and that they should not be fired unless employers can prove just cause for doing so. However, the federal civil service system does not apply to state and local governments. States and cities have adopted their own civil service systems, but differences exist across places in terms

---

[57] J. Morgan Kousser, *The Shaping of Southern Politics* (New Haven, Conn.: Yale University Press, 1974).

[58] Zoltan Hajnal, Paul Lewis, and Hugh Louch, *Municipal Elections in California: Turnout, Timing and Competition* (San Francisco: Public Policy Institute of California, 2002).

[59] Cox and Kousser, "Turnout and Rural Corruption."

[60] John H. Fund, "How to Steal an Election."

[61] See John H. Fund, "How to Steal an Election"; Kevin Phillips and Paul Blackman, *Electoral Reform and Voter Participation* (Washington, D.C.: AEI Press, 1975); Gist, "Progressive Reform in a Rural Community"; and Mayfield, "Voting Fraud in Early Twentieth-Century Pittsburgh," for dates on the introduction of these reforms across states.

[62] Walter Dean Burnham, *Critical Elections and the Mainsprings of American Politics* (New York: Norton, 1970), 81.

[63] John Lapp, "Election: Identification of Voters," *American Political Science Review* 3, no. 1 (1909): 62–63.

[64] Jerrod Rusk, "Communications," *American Political Science Review* 65 (1971): 1152–57; and Jerrod Rusk, "Comment: The American Electoral Universe," *American Political Science Review* 68 (1974): 1028–49.

of how many public jobs are classified as civil service and how many public employees serve at the pleasure of elected officials. Public jobs that do not fall under state or local civil service rules can still be awarded by political appointments.

Federal civil service rules did not apply to state and local government employees. Progressive reformers promoted the adoption of civil service rules on a city-by-city basis after 1900. By 1935, at least 450 U.S. cities had adopted some form of a civil service system. At least 200 more had adopted a civil service–merit system by 1938, including 80 percent of cities over 100,000.[65] This transferred the routine, day-to-day tasks of city governments from political loyalists to bureaucrats. By 1939, federal law required that states adopt some form of civil service for state workers, and in the 1960s, many states began requiring that their cities develop civil service–merit systems to depoliticize the hiring and firing of public employees. By the 1990s, most (but not all) states required their cities to adopt merit-based civil services.[66]

Today, cities vary in terms of how many city positions are classified as political appointments or civil service. In most places, only a few "policy advisor" positions are left for elected officials to appoint. In less reformed cities, a strong mayor may still control numerous appointments to numerous city jobs and boards. A contemporary mayor of Chicago is estimated to control the appointment of 900 to 1,200 city positions.[67]

Corrupt Practices Acts After 1900, several states adopted laws to make it illegal to use bribes in elections and illegal to impersonate someone else when voting. An Oregon Corrupt Practices Act passed by voter initiative in 1908 designated as corrupt "the unlawful expenditure of money for election purposes; which covers the giving of cigars and tobacco; undue influence, including the threat of even a 'spiritual injury,' [im]personation; bribery; betting by a candidate on any pending election, or furnishing money therefore; seeking nomination for a venal motive, and not in good faith." Some states also attempted to regulate elections by limiting campaign expenditures.[68]

Strict Rules for Public Contracts Most states also now require cities to abide by strict rules when spending public money. These rules are designed to limit the ability of public officials to use public funds for their own benefit (or for the benefit of their supporters). These rules govern how public employees can make routine purchases and how contracts for public work shall be put to bid (most require sealed bids that conceal the identity of the firm bidding for the job). Other rules require detailed public records of expenditures and require that city departments be subjected to external audits.

Local Direct Democracy Many reform advocates also promoted the adoption of the direct initiative, referendum, and recall for use in cities and counties. We discussed these institutions in Chapter 4. Initiatives were seen as a way to advance reform goals that might not be approved by a city council. In 1893, California changed its law to allow the initiative in every county. Nebraska granted residents of all its cities the right to use initiatives in 1897. By 1911, state laws were changed to allow initiatives in cities in 11 states, mostly in the West.[69]

---

[65] Pamela Tolbert and Lynne Zucker, "Institutional Sources of Change in the Formal Structure of Organizations: The Diffusion of Civil Service Reform, 1880–1935," *Administrative Science Quarterly* 28 (1983): 22. Also see H. George Frederickson, Bret Logan, and Curtis Wood, "Municipal Reform: A Well Kept Secret," *State and Local Government Review* 35, no. 1 (2003): 7–14.

[66] Frederickson, Logan, and Wood, "Municipal Reform."

[67] Author's personal communication with Ron Michaelson, former executive director of the Illinois State Board of Elections.

[68] Leon E. Aylsworth, "Corrupt Practices," *American Political Science Review* 65 (1909): 50–56.

[69] John Matsusaka, *For the Many or the Few* (Chicago: University of Chicago Press, 2004).

Municipal Reforms as a Continuum and Constant Process

Research suggests that municipal reform efforts had greater success in places where there were fewer working-class and immigrant voters, as these voters were the major supporters of the urban party machines. This means that some of the reforms discussed above were less likely to end up being adopted in older cities and were more likely to be adopted in smaller communities and in places outside the northeastern states.[70] Cities with high percentages of Irish immigrants were particularly resistant to adopting reforms during the Progressive era, as were northern cities that had a machine presence during the Reform era (e.g., Albany, New York; Baltimore; Boston; Chicago; Cleveland; Hartford, Connecticut; Jersey City, New Jersey; New Haven, Connecticut; Indianapolis; Philadelphia; Toledo, Ohio; and Youngstown, Ohio). Western cities as well as cities without established machines, were more likely to adopt several of these reforms during the Progressive era (e.g., Colorado Springs, Colorado; Pasadena, Sacramento, and San Jose, California; and Wichita, Kansas).[71]

The structure of any city's political institutions today can be categorized in terms of a continuum, with cities employing fewer of these reforms at one end of the continuum and many reforms at the other. Cities now show limited variation regarding whether they have corrupt practices rules, civil service systems, or strict rules about public spending. But a large amount of variation still exists across cities in terms of how these rules work and in who ultimately administers the city. These rules mean that cities also vary in terms of how much direct control elected officials ultimately have on how their city is administered.

Events associated with the 1991 Los Angeles Police Department arrest and beating of motorist Rodney King provide a dramatic example of this. The structure of political institutions that existed in Los Angeles when the beating was videotaped placed that city much farther toward the reform end of the continuum than a city like New York. Cities like Los Angeles that adopted their charters during or after the Progressive reforms employ a large number of the reforms listed above. Rigid civil service rules and relatively weak executive authority granted to the mayor meant that Los Angeles Police Chief Daryl Gates could not be fired, despite overwhelming political pressure on the city to do so. A classic reformed city would likely have a council–manager system employing a professional city manager and a weak mayor (or no mayor). The council would be elected at large in nonpartisan elections scheduled when no higher-profile partisan races are being contested. A mayor of New York, in contrast, has much more power to fire city employees.

Larger cities, particularly those in eastern states where political institutions were more firmly established before the Progressive-Reform era began, are more likely to be located on the less reformed end of the continuum; that is, they are more likely to have partisan elections, council elections by district, large city councils, and nearly all city affairs controlled by elected officials. This does not mean that former machine cities, such as Chicago and New York, have been insulated from the reform movement; both of these mayor–council cities now have some reform institutions (such as civil service). As Table 9.2 illustrates, cities with mayor-council systems are still "less reformed" in that they are more likely to have larger councils (even when population is accounted for), with a high proportion of the council representing individual districts. Mayor–council cities listed in Table 9.2 average 15 seats in size, with 83 percent of seats elected from districts. In contrast, council–manager city councils listed in Table 9.3 average nine seats in size, with 68 percent elected by district.

---

[70] James Weinstein, *Corporate Ideal in the Liberal State, 1900–1918* (Boston: Beacon Press, 1968).

[71] James Gimpel, "Reform Resistant and Reform Adopting Machines: The Electoral Foundations of Urban Politics," *Political Research Quarterly* 46, no. 2 (1993): 371–82.

It is important to remember that city institutions are flexible and change frequently in response to crises and public demands for reform. The reform of municipal institutions is a continuing process. After the Rodney King incident, Los Angeles went through a process of reevaluating its charter, and proposals for stronger mayoral power emerged. And as noted above, larger council–manager cities, including some listed in Table 9.3, are also considering changing their institutions to provide for greater political accountability in the form of a strong, directly elected mayor.

Consequences of Municipal Reforms

One thing that occurred after the Reform era was that reformed cities became more efficient and had less political corruption. The cumulative effect of many of these reforms may be efficient, professional, modern city administration that is more capable of managing the "housekeeping" functions of cities. Building codes and public health standards are now much more likely to be implemented and administered by civil servants following standard operating procedures. Business licenses and lucrative contracts to provide services to a city are more likely to be granted on the basis of standard operating procedures rather than political favoritism. Public works projects are now far more likely to be constructed by qualified contractors who offer the lowest bid. Well-regulated public utilities now provide many cities with water, power, street lighting, and sewerage. Police enforce laws with greater objectivity, and politicians cannot easily enrich themselves by directing the police to "selectively" enforce laws. Of course, it is difficult to prove that reforms themselves made cites more efficient

and less corrupt. Since the early 1900s, all U.S. cities, reformed and unreformed alike, are probably governed better today.

Nonpolitical Administration?

The discussion of party machines in this chapter suggests that patronage, corruption, and other inefficiencies may have inflated public spending in unreformed cities. We also might expect public spending to be higher in unreformed cities because classic machines were designed to be responsive to many different groups that might demand city services. Reforms such as at-large, nonpartisan elections and council–manager systems could insulate city officials from such demands. One influential study did find less taxing and spending in reformed cities,[72] but subsequent research found few differences in city finances in reformed versus unreformed cities.[73] Council–manager systems may limit how much direct influence elected officials have on how city money is spent, but this need not mean that these cities spend less or that their appointed managers are insulated from political pressures. Modern city managers face pressure from elected officials for changes in how (and to whom) services are delivered and for changes in how cities are managed.[74]

Efficiency-Accountability Trade-Off?

Some observers suggest that gains in administrative efficiency may come at the price of less direct control of city government by citizens. With so many administrative functions now supervised by appointed city managers and public employees protected against being fired for political reasons, it may be more difficult for a majority of voters to hold their government accountable at the ballot box for

---

[72] Robert Lineberry and Edmond Fowler, "Reformism and Public Policies in American Cities," *American Political Science Review* 61 (1967): 701–16.

[73] David Morgan and John Pelissero, "Urban Policy: Does Political Structure Matter?" *American Political Science Review* 74 (1980): 999–1006.

[74] James H. Svara, "The Politics-Administration Dichotomy Model as Aberration," *Public Administration Review* 58 (1998): 51.

unpopular actions. Rigid bureaucratic rules, civil service protections, and "red tape" may make it difficult for elected officials to put political pressure on city administrators, but these rules ensure that politicians can't use their position to enrich themselves and their friends. A study of nonpartisan city council members also found that unlike machine politicians, nonpartisan elected officials may care little about getting reelected and thus have little regard for public opinion.[75]

Another side exists to the efficiency-accountability trade-off, however. Cross-national studies show that high levels of political corruption increase cynicism about politics and depress respect for the rule of law.[76] Public corruption causes people to retreat from conventional politics. In contrast, reforms that root out political corruption may increase public confidence in democracy.

Barriers to Mass Participation

Several studies find that the combined effects of reforms, such as off-year elections and nonpartisan elections, act to depress voter participation in reform cities.[77] These reforms make local elections less visible to many people and make it more difficult for many people to evaluate candidates. We provided more discussion of this in Chapter 3. For much of the 20th century, turnout for local elections was higher in large machine cities than in large reform cities.[78] Lower turnout may lead to substantial reductions in the representation of Latinos and Asian Americans on city councils and in mayors' offices. African Americans win

office less often when turnout is depressed by off-year elections.

Class and Racial Bias

Scholars have also noted that politics and elections in reform cities such as Houston and San Jose became dominated by powerful nonpartisan "slating groups" that promoted the election of white professionals, business owners, and land developers.[79] Some of these groups were just as dominant in local politics in reform cities as party organizations were in machine cities.[80] Class and racial bias in local politics may be affected by low turnout, itself a product of some reforms. Turnout can be lower than 10 percent in some off-year, nonpartisan local elections. Although there may not be large differences in who votes and who does not vote in high-turnout national elections, very low turnout in local elections may increase the class and racial differences between voters and nonvoters.[81] This may distort democracy because elected officials may be more attentive to the interests of voters than nonvoters. Low turnout rates also result in less representation of Latinos and Asian Americans as mayors and on city councils than they might receive when turnout is higher. At-large elections can further increase the influence of middle-class and upper-class groups in local politics by reducing opportunities for representation of African Americans and ethnic minorities (see Chapter 3). Maintaining lower levels of minority officeholders has consequences for who gets what from city government. Fewer minorities

[75] Kenneth Prewitt, "Political Ambitions, Volunteerism, and Electoral Accountability," *American Political Science Review* (1970): 5–17.

[76] Todd Donovan, David Denemark, and Shaun Bowler, "Trust, Citizenship and Participation: Australia in Comparative Perspective," in *Australian Social Attitudes: The 2nd Report*, ed. David Denemark et al. (Sydney: University of New South Wales Press, 2007).

[77] Albert Karing and B. Oliver Walter, "Decline in Municipal Voter Turnout: A Function of Changing Structure," *American Politics Quarterly* 11 (1983): 491–505; and Hajnal and Lewis, "Municipal Institutions and Voter Turnout in Local Elections."

[78] Jessica Trounstine, "Dominant Regimes and the Demise of Urban Democracy," *Journal of Politics* (2006): 879–93.

[79] Chandler Davidson and Luis Fraga, "Slating Groups as Parties in a 'Nonpartisan' Setting," *Western Political Quarterly* 41 (1988): 373–90; and Bridges, *Morning Glories*.

[80] Trounstine, "Dominant Regimes and the Demise of Urban Democracy."

[81] Albert Karing and B. Oliver Walter, "Decline in Municipal Voter Turnout: A Function of Changing Structure," *American Politics Quarterly* 11 (1983): 491–505.

INSTITUTIONS MATTER

HOME RULE CHARTER

The U.S. Constitution does not mention local governments or specify anything about the powers of local governments (the 10th Amendment does state that powers not delegated to the federal government via the U.S. Constitution are "reserved" to the states). After the American Revolution and after the ratification of the U.S. Constitution, the states assumed the role of defining what local governments would do, just as colonial governments had done before. Today, states and cities outline the powers of governments in **municipal charters**. A local government's charter defines how it will be governed by listing rules about the powers of local officials and the conduct of elections. Each state government may define the powers of local government as it sees fit. Within any one state, state law may allow large cities and counties different charter arrangements than smaller places. State constitutions and laws thus define what the role of towns, cities,

villages, counties, and other local governments will be.

One class of local government charter is the home rule charter. Home rule is when the state government delegates power about setting up local political arrangements to a local government. A home rule charter can give local governments—or a specific local government— substantial discretion to decide how it will arrange its government, how it will conduct elections, what services it will provide, how it will raise and spend revenues, and how it will hire and fire employees. Home rule charters could grant a local government the autonomy to decide how to operate across all these areas. A more limited home rule charter could let local governments make their own decisions in some areas but not others. If powers are not delegated to the local government, then state laws define how things will operate locally. During the Progressive Reform era, some reformers believed it was better to let each city have home rule to best identify how it should restructure its political institutions.

---

in offices mean fewer minority citizens holding city jobs.[82]

At-large elections may also change how council members do their jobs. One study concluded that districted, partisan elections were more likely to produce representation that mirrors the community and that partisan elections made it easier for voters to hold elected officials accountable.[83] At-large elections have also been found to be used, intentionally, to disenfranchise blacks in southern cities and

counties.[84] Council–manager governments are also seen as being slower in their responsiveness to the demands of emerging political groups in a city.[85] Another study found that mayor–council cities were more responsive than council–manager cities in responding to social and racial cleavages in a city[86] and incorporating minorities into city jobs.[87] Minority mayors may have more ability to affect what government does and serve their constituents in mayor–council systems.[88]

---

[82] Peter K. Eisinger, "Black Employment in Municipal Jobs: The Impact of Black Political Power," *American Political Science Review* 76 (1982): 380–90; Lana Stein, "Representative Local Government: Minorities in the Municipal Workforce," *Journal of Politics* 48 (1986): 694–713; and Thomas Dye and James Renick, "Political Power and City Jobs: Determinants of Minority Employment," *Social Science Quarterly* 62 (1981): 457–86.

[83] Susan Welch and Timothy Bledsoe, *Urban Reform and Its Consequences* (Chicago: University of Chicago Press, 1988).

[84] Chandler Davidson and George Korbel, "At-Large Elections and Minority Group Representation: A Re-examination of Historical and Contemporary Evidence," *Journal of Politics* 43 (1981): 982.

[85] Charles H. Levine, Irene S. Rubin, and George Wolohojian, "Resource Scarcity and the Reform Model: The Management of Retrenchment in Cincinnati and Oakland," *Public Administration Review* 41 (1981): 627.

[86] Lineberry and Fowler, "Reformism and Public Policies in American Cities."

[87] Stein, "Representative Local Government."

[88] Albert Karing and Susan Welch, *Black Representation and Urban Policy* (Chicago: University of Chicago Press, 1980).

Summary

In this chapter, we examine how the United States began as a rural nation but experienced rapid urbanization in the mid-1800s. The growth of cities outpaced the growth of effective government, and urban machines emerged in this context with a style of politics that thrived for decades. The machine style emphasized personal bonds over substantive government services. The style is well-represented by a machine politician who was quoted as saying that he wanted to be sure that there has to be someone in every ward of his city that "any bloke can come to—no matter what he's done—and get help. Help, you understand; none of your law and justice, but help."[89] The personal touch of machine politicians might have helped some people find jobs or fix problems with the law,[90] but it could not assure that all people were treated equally before the law. The absence of law, justice, and effective municipal services made machines a target for reforms that redesigned local political institutions. The modern bureaucratic city, for all its cold impersonal character, is designed to have routine standards that public employees must follow if everyone is going to be treated the same.

This chapter also illustrates how changes in political institutions can affect who gets what from local government. The reforms adopted during the Progressive era altered how people become engaged with local politics. Some reforms were clearly designed to limit which sort of people would be mobilized. Many of these reforms survive to this day, but others, such as at-large elections, are often challenged and rejected. Overall, the municipal reforms discussed here may have subtle effects on how a modern city is governed. Elected officials in reformed cities have less direct influence over some administrative matters than their counterparts in cities that adopted few reforms. For all their supposed separation of politics and administration, highly reformed cities may differ from contemporary "unreformed cities" not so much in how efficiently they are governed but in who governs. Institutions that increase participation, increase diversity in representation, and guarantee electoral competition—such as partisan local elections, local elections held during presidential contests, and representation by district—may create a more pluralist form of local politics. By pluralist, we mean a form of politics where more voices are heard and where it is difficult for any single group to consolidate power.

Key Terms

Civil service

Clientele politics

Council–manager system

Dillon's rule

Home rule

Jacksonian democracy

Model city charter

Muckraking journalists

Municipal charters

Party machines

Patronage

Pendleton act of 1883

Populist era

Precinct

Precinct captain

Progressive era

Straight-ticket ballot

Strong mayor–council system

Tammany hall

Urbanization

Ward

Weak mayor–council systems

[89] Lincoln Steffens. 1931. *The Autobiography of Lincoln Steffens*. Harcourt, Brace & World, Inc: New York.

[90] Gustavus Myers, *History of Tammany Hall* (New York, 1917).

10

State and Fiscal Politics

INTRODUCTION

conomic boom and bust can have dramatic effects on state and local budgets. California provides one example. The 1990s boom in technology sector stocks created many instant millionaires in California. It also propelled state tax revenues higher as these new millionaires paid income and capital gains taxes. Increased economic activity associated with the tech boom meant the state collected more revenues while tax rates remained fixed. There was so much new money, that the state spent lavishly. Elementary class sizes were reduced, college tuition was frozen, teachers were paid more, public employee pension plans became more generous, and more children were covered by state health care programs. Some taxes were cut.

The "dot-com" bubble burst when many firms failed to become profitable. Businesses closed, tech jobs were eliminated, businesses cut investments, spending declined, and profits plunged. As a result, there was little stock profit to tax. Tax revenues started to dry up in 2002, and the state soon faced a $38 billion dollar deficit—more than an average state budget. The state faced tough choices: raise college tuition, cut spending, raise taxes, borrow money—or all of the above. California's boom and bust experience is an extreme case, but it is not unique. Although the federal government can ride out economic cycles with deficit spending, states generally need to have a balanced budget. Unlike their federal counterparts, state and local elected officials have less room to hide from tough choices associated with budgeting. This chapter examines how and when states make choices about taxing and spending and what some of the consequences of these choices might be.

State and local governments provide people with a wide array of services—literally from birth to death. States, counties, and cities run hospitals and health care systems, child care programs, elementary education, and colleges and universities. They provide for public safety by enforcing building codes, inspecting restaurants, maintaining drinking water systems, and operating police and firefighting services. Some jurisdictions even run cemeteries.

One of the most difficult tasks of governing is generating the revenue required to fund the wide range of public services that people expect and demand and then balancing limited revenues with those demands for services and programs. Matters are complicated by the fact that people do not agree on what the government's spending priorities should be and by disagreement over which taxes should be used to fund government. Fiscal politics involves policies and decisions relating to raising and spending public money. Fiscal policy—or budgeting—is how state and local elected officials figure out who gets what from government and at whose expense.

People generally do not like to pay taxes, but a fundamental trait of a sovereign government is that it has some ability to coerce citizens to pay their taxes.

Governments face constraints raising revenue, yet nearly all elected officials have a spending program they will fight to defend—largely in response to demands from their constituents. For elected representatives, the act of budgeting involves balancing demands for expensive government programs against practical limits on how much revenue a government can or should raise. Budgeting is an attempt to deal with scarcity: There's never enough money to fund every possible government program that people might want. As we shall see, states and communities deal with scarcity in different ways, and their ability to balance demands for programs against limits on resources depends on many factors. Demands for government spending vary widely across places due to differences in state populations. More children, for example, may mean more demand for education; more elderly may mean more spending on health care. Demand may never overlap with public willingness to pay because some people may be willing to support taxes to pay for services that assist them, but they may be reluctant to support funds for public goods and services they don't use.

Criteria for Evaluating Taxes

The public's willingness to pay a particular tax (or a fee or charge) is one criterion we will use in this chapter when evaluating the revenue sources that state and local governments use. Willingness to pay, as we show below, may be a function of how visible a tax is. We also focus on additional features of taxes that are of interest to political scientists, economists, and, perhaps most importantly, government officials. As we examine different taxes, we see they differ in terms of **tax equity**—or who bears the burden of paying them. When a tax is **progressive**, the wealthier people pay a larger proportion of their total income to cover the tax than the less affluent pay of theirs, whereas when the tax is **regressive**, the poor pay a larger proportion of their income than the wealthy do to cover the tax.

Some governments may also be positioned to use taxes that are exportable. Exportable taxes are those mostly paid by people from other places (such as hotel taxes and taxes on natural resources, such as oil). Taxes also differ in their **elasticity**; that is, in how stable (or volatile) revenues from the tax are in times of economic boom and bust. Furthermore, some taxes may be "neutral" in their ability to alter the economic behavior of people and businesses. Others may create odd incentives that distort behavior. All these factors enter into the politics of which taxes governments use to fund public services.

Options for revenues also vary widely due to the economic structure of a state or community, institutional differences, and differences in popular support for taxation. California and New York have established income taxes and have rather liberal public preferences for government spending. Florida and Texas, in contrast, have voters who may be less sympathetic to public spending, and neither state has adopted a personal income tax. States also vary considerably on what can be taxed. Alaska can rely heavily on revenue from oil extraction, whereas Ohio cannot.

Where Does the Money Come From? Major Sources of Revenues

State and local governments spend about 17 cents of every dollar generated by the American economy, more than what is spent by the federal government. This reflects the fact that states spend the money they collect in taxes, charges, and fees and that states also spend billions of dollars that the federal government collects each year that are transferred to the states.

Each level of government competes for revenue—sometimes applying the same kind of taxes to the same sources. This is why, in some places, you may pay a state income tax in addition to your federal income tax or a local sales tax on top of your state's sales tax. However, the American fiscal environment has evolved such that the national government, the states, and local governments each have one particular revenue source, respectively, that they tend to rely upon for much of the resources they raise by taxation.

States vary in terms of how much revenue they raise and how they raise it. This makes it difficult to clearly define which states have the highest taxes. It depends on how we rank the states. The first two columns in Table 10.1 rank states according to how much they tax residents relative to the amount of income in the state per person. Ranked this way, Vermont, Maine, and New York tax the most and Alaska and New Hampshire the least.

The third column ranks states according to the total state and local taxes collected per resident (rather than as a function of state income). This illustrates how states compare in terms of the total dollars they collect

Table 10.1				
State and Local Taxes as a Percentage of State Income, 2007				
	State and Local Revenue as a % of per Capita Income, 2007	States Ranked by Revenue as a % of per Capita Income, 2007	States Ranked by Total Revenues per Capita, 2005	States Ranked by per Capita Income, 2005
Vermont	14.1	1	12	25
Maine	14.0	2	14	37
New York	13.8	3	3	5
Rhode Island	12.7	4	13	17
Ohio	12.4	5	21	29
Hawaii	12.4	6	9	19
Wisconsin	12.3	7	19	21
Connecticut	12.2	8	4	1
Nebraska	11.9	9	15	22
New Jersey	11.6	10	6	2
Minnesota	11.5	11	10	9
California	11.5	12	8	12
Arkansas	11.3	13	47	47
Michigan	11.2	14	22	24
Kansas	11.2	15	31	23
Washington	11.1	16	17	16
Louisiana	11.0	17	32	50

(continues)

State and Local Taxes as a Percentage of State Income, 2007—(continued)

	State and Local Revenue as a % of per Capita Income, 2007	States Ranked by Revenue as a % of per Capita Income, 2007	States Ranked by Total Revenues per Capita, 2005	States Ranked by per Capita Income, 2005
Iowa	11.0	18	28	30
North Carolina	11.0	19	37	35
Kentucky	10.9	20	46	43
West Virginia	10.9	21	33	48
Illinois	10.8	22	25	13
Maryland	10.8	23	11	4
Pennsylvania	10.8	24	23	18
Indiana	10.7	25	27	34
South Carolina	10.7	26	34	44
Utah	10.7	27	35	46
Massachusetts	10.6	28	7	3
Mississippi	10.5	29	50	49
Colorado	10.4	30	20	8
Arizona	10.3	31	45	38
Georgia	10.3	32	43	33
Virginia	10.2	33	18	7
Missouri	10.1	34	42	31
Idaho	10.1	35	40	42
Nevada	10.1	36	16	14
Oregon	10.0	37	30	28
Florida	10.0	38	26	20
North Dakota	9.9	39	24	32
New Mexico	9.8	40	29	45
Montana	9.7	41	38	41
Wyoming	9.5	42	2	10
Texas	9.3	43	39	27
South Dakota	9.0	44	49	26
Oklahoma	9.0	45	44	39
Alabama	8.8	46	41	40
Delaware	8.8	47	5	11
Tennessee	8.5	48	4	36
New Hampshire	8.0	49	36	6
Alaska	6.6	50	1	15

Source: Tax Foundation (2007); Tax Policy Center (2005); and U.S. Census (2005).

per person. Had we ranked states this way, Alaska and Wyoming would top the list, while South Dakota and Mississippi would be last. These rankings are affected by the state's level of wealth and the size of its population. But they also reflect the political and economic circumstances that shape the mix of taxes used in a state. New York has wealth to tap and relatively high taxes. Alaska and Wyoming are less affluent, but both generate tremendous revenues from resource taxes relative to the size of their populations.

The final column in Table 10.1 ranks states according to their level of per capita personal income, from the wealthiest (Connecticut) to the least affluent (Mississippi). Some states that are below average on this measure of wealth (for example, Maine and Louisiana) nonetheless rank relatively high on how much revenue they collect as a percentage of per capita income. Conversely, some affluent states (such as Virginia and Delaware) rank fairly low on taxes as a percentage of income. Again, this reflects political and economic circumstances in these states. Voters in Maine may be more receptive to higher taxes than Virginians. Delaware is uniquely situated to collect a substantial proportion of revenue from the unusually large number of businesses incorporated there. Delaware thus collects a great deal of revenue per capita but not much relative to its overall level of wealth per capita. Mississippi and Louisiana, in contrast, tax relatively high relative to their limited wealth, but those taxes generate much less revenue per capita than lower taxes do in affluent Delaware.

Below, we consider the various tools that state and local governments use to raise revenues and the political issues associated with some of these.

Income Tax

Nearly all states (41) tax personal income, and two more states (Tennessee and New Hampshire) tax just personal income from investments. In addition, Alaska and Florida tax corporate income. This means that Wyoming, Washington, Nevada, Texas, and South Dakota are the only states that lack taxation of personal or corporate income.[1] A handful of states allow local governments to levy an income tax.

A few states have **flat rates** for their income tax, but most state income tax systems place people into one of several brackets defined by how much they earn. Tax rates increase for each bracket, with people in the highest income brackets paying the highest tax rate. Even for people in the top brackets, state income tax rates are far lower than those levied by the federal government. An average state has about five brackets, with the tax rate for people in the lowest income bracket averaging about 2.6 percent and the rate for people in the highest bracket averaging about 6.5 percent. Vermont (9.5 percent), California (9.3 percent), and Oregon (9 percent) have the highest rates for top income brackets.[2] The proportion of all states' total personal income collected in state income taxes has increased steadily since the 1960s.[3]

Evaluating the Income Tax Supporters of the income tax note several features they find attractive. Advocacy groups note that states making use of an income tax have the most progressive revenue systems overall, whereas the poor pay a much larger proportion of their income in state and local taxes than the wealthy in states that lack an income tax (such as Washington, Florida, and Texas).[4] Income taxes are relatively easy for governments to collect (through payroll deduction), and revenues collected tend to be more stable in times of economic downturns when compared to sales taxes. Public opinion polls illustrate that voters find state income taxes more politically acceptable than federal taxes and property taxes, at least in states where the income tax already exists.[5] One study of the political consequences of adopting income taxes found that the party in control of the legislature that

---

[1] South Dakota does levy a tax on bank income.

[2] http://www.taxadmin.org/fta/rate/ind_inc.html.

[3] James Garand and Kyle Baudoin, "Fiscal Policy in the American States," in *Politics in the American States: A Comparative Analysis*, 8th ed., ed. V. Gray and R. Hanson (Washington, D.C.: CQ Press, 2004).

[4] Michael P. Ettlinger, John F. O'Hare, Robert S. McIntyre, Julie King, Neil Miransky, and Elizabeth A. Fray, "Who Pays? A Distributional Analysis of the Tax Systems of the 50 States," 1996 Center for Tax Justice report, Citizens for Tax Justice, 1996, http://www.ctj.org/html/whopay.htm.

[5] Shaun Bowler and Todd Donovan, "Public Responsiveness to Taxation," *Political Research Quarterly* 48 (1995): 79–99.

adopted the tax was usually reelected. When voters did punish politicians for adopting a state income tax, Republicans were much more likely to suffer than Democrats.[6] This may be due to the fact that Republican voters expect more fiscal prudence from Republicans than Democratic voters expect from Democrats.

Critics point out that income is already taxed by the federal government and that inflation can drive people who get **cost of living allowances (COLAs)** into higher tax brackets even though their real earning power does not increase. Income taxes may also distort the incentives that people have to work. And by taxing income that people save, it creates disincentives for savings, which makes less money available for investment and economic growth.

Sales Tax

Mississippi first adopted the sales tax in 1932, and another 11 states had adopted it by 1933.[7] Today, all but five states (Oregon, Alaska, Montana, New Hampshire, and Delaware) have a sales tax. About half of all tax revenue collected by state governments comes from the sales tax, with Mississippi, New Jersey, Tennessee, and Rhode Island having the highest rates (7.0 percent). In addition, nearly all states grant their local governments the power to levy an additional increment on top of the state rate. This is the reason why you might pay a different rate as you move from one county to the next inside a state. When local sales taxes are considered, residents in parts of several high-sales-tax states pay over 9 percent in state and local sales tax on their purchases (for example, Alabama, Arkansas, Oklahoma, and Tennessee).

Evaluating the Sales Tax One of the most noteworthy features of the sales tax is its relative political acceptability. Surveys of opinion demonstrate that when compared to other major revenue sources, state sales taxes are the most popular (or usually the least disliked). Taxes are collected at the point of sale on individual purchases, so they may not be as noticeable to the taxpayer as lump sum payments that can come due with property taxes and income taxes. For local governments, sales tax revenue can be particularly attractive because it offers the opportunity to get folks from out of town to bear some of the costs of funding services. As a tax on consumption, sales taxes may also create fewer distortions in people's incentives to work, save, and invest than an income tax does.

Susan Hansen's study suggests that most state governments that adopted a state sales tax between 1911 and 1977 survived the next election but that they faced a slightly greater threat of defeat than governments that adopted the income tax. Again, Republican governments that adopted the tax were at a greater risk of defeat than Democratic governments.[8]

The sales tax has two clear weaknesses, however. The first is the elasticity or stability of it as a revenue source. The total amount collected depends on how much people are spending on "big-ticket" consumer goods. When the economy cools and consumer confidence wanes, the demand for things, such as new cars, boats, TVs, computers, and construction materials, declines—and so does sales tax revenue. This problem is magnified when the sales tax applies only to goods and not to services.

The second issue is equity. People who earn less usually spend all their income, which means the sales tax applies to most of what they earn. People who earn more are able to save and invest some of what they earn, and the sales tax does not apply to that portion of their income. This means the poor pay much

---

[6] Susan Hansen, *The Politics of Taxation: Revenue without Representation* (New York: Praeger, 1983).

[7] Richard Winters, "The Politics of Taxing and Spending," in *Politics in the American States: A Comparative Analysis*, 7th ed., ed. V. Gray and R Hanson (Washington, D.C.: CQ Press, 1999).

[8] Hansen, *The Politics of Taxation.*

more of their overall income to sales taxes than the rich. It also means that states that rely heavily on sales taxes have the most **regressive tax** systems. Many states offset the regressive nature of this tax by exempting basic items, such as food and medicine, from the tax.

Due to growing exemptions and shifts in the nature of the economy, the base of what the sales tax applies to has been eroding over time. Over the past several decades, spending has shifted from goods to services (such as lawyers, health care, advertising, and consulting), and purchases are moving from the physical storefront to the virtual store online. Services are not always covered by state sales taxes (in part due to successful lobbying efforts by the affected groups), and states have particular difficulty collecting taxes from sales made via the Internet. As the base of the tax erodes, states are under pressure to raise sales taxes on the remaining items subject to the tax.[9] And if more exemptions are made for "basic" necessities, the remaining base of the sales tax becomes more dependent on big-ticket purchases, making revenues even more volatile.[10] Sales taxes may also distort behavior by creating incentives for people to travel to make purchases where taxes are lower or by encouraging them to shop online in order to avoid paying any sales tax.

Property Tax

Some states collect state property taxes, but for most states, the property tax contributes less than 2 percent to total state taxes collected. However, property taxes are the main source of revenues for local governments. Property taxes are typically levied as a flat rate proportion (1 percent), for example, multiplied by the assessed value of property. These rates are often referred to as mill levies. A 1 percent

mill levy is the same as saying the tax is $1 per $1,000 in assessed value of property, or the property value multiplied by .01. The amount one pays in tax is determined as much by the value of the property as by the tax rate. Most homeowners pay the same rate on residential property, with those having more valuable homes paying a higher tax amount overall. For example, a home assessed at $276,000 in Clark County, Washington, is subject to a 1.618 percent annual county property tax (or 0.00161 mill), a 2.766 percent state property tax (0.00276 mill), and various other property taxes. It would owe $446 a year in county property tax and $763 per year in state property tax (most state property tax rates are much lower than this).[11] All property taxes are usually collected on a single bill or two bills that arrive six months apart. This means that taxpayers are likely to be highly attentive to the total dollar amount they pay in property taxes (compared to what they pay in sales taxes—imagine if you received one large bill each year for all that you owed in sales taxes rather than paying it at each individual purchase). Depending on where the property is located, the bill may include taxes for the county, the city, the school districts, the state, and other special service districts (that is, library districts, port districts, and water districts).

In the first half of the 20th century, property taxes accounted for nearly all municipal revenues. Today, the local government revenue mix is quite different. Because cities, counties, and towns now use a wider range of taxes and fees to raise revenue while also receiving funds from the national government and their state governments, property taxes now contribute less overall to local budgets. Nonetheless, it is still the primary source of revenue for local governments. At the end of the 20th century, property taxes still generated 79 percent of all

---

[9] Winters, "The Politics of Taxing and Spending."

[10] W. Duncombe, "Economic Change and the Evolving State Tax Structure: The Case of the Sales Tax," *National Tax Journal* (1992): 308.

[11] State laws also determine what percentage of the assessed value of property is subject to the tax.

INSTITUTIONS MATTER

STATE AND LOCAL SALES TAX AND THE INTERNET

Traditional sales tax rules evolved in an era where goods were mostly sold to local people from local businesses. But what happens to the sales tax when more people make purchases via the Internet from businesses in other states? If the vendor has a physical presence in your state (such as a shop or warehouse), it must charge sales tax for your state and local governments. If no "bricks-and-mortar" presence exists, however, it is not required to collect the tax. Some worry that this gives online retailers a major advantage over local businesses. As the Internet became a common shopping destination, many large retailers like Wal-Mart, Target, Toys "R" Us, and Barnes and Noble that have physical stores in nearly every state avoid charging sales taxes by setting up separate legal dot-com entities that are, at least on paper, distinct from their traditional stores. The large online retailers argue that the old rules were obsolete and that it was too complicated to collected taxes for 50 states and thousands of local governments.

In theory, the buyer is supposed to pay the tax to the state if the online seller doesn't collect it. Given the difficulty of administering and monitoring Internet sales, states focused enforcement on a few "big-ticket" items, such as cars, and left large-volume sales areas, such as clothing, books, and music, untaxed. Sites like Travelocity.com also allow people who book rooms online to avoid paying local hotel taxes because rooms are purchased online. States may lose $38 billion annually in sales tax revenue by 2011 as retailers shift sales to the Internet—with some states losing nearly 10 percent of their total tax collections.[a] States have banded together to pressure retailers to voluntarily charge sales tax that can be distributed to the state where a buyer resides, and some large retailers (Walmart.com and ToysRUs.com) began to do so. By 2008, 22 states were participating in this "streamlined" Internet sales tax system to make it easier for retailers to collect sales taxes from online sales. However, absent federal legislation, states cannot force online retailers to pay the tax. The high-tech industry has lobbied successfully in Washington, D.C., against giving states power to enforce their sales tax collections for purchases made online.[b]

[a] Donald Bruce and William F. Fox, "State and Local Sales Tax Revenue Losses from E-Commerce: Updated Estimates" (Chattanooga: University of Tennessee, Center for Business and Economic Research, 2001).
[b] Brian Krebs, "Internet Sales Tax Effort on Hold Now," Washington Post, 17 December 2003, http://www.washingtonpost.com/wp-dyn/articles/A5949-2003Dec16.html.

local tax revenues.[12] Cities, counties, school districts, and special districts each levy their own property taxes.

The Property Tax Evaluated   One traditional rationale for the property tax is that it taxes people who benefit the most from local public services. Property values are increased by public services, such as fire, police protection, and quality schools, so property taxes target people who benefit from these services. Historically, real property (land, homes, and farms) was the

place where most Americans held their wealth. When fewer people owned property and fewer people invested their wealth in stocks and bonds, the wealthy had a greater share of their assets in real property. This made a tax on property relatively progressive.

In the contemporary era, however, homeownership is no longer something reserved for the wealthy. About two-thirds of American families now own a home. Moreover, for most middle-class families, a home is their primary

[12] National Council of State Legislators, *A Guide to Property Tax: Property Tax Relief*, report on property tax (Denver, CO: National Council of State Legislators, 2002).

investment and thus represents most of their wealth. In contrast, the wealthiest people today have much more of their wealth invested in paper assets. Property taxes—a flat rate—thus cost the poor (if they can buy a home) and the middle class a larger share of their wealth than they cost the wealthiest people. Some economists suggest contemporary property taxes are highly regressive.[13]

Property Taxes and Tax Rebellions Property taxes are consistently rated as the most unpopular tax by Americans.[14] Voters are particularly sensitive to property taxes. With sales and income taxes, marginal changes in rates don't tend to translate into increased hostility to the tax. Unlike the sales tax, property tax payments are made in a lump sum (unless built into monthly mortgage bills), which may add to the sting of the tax. One of the biggest political liabilities of the tax is that inflation in home values can drive up a person's tax burden much faster than any increase in their income. In booming housing markets, home prices may increase by 15–30 percent per year. Local governments are often required by law to reassess home values frequently, leading some homeowners to find steep increases in their property tax bills virtually overnight. Tax bills increased dramatically, not because elected officials raised the rates but because market demand increased home values.

This dynamic of rising home prices driving tax bills higher fueled a rebellion against property taxes in California (Proposition 13 in 1978) and Massachusetts (Proposition 2½ in 1980) and led to an antitax movement[15] that has consequences to this day.

The success of ballot measures in several states and general demands for "tax relief"

pressured legislatures across the nation to enact various laws that exempted property owners from new tax burdens resulting from rapid increases in the value of their homes and land. Today, many states make various exemptions for low-income households, veterans, and the elderly. Exemptions for agricultural land allow owners to resist pressures of selling to developers in order to avoid a growing tax burden. Exemptions, although popular, come at a cost of lost tax revenues for each level of government that collects property tax.

Property tax revolts are not limited to the nation's hottest real estate markets and persisted long beyond the 1980s. In 2006, activists in 20 states were pushing for new property tax limits. Becky and Don Fagg of Lexington, South Carolina, saw their property taxes double in just five years as out-of-state buyers drove up local real estate prices and property assessments. The increased tax burden threatened their retirement plans, motivating Mrs. Fagg to form a group dedicated to abolishing taxes on a person's primary residence.[16] On the Olympic Peninsula in Washington that same year, Shelly Taylor and Jill Wilnauer reacted to rapid increases in their property taxes—increases produced by the heated local real estate market—by forming a group to press their state legislature to limit increases in the assessed value of homes to 1 percent per year. Hundreds of people crammed into a hall to attend the group's meeting where they announced their proposed constitutional amendment. The Washington amendment had not advanced as of 2008, but South Carolina used higher than expected sales tax revenues to reduce what homeowners would pay in property taxes in 2008.

[13] Daniel B. Suits, "Measurement of Tax Progressivity," *American Economic Review* 67, no. 4 (1977): 747.

[14] Bowler and Donovan, "Public Responsiveness to Taxation."

[15] David O. Sears and Jack Citrin, *Something for Nothing in California* (Berkeley: University of California Press, 1982); David Lowery and Lee Sigelman, "Understanding the Tax Revolt: Eight Explanations," *American Political Science Review* (1981): 963–74; and Daniel A. Smith, *Tax Crusaders and the Politics of Direct Democracy* (New York: Routledge, 1999).

[16] Rafel Gerena-Morales, "Across U.S., Rising Property Taxes Spark Revolts," *Wall Street Journal*, 1 February 2006, p. B4.

Other Revenue Sources

Given the political difficulties of relying on traditional tax sources, such as income, property, and general sales taxes, states and communities also generate revenues from taxes that are more narrowly targeted as well as direct charges for services. Over the last two decades, state and local governments are relying more heavily on some of these "other" sources of revenues and have been using them more than ever before.

Selective Sales Taxes

General sales taxes apply to most common purchases. Additional sales taxes are often levied on select items, such as fuel, alcohol, tobacco products, and public utilities. Sometimes, these taxes are referred to as excise taxes, or **sin taxes**, because they target behavior—such as drinking or smoking—that many people believe should be discouraged. If higher taxes actually cause people to consume less of the targeted item, the state may benefit. If demand for the item is **elastic** and responds to increases in prices, higher taxation will lead to less consumption of the item targeted with the tax. But if the tax applies to something that has **inelastic demand**—that is, something people must have regardless of the cost—a higher sin tax might not lower consumption.

Motor Vehicle Fuel Most of the revenues collected in this category come from state taxes on gasoline and diesel. Fuel taxes are charged per gallon, with a state rate added on top of the $0.18 per gallon in tax going to the federal government. Most states add about another $0.20 per gallon—Alaska has the lowest ($0.08 per gallon), with Pennsylvania, Rhode Island, and Wisconsin having the highest (over $0.30 per gallon). The political acceptability of gas taxes used to be enhanced by the fact that the funds are often dedicated to transportation projects.[17] Yet, when gas prices shot up in

2008, people bought fewer gallons of gas. This causes state and federal revenues dedicated to transportation to shrink. At the same time, hostility to high gas prices has led some states to consider cutting their fuel taxes. General sales tax is also collected on what people pay at the pump. As people paid more (for less gas), some states were enjoying windfall increases in general sales tax revenues.

Tobacco Products The proportion of state revenues from cigarette and tobacco taxes has been increasing recently. In several states that experienced tax rebellions in recent decades, citizens have actually voted to raise their state taxes. Or, at least, they voted to raise taxes on people who smoke.

On average, cigarette taxes have increased from $0.21 per pack in 1996 to $0.77 by 2006. Cigarette taxes have proved popular in part because they target an unpopular minority (smokers), with increases often linked to spending on public health programs. Voters in Washington and California, for example, approved cigarette tax increases that earmarked funds for health care (and antitobacco education). As a result of these taxes, cigarette prices now vary substantially across states. As of 2008, New York charged the most: $2.75 tax per pack. New Jersey ($2.57), Rhode Island ($2.46), and Washington ($2.02) were the next highest, respectively (Alaska, Arizona, Maine, Maryland, and Michigan charged $2.00 per pack). Smoking is a much more affordable habit in the South, particularly in tobacco-producing states. South Carolina ($0.07), Missouri ($0.17), Mississippi ($0.18), Kentucky and Virginia (both at $0.30), and North Carolina ($0.35) have the nation's lowest cigarette taxes.[18]

Alcoholic Beverages On average, states charge $0.24 in tax on a gallon of beer. Hawaii, which has no neighboring state to buy

---

[17] Garand and Baudoin, "Fiscal Policy in the American States."

[18] Data in this section are from the Federation of Tax Administrators, http://www.taxadmin.org.

from, has the highest rate ($0.93 per gallon) and the nation's most expensive beer. Some of the cheapest beer in the United States can be found in Missouri (the home of Anheuser-Busch/Budweiser—which controls 45 percent of U.S. beer sales), Colorado (the home of Coors—which controls 10 percent of U.S. beer sales), Oregon (center of the U.S. microbrewing industry), and Wisconsin (the home of many thirsty Green Bay Packer fans, Miller, Pabst, and Stroh's Brewing—the latter three control 33 percent of U.S. beer sales). Beer taxes in each of these states and in Wyoming are under $0.08 per gallon. The distribution of beer taxes suggests that industries are able to avoid sin taxes in states where the industry is a key part of the economy. Wine taxes are also low in California ($0.20 per gallon), the nation's largest wine-producing state, and high in Alaska ($2.50) and Florida ($2.25), where wine should probably not be produced.

Direct Charges

Some of what state and local governments do can be funded by direct charges to the people who use a service, also know as **user fees.** For every $3.60 that state and local governments collect in taxes, another $1.00 is collected in user charges and fees. States generate billions in revenue by charging users of hospitals, highways, higher education, and other services. User charges for hospitals, sewers, garbage collection, airports, and parks contribute tens of billions of dollars to local government revenues. For the most part, none of these services are fully funded by charges to users, but fees reduce the amount of revenue from general taxes that would otherwise be used as funding.

Despite the names, user fees and charges are a source of revenue, just like any other tax. States and local governments have come to rely more heavily on fees and charges in recent years because they make it possible to avoid increasing visible taxes, such as sales or income tax. Critics of direct charges and fees argue that they can be highly regressive because people at all income levels often pay the same flat fee.

Estate Tax

Estate taxes are levied on savings and properties that a deceased person passes on to heirs. Critics of estate taxes argue that they force "family farms" to be broken up upon the death of a property owner and that they amount to double taxation because the property taxes are already paid by the person accumulating the wealth. Political opponents of estate taxes have successfully rebranded these as "death taxes," although they can be levied on the living person inheriting a person's wealth (rather than the dead person). Federal and state estate tax programs typically made exemptions for family farms, and as of 2005, the minimum value for an estate to owe the tax ranged from $670,000 to $1.5 million. This meant that the vast majority of people inheriting money are not affected by the tax.[19] Advocates of the estate tax—including Bill Gates Sr., father of one of the world's richest men—note that the estate tax is fair because it taxes wealth that was not earned by the person receiving it. Estate taxes may also be a way to tax accumulated wealth that has avoided taxation during a person's lifetime. The estate tax is also one of the few instruments of progressive taxation available to government. Gates estimates that the repeal of the estate tax would largely benefit future heirs of the United States' wealthiest estates—several of whom have funded the successful anti-estate tax lobbying effort.[20]

Lotteries

Lotteries were promoted as a politically painless way to raise revenues that could be earmarked for public education.[21] Although

---

[19] Elizabeth McNichol, Center for Budget and Policy Priorities, 2004, http://www.cbpp.org/2-18-04sfp.htm#_ftn1.

[20] William Gates Sr. and Chuck Collins, "Tax the Wealthy: Why America Needs the Estate Tax," *American Prospect*, June 17, 2002.

[21] David Broder, *Democracy Derailed: Initiative Campaigns and the Power of Money* (San Diego, Calif.: Harcourt, 2000), 83–84.

they are classified as a regressive tax,[22] most tickets are purchased by middle- and upper-income people.[23] Forty-one states now have lotteries, with North Carolina adopting a lottery in 2006. Most states have their lottery funds earmarked for education. North Carolina's gambling revenues—estimated at over $1 billion through 2010—are earmarked for education, but this allowed the state to reduce general revenues spent on education.[24] The North Carolina case suggests that lottery funds may simply replace general revenue funds spent on education, resulting in no net gain for schools. However, one national study found that earmarking rules matter. Every dollar of lottery profit earmarked for education increased state education spending by more than would be the case if the funds were not prededicated to education.[25]

In 2004, 15 states had lottery sales well over $1 billion each, with nearly $50 billion in sales nationally.[26] However, only $14 billion of that was profit that contributed to state revenues. Most states dedicate their lottery revenues to education. However, because only a fraction of ticket sales end up as revenues, lotteries contribute a very small percentage to state funds, even to education budgets. One estimate is that states receive only 30 cents in revenue for every dollar wagered and that the yield has been in decline since the 1990s. In California, where profits are dedicated to education, the lottery provides less than 2 percent of all funds for the state's K–12 system.[27] Some evidence reveals that the market for the lottery is saturated: With so many states now running lotteries and with competition from the growing tribal gambling industries, more places now exist for a limited number of gamblers to risk their money. States respond to declining sales by increasing payouts, which can result in modest revenues.

Gambling

All but two states (Hawaii and Utah) have dropped their prohibitions against all forms of gambling. The recent expansion of legal gambling facilities means that taxes on gross receipts from casino gambling are one of the faster-growing sources of state revenues. Indian nations are major players in expanding the American gambling industry (the industry prefers to refer to the business as "gaming," not "gambling"). A tribe negotiates a compact with its state government about the scope of casino operations allowed in exchange for a certain share of the casino revenues. As tribes and states become more dependent on each other in this way, tribes have become some of the largest campaign donor for legislators in some states. For Nevada, gambling revenues are a method to export the state's tax burden to people from out of state.

Severance Taxes

Some states are blessed with valuable natural resources that provide a major source of revenues. Severance taxes are levied on resources "severed" from the earth or sea and are applied to resource extraction industries, such as fishing, mining, and oil and natural gas production. Taxes are levied on the volume of the resource extracted. When market prices for the resource are up, these revenues boom. If prices collapse,

[22] John Mikesell and C. Kurt Zorn, "State Lotteries as Fiscal Saviors or Fiscal Fraud," *Public Administration Review* 46 (1986): 311–20.

[23] Daniel B. Suits, "Gambling Taxes: Regressivity and Revenue Potential," *National Tax Journal* 30 (1977): 25–33.

[24] Mosi Secret, "Lottery Will Replace $1B in State Money: Bill Was Changed after Passage," *Independent Weekly*, 8 February 2006, http://indyweek.com/gyrobase/Content? oid=oid%3A27511.

[25] Neva Kerbeshian Novarro, "Does Earmarking Matter? The Case of State Lottery Profits and Educational Spending," Stanford Institute for Economic Policy Research Discussion Paper no. 02–19 (Stanford, Calif.: Stanford Institute for Economic Policy Research, 2002).

[26] http://www.naspl.org/ranksales.html.

[27] California Department of Education, *State Lottery Fact Book 2004* (Sacramento: California Department of Education, 2004).

so do revenues. High energy prices as of 2008 meant that severance revenues were booming in resource-rich states. Alaska generated over 50 percent of state revenues from severance taxes, and Wyoming collected 45 percent. Three more states (New Mexico, North Dakota, and Oklahoma) collected at least 10 percent of state revenues from severance taxes. Texas collected more than twice as much as any state ($1.9 billion), but given Texas' diverse revenue system, this is only about 6 percent of the state's total tax collections. Most states lack the natural resources that make severance taxes a significant source of revenues.

Tax and Expenditure Limits

Property tax revolts of the 1970s produced various policies designed to curb the growth of taxation and government spending. Known collectively as **tax and expenditure limitations (or TELs)**, these policies set formulas that determine by how much revenue and spending can grow. These formulas typically limit growth in spending or future revenues collected from existing sources to some level that keeps pace with inflation or population growth (or some combination). By 2005, 30 states had adopted some form of TELs: 23 had spending limits, four had tax revenue limits, and three had both.[28] Sixteen states also required legislative **supermajority votes** in order to pass a tax increase.

Substantial academic debate continues over whether TELs actually limit the growth of government expenditure over the long term. Several observers blame (or credit) California's Proposition 13 of 1978 with a dramatic reduction in revenue available for public services, particularly schools.[29] Others note that although property tax limits and spending limits affected which level of government raised revenues (shifting taxation from one level of government to another), overall spending was largely unaffected.[30] The first generation of TELs—particularly those enacted by legislators rather than via ballot initiatives—may not have had much effect on limiting the growth in taxation and spending.[31] It is difficult to evaluate the effects of these policies because the same formula limiting revenue growth (for example, a limit tied to population growth) might have quite different effects in a state with rapid population growth than in a state with no population growth.[32]

A second generation of TELs adopted in the 1990s and more recently may have more teeth than those adopted in the 1970s and 1980s.[33] Colorado's Taxpayer Bill of Rights (TABOR) serves as an example. In addition to strict formulas limiting revenue growth, TABOR required a public referendum to approve any tax increase proposed in the legislature. One critical case study of TABOR suggests that it resulted in substantially reduced levels of government spending, with education and health care suffering.[34]

---

[28] National Council of State Legislators, http://www.ncsl.org/programs/fiscal/tels2005.htm.

[29] Peter Schrag, *Paradise Lost: California's Experience, America's Future* (Berkeley: University of California Press, 2004).

[30] Elisabeth Gerber, Arthur Lupia, Mathew McCubbins, and D. R. Kiewiet, *Stealing the Initiative: How State Government Responds to Direct Democracy* (Upper Saddle River, N.J.: Prentice Hall, 2001).

[31] Shaun Bowler and Todd Donovan, "Evolution in State Governance Structures," *Political Research Quarterly* (2004): 189–196; and James Alt and Robert Lowry, "Divided Government, Fiscal Institutions, and Budget Deficits: Evidence from the States," *American Political Science Review* 88 (1994): 811–28.

[32] Ronald Shadbegian, "Do Tax and Expenditure Limitations Affect the Size and Growth of Government?" *Contemporary Economic Policy*, January 1996, 22–35.

[33] Michael New, "Limiting Government through Direct Democracy: The Case of State Tax and Expenditure Limitations," Cato Policy Analysis no. 420 (Washington, D.C.: Cato Institute, 2001).

[34] Bell Policy Center, *Ten Years of TABOR: A Study of Colorado's Taxpayer's Bill of Rights* (Denver, Colo.: Bell Policy Center, 2003).

Fiscal Federalism

State and local governments receive substantial money from the federal government to promote the federal government's goals in areas such as health care, urban renewal, education, and transportation. The relative power of the federal government and the states is often measured in dollars, with the efforts of federal and state governments to exert control over policies limited by their willingness to pay for such authority. In 2006, the amount of annual transfers from the federal government to states and localities was more than $427 billion, including $62 billion in capital investments.[35]

The federal government's largess in aid to the states and their localities does not come free. The federal government uses a number of mechanisms to compel the states to spend the money according to the wishes of Congress. The federal government provides grant-in-aid to state and local governments. There are two general types of grants that the federal government uses to distribute funds to subnational governments.

General Funds versus Non-General Funds

All these various revenues may end up in different budgets before they are spent. Revenues collected from the general sales tax, income tax, and property tax often end up in a state or local government's general fund budget. Some states may also put their lottery revenues and other miscellaneous funds in their general budget. General fund revenues can typically be used for any purpose, so politicians have substantial discretion over how such revenues might be spent. Budget battles in the legislature or between the legislature and

the governor largely center on what should be done with general fund revenues.

Revenues that are collected for a specific purpose or transferred to a state or community for a specific program often end up in a non-general fund budget. As example, most money that comes as transfers from the federal government is allocated to fund health and welfare programs and cannot be spent on other things. Likewise, tuition and fees collected by universities are dedicated to fund universities and cannot be spent on other programs. Gas taxes are often dedicated to road construction and transportation only, and most states earmark their lottery funds for education. This means that budget writers often have very little discretion over how non-general fund revenues can be spent. Over half of a state's total revenues may end up in a non-general fund budget. In Virginia's 2004–2006 budget, for example, 53 percent of all state revenues went into the non-general fund.

Adding It All Up: Variation in State Revenue Packages

Every state and local government has its own unique combination of revenue sources. When state revenue sources are displayed graphically, it's often in the form of a pie, with larger slices depicting the major revenue sources. Unfortunately, there's not one single pie to consider, as the overall mixture of state or local revenue can be expressed at least three ways. The first is to think in terms of the tax revenues a government generates on its own. But state and local taxes are only part of the story—governments also generate substantial revenues by charging for services. This means we must also consider these additional nontax revenues as part of a government's revenue package.

---

[35] Todd Donovan and Shaun Bowler, "Responsive or Responsible Government," in *Citizens as Legislators*, ed. S. Bowler, T. Donovan, and C. Tolbert (Columbus: Ohio State University Press, 1998); and James Clingermayer and B. D. Wood, "Disentangling Patterns of State Debt Financing," *American Political Science Review* (1995): 108–120. In contrast, see D. R. Kiewiet and K. Szakaly, "Constitutional Limitations of Borrowing: An Analysis of State Bonded Indebtedness," *Journal of Law, Economics and Organizations* (1996): 62–97.

Finally, much of what state and local governments spend comes from funds transferred from other, higher levels of government, so a third way to express a government's revenue mix is to include all "own-source" revenues (taxes and other sources) plus transfers from other levels of government.

The Mix of State Revenues

The 50 states combined had nearly $1.3 trillion in annual revenue in 2005. To put that amount in perspective, the federal government collected about $1.5 trillion in annual revenue the same year (excluding Social Security).[36] Figure 10.1 illustrates the sources of all funds available to state governments. Of the $1.3 trillion available, about $874 billion were generated by states. This includes about $648 billion collected via state taxes, $123 billion in direct

charges and fees collected by states, and about $103 billion from miscellaneous state revenue sources. Federal funds and direct charges allow states to spend about twice what they collect in taxes. Direct charges apply to users of state services and include college tuition, road tolls, park fees, and the like. As noted in Chapter 2, the federal government redistributes substantial funds back to the states each year—over $400 billion—mostly to fund health and welfare expenses shared between the state and federal governments.

About 74 percent of all state-generated (or own-source) revenues come from taxation, with another 14 percent from direct charges for services and 12 percent from interest earned on investments and other miscellaneous sources. Most revenue from direct charges for public services (paid only by those who use the

---

Figure 10.1

Sources of All State Revenues, 2005

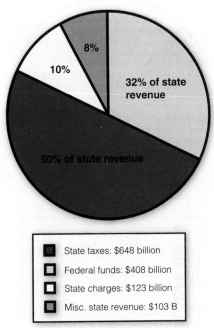

- State taxes: $648 billion
- Federal funds: $408 billion
- State charges: $123 billion
- Misc. state revenue: $103 B

Note: Total state revenues from all sources = $1.282 trillion. Total excludes $335 billion generated from insurance trust funds.

Source: U.S. Census Bureau, "Census of Governments 2005," http://www.census.gov/govs/state/0500usst.html.

---

[36] U.S. Census Bureau, http://www.census.gov/prod/2004pubs/04statab/stlocgov.pdf.

services) comes in the form of tuition for higher education. This is one of the fastest-growing sources of funds for state governments.

Figure 10.2 focuses more narrowly on what the average state's mix of tax revenues might look like: about one-third coming from general sales tax (plus another 15 percent from "selective" sales taxes on things like gas, cigarettes, and alcohol), about one-third from individual income taxes (plus another 6 percent from corporate income taxes), 6 percent from license fees (mostly on vehicles), and the rest from miscellaneous taxes. Taxes bring in most, but by no means all, the revenues that states generate.

States vary tremendously in the mix of revenues they use to fund public services. A balanced package of revenues—just like a balanced stock portfolio—helps bring stability to a state's budget process through periods of economic recession. But can states thrive without having both an income tax and a sales tax, the two main pillars of revenue systems? A few states endowed with natural resources or specialized industries avoid having to rely on one of the major taxes (income and sales). Alaska and Texas have generated tremendous revenue from oil and gas. Wyoming has profited from mining, Nevada from gambling, and Florida from tourism. These revenue sources export the burden of state taxes to people in other states and allow these states to get by without income taxes. However, they may face budget crises when prices of their key commodity crash or if the tourist industry crashes (as Florida and Nevada learned after September 11, 2001).

Figure 10.2

Sources of Tax Revenue Generated by State Governments, 2005

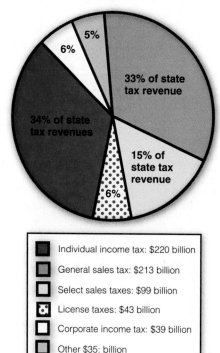

Individual income tax: $220 billion

General sales tax: $213 billion

Select sales taxes: $99 billion

License taxes: $43 billion

Corporate income tax: $39 billion

Other $35: billion

Note: Total state revenues generated by state taxes = $649 billion.

Source: U.S. Census Bureau, "Census of Governments 2005," http://www.census.gov/govs/state/0500usst.html.

Absent major tourism or natural resources, few states have the luxury of funding their operations without sales and income taxes—which, as just mentioned, are the two main pillars of state revenue. Those that have only one must rely heavily on it. Oregon lacks a sales tax, so it collects 70 percent of state revenues from the income tax. Washington lacks an income tax, so it must collect 60 percent of its revenues from the sales tax. New Hampshire has neither a general sales nor a general income tax and manages to balance its budget via frugality and having local governments fund many services. Although no state is average, most have revenue packages that look less like Washington, Oregon, Alaska, or New Hampshire and more like what is shown in Figure 10.2.

The Mix of Local Revenues

When transfers from higher levels of government are factored in, local governments collect about $1.16 trillion in revenues. Local governments, including cities, counties, school districts, and other special districts, collect just over $700 billion in locally generated taxes and charges, with the majority of this coming from the property tax.

Figure 10.3 illustrates that local governments collect 39 percent of this $1.16 trillion from local taxes, with a similar proportion of funds coming from transfers (mostly from their states). Most of these transfers are state funds dedicated to school districts and to cities and counties to cover their costs of running health programs. Another 16 percent of local funds come from direct charges, mostly for hospitals and utilities.

When we focus only on the revenues that local governments collect themselves, we find that a local government's revenue package looks quite different from a state's revenues. Although most locally generated revenues

---

Figure 10.3

Sources of All Local Government General Revenues, 2005

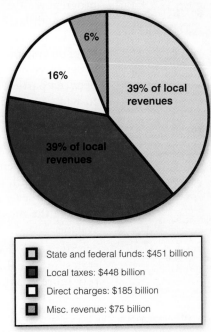

- 6%
- 16%
- 39% of local revenues
- 39% of local revenues

☐ State and federal funds: $451 billion
■ Local taxes: $448 billion
☐ Direct charges: $185 billion
■ Misc. revenue: $75 billion

Note: Total local revenues = $1.159 trillion. Excludes $47 billion in revenues from insurance trusts and $99 billion from utilities.

Source: U.S. Census Bureau, http://www.census.gov/govs/estimate/0500ussl_1.html.

come from local taxes, local governments rely much more on charges and fees than states do. Twenty-six percent of locally generated revenues come from user fees and charges for services, compared to 14 percent for state-generated revenues.

Figure 10.4 breaks down the sources of the $448 billion in taxes generated by local governments. Again, we see a substantially different picture when we compare locally generated tax revenue (Figure 10.4) to tax revenue generated at the state level (Figure 10.2). Local governments have a much less diversified tax portfolio compared to states, and they rely heavily on the property tax. School districts and special districts (districts that provide services such as fire protection or libraries) rely almost exclusively on property taxes.

"Cash Reward," "Trucks & Bucks," "Lucky Times," "$25,000 Jackpot," and "Pot o' Gold" are some of the Oklahoma Lottery games available.

Who Bears the Burden of State and Local Taxes?

Other than the income tax, most revenues that states and communities rely on are relatively regressive compared to the federal tax structure. That is, those who earn less income pay more of their income in state and local taxes. At the same time, the wealthiest people, having far more income, pay more of the total dollars collected. Just as states and cities differ in the revenue packages they use, they also differ in terms of how regressive their taxes are. As Table 10.2 illustrates, the poorest 20 percent of a state's population can pay 12 to 18 percent of their income in state and local taxes, whereas the richest residents in the same state pay as little as 2 or 3 percent of their income in state taxes. In some states (Delaware, Hawaii, Minnesota, and Montana), all income groups pay about the same share of their income in state taxes.

Why such differences? States that adopted the income tax early tend to rely on it more heavily, making their tax systems more progressive. A state's economy matters as well. States with larger manufacturing sectors and with wealthier people have more progressive revenue systems. Taxation may also be more progressive in states with strong competition between parties. A party out of power trying to win support from a broad base of voters may have an incentive to propose increased government spending for the poor and middle class financed by taxes on the rich.[37] Economic growth and Democratic governors are also associated with more progressive taxation.[38] States that never adopted the income tax tend to have the most regressive overall revenue systems.

Since the tax revolt of the late 1970s, states and local governments have begun to rely more heavily on user fees (particularly

[37] David Lowery, "The Distribution of Tax Burdens in the American States: The Determinants of Fiscal Incidence," *Western Political Quarterly* (1986): 137–58; and V. O. Key, *Southern Politics in the State and Nation* (New York: Knopf, 1949). This effect may depend on the period being studied. See B. R. Fry and R. F. Winters, "The Politics of Redistribution," *American Political Science Review* 70 (1970): 508–22.

[38] Neil Berch, "Explaining the Changes in Tax Incidence in the States," *Political Research Quarterly* 48 (1995): 629–41.

Figure 10.4

Local Tax Revenues by Source, 2005

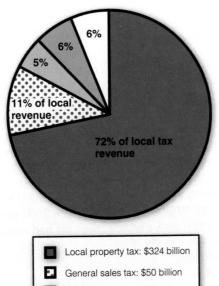

6%

6%

5%

11% of local revenue

72% of local tax revenue

Local property tax: $324 billion

General sales tax: $50 billion

Local income tax: $26 billion

Misc. taxes: $26 billion

Selective sales tax: $22 billion

Note: Total local tax revenues = $448 billion.

Source: U.S. Census Bureau, 2005, http://www.census.gov/govs/estimate/0500ussl_1.html.

Table 10.2

The Ten Most Regressive State Tax Systems*

State	Taxes as a % of Income	Poorest 20%	Middle Top 1%
Washington	17.6	11.2	3.3
Florida	14.4	9.8	3.0
Tennessee	11.7	8.9	3.4
South Dakota	10.0	8.4	2.3
Texas	11.4	8.4	3.5
Illinois	13.1	10.5	5.8
Michigan	13.3	11.2	6.7
Pennsylvania	11.4	9.0	4.8
Nevada	8.3	6.5	2.0
Alabama	10.6	9.6	4.9

*Taxes as shares of income for nonelderly residents.

Note: States listed in bold have no income tax.

direct democracy states) and specific sales taxes, such as cigarette taxes—trends that may make revenues more regressive over time.

When Do Taxes Go Up or Down?

Tax "innovation," or the adoption of new taxes, is a function of need and political opportunity. Factors that increase the need for new revenues also increase the likelihood that a government might adopt a new tax or raise an old one. Perhaps the most important thing motivating a state to adopt new taxes is, not surprisingly, fiscal hardship. States have not typically adopted new sales and income taxes during prosperous years. Although such taxes are unpopular, a fiscal crisis may make tax increases more palatable for voters and reduce the risk elected officials face when they increase taxes.[39]

Some research suggests that politicians also wait until after an election year to raise unpopular taxes, but the frequency of tax increases the year after a general election also reflects that some states budget for two years (a biennial budget). Budgets that might reflect promises from the previous election are drawn in the first year of the biennium, after a new governor and legislature may have been elected. Less unpopular revenue sources—like the lottery or targeted user fees—may be more likely to be adopted in an election year as politicians try to avoid highly unpopular tax increases. New taxes adopted in one state may also be more likely if a neighboring state has already adopted the tax.[40] One prominent study suggests new taxes are more likely when the same party controls both the legislature and governor's office,[41] but others find

evidence that this is not the case.[42] Similarly, politicians are more likely to increase existing taxes when the political costs are lowest, that is, when the next election is far away and the economy is bad.[43]

Taxes also go down. States often implement tax cuts when the economy is strong and revenues are growing. During the boom of the mid- to late 1990s, 44 states enacted tax cuts. Tax cuts are often packaged as a means to stimulate a state's economy, although one think tank report suggests that states with the largest tax cuts of the 1990s had the biggest fiscal problems and were more likely to have their credit rating downgraded in the next decade. Between 2001 and 2006, states with the largest tax cuts had weaker job growth.[44]

What Are the Effects of Taxes?

Do taxes help or hurt long-run economic development? This is one of the more contentious questions in politics as well as in the academic world of economists and political scientists. Some economic theory assumes that growth depends on the development of physical and human capital; that is, on the amount that machines and people can produce. Human capital includes education, skill, and training. Physical capital can be seen in factories, tools, roads, and equipment. Traditional models of growth assume that taxes are just part of some equilibrium level of capital and that economic growth results from technical changes that increase productivity.

---

[39] Hansen, *The Politics of Taxation.*

[40] Francis Berry and William D. Berry, "State Lottery Adoptions as Policy Innovations," *American Political Science Review* (1990): 395–415.

[41] Hansen, *The Politics of Taxation.*

[42] Francis Berry and William D. Berry, "Tax Innovation in the States: Capitalizing on Political Opportunity," *American Journal of Political Science* (1992): 715–42.

[43] Francis Berry and William D. Berry, "The Politics of Tax Increases in the States," *American Journal of Political Science* (1994): 855–99.

[44] Nicholas Johnson and Brian Filipowich, *Tax Cuts and Continued Consequences* (Washington, D.C.: Center for Budget and Policy Priorities, 2006).

But things are more complex than this. There are different types of taxes—some might discourage the formation of human and physical capital, some might have fewer effects, and other taxes might actually encourage capital formation. And different taxes have different effects on how people spend their money and invest. In other words, the relationship between taxes and economic growth depends on how the money is raised and what it is spent on. Taxes that are spent on education, for example, can generate positive effects on the formation of human capital—effects that a private market might not produce.[45] However, the personal income tax might also discourage entrepreneurial activity.[46] Taxes on corporate earnings, on the other hand, might discourage economic growth,[47] but when corporate taxes are low relative to high personal income taxes, entrepreneurial activity might be encouraging because people have greater incentives to incorporate businesses.[48]

Some studies show positive effects of state taxation on state economic growth, and some studies find negative effects.[49] Results are sensitive to the statistical methods used, the time period examined, and the tax or spending patterns that are examined. Studies of state taxing and spending from the 1950s found no relationship between taxes and growth.[50] Some studies from the 1970s and early 1980s found a negative relationship, with one noting that welfare spending harmed economic growth, whereas business taxes increased growth.[51] Further evidence shows that state tax increases used to fund welfare payments depress economic growth;[52] however, state taxes spent on education, highways, and public health and safety have been shown to have favorable impacts on the location decisions of businesses.[53]

One overview of these studies concluded that most found "a weak or insignificant relationship between taxes and economic performance" because they failed to account for what taxes were spent on. Taxes dedicated to health, education, and highways were found to have a positive effect on private investment and employment in a state, but welfare spending had a negative effect. The authors concluded that their findings should not be interpreted as a prescription for curtailing welfare spending. They noted, rather, that states face a "vicious cycle" in a prolonged economic slump. They risk crowding out public investment in health, education, streets, and highways if they increase welfare spending alone, but raising taxes to fund public investment and welfare may further depress the economy.[54]

[45] Robert Lucas, "On the Mechanics of Economic Development," *Journal of Monetary Economics* (1988): 3–42; and Enrico Moretti, "Estimating the External Return to Higher Education," *Journal of Econometrics* (2003): 175–202.

[46] William M. Gentry and R. Glenn Hubbard, "Tax Policy and Entrepreneurial Entry," *American Economic Review* (2000): 283–87.

[47] Young Lee and Roger H. Gordon, "Tax Structure and Economic Growth," *Journal of Public Economics* (2005).

[48] J. B. Cullen and Roger H. Gordon, "Taxes and Entrepreneurial Activity: Theory and Evidence for the U.S.," NBER Working Paper no. 9015 (New York: National Bureau of Economic Research, 2002).

[49] James Heckman "A Life-Cycle Model of Earnings, Learning, and Consumption," *Journal of Political Economy* 84, no. 4: S11–S44; in contrast, see P. A. Trostel, "The Effect of Taxation on Human Capital," *Journal of Political Economy* (1993): 327–50.

[50] Clark C. Bloom, *State and Local Tax Differentials and the Location of Manufacturing* (Iowa City, Iowa: Bureau of Business and Economic Research, 1955); Wilbur Thompson and John M. Mattila, *An Econometric Model of Postwar State Economic Development* (Detroit, Mich.: Wayne State University Press, 1959); and Dennis W. Carlton, "Why New Firms Locate Where they Do," in *Interregional Movements and Regional Growth*, ed. W. Wheaton (Washington, D.C.: Urban Institute, 1979).

[51] Thomas Romans and Ganti Subrahmanyam, "State and Local Taxes, Transfers, and Regional Economic Growth," *Southern Economic Journal* (1979): 435–44; and Robert J. Newman, "Industry Migration and Growth in the South," *Review of Economics and Statistics* (1983): 76–86.

[52] Romans and Subrahmanyam, "State and Local Taxes"; and L. Jay Helms, "The Effect of State and Local Taxes on Economic Growth: A Time Series-Cross Sectional Approach," *Review of Economics and Statistics* 67 (1985): 574–82.

[53] Helms, "The Effect of State and Local Taxes on Economic Growth."

[54] Alaeddin Mofidi and Joe A. Stone, "Do State and Local Taxes Affect Economic Growth?" *Review of Economics and Statistics* (1990): 686–91.

Trends in State and Local Revenues

Governments have grown in size since the 1950s. With this growth and with changes in the economy, the mix of revenues that now fund state governments has changed. Federal revenues sent to the states increased sharply from 1955 through 1975 and now play a larger role in state budgets than they did 50 years ago. States now collect about twice as much of their overall revenues from income taxes than they did 50 years before and have been relying more on fees and charges (tuition) to fill out their revenue portfolios since the 1980s. Although states have increased their reliance on federal funds, income taxes, and fees, a much smaller proportion of state revenues is now generated by selective sales taxes on gasoline.[55]

As states struggle to recover from the 2002 recession, they appear to be relying on ways to raise revenues that present the least political challenges. An overview of budget proposals from the state's governors for 2006–2007 found that the largest increase in revenues would be coming from cigarette taxes (nearly $1 billion in new revenues). The next largest source of new funds was from fees (tuition). Governors proposed much more modest increases in state sales taxes while reducing net revenues collected via the personal income tax.[56] If these choices mark a trend, state revenue sources may grow more regressive over time.

Where Does the Money Go? Government Spending

Discussing state and local revenue sources before examining what government spends the money on is a bit like putting the cart before the horse. Revenues are generated in large measure to satisfy public demands for programs and services and to fund budget drivers—the major programs that state and local governments operate.

Figures 10.5 and 10.6 illustrate the major program spending areas for state and local governments, respectively. State and local governments combine to spend about $2.6 trillion: $1.3 trillion by the 50 states and $1.3 trillion by local governments.

Social Services: Health Care

Thirty-six percent of money spent by states funds social services. Social service spending, the largest and fastest-growing component of state budgets, is dominated by health care. When looking at Figure 10.5, it is important to remember that a large part of overall state spending is financed by the federal government. Most of the federal dollars going to states are from the **Medicaid** program. Medicaid accounts for most of state social service spending—about 20 percent of all state expenditures.[57] Given the absence of national health care insurance and the high costs for private health insurance, states are left with much of the responsibility for providing health care to the 47 million Americans who are uninsured. Federal funds come with standards that define minimal levels of service the states must provide, and federal dollars are given to match state spending on Medicaid. If states want to provide additional health care beyond the minimal standards—for example, offering prenatal care or providing basic health care insurance for the working poor— they must spend more. A growing proportion of social service spending is used to fund prescription drug purchases.

---

[55] Garand and Baudoin, "Fiscal Policy in the American States," 293.

[56] National Association of State Government Budget Officers, "Fiscal Survey of the States 2005," http://www.nasbo.org/Publications/fiscalsurvey/fsfall2005.pdf.

[57] Kenneth Feingold et al., "Social Program Spending and State Fiscal Crisis," Urban Institute Occasional Paper no. 70 (Washington, D.C.: Urban Institute, 2003).

Figure 10.5

Major State Government Spending Programs, 2005

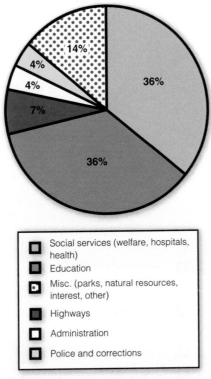

Note: Total direct state expenditures = $1.281 trillion. Excludes $167 billion in insurance trust and pension payments.

Source: U.S. Census Bureau, "State and Local Government Finances by Level of Government and by State: 2005," 2005, http://www.census.gov/govs/state/0500usst.html.

Because spending on hospitals, long-term care for the elderly, mental health, and other health care-related services comprise the single largest part of a state's budget, health care spending is the largest target for cuts in times of economic downturn. Given the size of health care in the overall state budget, it is nearly impossible to reduce spending without rolling back reimbursement rates paid to health care providers (doctors, hospitals, and nursing homes), freezing reimbursement levels, or cutting back on the number of people eligible for benefits. In times of fiscal crunch, states will cut back on health care, even if it means losing federal Medicaid matching dollars.[58] Nonetheless, the proportion of state spending on health care has been growing. Local governments, in contrast, spend much less on social services, as these programs are largely administered by the states.

Social Services: Aid to the Poor

Assistance to the poor, or welfare programs, works in a similar manner as medical benefit programs. Federal government funds are sent to the states and topped up by a state if it expands services offered or people who are eligible. Cash assistance to the poor represents a much smaller proportion of state spending on social services than health care: less than 20 percent of all social service spending.

[58] Feingold et al., "Social Program Spending and State Fiscal Crisis."

Figure 10.6

Major Local Government Spending Programs

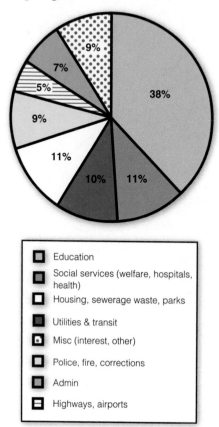

Note: Total direct local government expenditures = $1.3 trillion. Excludes $27 billion in insurance trust expenditures.

Source: U.S. Census Bureau, "Census of Governments." http://www.census.gov/govs/estimate/0500ussl_1.html.

Social welfare programs include transferring cash to individuals and providing services. In 1996, Congress passed the Temporary Assistance to Needy Families (TANF) block grant program and shifted much of the responsibility for welfare assistance programs from the national government to the states. The TANF program also represented a contraction of total welfare benefits. By 1998, states and communities were spending 20 percent less on cash assistance to the poor than they were in 1992.[59]

Education

The second-largest area of direct state spending illustrated in Figure 10.5 is education—35.6 percent of total spending by the states. But if we consider state money spent by local school districts, education would be the single largest area of state spending. The amount of state funds spent on education is actually much larger than what is suggested by Figure 10.5 because states transfer hundreds of billions of dollars to local governments to fund

[59] Mark Rom, "Transforming State Health and Welfare Programs," in Gray and Hanson, *Politics in the American States*, 8th ed.

K–12 schools. Local schools have their own revenue source (local property taxes), but state funds are used to supplement what schools raise in local taxes. Because these funds are actually spent at the local level, they are included in our picture of the local government spending mix (Figure 10.6). If we had illustrated state spending just as a percentage of state-generated funds (excluding federal funds for social programs), education would be the largest area of state expenditure. Figure 10.5 illustrates funds that are spent directly by the state and omits state funds spent by local school districts.

Unlike local K–12 schools, state colleges and universities have no local tax revenues and are totally reliant on state funds and tuition they collect from students. The majority of direct state spending on education (80 percent) goes to operate universities and colleges. The National Association of State Budget Officials notes that "when the state fiscal picture darkens, higher education often is the first category of spending to cut." Colleges and universities are an easy target because they are one of the largest state services that allow costs, however painful, to be transferred to users (students or their parents). Many states responded to the 2002 fiscal crisis by accelerating the shift toward financing higher education with higher direct charges (fees and tuition), while reducing general fund revenues spent. Over the decade that ended in 2004, tuition and fees increased 47 percent at public four-year universities.[60]

Figure 10.6 illustrates that education is the largest component of local government spending—38 percent of all local expenditures, 94 percent of which is spent on elementary and secondary education (K–12 schools). Most of this money is raised by local property taxes or provided by the states and is spent by local school districts. The largest cost of education is labor: paying salaries for teachers, counselors, school administrators, technology staff, cooks, and so on.

Pensions and Unemployment

A major component of state expenditures is payments from insurance and trust funds. States spend about as much on these programs as on higher education, but they are considered "off budget" because they have their own funding sources. States maintain various trust funds to provide unemployment coverage for state residents or to provide compensation to residents who cannot work because they were injured on the job. States also maintain pension funds to cover their own employees' retirement payments, some of which provide rather generous benefits. In theory, these can be "pay as you go" programs. Workers pay weekly or monthly contributions into an unemployment insurance fund, for example, and are eligible for benefits if they lose work. Likewise, the state, as an employer, matches public employees' contributions to public pension funds to create a pool of money to cover future retirement benefit costs for state workers and public school teachers. Pension funds may be invested in order to increase their value.

In practice, things do not always work this way. When revenues are low, some states and cities forgo contributing to trust funds or borrow from the funds in order to make it appear that their budgets balance. In 2002, state and local employee pension funds were $30 billion in deficit. States have full responsibility for workers' comp and unemployment programs, so these programs do not factor into the local spending mix. For many state governments and some local governments, obligations to fully fund public employee retirement pension accounts may be a looming crisis. It is easy to forgo collecting revenues to cover the costs of pension funds, but if the deficits in such accounts grow over time, it may be harder to make up lost ground. A 2004 survey of cities found 79 percent reporting that their pension funds' fiscal health was eroding. San Diego's public employee pension fund was nearly $2 billion

---

[60] National Association of State Budget Officers, *State Expenditure Report* (Washington, D.C.: National Association of State Budget Officers, 2003).

in deficit in 2004. The city had been providing lavish benefits while reducing payments into the fund. When a stock market crash reduced the value of the fund, the city faced bankruptcy.[61]

Transportation and Highways

About 7 percent of state spending and 5 percent of local spending are for transportation. Most state expenditures on transportation are funded by earmarked revenues placed in special non-general fund accounts, usually from gasoline taxes. Federal funds are also directed to the states for highway construction and cover about 30 percent of transportation spending. States also finance highways with bonds. Transportation represents the largest part of state spending in capital budgets. States spend more on transportation infrastructure than they do on building prisons, universities, housing, and all other infrastructure combined.

Government Administration and Debt Interest

Four percent of state and 7 percent of local expenditure are used to operate public buildings, run court systems (including paying public defenders, judges, and prosecutors), and fund general administrative costs.

Public Safety, Police, and Prisons

Four percent of state spending and 9 percent of local spending finance public safety programs. At the state level, 66 percent of public safety costs fund corrections operations (mostly salaries for prison guards and other staff); most of the remainder pays for state troopers (highway patrols). The operation of prisons is a growing part of state budgets. At the local level, most spending in this area supports local police forces.

Do State and Local Spending Actually Reflect What People Want?

Much of governing involves responding to the popular demands for spending. Thus, if a state's population consistently tells politicians they want more spent on schools and playgrounds, we might expect more spent on schools and playgrounds. But there are other factors that might drive spending away from what most voters (or the average voter) might want. This raises at least two questions: how much do state and local spending reflect what people really want? And how much should they reflect what most people want?

In addition to trying to determine the preferences of the general public, elected officials hear from many different interest groups who each want some unique benefit just for themselves: a tax break here, a new road there, higher salaries for prison guards or professors, more spending on somebody's favorite program—public funds to help all sorts of relatively narrow concerns. In many legislative hearings, representatives of rather narrow constituencies may outnumber everyone else.

Governing involves the need to balance these demands and the ability to anticipate other things that also need to be done. These may include things the public might not be paying much attention to or that they might not want to spend much money on. Courts may require states to reduce prison crowding. The business climate may be threatened by traffic gridlock, forcing politicians to find ways to fund transportation projects that only benefit part of a state. Bridges, levees, and tunnels need maintenance or modernization. The fact that these matters may require public investment does not necessarily mean that the public supports such spending.

---

[61] John Ritter, "San Diego Now Enron by the Sea," *USA Today*, 24 October 2004.

Why Is Spending Higher in Some States?

It might come as little surprise that states with more wealth tend to spend more.[62] Wealthy states have a greater tax base, and they also have more complex economies that create demands for rules and regulations—the basic stuff of government. Federal funds, rather than replacing state money, also seem to increase state spending. States that receive more money from the federal government also spend more of their own funds for public services.[63]

One of the primary determinants of spending, however, is political. States where people have more liberal opinions tend to elect liberals, who, regardless of party, spend more on public services. States where people have more conservative opinions tend to elect conservatives, who spend less. Even after accounting for a state's income, liberal states spend more per pupil on education and have more expansive Medicaid and welfare programs.[64] States also spend more on welfare when less affluent voters turn out in higher proportions in state elections.[65]

Budgeting

Deficits and Balanced Budget Requirements

If the federal government decides it wants to spend more than it is collecting in taxes, it can. The federal government can finance its operations by selling long-term U.S. Treasury bonds. Investors buy the bonds and earn interest on their investment over time. This allows for long-term borrowing to finance the

annual operations of the federal government. In recent decades, the federal budget has been in deficit more years than not, which means a large percentage of each federal budget includes funds to pay interest on bonds that are outstanding. Critics of chronic federal deficits look to state **balanced budget rules** as a model for fiscal reform.

Borrowing

State governments cannot run deficits—at least not in the same way the federal government does. Virtually all states—Vermont is the only exception—have constitutional rules that require annual (or biannual) spending to not exceed revenues. Many states actually write two budgets, with balanced budget rules applying to the state's **operating budget**. Operating funds cover spending on services, salaries, and purchases of supplies. States might borrow funds in the short term to manage cash flow problems during the year (some tax collections peak in certain months, but government expenses, such as paying salaries, are more constant). Short-term debts are supposed to be repaid by the end of the budget cycle. **Capital budgets** can be a separate matter; states and local governments issue long-term bonds to finance capital investment in roads, bridges, buildings, and other infrastructure. Capital budgets may be funded with long-term borrowing, which is a form of deficit spending. Borrowing, rather than paying costs up front, can be seen as a fair way of paying for infrastructure that will be in use for years. Paying for a road, a bridge, or a sports arena all at once means that some of those who paid for it will die or move away before the project is completed and thus never benefit from it.

---

[62] Dye, *Politics Economics, and the Public*; and Richard Hofferbert, "The Relationship between Public Policy and Some Structural and Environmental Variables in the American States," *American Political Science Review* (1966): 73–82.

[63] Garand, "Explaining Government Growth in the US States."

[64] Robert S. Erikson, Gerald C. Wright, and John P. McIver, *Statehouse Democracy: Public Opinion and Policy in the American States* (Cambridge: Cambridge University Press, 1993), 85.

[65] Kim Q. Hill and Jan Leighley, "The Policy Consequences of Class Bias in State Electorates," *American Journal of Political Science* (1992): 351–65.

In addition to having balanced budget rules, some states require that voters approve the sale of any bonds that will be used to finance long-term borrowing. Some also require a supermajority vote in the legislature before the proposal can go to voters for approval.

Do Budgeting Rules Matter?

But do these budgeting rules really make any difference? Some balanced budget rules have weak provisions for enforcement. Most studies suggest that tough rules do work at preventing deficits when they are combined with limits on government borrowing, but weak rules do not.[66] Some rules simply require the governor to submit a balanced budget to the legislature or require the legislature to enact a balanced budget at the start of the fiscal year. But a state with such rules may still be allowed to run a deficit if revenue or spending estimates end up wrong.[67] Rules that simply require the budget to be balanced when written may be less effective than rules that require it to be balanced at the end of the year. Likewise, constitutional rules may be more effective than regular laws that politicians can easily amend. Finally, balanced budget rules may be more effective when enforced by an independently elected state supreme court than when enforcement depends on a court appointed by the politicians who write the budget.[68] One study noted that balanced budget rules were more effective when Republicans were in office.[69]

Some rules regulating long-term capital borrowing don't necessarily lead to less state indebtedness. Requiring a supermajority vote in the legislature for transportation infrastructure bills, for example, may create incentives to place a transportation project in every representative's district.[70] Even voters seem more likely to approve state-level borrowing if a project is proposed for their local area.[71]

Budget Surpluses

Independent of whatever these balanced budget rules may produce, states have a fairly predictable record of not only balancing their budgets but also ending with a surplus. In many years, states maintain a surplus "rainy day fund" to be used in times of crisis. When 50 state budges were considered across a 40-year period starting in 1961 (that is, 2,000 different budgets), 83 percent produced surpluses. Texas and New Mexico ran in the black every single year. Although Massachusetts (52 percent of budgets had a surplus), Hawaii (55 percent), and Rhode Island (60 percent) were least likely to run surpluses, they usually did.[72] With state governments usually running surpluses, they soften the effects that federal deficits might have on the national economy. States and communities run deficits at their own peril. Lenders charge states more in interest if they have more debt (relative to the size of their economies).[73]

---

[66] James Poterba, "Budget Institutions and Fiscal Policy in the U.S. States," *American Economic Review* 86, no. 2 (1996): 395–400.

[67] James Poterba, "Balanced Budget Rules and Fiscal Policy: Evidence from the States," *National Tax Journal* (1995): 329–36.

[68] Hening Bohn and Robert P. Inman, "Balanced Budget Rules and Public Deficits: Evidence from the U.S. States," NBER Working Paper no. W5533, 1996, http://ssrn.com/abstract=4069.

[69] James Alt and Robert Lowry, "Divided Government, Fiscal Institutions, and Budget Deficits: Evidence from the States," *American Political Science Review* 88 (1994): 811–28.

[70] Kiewiet and Szakaly, "Constitutional Limitations of Borrowing."

[71] Shaun Bowler and Todd Donovan, *Demanding Choices: Opinion, Voting, and Direct Democracy* (Ann Arbor: University of Michigan Press, 1998).

[72] Garand and Baudoin, "Fiscal Policy in the American States."

[73] Tamim Bayoumi, Morris Goldstein, and Geoffrey Woglom, "Do Credit Markets Discipline Sovereign Borrowers?" *Journal of Money, Credit and Banking* 27 (1995): 1046–59.

Boom to Bust Budgeting

When the national economy was booming and tax revenues were rising, it was relatively easy for states to adopt new spending programs while also balancing budgets or running a surplus. When the national economy cooled in 2008, 41 states faced deficits in their 2008 or 2009 budgets. Many were left with spending commitments made during an earlier period of strong revenue growth.

Budgeting in recession years, however, can encourage great creativity. In addition to cutting spending and raising taxes, states responded by delaying payments they owed, raising tuition, offering early retirement programs to lower salary costs, expanding gambling, raiding transportation and pension funds, mortgaging funds awarded in a settlement with tobacco companies, and borrowing money to fund operations. Some managed to use rainy day funds to help balance their budget. Smokers helped several states balance their books by paying higher cigarette taxes. States often cut spending on their largest programs (health care) during recessions, when the need is greatest for public services and economic stimulus produced by government spending. The 2008 recession was not bad news for all states. Revenues boosted by high energy prices left Alaska, North Dakota, and Wyoming with surpluses and the ability to increase spending on their colleges and universities.

Summary

In surveys of state and local fiscal politics from previous decades, the taxing and spending patterns of states and communities were often explained largely in terms of "environmental" factors. That is, wealthy states were said to spend more because they had more. Political factors, such as public opinion, budgeting rules, and other partisan and institutional forces, were largely dismissed because most studies found little effect of politics on fiscal policy.

The dismissal of political and institutional forces was probably a mistake resulting from flawed measures of political influence and from a lack of investigation. We now have detailed measures of state public opinion and decades of research examining the effects that taxing and spending limits (TELs), balanced budgeting rules, direct democracy, and popular opinion have on taxation and spending. Although some debate the magnitude of the effects of such rules or of public opinion, it is clear that politics matters, perhaps more than anything else, in determining who gets what from government via fiscal policy.

Key Terms

Balanced budget rules

Capital budget

Cost of living allowances (COLAs)

Elastic demand

Elasticity

Flat rate tax

Inelastic demand

Medicaid

Operating budget

Progressive tax

Regressive tax

Sin tax

Supermajority vote requirement

Tax equity

Tax and expenditure limits (TELS)

User fees

Adjudication: To settle a dispute by judicial procedure.

Adjudicator: Legal professional trained in resolving disputes between parties outside of the courtroom.

Administrative rules: Regulations, restrictions, and requirements written by executive agencies and used to implement public policy enacted through the legislature, the courts, or the governor.

Administrative rules review committee: The state legislative committee whose job it is to check whether the thousands of rules that a state's executive agencies propose each year follow the intent of the legislation that authorized that agency to establish those rules.

Adversarial argument: As in a courtroom, when two parties to a dispute make their best arguments to a neutral third party, who then decides the dispute. This is as opposed to a negotiated settlement, where the parties work back and forth between themselves to resolve the dispute.

Amend: To modify a bill in the lawmaking process.

Amendatory veto: The power of some states' governors to send a passed bill back to the legislature asking for specific changes in it before he or she will sign it.

Appropriations bill: A bill that authorizes a state agency to spend money in specific ways.

Articles of Confederation: The country's first constitution, ratified in March 1781.

Astroturf campaign: An artificial campaign orchestrated by an interest group to appear as though it is growing naturally from the grassroots.

At-large elections: Many elections for local government, such as city or county councils (or commissions), are often contested such that every voter in the jurisdiction votes on every council position up for election. Voters cast one vote per position being contested. Rather than representing a specific geographic area within the jurisdiction, elected officials represent the entire jurisdiction. At-large elections can allow a cohesive majority group to sweep every position.

Balanced budget rules: A requirement that a state's budget has revenues equal to spending. Rules may apply to projected revenues and spending or to actual levels.

Bench trial: Trial with no jury, where the judge or judges alone decide the outcome.

Bicameral: Having two chambers, such as in 49 state legislatures and Congress, which have a house of representatives (called by another name in some states) and a senate.

Bill: A proposed law that is formally introduced by a legislator for consideration by his or her chamber.

Bill of Rights: The first ten amendments to the U.S. Constitution, ratified in December 1791, which ensure the protection of individuals and the states from the national government.

Bill sponsor: The legislator who proposes that a bill be considered by his or her chamber.

Bipartisan Campaign Reform Act of 2002: Also known as BCRA, this act not only banned federal political parties from using soft money for federal election activity but also restricted some activities of state and local parties.

Blanket primary: Primary elections nominate candidates for the general election. In a blanket primary election, candidates from all parties are listed on the same ballot. Voters participate regardless of their party affiliation, and are able to select candidates of different parties for different offices.

Block grants: Fixed-sum federal grants allocated by formula that give state and local governments broad leeway in designing and implementing designated programs.

Bureaucracy: The administrative structure of any large, complex organization, like a government, that is characterized by hierarchical control and fixed rules of procedure.

Campaign finance regulations: Rules and statutes regulating the ways in which money can be gathered and spent by political campaigns, defining what is required, permissible, and impermissible.

Capital budget: The portion of state spending on infrastructure, such as buildings, bridges, and roads. Capital budgets may be exempt from balanced budget rules.

Casework: The activities of a legislator and his or her staff in helping constituents with specific problems, usually with state government. For example, a legislator may help a constituent solve a problem with getting a driver's license or adjusting a state tax bill.

Categorical grants: Grants from the federal government to states and cities that are for specific purposes as defined by Congress.

Caucus: Used by parties to nominate candidates, with party members informally meeting, deliberating, and casting a vote for their preferred candidate.

Centralization: Empowering a national governing authority with unitary control and authority.

Chamber floor: Where and when the members of one chamber (the house or senate) meet as a group to debate and vote on legislation.

Citizen legislature: A state legislature that is largely a part-time body, whose members are paid a modest salary, have little staff, meet infrequently, and are expected to have careers and interests other than the state legislature.

Civil service: Appointed administrators and public employees. Civil service jobs are usually awarded based on merit exams and qualifications rather than political connections.

Civil service system: A system of hiring, promoting, and firing government workers based on job-related criteria rather than on political connections or other biases.

Class action lawsuit: A lawsuit brought by one party on behalf of a group of individuals all having the same grievance.

Clean money and public financing of campaigns: Some states provide public funds for candidates seeking political office if they agree to limits on the contributions they receive from private sources.

Clientele politics: A style of politics where the people in control of government provide something of value in exchange for political support. Support for clientele parties is based on what sort of favors a party can supply or the personal contacts that the party builds with supporters.

Closed primary: A primary nomination election in which voters registered with a political party are permitted to vote only for candidates of the party with whom they are registered.

Coercive federalism: A federalist arrangement whereby the federal government spearheads and funds programs; also referred to as creative federalism.

Collective action problem: The problem of coordinating a group of people to achieve a common goal.

Commerce Clause: Gives Congress the power "to regulate Commerce with foreign Nations, and among the several States, and with the Indian Tribes." Used by Congress to expand its power vis-à-vis the states.

Committee jurisdiction: The policy area and bills that a legislative committee has the responsibility to consider in its deliberations.

Common law: The system of laws originated and developed in England, based on court decisions, the doctrines implicit in those decisions, and customs and usages rather than on codified written laws.

Commutation: The power of some governors unilaterally to reduce the sentence of a person convicted of a crime.

Comparative method: An approach to political analysis that entails comparing units of analysis (such as states or communities) on more than one characteristic to help understand the relationships among those characteristics.

Confederal system: Also known as a confederacy, a system of governance whereby the national government is subject to the control of subnational, autonomous governments.

Conference committee: A temporary legislative committee made up of equal members of the senate and house who meet to reconcile the differences between the versions of a bill passed by the two chambers and to propose a single version for both chambers to consider.

Conflict of interest: A situation in which a government decision maker may personally benefit from his or her official actions or a judge has a personal interest in the outcome of a case that may bias his or her actions in that case.

Constitutional initiative: An initiative measure that amends a state's constitution or adds new language to a constitution. Constitutional measures can alter rules about a state's political process. If approved by voters, constitutional measures are typically more difficult for elected officials to amend or repeal than statutory initiatives.

Contiguous: Areas of land that touch (except for islands).

Contract lobbyist: A professional lobbyist who temporarily works on behalf of a client.

Cooperative federalism: A federalism arrangement whereby responsibilities for most governmental functions are interdependent, shared between the federal and state governments.

Cost of living allowances (COLAs): A pay increase that matches the rate of inflation. COLAs maintain a fixed level of purchasing power, not an increase in purchasing power.

Council–manager system: Form of city government in which an elected council acts as a legislature, with no mayor. An appointed, professional city manager is hired to oversee executive functions. Some council–manager systems have one council member serve as a ceremonial mayor with no formal powers.

Court of last resort: Those courts whose decisions cannot be appealed to another court; these courts have the final word on a given set of laws. Typically called the supreme court (or something similar).

Cracking: Dispersing a party's voters among many districts so it will win fewer district races.

Cumulative voting: A form of voting in at-large elections for city councils and other bodies. Voters are given as many votes as positions up for election on the council. Rather than casting one vote per council position, voters can, if they want, give one candidate multiple votes. This makes it less likely that a cohesive majority will sweep all positions up for election.

Decentralization: Devolving to citizens or their elected representatives more power to make decisions, including the formation and implementation of public policies.

Defendant: The person or institution against whom an action is brought in a court of law; the person being sued or accused of a crime.

Descriptive representation: The idea that a representative should reflect the characteristics of the people (the constituents) whom she (or he) represents. Characteristics could include race, ethnicity, gender, and other traits related to the identity of the representative's constituents.

Devolution: The decentralization of power and authority from a central government to state or local governments.

Dillon's rule: Concept about the nature of local government powers (or "municipal corporations") from John F. Dillon, scholar and judge, circa 1872. Whereas states may be seen as having powers beyond those listed in the U.S. Constitution, local governments have only those powers explicitly granted to them by a state. Cities, counties, school districts, and "special districts" are thus legal entities created by their states.

Direct initiative: A measure proposed by a citizen or group. If the proposal qualifies with sufficient signatures, it is voted on directly by the public and becomes law if approved.

Direct primary: An election in which voters select one candidate affiliated with a political party for each elected office; the party nominees later face one another in a general election.

Director of state courts: Administrator hired by a court system to handle the bureaucratic chores of the system, including personnel and budget issues.

District magnitude: The number of people elected to represent a political jurisdiction. In most American legislative races, district magnitude equals one. In at-large races, in multimember districts, and in most proportional representation systems, district magnitude is greater than one.

Disturbance theory: A macrolevel theory that assumes groups emerge in response to societal changes.

Divided government: When two of the three legs of the legislative process (the governor, the house, and the senate) are controlled by different parties.

Docket: A calendar of the cases awaiting action in a court.

Double jeopardy: The prosecution of a defendant for a criminal offense for which he or she has already been acquitted; this is prohibited by the Fifth Amendment to the U.S. Constitution.

Drug courts: Trial courts of limited jurisdiction used in some states and localities to prosecute certain minor drug and related offenses, with a focus on reducing recidivism and drug abuse treatment. Judges and lawyers working in these courts specialize in the issues surrounding drug abuse and addiction.

Dual federalism: A system of federalism whereby governmental functions are apportioned so that the national and subnational governments are accorded sovereign power within their respective spheres; sometimes referred to as "layer cake" federalism.

Earmark: In the context of government budgeting, the reservation of the revenue from a certain fee or tax into its own fund to be spent only for a specified purpose.

Earned media: Generating newsworthy events or stories for free publicity.

Efficacy: The sense that one's effort at something can make a difference. Personal efficacy is the sense that you are able to understand politics. External efficacy is the belief that public officials will respond to your political acts.

Elastic demand: Demand for something is said to be elastic if it responds to changes in price. If a tax raises the price of something that has elastic demand, such as travel or some luxury items, the tax may reduce consumption of the good.

Elasticity: The responsiveness of something to a change in price.

Electioneering: Explicitly supporting or opposing candidates or political parties, including recruiting and endorsing candidates, fundraising, phone banking, canvassing, and advertising.

Ex post oversight: When the legislature investigates how well an agency is carrying out the intent of a law.

Executive budget: A reform of the Progressive era under which the first proposal of the budget for a government's next fiscal year is put together by the chief executive, whether it is the president, governor, or mayor.

Federal preemption: Federal government taking regulatory action that overrides state laws.

Federalism: The structural relationship between a national government and its constitutive states.

Fiscal illusion: One explanation of government growth is fiscal illusion. The idea is that when states collect revenues by withholding taxes from paychecks or by taxing corporations, taxes are hidden. People might thus underestimate the true cost of public services, causing them to support more spending. James C. Garand, in "Explaining Government Growth in the U.S. States," contends that little empirical evidence supports this explanation.

Flat rate tax: A flat rate income tax applies the same tax rate to everyone, regardless of their income levels.

Free-rider problem: When the benefit of some valuable good or service cannot be restricted to those who pay for it.

Full veto: The power of the chief executive to block the passage of an entire passed bill, subject to override by a supermajority vote of the legislature.

Functional party model: A theory that parties are pragmatic, self-interested organizations, striving to maximize votes in order to win elections and control political office.

Gatekeeping: Determining which questions and decisions will and will not be considered.

General jurisdiction: Referring to courts that deal with virtually any type of case.

General Revenue Sharing (GRS): A federal grant-in-aid program that provides financial aid to subnational units but does not prescribe how those units are to allocate the funding.

Gerrymander: The process of drawing governmental district boundaries for political advantage.

Good-Time Charlie: Some state governors in the mid-20th century who were less active in attacking public policy problems and less educated, older, and less qualified than most governors serving since that time; the term was coined by political scientist Larry Sabato.

Grandfather clause: Exemptions to post–Civil War rules granted to whites, based on the fact that they had a father or grandfather who was a citizen prior to the Civil War. As slaves (noncitizens), blacks were excluded by grandfather clauses.

Gubernatorial powers: Institutional and informal tools that a governor can use to develop and promote public policy, manage the state bureaucracy, and act as an intergovernmental relations (IGR) manager, among other duties.

Head of state: The main public representative of a government.

Home rule: The delegation of power from a state government to local governments. Home rule charters define the boundaries of local government autonomy and result in less state control over local government affairs.

Hypothesis: A potential answer to a research question that is based on theory and that will be tested by observing data in the world.

Implementation: The execution by government agencies of laws passed by the legislature.

Incorporation of the Bill of Rights: A legal doctrine whereby parts of the U.S. Bill of Rights are applied to the states through the Fourteenth Amendment's Due Process Clause.

Incumbent: The person currently holding a position.

Incumbent-protection district: A governmental district drawn to give electoral advantage to the incumbent.

Indirect initiative: A measure proposed by a citizen or group. If the proposal qualifies, it is directed to the state legislature. The legislature can vote to approve the measure as written or refer it to the voters for approval. The legislature may also refer an alternate proposal along with the initiative proposal.

Individualistic political culture: The general and informal set of beliefs and attitudes that politics in a state or community is a place where individuals can work to advance their personal economic and social interests largely the same as they would do in private business.

Inelastic demand: Demand for something is said to be inelastic if it does not respond to changes in price. If a tax raises the price of something that has inelastic demand, such as basic foods, medical care, or things that people are addicted to, the tax may not reduce consumption of the good.

In-house lobbyist: A professional lobbyist who is a permanent employee of an interest group.

Injunction: A court order prohibiting someone from taking some action.

Interest group: A formally organized body of individuals, organizations, or public or private enterprises sharing common goals and joining in a collective attempt to influence the electoral and policy-making processes.

Interest group system density: The number of functioning groups relative to the size of a state's economy.

Interest group system diversity: The spread of groups in a state across social and economic realms.

Intergovernmental relations: The interactions among the federal government, the states, and local governments.

Intermediate courts of appeal: Courts that hear appeals of trial decisions and are concerned with whether the trial was fair and conducted with proper procedures. ICAs were developed as a way to take the burden of routine appeals off of supreme courts so that supreme courts can focus on the most important cases.

Issue advocacy: A form of political speech focusing on issues of public concern that mentions issues and the positions taken on those issues by elected officials or candidates, but stops short of expressly advocating the support or defeat of those elected officials or candidates.

Jacksonian democracy: A broad philosophy of government, associated with the era when Andrew Jackson was president (1829–1837), which emphasized executive power, broad suffrage (for white males), the election of many public officials, laissez-faire economics, and patronage appointments for government employment.

Judicial review: The power of a supreme court to judge whether a law is in violation of the state constitution and, if so, to nullify that law.

Jurisdiction: Geographical or topical area over which a court, institution, or official has power and authority.

Jury: A randomly selected group of citizens who are sworn by a court to hear and render a verdict and/or set a penalty in a trial.

Lame duck: An elected official who will not or cannot run for his or her current office in the next election; also, any official who has been voted out of office and is serving in the last days of a term before the new official is sworn in.

Land Ordinance of 1785: An act of Congress that set a process to sell land west of the Appalachian Mountains, north of the Ohio River, and east of the Mississippi River for $1.00 per acre. The act set rules for the creation of townships in the area.

Legal brief: A document stating legal facts and arguments.

Legislative intent: What the legislature meant for a piece of legislation to do when it passed it.

Legislative professionalism: When a legislature is established to be largely a full-time body, with members who are paid a living wage, have plenty of staff, and believe that legislating is their primary job.

Legislative referendum: Legislation approved by the legislature but referred to the voters for final approval. Some legislation, like constitutional amendments (in most states) or bond issues (in some states and communities), must be referred to voters for final approval.

Legislative turnover: The degree to which the membership of a legislature changes after an election.

Leviathan: The model of government as an entity that seeks to increase revenues beyond even what the public might demand.

Limited jurisdiction: Referring to courts that handle cases on only certain topics, such as traffic courts or probate courts.

Line-item veto: The power of some governors to block only parts of passed appropriations bills from becoming law, subject to override by a supermajority vote of the legislature.

Literacy tests: Post–Civil War rules that denied blacks the vote; literacy tests included tests designed to be too difficult for most people to pass. The test could ask people to interpret passages from the U.S. Constitution and allowed local officials the discretion to judge if answers were right or wrong. Whites who failed the tests could vote based on a grandfather clause.

Lobbying: Communicating with elected officials in general as well as the systematic effort to shape public policy by pressuring governmental officials to make decisions in line with the goals of an organized interest. The term lobbying comes from the fact that representatives were often approached in the lobby of legislative buildings.

Louisiana Purchase: The purchase of the French Territory of Louisiana (more than 500 million acres of land) from France in 1803. The purchase included land that is now Arkansas, Kansas, Missouri, Iowa, Nebraska, and Oklahoma as well as much of what is now Louisiana, Colorado, Minnesota, Montana, North and South Dakota, and Wyoming.

Machines: A term for local political party organizations that used patronage and clientele politics to control elections in many U.S. cities.

Majority-minority district: Legislative districts where district lines are drawn so that people from a specific minority group comprise a majority of voters in the district.

Malapportionment: When the districts in a legislative chamber are not equal in population.

Media market: Region where the population is exposed to the same (or similar) media offerings, including the same television and radio stations and newspapers.

Mental health courts: Trial courts of limited jurisdiction used in some states and localities to prosecute certain offenses by those who have a mental illness, with a focus on reducing recidivism by treating the mental illness. Judges and lawyers working in these courts specialize in the issues surrounding mental health.

Merit Plan: A method used to select at least some judges in 24 states whereby (1) a panel of experts recommends a few candidates for a judicial opening to the governor, (2) who then appoints one person to that position for a trial period, and (3) after which the judge faces a retention election to see whether he or she will earn a full term.

Meyer v. Grant: A 1988 U.S. Supreme Court ruling against a Colorado law that made it a felony to pay for the collection of signatures on initiative and referendum petitions. The Court ruled that spending to collect signatures was "core political speech" and that no state could ban campaign spending on signature collection. Since 2005, however, two federal appellate courts (the 8th Circuit and 9th Circuit) have permitted states to ban payment per signature, thus requiring that paid petitioners receive a salary or an hourly wage.

Mobilization of bias: The benefiting of private, organized interests in an interest group system.

Model city charter: Recommendations for how city political institutions should be arranged. Model charters published by the National Municipal League (now called the National Civic League) have been published since 1900.

Moralistic political culture: The general and informal set of beliefs and attitudes that politics in a state or community is intended to enhance the public good and for the uplifting of the have-nots of society.

Muckraking journalists: Journalists and authors who exposed issues of political corruption, public health dangers, and child labor practices. The writing of muckrakers was featured in newspapers and magazines, such as *Cosmopolitan, Harper's Weekly,* and *McClure's.* Some famous muckrakers included Thomas Nast, Lincoln Steffens, and Upton Sinclair.

Multimember district (MMD): Legislative districts that elect more than one representative. Some state legislative districts and many local councils have more than one representative elected per district.

Multiparty politics: Political systems where three or more parties are able to win office. The United States, in contrast, is dominated by two-party politics.

Municipal charters: The set of rules that define how cities are structured, what the powers of local officials are, and how local elections shall be conducted.

National Governors Conference: Bipartisan association of the 55 state and territorial governors, supported by research and training staff.

National Supremacy Clause: Stipulates that the U.S. Constitution and national laws and treaties "shall be the supreme law of the land."

Necessary and Proper Clause: Also known as the Elastic Clause, it grants Congress the power to make all laws that shall be "necessary and proper for carrying into execution the foregoing powers"; that is, the other congressional powers listed in Article I, Section 8, of the Constitution.

Neutral competence: The value that a government agency should implement policy based only on original legislative intent and its workers' professional norms and training rather than by nonlegislative political pressure.

Nonpartisan blanket primary: All candidates, regardless of their party, face off in the same primary election, with a candidate winning the election outright if he or she wins more than 50 percent of the vote.

Nonpartisan primary: An election to nominate candidates for the general election where candidates have no party labels and all voters can participate. Used in many local elections and at the state level in Nebraska.

Nullification: A constitutional theory, advanced most notably by John C. Calhoun and other advocates of states' rights, espousing the right of a state to declare null and void a law passed by the U.S. Congress that the state found to be unconstitutional or disagreeable.

Office-block ballot: Groups together all candidates running for a single political office by the political office rather than by their party.

Open primary: A primary nomination election. Any registered voter, including independents, can participate. Voters must decide which party's primary they will participate in and can choose only among that party's candidates.

Operating budget: The part of a state's budget dedicated to paying for current operations, such as public services and public employee salaries.

Original jurisdiction: The right of a court to be the first to hear a case; where a case must begin its path through the judicial system.

Out-of-court settlement: An agreement made privately between the parties to a civil suit before a trial court decision.

Outsider gubernatorial candidates: Candidates for governor who are not traditional politicians but who have achieved success in other ways, such as in business or as entertainers.

Override: When the legislature passes a law despite a gubernatorial veto, usually by a supermajority vote in each chamber.

Packing: Concentrating one party's voters into a few districts so as to "waste" those votes over 50 percent, allowing the other party to win more district races.

Pardon: The power of some governors to throw out the conviction of a person convicted of a crime.

Participation bias: The difference between the general population of eligible voters and the people who actually participate in elections. Bias in participation exists if participants are substantially different than nonparticipants.

Partisan dealignment: The weakening of the attachment that voters have to a political party.

Partisan primary: A primary election to decide a party's nominee for the general election ballot.

Party boss: The head of an urban or state party machine who controls elections and the disbursement of patronage.

Party caucus: All the legislators in a given chamber from a given party, such as the house Democrats or the senate Republicans.

Party fusion: Permits two or more parties to nominate the same candidate for office, with the candidate's name appearing on the ballot alongside the name of each party by which he or she is cross-endorsed.

Party identification: Also known as PID, it is the strength of an individual's attachment to a political party.

Party-column ballot: Groups together all candidates running for different political offices by their party affiliation, making straight-ticket voting possible.

Patronage: Favors and benefits that elected officials provide their supporters. Nineteenth-century party machines used city jobs as one source of patronage to reward loyal supporters.

Patronage appointments: The rewarding of government offices to loyal supporters in exchange for their political support.

Patronage job: A government job obtained at least in part through political connections rather than entirely by personal merit; used by elected officials to reward their political supporters and secure loyalty from the bureaucracy.

Pendleton Act: The Civil Service Reform Act of 1883, which created a modern civil service for the federal government. This made it more difficult for politicians to place their supporters in federal government jobs.

Petition: To make a formal request.

Plaintiff: The party that starts a lawsuit in a court of law.

Plea bargaining: A deal in which the defendant in a criminal case agrees to plead guilty to a lesser charge if the prosecutor agrees to drop a more serious charge.

Pluralism: A political theory that assumes conflict is at the heart of politics and that the diversity of interests will lead to consensual outcomes through discussion and debate.

Policy agenda: The public problems and solutions that are discussed and addressed by policy makers at a given time.

Political accountability: The value that government agencies should implement law following closely the wishes of current elected officials.

Political action committee (PAC): A legal entity that allows like-minded individuals who belong to a corporation, labor union, or virtually any other organization to bundle their contributions and give them to candidates or political parties.

Political capital: The intangible goodwill or support for an elected official that can be used to influence the actions of other officials informally.

Political ideology: A relatively coherent and consistent set of beliefs about who ought to rule, what principles ought to be used to govern, and what policies rulers ought to pursue.

Political institution: The rules, laws, and organizations through which and by which government functions.

Poll tax: A tax or fee that must be paid in order to secure the right to register or to vote.

Popular referendum: Legislation approved by the legislature (or a local government) that is put to a popular vote as a result of a successful petition for a referendum. It allows voters to have the final decision on legislation written by elected officials.

Populist era: The 1890s, during which time the Populist political movement was influential, particularly in the West. Populists advocated greater popular democracy, government control of key industries, and a national income tax.

Populist Party: A "third" American political party that had its greatest success in the 1890s. Populists were elected to state legislatures as well as to the U.S. House and Senate. The party called for political reforms, including direct democracy, direct election of the U.S. Senate, and direct election of the president.

Pork barrel: A derogatory and subjective term referring to government spending that is focused on a single geographic area, such as a bridge or a park, suggesting that such spending is wasteful and politically motivated.

Potential interest: An interest that is yet to be organized but has some latent acceptance in society.

Precinct: One of the smallest geographic units in a town, city, or county. Precincts comprise several city blocks. A neighborhood might consist of several precincts.

Precinct captain: A party machine operative who worked to organize a city neighborhood on behalf of the party machine.

Primary election: An election to decide which candidates will be able to be listed on the general election (November) ballot.

Privileges and Immunities Clause: Ensures that residents of one state cannot be discriminated against by another state when it comes to fundamental matters, such as pursuing one's professional occupation or gaining access to the courts.

Problem-solving courts: Trial courts of limited jurisdiction whose focus is less on prosecuting crimes or settling lawsuits than on helping the parties in the case work out certain types of especially difficult problems; for example, family court, drug court, and mental health courts can be thought of as problem-solving courts.

Progressive era: A period of political change and reform during the early decades of the 20th century. Some Progressives hoped to reform politics by limiting the power of corporations and political parties.

Progressive tax: A progressive tax has wealthier people pay a larger proportion of their income to cover the tax. The less affluent pay a lower share of their income toward the tax.

Progressives: Members of the political party and social movement of the early 20th century whose aim was to improve government and public policy through rationality and broadening political participation.

Proposition 13: A constitutional initiative approved by California voters in 1978. One of the first major antitax initiatives, Proposition 13 froze property values at 1977 levels, limited future increases in property taxes, and is credited with setting an antitax mood that helped propel Ronald Reagan to the White House.

Public goods: Policies or actions providing broad benefits rather than narrow benefits to a specific group.

Racial gerrymandering: Drawing boundaries for legislative districts on the basis of race.

Rank-and-file legislator: Legislator who does not hold a leadership position in his or her chamber.

Reapportionment revolution: The political upheaval in the states in the 1960s following the U.S. Supreme Court's mandate that they redraw their legislative and congressional districts to be equal in size in each chamber.

Recall: A vote to remove an elected official from public office. Recall proposals qualify if sufficient signatures are collected.

Recidivism: The tendency to relapse into a previous pattern of behavior, especially criminal behavior.

Reconstruction: The post–Civil War era (1865–1877) when government and public policy in the 11 states of the former Confederacy were dominated by the federal government, immigrants from the northern states ("carpetbaggers"), and freed slaves and where those sympathetic with the Confederacy were shut out of the political process.

Recuse: To disqualify from participation in a decision on grounds such as prejudice, personal involvement, or conflict of interest.

Redistricting: The redrawing of political districts, as required after each census to keep them equal in population.

Reduction veto: The power of some state governors to reduce the level of spending authorized in an appropriations bill passed by the legislature, subject to an override by a supermajority vote of the legislature.

Regressive tax: A regressive tax is one in which the less affluent pay a greater share of their income to cover the tax. The wealthy pay a lower share of their income toward the tax.

Responsible party model: A theory advanced by 18th-century Irish philosopher Edmund Burke that parties should be ideologically consistent, presenting voters with a clear platform and set of policies that are principled and distinctive. Elected officials are expected to be held responsible for implementing the party's program and policies.

Retention election: An election in which the issue on the ballot is whether an incumbent should be kept in office (yes or no) rather than one that offers a choice between two or more competing candidates.

Roll call: When legislators are required to cast a recorded vote on a bill or motion, whether in a committee or on the chamber floor.

Runaway jury: A subjective and pejorative term used to describe a jury whose verdict, in the judgment of the describer, goes against the obvious facts in the case.

Selective benefit: The provision by a group of some material, purposive, or solidarity incentive that can be enjoyed only by members of the group.

Self-financing candidates: Candidates for office who mainly use their own money for their campaign expenses.

Semiclosed primary: Voting in a party's primary is permitted for voters who are registered with the party or as independents.

Semiopen primary: Registered voters may vote in any party's primary, but they must publicly declare for which party's primary they choose to vote.

Sin tax: A tax on an item or behavior that is unpopular or a tax on a product that the state seeks to reduce consumption of.

Single-member district (SMD): Legislative district in which only one legislator from the same chamber serves.

Single-subject rule: Rules that require that an initiative address only one question or issue. Twelve states have such rules for their initiative process. The definition of a single subject varies widely, as does how courts interpret them. Some courts have become more assertive in rejecting initiatives on the grounds that this rule is violated.

Small claims courts: A trial court of limited jurisdiction that deals only with civil suits of less than a specified amount of claimed damages (e.g., $5,000) and in which the plaintiff and defendant are not represented by legal counsel.

Social capital: Networks of trust and reciprocity built from participation in voluntary social groups.

Soft money: Campaign funds not regulated by federal election laws, originally intended to be used for party building and for state and local general electioneering activities.

Special session: An extraordinary meeting of the legislature after its regular session has adjourned, usually called by the governor to consider a very limited policy agenda.

Spoils system: An informal system in which political appointments are rewarded on the basis of political considerations rather than fitness for office.

Standing committee: An at least semipermanent legislative committee that evaluates legislation in a particular area of policy.

State of the State address: In most states, the annual address by the governor to the state legislature at the beginning of its session in which he or she describes the condition of the state and presents a policy agenda for the coming legislative session.

Statutory initiative: An initiative measure that amends a regular law or adds a new law to the statute books. If approved by voters, statutory initiative measures have the status of laws passed through the regular legislative process. Statutory initiative laws are thus typically easier for elected officials to amend (or repeal) than constitutional initiative laws.

Stay of execution: The power of governors in most states with capital punishment to delay temporarily executing a condemned person.

Straight-ticket ballot: A type of ballot that allows (or requires) voters to cast their votes for candidates of a single political party.

Street-level bureaucrats: Government workers who have direct contact with the public, such as police officers, teachers, and driver's license examiners.

Strong mayor–council system: Form of city government where an elected mayor holds many executive functions, including influence over budgeting, appointment of department heads, and veto powers. Sometimes referred to as a mayor–council system.

Supermajority: A portion of a vote that is greater than one-half, such as two-thirds or three-fifths.

Supermajority vote requirement: A rule that requires more than a simple majority vote to approve a budget; for example, 60 percent or a two-thirds majority.

Supreme court: The highest court in a judicial system, with final appellate jurisdiction over cases of law in that system.

Tammany Hall: A machine that controlled New York City politics during the late 1800s.

Targeting electoral strategy: Focusing campaign resources where they will be most effective, especially by supplying more resources to close races and fewer to those in which a candidate will likely either lose or win.

Tax and expenditure limits (TELS): Rules that limit how much a state legislature may increase revenues or spending in an annual budget.

Tax equity: Tax equity refers to which income groups bear the burden of a tax.

Term limits: The requirement that a person can be elected to a certain office only for a specified number of terms or years.

Top-two primary: Allows eligible voters, irrespective of their party affiliation, to vote in a primary for any candidate running on any party ticket, with the top candidates from each political party squaring off in the general election.

Tort: Damage, injury, or a wrongful act to person or property—whether done willfully or negligently—for which a civil suit can be brought.

Traditionalistic political culture: The general and informal set of beliefs and attitudes that politics in a state or community is the domain of social and economic elites and that the have-nots ought not to get involved in politics.

Trial court: A court before which issues of fact and law are tried and determined for a legal case.

Trial transcript: The official, verbatim, and written record of what was said during a trial.

Two-party contestation: When both major parties have a general election nominee in a race for a given office.

Unfunded mandate: A public policy that requires a subnational government to pay for an activity or project established by the federal government.

Unicameral: Having only one chamber, such as the Nebraska Legislature, which has a senate but no house.

Unified government: When all three legs of the legislative process (the governor, the house, and the senate) are controlled by the same party.

Unitary system: A system of governance with a strong central government that controls virtually all aspects of its constitutive subnational governments.

Urbanization: The sociologist Louis Wirth defined urbanization as a process where a city grows in size, density, and heterogeneity.

User fees: A direct charge for use of a service, charged to the user of the service. Examples include tuition and hospital charges.

Veto-proof majority: When the legislative majority party has a supermajority of members large enough to override a gubernatorial veto, if all majority party members vote to do so.

Voting cue: A simple signal about how to vote, in lieu of more detailed information; for example, a candidate's political party.

Voting Rights Act: A law passed by Congress in 1965 designed to remove racial barriers to voting. The original law gave the federal government authority over local voter registration procedures in several southern states. It has been amended and reauthorized by Congress several times since 1965.

Voting-age population: All U.S. residents age 18 and over.

Voting-eligible population: All U.S. citizens age 18 and over who are not excluded from voter eligibility due to criminal status (felony convictions, incarceration, or parole) or due to being declared incompetent to vote.

Ward: Also known as a district. Districts and wards elect their own representatives to a city council.

Watchdog: A group that monitors and publicizes the actions of government officials and agencies and pulls a public alarm when something is awry.

Weak mayor–council systems: Form of city government where a mayor has limited formal power. In the machine era, a city council in weak mayor systems had influence over executive and administrative functions such as hiring and purchasing. Sometimes referred to as a council–mayor system.

Wedge issues: Controversial issues placed for a public vote via the initiative or referendum process by one political party or group, with the goal of dividing candidates and supporters of a rival party or group.

Winner-take-all: Also known as plurality election rules. When a single person represents a jurisdiction or just one person can win an elected position, the candidate with the most votes (the first to win, so to speak) is elected.

Writ of certiorari: The discretionary review of a lower court's ruling.

A

Abrahamson, Shirley S., 230
Abramowitz, Alan, 114
Addams, Jane, 259
Adrian, Charles, 260, 262, 266
Aldrich, John, 107, 116
Allswang, John, 95
Alozie, Nicholas O., 243
Alt, James, 121, 289, 304
Alvarez, Michael, R., 66
Anderson, Jennifer, 130, 136, 139
Ansolabehere, Stephen, 152
Arceneaux, Kevin, 8, 16, 99, 158
Atkeson, Lonna Rae, 68, 188
Aylsworth, Leon E., 270

B

Bachrach, Peter, 124
Baker, Gordon E., 152
Baldauf, Scott, 216
Banchero, Stephanie, 214
Banducci, Susan, 66, 88, 93
Banfield, Edward, 256
Barabas, Jason, 153, 157
Baratz, Morton S., 124
Bardwell, Kedron, 73
Barnello, Michelle A., 8, 158
Barnes, James A., 217
Barrilleaux, Charles, 4, 17, 196, 121, 204, 213
Battista, James Coleman, 169
Baudoin, Kyle, 281, 286, 298, 304
Baum, Lawrence, 222, 239
Bayoumi, Tamim, 304
Beard, Charles, 89
Becker, Lawrence, 169
Beer, Samuel, 24, 37
Behr, Roy, 124
Behrens, Angela, 62
Bender, Edwin, 134
Benesh, Sara C., 242
Benhabib, Seyla, 42
Berch, Neil, 294
Berinsky, Adam, 66, 70
Berkman, Michael B., 145, 150, 175, 196
Bernick, Lee, E., 196
Berry, Francis, 296

Berry, Jeffrey, 107, 136
Berry, William D., 16, 114, 136, 149, 150, 175, 296
Beyle, Thad, 188, 190, 194, 196, 198, 202, 205
Bibby, John, 108, 109, 115, 116, 120, 122
Billeaud, Jacques, 216
Binder, Norman, 76
Blackman, Paul, 269
Blais, Andre, 66
Blatter, Joachim, 216
Bledsoe, Timothy, 274
Bloom, Clark C., 297
Blumenthal, Ralph, 216
Bluth, Alex, 133
Boatright, Robert, G., 151
Bobo, Lawrence, 76
Boehmke, Fredrick, 128, 138
Bogen, David, 31
Bohn, Hening, 304
Bonneau, Chris W., 239, 240
Bowler, Shaun, 59, 60, 61, 66, 67, 68, 73, 81, 83, 84, 88, 89, 91, 93, 94, 96, 98, 101, 103, 242, 273, 281, 285, 289, 290, 304
Bowman, Ann, 39, 175
Boyansky, Bill, 175
Brace, Paul, 114, 233, 243, 244
Brady, Henry E., 52, 54, 55, 57, 70
Bratton, Kathleen A., 161, 243
Breaux, David, 150
Bridges, Amy, 63, 253, 257, 273
Brockington, David, 66, 67
Broder, David, 85, 287
Broder, John, 130
Bruce, Donald, 284
Bryan, Frank, 64
Burden, Barry, 94
Burke, Edmund, 108
Burklin, Wilhelm, 85
Burnham, Walter Dean, 63, 70, 269
Butler, David, 153
Button, James, 161
Byrne, Julie, 249

C

Cain, Bruce, 81, 97, 99, 153, 178, 180, 189
Camissa, Anne Marie, 162, 168
Camobreco, John F., 8, 99, 158

A

AARP (American Association of Retired Persons), 127
abanet.org, 239
abortion rights, 134
absentee voting, 66, 68
Addams, Jane, 259
adjudication, 224
adjudicator, 227
Administrative Law Review, 112
administrative rules, 212
administrative rules review committees, 167
Administrative Science Quarterly, 270
adversarial argument, 224
AFDC (Aid to Families With Dependent Children), 35, 39, 56, 71
AFL-CIO (American Federation of Labor- Congress of Industrial Organizations), 128
African-American and Latino State Legislators, 160–161
African Americans
  governors, 195
  migration to the North, 13
  political participation, 273
  poverty, 13–14
  representation, 75–76, 145, 160, 273, 274
agribusiness, 125
Agricultural Adjustment Act, 35
Aid to Families With Dependent Children (AFDC), 35, 56
Alabama
  African-American and Latino State Legislators, 160
  campaign finance, 117
  conservative, 115
  direct democracy in, 81
  gubernatorial election cycle, 187
  gubernatorial powers, 203
  higher education spending, 11
  Hurricane Katrina, 46
  ideologically conservative, 114
  initiatives, 103
  interest groups, 141
  interparty competition, 119
  interparty competition 1999–2006, 121
  judicial selection, 235
  legislative professionalism, 176
  literacy test, 59
  lobbying laws, 131
  Montgomery, 56

party of governor, 10
political ideology, 16
primaries, 110
registered voters, 1965, 59
representation, 75
Selma, 56
state legislature, 147
taxes, 280, 295
voter participation presidential election 2008, 58
voter turnout, 121
women, in state legislature, 8
Alaska
  direct democracy in, 80, 89
  gubernatorial election cycle, 187
  gubernatorial powers, 203
  higher education spending, 11
  interest groups, 141
  interparty competition, 119
  interparty competition 1999–2006, 121
  judicial selection, 235
  legislative professionalism, 176
  literacy test, repealed, 59
  lobbying laws, 131
  party of governor, 10
  primaries, 111
  revenue, 292
  state legislature, 147
  tax base, 12
  taxes, 280, 287
  term limits, 177
  voter participation presidential election 2008, 58
  women, in state legislature, 8
Alaska Hire Law, 31
Albany, New York, 130
Alliance for a Better California, 133
alternative local election systems, 67
amend, 163
amendatory veto, 197
amended, 165
American Association for Justice, 125
American Association of Retired Persons (AARP), 127
American Bar Association, 239
American Bar Association Report, 38
American Bar Foundation Research Journal , 238
American Economic Review, 285, 297, 304
American Enterprise Institute, 44

Governor's Institutional Powers

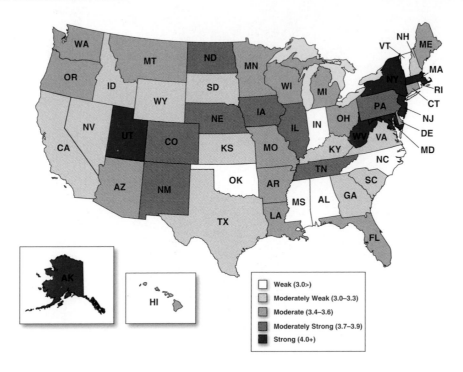

Weak (3.0>)
Moderately Weak (3.0–3.3)
Moderate (3.4–3.6)
Moderately Strong (3.7–3.9)
Strong (4.0+)

Note: This figure compares governorships' institutional power based on appointments, independently elected executives, tenure potential, the state budget, party control of the legislature, and the veto.
Source: A modification of an index developed in Thad Beyle and Margaret Ferguson, "Governors and the Executive Branch," in *Politics in the American States*, 9th ed., ed. Virginia Gray and Russell L. Hanson (Washington, D.C.: CQ Press, 2008).

★★★

State Legislative Term Limits

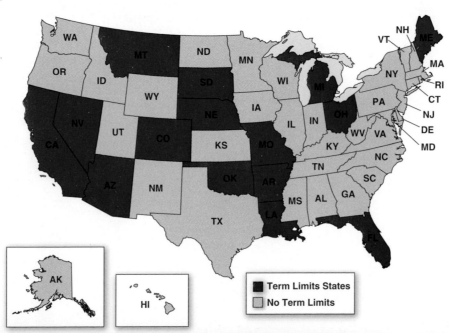

Term Limits States
No Term Limits